Cheseldine and Gerard Families

of Maryland

by

Edwin Warfield Beitzell

1949

1999 Revised, Edited and
Additional Material Added by:

Thomas Brent Cheseldine and Beverly Wild
With Additional Material and Great Assistance from
Alton Fred Cheseldine and Theresa Cheseldine Saylor

HERITAGE BOOKS
2008

HERITAGE BOOKS

AN IMPRINT OF HERITAGE BOOKS, INC.

Books, CDs, and more—Worldwide

For our listing of thousands of titles see our website
at
www.HeritageBooks.com

Published 2008 by
HERITAGE BOOKS, INC.
Publishing Division
100 Railroad Ave. #104
Westminster, Maryland 21157

Copyright © 2000 Thomas Brent Cheseldine
and Beverly Wild

Other Heritage Books by Edwin W. Beitzell:
Life on the Potomac River

International Standard Book Numbers
Paperbound: 978-0-7884-1650-7
Clothbound: 978-0-7884-7711-9

Table of Contents

Introduction

After 328 years in Southern Maryland, the Cheseldine family held their first reunion in Newburg, Maryland on October 5, 1997.

The event, which was attended by 170 people, had been planned only since June, when Thomas Brent of Wakefield, RI, and his sister, Theresa Saylor of Lower Marlboro, Maryland, were invited on a five hour tour of 16,400 acres of land in St. Mary's County that had once belonged to their ancestors, including St. Catherine's Island, St. Clement's Manor and White's Neck. The tour guide, Alton Fred Cheseldine of Temple Hills, Maryland, is the only person alive who has been researching the family longer than Brent and Saylor.

Any Cheseldine living in America today could be a descendant of Kenelm and Mary Cheseldine. Kenelm Cheseldine, the second son of a minister with the Church of England, emigrated to the United States from Braunston Manor, England, after his father's death in 1669. He brought with him to the colonies an extensive library that he had collected as a lawyer. Upon his arrival, he bought 540 acres of land in Kent County on the Eastern Shore and settled there with his wife, Bridgett Faulkner.

Kenelm was in his 20's when Faulkner died, and he remained in Kent County for six to seven years before marrying again.

His second wife, Mary Gerard, brought to the marriage in 1677, a dowry containing ____ acres of land in St. Mary's County, part of the 16,400 acres of land that had been granted to her father, Sir Thomas Gerard, by Lord Baltimore, beginning in 1637. Kenelm and Mary had four children.

Kenelm was a powerful orator and held several prestigious posts, including Ambassador to England for Maryland, Speaker of the Maryland General Assembly and Maryland State Attorney General.

Before his death in 1708, he had helped to found the new capital of Maryland at Annapolis in 1694 and King William School, the first free school in Maryland, in 1696. King William School was later renamed St. John's College.

So began a distinguished family history that remained buried for decades after the land records were destroyed in a courthouse fire in the early 1800s. Later, the facts were uncovered by Edwin Bietzell of Leonardtown, Maryland who spent half of his life writing a manuscript about the Gerard and Cheseldine families. Edwins mother was a Cheseldine.

Theresa and Thomas Brent Cheseldine first learned of Mr. Beitzell's manuscript when teenagers growing up in their family home in Washington, DC. Beverly Wild and Thomas Brent met at the family reunion and decided to work together to bring this history up to date.

When Mr. Bietzell died, his wife, Josephine, gave the manuscript and six other books he had written to Alton Fred Cheseldine. Fred spent many years revising and adding material. In 1997 he supplied his copy of the manuscript with revisions so Brent and Wild could add their contributions and bring this book to publication.

The Cheseldine family reunion at the home of Wilda and Joseph Edward Cheseldine at Newburg, Maryland (near Cobb's Island) brought together those members who had been working on the history and this book is the result.

GERARD AND CHESELDINE FAMILIES

Foreword

Both Gerard and Cheseldine are old and honorable family names in Maryland. Indeed, Maryland historians have been remiss in their treatment of both the first Kenelm Cheseldyne and his father-in-law, Thomas Gerard. Between them they were in the forefront in the affairs of the Province for the first 70 years of its existence. Even a casual perusal of the state records, the Archives of Maryland will prove this fact. Whether it was fighting off Indians or claimants to Lord Baltimore's land, formulating laws for the government and betterment of the Province, in the Assembly and in the Council, putting down rebellion or promoting a revolution, they were active and fearless participants. Consequently, it is unfortunate that Maryland historians have put so much stress on certain minor events, such as Gerard's locking of the chapel or Cheseldyne's alleged negligence in riding the Circuit Court, when these men should be remembered for their many important contributions during the most critical years of the state's existence.

Both are deserving of better treatment even though we, in this day, may not agree with all of their actions. Further, early Maryland history is very much confused, "many pages are missing" and with the passage of some three hundreds years it is difficult, if not impossible, to determine at this date the motives underlying the actions of many of the leaders of the Province. In recent years a marker honoring Thomas Gerard has been placed at Colton's (Longworth) Point, at the approximate site where the Catholic Gerard erected, prior to 1642, an Anglican Chapel for the use of his family and friends who were members of the Church of England. It is hoped that some day an appropriate marker will be placed in St. Anne's Churchyard at Annapolis, MD, where Kenelm Cheseldyne is buried.

Although the members of the family have scattered, several Cheseldines of the present generation have fine farms on the old Cheseldine plantation on White's Neck, having maintained possession for three hundred years, through some eleven generations. Many other members of the family have homes in what was originally St. Clements Manor which in the early days stretched from the head of St. Clements Bay over to the Wicomoco River. Farmers, boat builders, rivermen or whatever their walk in life, they are a sturdy and independent people, good neighbors. good friends and good citizens.

The records of Thomas Gerard and the first two generations of the Cheseldine family in Maryland are fairly complete and cover the period from 1638 to 1725. Since they were prominent in the affairs of the Province many of their activities have been included in the official records of Maryland, namely, the Maryland Archives. However, much research has been necessary to trace the family affairs from 1725 to 1800 for while the family continued to be large landholders and prominent citizens they dropped out of the political life of the state. Also during this period private cemeteries were used for burial which have largely disappeared over the years and in addition deed records in St. Mary's County prior to 1831 have been destroyed by fire. Consequently record sources for this period are meager. Fortunately Hilda, G. Frederick, Alton G., and Alton F. Cheseldine and some of the elder members of the family have lent willing hands in the search and the associated work so that, in all, the task has been a pleasant one.

We know that there is much information that we have not uncovered and it is our hope that this family record will be supplemented by such additional information from members of the family we have not had the opportunity of contacting. Spaces have been provided for entering dates of birth, marriage, etc. for the record. It is hoped that a copy of this and other information of interest will be forwarded to the undersigned and as additional information is received the family record can be reissued in more complete form. Your cooperation is invited and will be greatly appreciated.

> Edwin W. Beitzell
> February 1, 1949
> Abell, Maryland

Note: Edwin is now deceased.

The undersigned is attempting to continue this valuable work of maintaining the history of our family.

Please send all updated information, including errors, omissions and additions to the family to:

> Beverly Wild
> 2917 Needlewood Lane
> Bowie, MD 20716-1211

Supplement

After the first edition of this book is published, we expect to hear from many members of the branches of the families covered, with additional information and/or corrections. We welcome this. When sufficient new material has been accumulated, we plan to publish a Supplement that would be available to those who have purchased a copy of this book and possibly add the Supplement to any new editions that may be printed.

We are especially interested in receiving information about Kenelm Cheseldine's activities in Kent County, Maryland, before he married Mary Gerard. Also about his life in England before he came to America, from what port and on what ship he arrived, location of any of his books or other possessions that are still existing.

Please send any information or inquiries to:

Beverly Wild
2917 Needlewood Lane
Bowie, MD 20716-1211
Bwild@sfa.com

The Editors

CHESELDYNE

Cheseldine Family

in

England

The Cheselden Family
(in England)

1. Robert Cheselden (1)

The history of the Cheseldine (Cheselden, Cheseldyne) Family has been traced back in England to the reign of Edward III, (1327 - 1377). During the political disturbances of Edward's reign, (The Hundred Years War). Sir William de Brughe was one of the Judges who was forced to forfeit his land. In 1382, during the reign of Richard II (1377 - 1399), he purchased Braunston Manor in Rutland County, England, jointly with his son-in-law, Theobold Warde, son of Simon Warde of Nevill, who had married his daughter and heir, Anne. Theobold Warde died in the summer of 1391 and upon her father's death, some years later, Braunston passed to Anne, subject to the dower of her mother, Margery. In 1392, Anne married, secondly, Robert Cheselden, and in 1427 they made a settlement for her mother's third part. Her mother died the following year, 1428. In an inquisition taken after Anne's death on April 23, 1445, it was stated that she held the Manor of Braunston by Knight's service to Humphrey, Duke of Buckingham, at his Castle of Dikeham and the Manor was then "valued at 12 marks per annum, over and above all reprises". Anne and Robert also had custody of the King's Forest at Rutland from 1430 to 1445 and the family continued custody until the reign of Edward IV, (1461). Anne died seized of the Manor on March 7, 1445, and her husband, Robert, and son, John, having died before her, she was succeeded by her grandson, John Cheselden (No. 3) who was born in 1422. (See: The Victoria History of the County of Rutland, The Rutland Visitation of 1618 - 1619 and 1681 - 1682, the History and Antiquity of Rutlandshire and the History and Antiquities of Leicestershire.) Children:
    2.   I. John Cheselden (2) B. about 1395. D. before 1445.

2. John Cheselden (2)

Son of Robert Cheselden and Anne (de Brughe Warde) Cheselden, born about 1395, he married Elizabeth (Scarle), about 1420, daughter and co-heir of _____Scarle. Through this marriage the Manor of Scarle (Scarlies, Skarley) in Uppingham was acquired.

Later it was known as Cheselden Manor. Due to the family's land holdings at Alexton, in the County of Leicester, Mr. Cheselden was known as John Cheselden of Alexton. He died prior to the death of his mother, Anne Cheselden, in 1445, and left two sons, and perhaps, other children. Children:
  3.   I. John (3) B: about 1422.
  4.   II. William (3) B. about 1445.

3. John Cheselden (3)

Son of John Cheselden (No. 2) and Elizabeth (Scarle) Cheselden, born about 1422, he married, about 1447, _____ (Nowers) of Buckingham County. He was living at Alexton in 1471, and had two sons and, perhaps, other children. Children:
  5.   I. John (4) B. about 1445.
  6.   II. William of Groby (4) B. M. Emme _____, and had two children, Elizabeth and William.

4. William Cheselden (3)

Son of John Cheselden (No. 2) and Elizabeth (Scarle) Cheselden, born about 1445.

5. John Cheselden (4)

Son of John Cheselden (No. 3) and _____ (Nowers) Cheselden, born about 1445, he married the daughter of William Marbury of Northampton. They lived at the Manor of Braunston at Uppingham in Rutland County. The names of three children are recorded. Children:
  7.   I. John (5) B. about 1470
  8.   II. Thomas (5) B.
  9.   III. Richard (5) B. Lived on the family estate at Northampton.

6. William Cheselden (4)

Son of John Cheselden (No. 3) and _____ (Nowers) Cheselden, born _____. Married Emme _____, and had

two children. Children:
     9A.   I. Elizabeth (5) B.
     9B.   II. William (5) B.

7. John Cheselden (5)

Son of John Cheselden (No. 5) and _____ (Marbury) Cheselden of Northampton, born about 1470. Married Elizabeth, daughter of _____ Neville of Gothurst. They lived at Braunston Manor. Children:
    10.   I. Edward (6) B.
    11.   II. Elizabeth (6) B.
    12.   III. Eusebius (6) B.
    13.   IV. William (6) B.

8. Thomas Cheselden (5)

Son of John Cheselden (No. 5) and _____(Marbury) Cheselden of Northampton, born _____.

9. Richard Cheselden (5)

Son of John Cheselden (No. 5) and _____ (Marbury) Cheselden of Northampton, born _____.

10. Edward Cheselden (6)

Son of John Cheselden (No. 7) and Elizabeth (Neville) Cheselden of Gothurst, born about 1492, he married Bridget, daughter and heir of William Montgomery of Eckston in Northampton County, whose wife was Elizabeth Aynesworth. The Manor of Scarlies or Cheselden at Uppingham, was settled on Edward and Bridget in 1515, at the time of their marriage, with remainders to his brothers and sister. In 1540, Edward granted the Manor to his son, George, who was seized of it at the time of his father's death, in 1549. No other children were mentioned. Children:
    14.   I. George (7) B. about 1516.

3

11. Elizabeth Cheselden (6)

Daughter of John Cheselden (No. 7) and Elizabeth (Neville) Cheselden of Gothurst, born _____ .

12. Eusebius Cheselden (6)

Son of John Cheselden (No. 7) and Elizabeth (Neville) Cheselden of Gothurst, born _____ .

13. William Cheselden (6)

Son of John Cheselden (No. 7) and Elizabeth (Neville) Cheselden of Gothurst, born _____ .

14. George Cheselden (7)

Son of Edward Cheselden (No. 10) and Bridget (Montgomery) Cheselden, born about 1516, he married in 1537, (1) Anne daughter and heir of Thomas Skeffington of Groby, brother of Sir William Skeffington. After the death of Anne, he married, (2) Alice, daughter of Roger Wilston of Uppingham. A coat of arms was granted George Cheselden, Gentleman, in January, 1560. The patent reads as follows: "A patent Graunted by Lawrence Dalton, Esqr. als Norroy the last of January 1560, 3rd year of reign of Queen Elizabeth to George Cheselden of Uppingham, gent. sonne of Edward, sonne of John, sonne of John Cheselden late of Allexton in Con. Leicester." This patent was in the hands of Edward Cheselden of Borough in 1681.
Children: - First Marriage
     15.   I. Kenelm (8) B. about 1538. D. 1596.
     16.   II. John (8) B. _____ .
Children: - Second Marriage
     17.   III. James (8) B. ____ .
     18.   IV. Edward (8). B. _____ .
     19.   V. Thomas (8) B. _____ .

15. Kenelm Cheseldyne (8)

Son of George Cheselden (No. 14) and Ann (Skeffington) Cheselden of Groby, born about 1538, he married Winifred, daughter of Francis Say of Wilby, in the County of Northampton, Gentleman. He died in 1596, leaving Braunston Manor to his grandson, Kenelm, and is buried in the Church at Braunston. The inscription in brass on his handsome tomb reads; "Here lyeth Kenelme Cheseldyne of Uppingham, Esquire, who lineally defended from Anne Broogh, daughter and heir to Lord Broogh, who married Winifred, daughter of Francis Say of Wilby, in the County of Northampton, Gent., and had by her XI sons and III daughters who deceased the 2 of August 1596, leaving Edward his son and Heir succeeding.

As I was foe are ye,
As I am foe shall ye be"

Children:
20.   I. Edward (9) B. about 1570.
21.   II. Ann (9) B. M. James Green, of London, ale brewer.
22.   III. Alice (9) B. M. Isley Cromwell of Lenton in the
        County of Notts.

16. John Cheselden (8)

Son of George Cheselden (No. 14) and Ann (Skeffington) Cheselden of Groby, born_____.

17. James Cheselden (8)

Son of George Cheselden (No. 14) and Alice (Wilston) Cheselden of Uppingham, born_____.

18. Edward Cheselden (8)

Son of George Cheselden (No. 14) and Alice (Wilston) Cheselden of Uppingham, born_____.

19. Thomas Cheselden (8)

Son of George Cheselden (No. 14) and Alice (Wilston)

5

Cheselden of Uppingham, born_____.

20. Edward Cheseldyne (9)

Son of Kenelm Cheseldyne (No. 15) and Winifred (Say) Cheseldyne of Wilby, born about 1570, he married Bridget, daughter of Anthony Fawkener of Uppingham. They resided at Cheselden Manor and later at Braunston Manor until Edward's death on June 13, 1642. The following inscription appears on his tombstone; "Hic Jacet Corpus Edwardi Chefeldyn de Braunston in Com. Rotel Armigeri qui obit 13 die Juny Anne Domini 1642." On April 1, 1619, Edward and Bridget sold Scarlies or Cheselden Manor in Uppingham, which had been in the possession of the family about 200 years, to Bridget's kinsman, Everard Fawkener. This indenture still exists. An indenture, on vellum, and in fine condition, leasing three portions of Braunston Manor for sixty years to Edward and Bridget dated October 15, 1627, and signed by Edward's son, Kenelm Cheseldyne, was in the possession of Edwin Warfield Beitzell in 1949. It reads as follows;

Dated 15th October 1627

Kenelm Cheselden the son	Lease of three closes
to	at Braunston for
Edwd. Cheselden the father	three score years
and Bridget Cheselden	

THIS INDENTURE made the fifteenth day of October in the Thirde yeare of the raigne of our soveraigne Lord CHARLES by the grace of god of England Scotland ffrance and Ireland Kinge Defender of the fayth & c BETWEEN Kenelme Cheseldyne sonne and heir apparente of Edwarde Cheseldyne of Braunston in the Countye of Rotel Esquire of the one parte And the said Edwarde Cheseldyne ffather of the said Kenelme and Bridgett his wyffe of the other parte WITNESSETH that the said Kenelme Cheseldyne (as well for and in consideracon of the yearlye rents hereafter reserved as for dyvers other good causes and consideracons (to) him thereunto movinge) hath demysed granted lett and to farme letten and by these presents Doth Demyse grante lettand to ffarme lett unto the said Edwarde Cheseldyne and Bridgett his wyffe ALL that closse or inclosed grounds in the feylde of Braunston aforesaid called or knowne by the name of Woodstyle Closse (contayneinge by estimacon Twelve acres (be yt more or lesse) and all those his Twoe other Closses or inclosed

6

grounde in the feylde of Braunston aforesaid the one of them called or Knowne by the name of Bastfarde Closse, and the othercalled or knowne by the name of Crosfte Hill Closse, both wch Twoe Closses contayne in the whole by estimacon Twelve acres (be they more or lesse) TOGEATHER with all wayes easements proffytts and comodytes to the aforesaid Three Closes and any parte thereof belonginge or in any wayes appertayneinge TO HAVE AND TO houlde the aforesaid Three Closes and premyses and every parte and parcell thereof wth these appertnnces to the said Edward Cheseldyne and Bridgett his wyffe and their assignes for and enueinge and unto the full ende and tearme of Threescore years from henceforth nexte and ymedyatelye ensewing fully to be complete and ended yf the said Edward Cheseldyne and Bridgett his wyff or eyther of them shall soe longe lyve YELDINGE AND PAYINGE therefore to the saide Kenelme Cheseldyne, his heires executres and assignes the yearlye rente or somme of ffyve pounds of lawfull English money at the twoe usually feaste dayes or tearmes in the yeare (That is to say) at the feaste of the Annunciacon of our blessed Layde St. Marye the virgin and St. Michaell the Archangell by even and equall portions. The first paymente to beginne at the feaste of the Annunciacion of our blessed St. Marye the virgin nexte enseuinge the date hereoff AND IF IT shall happen the said yearly rent of ffyve pounds or any parte or parcell of the same to be behind and unpaid by the space of Thirtye Dayes nexte after any of the said feaste or Days of paymt. before lymyted wherein the same oughte to be payde and the aforesaid (being lawfullye Demanded at or in the capitall messuage or tenemente in Braunston aforesaid) wherein the said Edward Cheseldyne doth nowe dwell that then and from thenceforth yt shall and may be lawfull to and for the said Kenelme Cheseldyne his heirs and assignes into the premyses above Demysed and everye part therof to reenter and the same to have agayne and repossesse as in his or their former estate this Indenture or any thinge herein contayned to the contrarye notwithstandinge AND THE SAID Edward Cheseldyne and Bridgett his wyffe for themselves and oyther of them their and eyther of their executors and administrators Doe Covenente and grante to and with the said Kenelm Cheseldyne his heirs and assignes by these presents that only the said Edward Cheseldyne and Bridgett and their assignes shall and will well and yrewlye pay the aforesaid yearlye rente of ffyve to the sayed Kenelme his heirs and assignes at the Dayes and tymes before in these

7

presents lymted and appoynted for the paymente of the same accordinge to the trewe yntente and meaneinge of the presents and shall and wile lykewyse from tyme to tyme and at all tymes hereafter Dureinge the said terme mayntayne and keepe the moundes and fences of the aforesaid premises and every parte therof in tenantable repayres and soe leave the same at the expiracon of the aforesaid terme. And further that nyther the said Edward nor Bridgett nor their nor eyther of their assignes or undertenants shall or will at any tyme hereafter dureigne the said terme plough up the aforesayd premyses or any parte thereof AND THE SAID Kenelme Cheseldyne for himselfe his heirs and assignes Doe Covenente & grante to and with the said Edward Cheseldyne and Bridgett his wyffe and eyther of them or their and oyther of the executors and assignes by these presents. That they the said Edward and Bridgett and their assigns shall or lawfully may have houlde possesse and enjoy the aforesaid premyses and every parte thereof (underthe rente Condicons and Covenente herin expressed which which on the Lessees or tenants parte are to be performed accordinge to the trewe yntente & meaneinge of the presents without the lett trowble or molestacion of the said Kenelme his heirs or assignes or any lawfullye claymeinge from by or under them or any of them.

IN WITNESS whereof the partyes first above named to these presents Indentures have interchangeablye sett their hands and seales the day and yearefirste above written. Anno Dom 1627 Sealed & Delivered in the presence of Thomas Phillips Ken. Cheseldyne Thomas Blakesley Henrie Courtine.

Edward transferred a piece of land in Uppingham to Edward, his youngest son on May 20, 1642. This indenture still exists. Bridget lived until 1653. She is buried at St. James Church at Braunston. The inscription on her tomb reads; "Here lyeth the body of Bridget Chefeldyne, wife of Edward Chefeldyne of Braunston, in the County of Rutland, efg, who died the 17 day of December, 1653." Children:

23.   I. Kenelm (10) B. 1603. D. 1667.
24.   II. Anthony (10) B.
25.   III. Everard (10) B.
26.   IV. Lyon (10) B.
27.   V. Edward (10) B.
28.   VI. Elizabeth (10) B. M. Rev. Toby Turner
29.   VII. Wynborow (10) B. 1619. D. July 5, 1673

21. Ann Cheseldyne (9) Green

Daughter of Kenelm Cheseldyne (No. 15) and Winifred (Say) Cheseldyne of Wilby, born _____. Married James Green, of London, an ale brewer.

22. Alice Cheseldyne (9) Cromwell

Daughter of Kenelm Cheseldyne (No. 15) and Winifred (Say) Cheseldyne of Wilby, born _____. Married Isley Cromwell, of Lenton in the County of Notts.

23. Kenelm Cheseldyne (10)

Son of Edward Cheseldyne (No. 10) and Bridget (Fawkener) Cheseldyne, born in 1603, he was ordained as a Minister of the Church of England in 1624. He married about this time, Grace, the daughter of Stephen Dryden, who was a brother of Sir Erasmus Dryden, Knight and Baronet. Stephen Dryden resided at Bulwick in the County of Northampton. In 1655, Kenelm was appointed Vicar of Bloxham in Lincoln County where he died in 1667. At the time of the move to Bloxham, in 1655, Kenelm, together with his son, Thomas, conveyed the Manor of Braunston, which had been in the family for two and a half centuries to William Whitby, who, with William Clark and Stephen Cheseldyne sold it in 1668 to Giles Burton. Children:

30.   I. Thomas (11) B. M. Jane, daughter of Richard Munne, on October 4, 1659.
31.   II. Kenelm (11) B. about 1640. D.December 6, 1708. *Immigrated to America. First Cheseldyne in America. Kenelm is buried in Annapolis, MD.*

24. Anthony Cheseldyne (10)

Son of Edward Cheseldyne (No. 20) and Bridget (Fawkener) Cheseldyne, born_____.

25. Everard Cheseldyne (10)

Son of Edward Cheseldyne (No. 20) and Bridget (Fawkener) Cheseldyne born_____.

26. Lyon Cheseldyne (10)

Son of Edward Cheseldyne (No. 20) and Bridget (Fawkener) Cheseldyne, born_____.

27. Edward Cheseldyne (10)

Son of Edward Cheseldyne (No. 20) and Bridget (Fawkener) Cheseldyne, born_____. Married Joan Paull, eldest daughter of William and Jane Paull, in December, 1647, as disclosed in a marriage settlement indenture, still in existence, dated December 1, 1647, whereby the transfer of certain lands in Leicestershire to Edward Cheseldyne were the consideration involved upon his marriage to Joan. The indenture was signed by William Paull, Gentleman, of Owston in the County of Leicester, Father, and George Paull, Brother and heir of William Paull. Joan died March 30, 1703, age 83, and Edward died August 31, 1688, age 71. Children:

31A. I. Edward (11) B. 1648. Married Phoebe, daughter of Maj. William Hubbert. Edward died November 15, 1691. Phoebe died December 25, age 64. They had:
A. Deborah (12) B. D. March 31, 1699, age 23.
B. Edward (12) B. D. October 8, 1722, age 41.

28. Elizabeth Cheseldyne (10) Turner

Daughter of Edward Cheseldyne (No. 20) and Bridget (Fawkener) Cheseldyne, born _____. Married Rev. Toby Turner.

29. Wynborow Cheseldyne (10)

Son of Edward Cheseldyne (No. 20) and Bridget (Fawkener) Cheseldyne, born _____. Died July 5, 1673.

30. Thomas Cheseldyne (11)

Son of Kenelm Cheseldyne (No. 23) and Grace (Dryden) Cheseldyne, born _____. Married Jane Munne, daughter of Richard Munne, on October 4, 1659.

Cheseldine Family

in

America

31. Kenelm Cheseldyne I (1)
The Immigrant
First Generation in America

Second son of Kenelm Cheseldyne (No. 23) and Grace (Dryden) Cheseldyne. The first of the Cheseldyne name in Maryland, was born at Braunston Manor in Rutland County, England, about 1640. His elder brother, Thomas, was heir of the family. Kenelm received a good education as a lawyer and practiced for some years in England. After the sale of the family Manor lands and upon the death of his father in 1667, he decided to try his fortune in the new English Province of Maryland. He arrived on the eastern shore in 1669, bringing with him an excellent law library and his father's divinity books which he willed to his descendants in 1708. Of the first seven years of his life in the Province, little is known, except that there were a number of land transactions from 1669 to 1676. In May, 1676, we find, from the Maryland Archives, that he is a member of the Assembly. Apparently, he arrived in the province with some means as he paid his own passage, had a good education, practiced law and had a very good library.

In 1677, he married, Mary Gerard, daughter of Thomas and Susannah Gerard, who had been willed St. Katherine's Manor (including the Island), White's Neck and Mattapany, plus 30,000 pounds of tobacco by her father. They made their home at Mattapany, although in his later years, he spent considerable time in Annapolis, MD. He also acquired Broad Neck and Dryden in St. George's Hundred, both in St. Mary's County; Westwood, in Charles County, Grantham., in Kent County; Grossers Hall, in Dorchester County, and West Lee Neck, in Wicomico County. In all he owned some 3,000 acres of land.

He was very prominent in the affairs of the Province and held many offices. He was a member of the Lower House of the Assembly, 1676 - 1704; a member of the Council, 1704 - 1708; Attorney General; Speaker of the House; Commissary General; one of the Chief Justices for St. Mary's County; Judge for the Probate of Wills; and Vestryman of William and Mary Parrish. He also was a practicing attorney, a member of many important committees and lent his talents in establishing King William College at Annapolis, now St. John's. He was a member of the Church of England and was one of the leaders of

13

the rebellion in 1689, when the Proprietary Government was overthrown.

On March 27, 1689, he was one of the signers of a public declaration that there was no truth in rumors that the Catholics were trying to persuade the Indians to rise up and murder the Protestants. However, on July 25, 1689, he was one of the signers of the "Declaration of the Reason and Motive for the Present Appearing in Arms of his Majestye's Protestant Subjects in the Province of Maryland", put out by the "Associators" wherein one of the justifications for their action was the stated belief that the Catholics were trying to stir up the Indians to murder the Protestants. The truth of the matter was that the Proprietary Government was extremely unpopular in some quarters, as it was in the time of Thomas Gerard. Lord Baltimore had just appointed William Joseph, a most tactless individual as Governor, who made several provocative challenges to the Colonists and who then, capped the climax by giving out royal order prohibiting the export of bulk tobacco out of the colonies. This, combined with the fact that the Catholic James was forced at this time to flee his throne in England, and William and Mary were proclaimed the rightful successors to the throne, gave the "Associators" their opportunity, and they seized it. It was a combination of dissatisfied elements, which included those who sought profit and power for themselves or sought to maintain their positions of prominence and those who were sincerely suspicious of evil and who had viewed with distrust the restriction of suffrage and the rise of special privilege. It is interesting to note that three of the leaders of the rebellion were sons in law of Thomas Gerard, namely, Kenelm Cheseldyne, Nehemiah Blackistone and John Coode.

Matthew Page Andrews in his "History of Maryland", states "In this Declaration (of reason and motive), there were many statements that were certainly false, others doubtful, while some charges were based upon an element of truth, in the abuses of representative government which had taken place under Charles Calvert's rule. The "Associators" then proceeded to threaten, plunder and imprison sundry citizens, Protestants and Catholics alike, realizing that if they should not be sustained by the King, it would go hard with them, the revolutionists induced all the older counties except, strange to say, Anne Arundel, which had largely promoted the rebellion under Cecil Calvert, to send addresses to the King (William) urging him to

14

take the government of the Province in his own hands. Counter petitions, however, were prepared by the proprietary's supporters, and the latter had a surprising number of names thereon, considering the risk they ran in thus objecting whilst in the power of their political opponents in America."

Kenelm Cheseldyne and John Coode were sent as deputies to England in November, 1690, by the "Associators" and apparently did an effective job as their party triumphed and King William sent over a Royal Governor (Copley) and Lord Baltimore's status was reduced to that of a Landlord, entitled only to his rents, etc. On June 3, 1692, Kenelm Cheseldyne was voted 100,000 pounds of tobacco by the lower house for his services to the Province during the revolution. Nehemiah Blackistone was given a vote of thanks by the Assembly.

It is frequently mentioned in written accounts that Kenelm Cheseldyne was dismissed from his office as a Judge in the Province, due to inattention and neglect of his office. Actually, in his latter years, about 1704, he was appointed against his will, to ride the circuit and act as a Judge of Assizes. The old gentleman was violently afflicted with the gout, and at his age could not stand the rigor of horseback to cover the circuit. so that there appears to be considerable justification for any inattention and neglect.

The following little anecdote, contributed by Virginia Cheseldyne Bailey, which has been handed down through the family, will give a glimpse in the social activities of the old days. During the leisure months of winter, interchange of visits among the families of the county was one of the principal modes of entertainment. The young people of the neighboring plantations would come with their equipage, maids, etc., and spend a few days or a week at the Cheseldyne Plantation, holding a kind of house party with dancing, feasting and love making. Then adding the young people of that plantation to their members, they would move on to the next plantation, visiting in turn all the plantations in their circle.

Kenelm died in 1708 and is buried in St. Anne's Churchyard, Annapolis, MD. His will is dated December 6, 1708, and a copy is included with this account. The date of the death of Mary, his wife, is unknown. Children:

2. I. Mary (2) B. 1678.
3. II. Susannah (2) B. 1680. D. 1730.
4. III. Kenelm, II (2) B. 1683. D. about 1717.
5. IV. Dryden (2) B. 1687. D. 1760.

Second generation begins
2. Mary Cheseldyne (2) Hay, Forbes

Daughter of Kenelm Cheseldyne (No. 31) and Mary (Gerard) Cheseldyne, born in St. Mary's County in 1678. Married (1) Thomas Hay in 1702. Married (2) George Forbes after 1703. George died in June, 1743. Mary was left two plantations by her father, Kenelm, in his will dated December 6, 1708, Broad Neck in St. Mary's County and Westwood in Charles County, one grandaughter Mary Hay was mentioned. A copy of the last page of the Deed to Broad Neck is included with this account, which shows Mary's signature. Mary's date of death is not known. Children: - First Marriage
      I. Mary Hay (3) B. _____. M. Thomas McWilliams.
      Children - Second Marriage
      II. James Forbes (3) B. _____. D. 1760

3. Susannah Cheseldyne (2) Greenfield

Daughter of Kenelm Cheseldyne (No. 31) and Mary (Gerard) Cheseldyne, born in St. Mary's County in 1680. Married Thomas Truman Greenfield. They had eight children. She is mentioned in her father's will merely as a residuary legatee. Susannah died in 1730. The name of one son is known. Children:
      I. "Captain" Thomas T. Greenfield (3) B.about 1721.
         D. November 29, 1744, at age 23 and is buried at
         Trent Hall.

4. Kenelm Cheseldyne, II (2)

Son of Kenelm Cheseldyne (No. 1) and Mary (Gerard) Cheseldyne, born in St. Mary's County in 1683. He was the executor of his father's will of December 6, 1708 and was left Mattapany, the adjoining plantation White's Neck, and St. Katherine's Island. He married about 1709, Mary Phippard. He died in 1717, in St. Mary's County, when only 34 years of age. He was Sheriff in 1709 and a member of the House of Delegates from 1712 to 1714 representing St. Mary's County. Mary married a second time in 1722 to Hugh Collins. Kenelm's children were as follows: Children:
    6.   I. Kenelm (3) B. about 1710.

7.   II. Mary (3) B. about 1712.
8.   III. Cyrenius (3) B. about 1715.

Note: The following is from an article, "Marriage and Family in 17th Century Maryland" by Lorena S. Walsh, Research Associate at the St. Mary's City Commission in Annapolis, MD, and taken from Testamentary Proceedings, XXIII, 349-377, and is reprinted in "The Chesapeake in the 17th Century", edited by Thad W. Tate & David L. Ammerman, 1979, pages 139-140.

From evidence about matches that failed, it can be deduced that colonists considered normal and exclusive sexual union, peaceful cohabitation, and economic support of the wife by the husband the minimal duties that spouses must perform. Testimony about the more positive ingredients of a marriage are more rarely encountered. A 1719 case of a contested administration, however, provided an explicit discussion of contemporary attitudes about marriage.

The case involved Kenelm Cheseldyne, a substantial landowner, who died in 1718, naming his wife, Mary, as administratrix of his estate. Cheseldyne had, in fact, never married the woman with whom he had been living. At Mary's request, a number of neighbors testified that they believed that she and Cheseldyne had been man and wife because Cheseldyne had behaved in ways that defined the manner of a husband, not a paramour.

The Cheseldynes' problems arose because, about 1712, they had "Marryed in private", without banns, license, clergyman, justice, or witnesses, after Mary, the then Widow Phippard, was pregnant, and possibly not until after the birth of the child. Although Cheseldyne asserted that "shee was his Lawfull wife" as much as other man's, proof of Cheseldyne's marriage depended soley on their word and on community acceptance.

John Greaves testified about why he considered the couple married. He related that while he was constable he had gone to arrest Mary Phippard at Cheseldyne's because she had recently borne an illegitimate child. Cheseldyne had forewarned him "from takine her away at his perill for that he would give his oath that there was not any such person as Mary Phippard," claiming Mary as his wife and declaring the child ligitimate. Because Cheseldyne had always acknowlledged Mary as his wife and because neighbors had believed they were married, Greaves had also accepted the union.

Sarah Turner, the midwife who had delivered the three children

17

of Kenelm and Mary, testified that they were man and wife because "the said Cheseldyne particylarly was at the birth of the second and seemed very fond of the child and (Mary). . . . . Cheseldyne called her his wife and took care of her as such and Owned the Children."

Benjamin Reeder, a neighbor, had inquired of Cheseldyne's kinsman. John Coode, whether or not the they were married. Coode had assured him that they had been married in private. Reeder had then believed that they were, and he testified that "afterwards. . . Cheseldyne came with her publickly to Church and helped her off and on her Horse and shewed her the respect due to a wife."

Another neighbor, Thomas Bolt, once went to Cheseldyne's house, and found him "walking in his Hall with one of the Children he had by (Mary). . . in his Armes and in discours about a certaine Mr. Donaldson who had been (at the house) but a small time before and was angry about (Mary's) . .giving the said Donaldson's Child Indian Bread in boiled Milk.. . Cheseldyne sayd that he thought his wife knew what was best for children for says he our own Children Eat the same."

The conception of a husband expressed by these neighbors was that he always acknowledged his wife, that he appeared with her in public, that he showed affection and respect for her, and that he supported her in a condition commensurate with his means. A husband also owned the children born of the union, showed affection toward them, and cared for them. In addition, he acknowledged his wife's joint authority in their upbringing.

In the same book, page 262, "Emergence of a Native Elite" by David W. Jordan, regarding 'longevity of Service for Councilors', we read: Longer service within these three bodies meant an important accumulation of experience with greater knowledge of procedures, organization, precedents, and greater skill in achieving objectives. A number of the earliest legislators with lengthier tenures were well educated men whose knowledge and experience vastly exceeded that of most other colonists, and these factors were particularly important to political stability. These men, although relatively few in number, held influential positions as speakers of the house or as chairmen of the embryonic committee system that falteringly emerged in the 1670s but flourished in the 1690s. They were undoubtedly instrumental in the very evolution of these positions of importance within the assembly. Significantly, many of them were lawyers by profession, and as such were among the very few in the colony with formal legal training. Men like Thomas Notley, Philemon Lloyd, Robert Carvile, Kenelm Cheseldyne, and Robert Smith understood the issues and their implications, appreciated the importance of how laws were phrased, and brought a new sophistication and stability to provincial politics.

5. Dryden Cheseldyne (2) Jowles, Forbes

Daughter of Kenelm Cheseldyne (No. 1) and Mary (Gerard) Cheseldyne, born in 1687. Married (1) Peregrine Jowles and (2) John Forbes, who died June, 1743. By her father's will, she was left the plantation Dryden, in St. George's Hundred, St. Mary's County, containing 483 acres together with all cattle, horses, chattels, etc, and one negro maid called Beso. Dryden died in 1760.

Last Will and Testament of Kenelm Cheseldyne (1)

In the name of God, Amen. The 6th Day of December Annoque Domini 1708. I, Kenelm Cheseldyne, of St. Marye's County, Gent., doe make and ordaine this my last will and testament in manner following.

1. I commend my soul into the hands of Almighty God my Creator and Jesus Christ my redeemer and the Holy Ghost my Santifier to which blessed and Holy Trinity one Eternall Deity be all Honor and Glory forever. Amen.

2. I will all my just debts be well and truly paid.

3. I give and bequeath unto my son Kenelm Cheseldyne, and the heirs of his bodie lawfully begotten, all my plantation, called Mattapany, in St. Marye's County, that I now live upon, and all that tract of land called White's Neck, adjoining to it and all that tract of land called St. Katherynes Island in the said County, upon Potomack River, and for want of such issue, I give the same to my three daughters, Mary Hay, Susannah Greenfield and Dryden Cheseldyne and to the heirs of their bodyes lawfully begotten forever, and

4. I give bequeath and devise unto my daughter, Mary Hay, wife of Thomas Hay, all that plantation called Broad Neck, in St. Marye's County, and all that plantation called Westwood lying in Charles County, for and during the term of her natural life, for the support and maintenance of her the said Mary for her life, and her daughter, Mary Hay, my grandchild, till day of marriage, and after the

death of the said Mary the mother, I give the same to my grandchild Mary her daughter.

5. I give bequeath and devise unto my daughter Dryden Cheseldyne, all that plantation in St. George's Hundred in St. Mary's County called Dryden, containing 483 acres, to her and the heirs of her body lawfully begotten, and if she dye without issue, then I give and devise that same, to my daughters Mary Hay and Susannah Greenfield, and their heirs of their bodyes lawfully begotten and in defect of such issue to my son Kenelm, and his heirs forever.

6. I give and bequeath unto aforesaid Daughter, Dryden, all cattle, horses, mares and all other personalty, chattels, that now are or shall be at the time of my death upon the aforesaid plantation called Dryden, and one negro girl called Beso, and a good feather bed, and furniture at the timeforesaid.

7. I will that none of my books be sold or lent out, but upon good caution to be returned again and that Dyvinaty books remain in my Executors hands, but to the use of all my said children, and returned and my law books I will unto the first child of any of my children shall have by Executors shall be capable of using them.

Lastly I make my son Kenelm Cheseldyne my sole and whole Executor, of this my last will and testament, to whom I bequeath all the remainder of my goods and chattels.

In witness whereof, I hereunto set my hand and seal the day and year above written. Sealed and acknowledged, in presence of Kenelm Cheseldyne. (Seal)

Witnesses
John Coode
Tho. Greenfield
G. Muschaw

Third generation begins
6. Kenelm Cheseldyne III (3)

Son of Kenelm Cheseldyne (No. 4) and Mary (Phippard) Cheseldyne, born in St. Mary's County about 1710. His aunt, Dryden, in testamentary proceedings, stated "When my brother Kenelm died in 1717, his son Kenelm 3rd was about 6 or 7 years of age". He lived on the family plantation, which he shared with his sister Mary, by the terms of his father's will. He married Chloe Nelson, and had eight children, perhaps others, and died in 1772. Judging by the inventory of his estate, it was very large and included some 30 slaves. Children:

9.   I. Kenelm (4) B. about 1740.
10.   II. Rubin (4) B. about 1745.
11.   III. Seneca (4) B. about 1750. D. June 15, 1816.
12.   IV. William (4) B. 17__.
13.   V. Caleslenleys Nelson (4) B. about 1750.
14.   VI. Mary (4) B. 1752.
15.   VII. Ursula (4) B. 1754.
16.   VIII. Elizabeth (4) B. 1755.

7. Mary Cheseldyne (3)

Daughter of Kenelm Cheseldyne (No. 4) and Mary (Phippard) Cheseldyne, born about 1712.

8. Cyrenius Cheseldyne (3)

Son of Kenelm Cheseldyne (No. 4) and Mary (Phippard) Cheseldyne, born in St. Mary's County, about 1715. He was left 20,000 pounds of tobacco in his father's will, to be lodged in the hands of his uncles Truman Greenfield and Peregerine Jowles to buy land for him. He married Ann Anderson, the daughter of John Anderson and they administered John Anderson's estate in 1755-1756. He died about 1762. Children:

17.   I. Cyrenius (4) B. about 1740.
18.   II. Gerard (4) B. about 1742.

Fourth generation begins

9. Kenelm Cheseldyne IV (4)

Son of Kenelm Cheseldyne (No. 6) and Chloe (Nelson) Cheseldyne, born in St. Mary's County about 1740. In the U. S. Census of 1790 he is shown as having five sons. However, in the census of 1800 for St. Mary's County he and his wife are shown as being over 45 years of age with three sons and two daughters. He married Elizabeth Neale on February 3, 1771, and served in the St. Mary's County Militia in the Revolutionary War. He died prior to 1810. Children:

21

19.   I. Kenelm (5) B. about 1775.
20.   II. Henrietta (5) B. 17__.
21.   III. Mary Neale (5) B. 1780. D. 1800.
22.   IV. Charles (5) B. 17__.
23.   V. William (5) B. 17__.
       Fourth generation begins

10. Rubin Cheseldyne (4)

Son of Kenelm Cheseldyne (No. 6) and Chloe (Nelson) Cheseldyne, born about 1745, he owned property in Kent and Dorchester Counties, probably land that was purchased by his great grandfather, the first Kenelm Cheseldyne, as deed records at Annapolis show that "Grantham" in Kent County was purchased in 1674 and "Grossers Hall;" in Dorchester County in 1672. Rubin apparently died without issue in 1765 and his estate was administered by Kenelm Cheseldine who with Ursula Haskins was listed as being next of kin.

11. Seneca Cheseldyne (4)

Son of Kenelm Cheseldyne (No. 6) and Chloe (Nelson) Cheseldyne, born in St. Mary's County about 1750 at White's Neck Farm. He served in the Revolutionary War and is shown as a member of the St. Mary's County Militia in 1780. He appears in the 1800 census of St. Mary's County, with five sons and three daughters. He married (1) Elizabeth Biscoe November 4, 1779 at St. Mary's County, and (2) Elizabeth Turner September 9, 1798 in Machoda, Westmoreland County, VA. In 1814, he sold 25 acres of White's Neck to Elizabeth Tarlton. He died June 15, 1816 at White's Neck Farm, and his will was probated in the same year. Children: - First Marriage
24.   I. Seneca Nelson (5) B. 1780. D. May 24, 1815.
25.   II. Kenelm (5) B. 1782. D. March 13, 1835.
26.   III. Henry (5) B. 1799.
       Children: - Second Marriage
27.   IV. Charles (5) B. 1800.
28.   V. Gerard R. (5) B. August 18, 1803.
29.   VI. Janey (5) B. 18__.
30.   VII. Chloe (5) B. 18__. D. February 10, 1847.
31.   VIII. Eliza (5) B. 18__.

32. IX. Mary Ann (5) B. 18___.
33. X. Elizabeth (5) B. 18___.

Seneca wrote two wills. The first will written and witnessed on March 24, 1815 reads as follows:

First Will of Seneca Cheseldine (No. 11)

In the name of GOD AMEN. I, Seneca Cheseldine, of St. Mary's County in the State of Maryland, being in perfect health of body and of sound ___ mind, memory and understanding, considering the certainity of death and the uncertainity of the time, thereof, make and publish this my last will and Testament in manner and form following that is to say:

First and Principally. I commit my Soul into the hands of the Almighty God and my body to the Earth to be decently buried at the direction of my Executor's therein after named and after my debts and funeral charges are paid and my bills thereof are taken out, I give and bequeath as follows:

I give and bequeath to my beloved wife Elizabeth Cheseldine the use of the whole of my estate both real and personal during her natural life, and after her death, I give the aforesaid real and personal property to be equally divided between my children as follows:

To my sons Seneca Nelson Cheseldine, Harry Cheseldine, Gerard Cheseldine, Janey Cheseldine, Charley Cheseldine, Chloe Cheseldine, Eliza Cheseldine, and Mary Ann Cheseldine. My wish and desire is that Chloe Cheseldine's part of my estate shall be delivered after my wife Elizabeth's death to my daughter Elizabeth Grant, and for her to make use of this said part for the maintenance and support of the said Chloe. And lastly, I do hereby constitute and appoint my dear wife Elizabeth Cheseldine, to be the sole Executrix of this my last Will and Testament ratifying and confirming this and none other to be my last Will and Testament. In testimony whereof, I have hereunto set my hand and affixed my Seal this 24, March, 1815.

Seneca Cheseldine (Seale)

Witnesses: Morris Shank, George Shank and Edward Scott.

Sometime after the first will was written, something must have happened to Seneca's wife Elizabeth, because he wrote and published a second will. He changed his mind about what he wanted to do with his estate.

Second Will of Seneca Cheseldine (No. 11)

In the name of God Amen. I, Seneca Cheseldine, of St. Mary's

County in the State of Maryland being of sound mind, memory and understanding concerning the certainty of death and uncertainty of the time thereof, and being desirous to settle my earthly affairs, and thereby, be the better prepared to leave this world when it shall please God to call me home, do therefore, make and publish this my last will and testament in manner and form following, that is to say:

First and principally I commit my soul unto the hands of almighty God and my body to the earth to be decently buried at the direction of my executor, herein after named and after my debts and funeral charges are paid, I devise and bequeath to my son Kenelm Cheseldine, this plantation called White's Neck whereon I now live, to him and his heirs forever with all the negroes, Rock House lots and kitchen furniture and all the plantation that may belong to same. My further wish and desire that my said son, Kenelm Cheseldine, shall keep my daughter Chloe with him as long as she may live, my further wish and desire that my son Kenelm shall keep together the rest of my children and do the best he can until the boys are able to be bound to whatever trade he may think most proper, and lastly I do hereby constitute and appoint my son Kenelm Cheseldine to be my sole executor of this my last will and testament revoking and annulling all former wills made by me heretofore ratifying and confirming this and none other to be my last will and testament.

In testimony whereof I have herewith put my hand and affix my seale this twelfth day of June in the year of our Lord, 1816.

Witnessed by: Kenelm Cheseldine, John Hammond and John Culberson.

Seneca was preceded in death by both of his wives and his oldest son, Seneca, who would have inherited the estate from his step mother, Elizabeth Turner, as was done in those years. The eldest son always inherited the estate. Since the eldest son, Seneca, died before his father, the next in line, Kenelm Cheseldine was the recipient of the estate of Seneca Cheseldine.

Evidently, Seneca's daughter , Chloe, had a physical or mental defect, as he wanted to make certain that she was cared for her entire life. Chloe was undoubtedly named for Seneca's mother.

Seneca and his brother Kenelm, and Mary Biscoe subscribed to the Oath of Allegiance in 1778.

12. William Cheseldine (4)

Son of Kenelm Cheseldine (No. 6) and Chloe (Nelson) Cheseldine, born in St. Mary's County, 1751. He enrolled July 12, 1776 in Col. Ewings Battalion of the Flying Camp from Maryland with Gerard Cheseldine. Also he is listed as serving in the St. Mary's County Militia on October 20, 1780. He is shown in the 1790 census with a wife Henrietta and three sons. His estate was inventoried by Caleslenleys Nelson and Seneca Cheseldine in 1799. Children:

    34.   I. William (5) B. 17__.
    35.   II. Charles (5) B. 17__.
    36.   III. Richard (5) B. 1785.

13. Caleslenleys Nelson Cheseldine (4)

Son of Kenelm Cheseldine (No. 6) and Chloe (Nelson) Cheseldine, born in St. Mary's County around 1750. He sold 175 acres of "Hardhsips Addition" to Robert Greenwood in 1799. His will was probated in 1800, which mentions his wife, Philippa, and two children, and leaves them a plantation, Mattapany. After Caleslenley's death, Philippa married secondly, Jeremiah Alston, January 17, 1802. Children:

    37.   I. Kenelm Greenfield (5) B. 1795.
    38.   II. Lydia (5) B. 17__.

14. Mary Cheseldine (4) Blackistone

Daughter of Kenelm Cheseldine (No. 6) and Chloe (Nelson) Cheseldine, born in St. Mary's County after 1750, married Nehemiah Herbert Blackistone, January 30, 1772.

15. Ursula Cheseldine (4) Haskins

Daughter of Kenelm Cheseldine (No. 6) and Chloe (Nelson) Cheseldine, born in St. Mary's County after 1750, married __ Haskins.

16. Elizabeth Cheseldine (4) Fulton

Daughter of Kenelm Cheseldine (No. 6) and Chloe (Nelson)

Cheseldine, born in St. Mary's County after 1750, married ___Fulton.

17. Cyrenius Cheseldine (4)

Son of Cyrenius Cheseldine (No. 8) and Ann (Anderson) Cheseldine, born in St. Mary's County around 1740. He had a son Cyrenius, born around 1765 and perhaps other children. He was appointed by the Orphans Court together with Kenelm Cheseldine and William Bean on February 11, 1812 to act as guardian to his grandchildren, the children of his son, Cyrenius. Children:
39.   I. Cyrenius (5) B. about 1765. D. about 1812.

18. Gerard Cheseldine (4)

Son of Cyrenius Cheseldine (No. 8) and Ann (Anderson) Cheseldine, Gerard enrolled in Maryland with William Cheseldine (No.12) on July 12, 1776, in Col. Ewing's Battalion of the Flying Camp. He does not appear in the 1790 census or in any other records and probably was killed in the Revolutionary War, or did not return to St. Mary's County when the war was over.
Fifth generation begins
19. Kenelm Cheseldine V (5)

Son of Kenelm Cheseldine (No. 9) and Elizabeth (Neale) Cheseldine, born in St. Mary's County about 1775. He is shown in the 1820 census of St. Mary's County as being about 45 years of age with five sons and three daughters. He married Fanny Tarlton on January 14, 1804 and served in the War of 1812 as a Corporal in Capt. Thomas Blackistone's Company, 45th Regiment. He died March 15, 1835. Children:
40.   I. Kenelm (6) B. 1805.
41.   II. John (6) B. 1807. D. February 9, 1890.
42.   III. James (6) B. 1810.
43.   IV. Wm. H. (6) B. 1824.
44.   V. George Washington (6) B. 18__.
45.   VI. Mary T. (6) B. 18__.
46.   VII. daughter (6) B. 18__.
47.   VIII. daughter (6) B. 18__.

20. Henrietta Cheseldine (5) Hayden

Daughter of Kenelm Cheseldine (No. 9) and Elizabeth (Neale) Cheseldine, born in St. Mary's County about 1778. Married November 11, 1800, Charles Hayden.

21. Mary Neale Cheseldine (5)

Daughter of Kenelm Cheseldine (No. 9) and Elizabeth (Neale) Cheseldine, born in St. Mary's County about 1780. She died about 1800. Her will was probated December, 1800.

22. Charles Cheseldine (5)

Son of Kenelm Cheseldine (No. 9) and Elizabeth (Neale) Cheseldine, born in St. Mary's County about 1780. In the 1820 census, he and his wife are shown, age about 40, with one son, believed to be Charles C., shown in the 1850 census, and two daughters. He served in the War of 1812 and apparently died before 1840, as he is not shown in that census. Children:

48.   I. Charles C. (6) B. 1804.
49.   II. daughter (6) B. 18___.
50.   III. daughter (6) B. 18___.

23. William Cheseldine (5)

Son of Kenelm Cheseldine (No. 9) and Elizabeth (Neale) Cheseldine, born in St. Mary's County after 1771. He married (1) Teresa Mason on September 29, 1794, and (2) Henny Gibson on May 2, 1797. For some reason, he does not appear in the census records. It is believed that William Cheseldine may have been his son and there were perhaps other children. Children:

51.   I. William C. (6) B. 1818.

24. Seneca Nelson Cheseldine (5)

Son of Seneca Cheseldine (No. 11) and Elizabeth (Biscoe) Cheseldine, born in St. Mary's County, 1780. Seneca died May 24, 1815. In his will of 1816, his father left the family plantation, White's

Neck, to his brother, Kenelm, with instructions that Kenelm was to care for and look after the rest of the children. Children:

52.   I. Gerard (6) B. 1818.
53.   II. daughter (6) B.18__.

25. Kenelm Cheseldine (5)

Son of Seneca Cheseldine (No. 11) and Elizabeth (Biscoe) Cheseldine, Kenelm Cheseldine was born in 1782 at White's Neck Farm, St. Mary's County, MD. He died on March 13, 1835 at White's Neck Farm. He inherited White's Neck Farm from his father, and raised the children of his father, who were living after his father died. (Note: DAR Application No. 671716 has some conflicting information, but Kenelm's brother, Seneca, preceded his father, Seneca, in death. The father, Seneca (No. 11) made two wills. The first will made his first son, Seneca, Executor of his estate. The second will made his third son, Kenelm, Executor and Recipient of his estate.)

On September 23, 1819, when he was 37 years old, Kenelm married Sophia D. Gardiner. Sophia was born about 1785 in St. Mary's County. They had four children, as family records show. Kenelm died in 1835, at the age of 53.

Sophia settled Kenelm's estate in 1841. She lived for a while in Washington, DC, with her daughter, Joanna Blackistone. Sophia married William Alston on January 5, 1841 and died a year later in 1842. Children:

54.   I. Biscoe (6) B. 1820. D. April 28, 1871.
55.   II. Posey (6) B. June 9, 1822. D. January 14, 1894.
56.   III. Kenelm Dent (6) B. 1824.
57.   IV. Joanna (6) B. 1826.

Estate Settlement for Kenelm Cheseldine of Seneca

St. Mary's County to wit. The 15th Day of February 1838. The account of Kenelm Cheseldine (of Seneca - late of St. Mary's County deceased) by Sophia D. Cheseldine and Morris Shanks, Administrators of the said deceased.

Estate Accounts for	$4,440.20
Payments and Disbursements	3,182.13
Balance Due (Disbursements)	1,258.28

Distribution as follows:

To Sophia D. Cheseldine, widow of the deceased, 2/3	$419.42
To Biscoe Cheseldine, son of the deceased, 1/5	209.71
To Posey Cheseldine, son of the deceased, 1/5	209.71
To Dent Cheseldine, son of the deceased	209.71
To Joanna, daughter of the deceased	209.71
Total	$1,258.28

26. Henry Cheseldine (5)

Son of Seneca Cheseldine (No. 11) and Elizabeth (Biscoe) Cheseldine. Born in St. Mary's County 1799.

27. Charles Cheseldine (5)

Son of Seneca Cheseldine (No. 11) and Elizabeth (Turner) Cheseldine. Born 1800.

28. Gerard R. Cheseldine (5)

Son of Seneca Cheseldine (No. 11) and Elizabeth (Turner) Cheseldine, born in St. Mary's County August 18, 1803, and is shown in the 1860 census as a retired merchant. He married on December 2, 1856, Mary Sophia Hammett, who died May 7, 1859. One daughter was born but died in infancy. Gerard moved to Cincinnati, OH. On July 24, 1860, Gerard was married in Baltimore, MD by Archbishop Kendrick to (2) Ellen Causin Greenwell of St. Mary's County (Beacon 8/2/1860). Ellen died prior to May 25, 1865. Gerard died January 24, 1882. Children: - First Marriage
    58.   I. Mary Sophia (6) B. April, 1858. D.June ,1859.
        Children: - Second Marriage
    58A   II. Eleanor (6) B. May 21, 1861. D. May 25, 1865.

29. Janey Cheseldine (5)

Daughter of Seneca Cheseldine (No. 11) and Elizabeth (Turner) Cheseldine. Born in St. Mary's County.

30. Chloe Cheseldine (5)

Daughter of Seneca Cheseldine (No. 11) and Elizabeth (Turner) Cheseldine. Born in St. Mary's County. Died February 16, 1847 in Longworth Point, St. Mary's County, MD. Buried Christ Episcopal Church at Chaptico, MD.

31. Eliza Cheseldine (5) Ellis

Daughter of Seneca Cheseldine (No. 11) and Elizabeth (Turner) Cheseldine. Married Sylvester Ellis, May 7, 1833.

32. Mary Anne Cheseldine (5) Grant

Daughter of Seneca Cheseldine (No. 11) and Elizabeth (Turner) Cheseldine. Married Daniel Grant, March 24, 1804. *May have been from first marriage.*

33. Elizabeth Cheseldine (5) Grant

Daughter of Seneca Cheseldine (No. 11) and Elizabeth (Turner) Cheseldine. Married _____ Grant.

34. William Cheseldine (5)

Son of William Cheseldine (No. 12) and Henrietta (surname unknown) Cheseldine.

35. Charles Cheseldine (5)

Son of William Cheseldine (No. 12) and Henrietta (surname unknown) Cheseldine.

36. Richard Cheseldine (5)

Son of William Cheseldine (No. 12) and Henrietta (surname unknown) Cheseldine, born in St. Mary's County about 1785, and married Mary Blackistone on January 1, 1807.

37. Kenelm Greenfield Cheseldine (5)

Son of Caleslenleys Nelson Cheseldine (No. 13) and Philippa (surname unknown) Cheseldine born in St. Mary's County about 1795. He married on October 19, 1821, in Longworth Point, St. Mary's County, MD, (1) Maria Thomas and in 1838 (2) Rachel D. Shaw. He served in the War of 1812 from Maryland in Capt. Blackistone's Company. In the 1830 census he is shown with his two sons and one daughter. He was left the plantation Mattapany in his father's will and his sister Lydia was mentioned as a residuary legatee. A number of property transfers in his name in the deed records at Annapolis, MD. He sold part of Mattapany to Nehemiah D. Mason on September 15, 1815, and 1 1/2 acres to Mary Knott in 1818. His mother, Philippa Alston, appears in this deed. On August 9, 1822, he sold 156 3/4 acres of Mattapany for $6,000 to William W. Bowling. On October 28, 1834, Kenelm G. and wife Maria sold 155 acres of Mattapany to Francis Knott. Kenelm is listed in the 1850 census with his son William E. and daughter-in-law Ann Elizabeth Cheseldine. Children:

   62.   I. William E. (6) B. 1828. D. February 20, 1865 in the Civil War.

   63.   II. Robert (6) B. 18__.

   64.   III. daughter (6) B. 18__.

38. Lydia Cheseldine (5) Bowling

Daughter of Caleslenleys Nelson Cheseldine (No. 13) and Philippa (surname unknown) Cheseldine born 17__. Married Charles Bowling.

39. Cyrenius Cheseldine (5)

Son of Cyrenius Cheseldine (No. 17) and _____. Born in St. Mary's County about 1765. However, very little has been learned concerning this Cyrenius other than he apparently died a young man about 1812 leaving seven sons under age. He appears in the 1800 Census for St. Mary's County with a wife, daughter of Stephen Tarlton, both about 35 years of age with seven sons. The Orphans Court of St. Mary's County on February 11, 1812, appointed his father Cyrenius, Kenelm Cheseldine and William Bean as guardians of the children. Children:

66.	I. Elijah (6) B. April 3, 1794. D. June 7, 1856.
67.	II. Richard (6) B. September 10, 1797. D. May 3, 1860.
68.	III. Kenelm (6) B. October 18, 1799.
69.	IV. Charles (6) B. January 11, 1802.
70.	V. Cyrenius (6) B. April 17, 1804.
71.	VI. John (6) B. March 9, 1806.
72.	VII. Gerard (6) B. September 7, 1810.

Sixth generation begins

40. Kenelm Cheseldine VI (6)

Son of Kenelm Cheseldine (No. 19) and Fanny (Tarlton) Cheseldine, born in St. Mary's County about 1805. He married Lucinda Ferguson on October 13, 1831, and the family is listed in the 1850 Census of St. Mary's. Lucinda died about 1859, and Kenelm prior to 1870. Children:

73.	I. Mary L. (7) B. 1834. D. 1915.
74.	II. Andrew Jackson (7) B. February 14, 1836. D. May 11, 1923.
75.	III. Ann Marie (7) B.May, 1837.
76.	IV. Sarah Elizabeth (7) B. May, 1842. D. March 1844.
77.	V. Jane Ann (7) B. March 17, 1844. D. June 27, 1914.
78.	VI. John Kenelm (7) B. August 19, 1847.
79.	VII. George W. (7) B. 1849.

41. John Cheseldine (6)

Son of Kenelm Cheseldine VI (No. 19) and Fanny (Tarlton) Cheseldine, born in St. Mary's County about 1807. He married (1) Ellen Watson on June 15, 1829 who died about 1838. (2) Julia Ann Cullison on March 26, 1839, who died prior to 1850. In 1828 he sold "Cross Hall" to John H. Milburn. On July 8, 1834 he bought land in White Plains from Cyrenius Cheseldine and in September of the same year he and Ellen sold land in White Plains to Richard Cheseldine. On May 20, 1842 John and Julia sold land in Hatches Thicket to John Mattingly. He was a farmer and was living in St. Mary's County in 1880. John died February 9, 1890, and is buried at All Souls Church. Children: 1st Marriage

80.   I. Mary Ellen (7) B. 1830.
81.   II. Mary J. (7) B. 1837
         Children: 2nd Marriage
82.   III. Ann Lucille (7) B. 1840.
83.   IV. John Nelson (7) B. 1844
84.   V. William A. (7) B. July 15, 1847. D. May 5, 1876.

42. James Cheseldine (6)

Son of Kenelm Cheseldine (No. 19) and Fanny (Tarlton) Cheseldine. Born in St. Mary's County around 1810. He married Jane Milburn on January 15, 1839. Apparently moved away from St. Mary's County as he does not appear in the Census records.

43. William H. Cheseldine (6)

Son of Kenelm Cheseldine (No. 19) and Fanny (Tarlton) Cheseldine. Born in St. Mary's County in 1824 and appears in the Census for that County in 1850. He married Susan E. Payne on May 24, 1851. Apparently moved away from the county as he does not appear in subsequent Census records. Children:
85.   I. Susan (7) B. 18__.

44. George Washington Cheseldine (6)

Son of Kenelm Cheseldine (No. 19) and Fanny (Tarlton) Cheseldine. Born in St. Mary's County around 1810. In a deed on record at Annapolis Hall of Records, he sold a part of "Hatches Thicket", which he stated he inherited from his grandfather, Stephen Tarlton, on February 5, 1833 to George W. Gibson. A similar sale was made on May 29, 1834 to Edward Joy and Richard H. Miles. He purchased St. Margaret's Island from Kenelm Cheseldine about 1830 and on March 24, 1835 he re-sold the Island to Richard H. Miles. Kenelm and Teresa Cheseldine and Washington and Mary Ann Cheseldine appear in this deed. Apparently Washington married Mary Ann (_____) about 1825 and moved to Charles County, Maryland. On May 1, 1838 George Washington and his wife Mary Ann bought land in "Hatches Thicket" from Edward Joy and re-sold it on January 11, 1839 to Richard H. Miles. He moved from Charles County to

Washington, D.C. and married there (2) Rose L. Compton on November 22, 1855. He ran a grocery store and was living at 21 9th Street, N.E. in 1880. Children:

    86.   I. Alfred W. (7) B. 18___.
    87.   II. Augustus D. (7) B. 1849.
    88.   III. Cora (7) B. 18___.
    89.   IV. Addie (7) B. 18___.

45. Mary T. Cheseldine (6) Clements

Daughter of Kenelm Cheseldine (No. 19) and Fanny (Tarlton) Cheseldine. Born in St. Mary's County after 1804. Married October 17, 1822 William Clements.

46. daughter Cheseldine (6)

Daughter of Kenelm Cheseldine (No.19) and Fanny (Tarlton) Cheseldine. Born

47. daughter Cheseldine (6)

Daughter of Kenelm Cheseldine (No.19) and Fanny (Tarlton) Cheseldine. Born

48. Charles C. Cheseldine (6)

Son of Charles Cheseldine (No. 22) and Elizabeth (Neale) Cheseldine Born in St. Mary's County in 1804. He married Ann Gibson (1) on April 3,1830 and (2) Henrietta Morgan on April 28, 1849, who was born in 1828. About 1830 he bought a part of "White Plains" from Kenelm Cheseldine. He also bought a part of "Hatches Thicket" from Richard and Ann Cheseldine on February 25, 1839. Henrietta died prior to 1870 and Charles prior to 1880. Children: 1st Marriage:

    90.   I. Mary (7) B. 1831
    91.   II. Jane (7) B. 1835.
    92.   III. Anna (7) B. 1838
    93.   IV. Clara E. (7) B. 1839
        Children: 2nd Marriage

94.　　V. Josephine (7). B. 1850.
95.　　VI. Thomas E. (7) B. 1856. D. prior to 1870.
96.　　VII. Roseanna (7) B. 1858. D. May 9, 1885.

49. daughter Cheseldine (6)

Daughter of Charles Cheseldine (No. 22) and Elizabeth (Neale) .Cheseldine. Born 18__.

50. daughter Cheseldine (6)

Daughter of Charles Cheseldine (No.22) and Elizabeth (Neale) Cheseldine. Born 18__.

51. William C. Cheseldine (6)

Son of William Cheseldine (No. 23) and Teresa (Mason) Cheseldine Born in St. Mary's County in 1818. He married Eleanor Thompson on July 12, 1842, who was born in 1824. On April 5, 1843 he transferred real estate to James Dean. The family appears in the 1850 Census and 1860 Census for St. Mary's County but do not appear subsequently. It is believed that they moved to Washington, D.C., as Philip, a son, appears in the city directory as an engineer at St. Elizabeth's Hospital in 1880. Children:
　97.　　I. William C. (7) B. 1843. D. June 8, 1864.
　98.　　II. Catherine (7) B. 1845
　99.　　III. John F. (7) B. 1847. D. prior to 1860.
100.　　IV. Ann V. (7) B. 1849. D. prior to 1860.
101.　　V. Thomas Philip (7) B. 1850.
102.　　VI. Ellen (7) B. 1852
103.　　VII. Mary (7) B. 1852
104.　VIII. Leddy (7) B. 1859 (Son)

52. Gerard Cheseldine (6)

Son of Seneca Nelson Cheseldine (No. 24), and Sophia D. Cheseldine. Born in St. Mary's County September 10, 1818.
This needs to be researched. This was thought to be another Gerard Cheseldine. (No. 72) Birthdate may not be correct.

53. daughter Cheseldine (6)

Daughter of Seneca Nelson Cheseldine (No.24) and Sophia D. Cheseldine. Born after 1818.

53A. Adeline Cheseldine (6)

Born 1832.

53B. Jackson Cheseldine (6)

Born 1834.

53C. daughter Cheseldine (6)

Born after 1834.

53D. daughter Cheseldine (6)

Born after 1834.

54. Biscoe Cheseldine (6)

Son of Kenelm Cheseldine (No. 25) and Sophia D. (Gardiner) Cheseldine. Born at White's Neck Farm in St. Mary's County in 1820. He inherited this land from his father, Kenelm, the son of Seneca and Elizabeth Biscoe Cheseldine. He was named for his grandmother. He married on November 25, 1856, Anna Rebecca Blackistone who was born 1832. Biscoe died on April 28, 1871, at age 51, at his home at White's Neck, of paralysis. He is buried at All Saints. (Beacon 6/15/1871). He left no will. Only two pages of the estate settlement are in the Probate Court of St. Mary's County, MD. John F. Dent purchased White's Neck Farm from the estate. Posey Cheseldine was paid $878.00, his share left by his father and grandfather. Anna moved to Washington, DC and was living at 209 10th Street, SW, in 1880. Her will is dated November 19, 1901 and mentions daughters, Maria Stuart Sullivan and Elizabeth B. Cheseldine, grand-daughter, Maria Knott and grandson George Knott. Children:

    114.   I. Ann S. (7) B. 1858. D. June 7, 1887.

115.   II. Rebecca (7) B. 1859. D. September 7, 1869.
116.   III. Maria Stuart (7) B. August 15, 1862.
117.   IV. Elizabeth B. (7) B. 1866.

55. Posey Cheseldine (6)

Son of Kenelm Cheseldine (No. 25) and Sophia D. Gardiner Cheseldine.   Born at White's Neck, St. Mary's County, on June 9, 1822.   He died January 14, 1894, in London, OH.   He went to Cincinnati, OH, as a young man still in his teens.   There was an uncle, who preceded him to Cincinnati, and he may have worked for this uncle, who was a merchant there.   After a couple of years, he went to Williamsburg, Clermont County, OH, where he opened his own store. He was very sucessful as a merchant as one finds out by reading the history of the area.   The History of Clermont County, page 209, states that Posey was one of the most prominent and successful merchandisers in Williamsburg, OH.   He married at the age of 25, (1) Nancy Sims, daughter of Sarah Crane and Samuel Sims.   She evidently had a long illness for her younger sister, Izora Sue, came to live with them.   Nancy died August 5, 1865.   Posey married (2) his wife's sister, Izora in 1866. She was born June 16, 1814, and died August 2, 1887. Posey must have believed deeply in education.   His home was well stocked with books.   Possibly his son Charles attended college, but it is well known that Charles's sons went to Ohio Wesleyan University.

Posey served on the Williamsburg Council from 1851 - 1855. In 1873 he left Williamsburg and went to London, Ohio.   He opened a store in London.   Over the years he opened several stores.   He owned a great deal of land.   It seems that he and his son, Samuel Dent, were in a lot of business deals together.   He was a member of the ME Church, and is buried in Williamsburg beside his wives. Children: - 1st Marriage.

118.   I. Samuel Dent (7) B. about 1847. D. September 2, 1902.
119.   II. Charles (7) B. April 10, 1863. D. February 23, 1908 Children: - 2nd Marriage
120.   III. Biscoe Kenelm (Pearl) (7) B. November 1, 1866. D. June 19, 1929.

Will of Posey Cheseldine

The last Will and Testament of Posey Cheseldine of London, Madison County, Ohio. In the Name of the Benevolent Father of all. I, the said Posey Cheseldine being of sound mind and memory, considering the uncertainity of continuance in life, and desiring to make such disposition of my worldly estate as I deem best, do make, publish and declare this to be my will and testament hereby revoking and annulling any and all former will or wills whatsoever by me made.

First: I desire all my just debts and funeral expenses to be paid, as soon as possible after my decease.

Second: I give and bequeath to my son Samuel D. Cheseldine one note No. 8 given by Charles Cheseldine payable to the order of Posey Cheseldine, calling for One Thousand ($1000) dollars, with six % interest after date, September 1st, 1892, payable 5 years and six months after date.

One note: No. 12 given by Charles Cheseldine, Payable to the order of Posey Cheseldine, calling for Two Hundred ($200) dollars with six % interest from date, dated September 1st, 1892 payable four years from date. I, also, give to Samuel Dent Cheseldine, my gold head walking stick to be kept in the family. This was a Christmas present from my children.

Third: To my son Charles Cheseldine I give and bequeath my homestead on East High Street, together with all the furniture, books and pictures. I also give him one fourth (1/4) of my undivided three fourth (3/4) interest which I now own, in the store room No. 317 Main Street, London, Ohio. I, also, give him one note of hand No. 6 F drawn by him made payable to Posey Cheseldine or order calling for One Thousand ($1000) dollars payable four years and three months after date-dated September 1st, 1892. I also give him one note No. 13 dated September 1st, calling for three hundred ($300) dollars payable four years after date payable to Posey Cheseldine or order.

Fourth: I give and bequeath to my son Biscoe Kenelm Cheseldine, Commonly called Pearl, my dwelling house situated on Elm Street, London, Ohio, Property bought of Johnathan Arnett. I, also, give and bequeath to him two fourths (2/4) of my undivided 3/4 interest in the store house building No. 37 Main Street, London, Ohio. I also give him my entire interest and credits in the store at South Charleston, Clark County, Ohio, now carried on under the firm name of P and PB Cheseldine, he is to pay all expenses due on the stock. I, also give him one note No. 7 calling for one thousand ($1000) dollars payable to Posey Cheseldine on order with six % interest after, date, dated September 1 st, 1892. I also give him one note No. 4 calling for five hundred ($500) dollars drawn by Charles Cheseldine payable to Posey Cheseldine on order, with six % interest after date dated September 1st, 1892, due three years after date. I, also, give and bequeath my gold watch and chain.

Fifth: I give and bequeath to my grand-daughter, Izora Cheseldine, daughter of B. K. Cheseldine and Maggy, his wife, one note No. 5 for Five Hundred ($500) dollars drawn by Charles Cheseldine, Payable to Posey Cheseldine on order three years and six months from date with six % interest after date, dated September 1, 1892. I, also give to my grand-child, Anna, daughter of B. K. and Maggy Cheseldine, his wife, one hundred ($100) dollars, also his son Kyle, one hundred ($100) dollars.

Sixth: I will and bequeath to my grandson Raymond, child of Charles and Pet Cheseldine one hundred ($100) dollars, to my grandchildren of Samuel Dent Cheseldine and his wife, Cate, twenty five ($25) dollars each making one hundred ($100) dollars in the aggregate, as follows: to Jenny $25, to Bessy $25, to Don $25, and to Sterling $25 dollars.

If after the above claims are all met there is any moneys or claims not disposed of I wish it to be equally divided between my children.

I nominate and appoint Samuel D. Cheseldine, Charles Cheseldine and Biscoe K. Cheseldine to be Executors of this will, that no bond or bonds be required during the administration of said trust. In witness thereof, I have hereunto set my hand and seal this 8th day of November in the year of 1892.

Posey Cheseldine   Seal
Witnessed by W. S. Murray and L. R. Watts

This will is filed in the Probate Court in Madison County, Ohio.

56. Kenelm Dent Cheseldine (6)

Son of Kenelm Cheseldine (No. 25) and Sophia D. (Gardiner) Cheseldine. Born at White's Neck Farm, St. Mary's County, MD in 1824.

57. Joanna Cheseldine (6) Blakistone

Daughter of Kenelm Cheseldine (No. 25) and Sophia D. (Gardiner) Cheseldine.. Born at White's Neck Farm, St. Mary's County, MD in 1826. Married George Wellington Blakistone on March or May 10, 1845 at Machodac, Westmoreland County, VA. Joanna died in 1856.

58. Mary Sophia Cheseldine (6)

Daughter of Gerard R. Cheseldine (No. 28) and Mary Sophia (Hammett) Cheseldine. Born in St. Mary's County April 1858. Died June 1858. Buried at Foster's Neck.

59. Eleanor Cheseldine (6)

Daughter of Gerard R. Cheseldine (No. 28) and Ellen (Causin) Greenwell Cheseldine. Born in St. Mary's County May 21, 1861. Eleanor died May 25, 1865. Her mother died prior to this date.

60. Open

61. Open

62. William E. Cheseldine (6)

Son of Kenelm Greenfield Cheseldine (No. 37) and Maria (Thomas) Cheseldine. Born in St. Mary's County in 1828 at Longworth Point. He married on February 7, 1850 Ann Elizabeth Cheseldine, born in 1832. William E. Cheseldine was a member of Company B 1st Maryland Infantry, U.S.A. He enlisted on December 12, 1864 and died in camp on February 20, 1865. After his death Ann married Joseph H. Phillips, on November 22, 1869 by the Reverend Mr. Wyatt. They had a daughter Elizabeth. She lived to be 103 years of age. She was a delight to know. Alton Fred Cheseldine recalls spending many hours in conversation with her on her front porch where one could look over the St. Clement's Island where the Maryland settlers landed. She enjoyed telling stories of the "old days". She was called Aunt Betty. Children:

40

121.   I. Annie (Nannie) E. (7) B. 1854.

122.   II. Susan F. (7) B. 1858.

123.   III. Richard Talbert (7) B. May 3, 1860. D. September 6, 1947.

63. Robert Cheseldine (6)

Son of Kenelm Greenfield Cheseldine (No. 37) and _____ Cheseldine. Born in St. Mary's County. Served in the U.S. Navy between 1861 - 1865 in the Civil War. St. Mary's County, Vol. 10, No. 7.

64. daughter Cheseldine (6)

Daughter of Kenelm Greenfield Cheseldine (No. 37) and_____ Cheseldine. Born

65. Open

66. Elijah Cheseldine (6)

Son of Cyrenius Cheseldine (No. 39) and Frances (Tarlton) Cheseldine. Born in St. Mary's County, April 3, 1794, he served in the War of 1812 in Capt. Thomas Blackistone's Company, the 45th Regiment. He married Sophia _____ Cheseldine, and died June 7, 1856. Elijah is buried at Christ Church. Children:

124.   I. Jeremiah (7) B. 1823.

125.   II. Jane M. (7) B. 1835.

126.   III. Alemedia (7) B. July 16, 1838.

67. Richard Cheseldine (6)

Son of Cyrenius Cheseldine (No. 39) and Frances (Tarlton) Cheseldine. Born in St. Mary's County September 10, 1797. He married January 31, 1820 Ann Weakley born 1810. On February 25, 1839 Richard and Ann sold a part of "Hatches Thicket" to Richard H. Miles. The family is listed in the 1850 Census and subsequent Censuses. Richard died May 3, 1860. Children:

127.   I. Richard Henry (7) B. 1826.

128.   II. Elizabeth (7) B. 1830.
129.   III. Mary Caroline (7) B. 1837.
130.   IV. Jane (7) B. 1841.
131.   V. Grayson L. (7) B. 1845.

68. Kenelm Cheseldine (6)

Son of Cyrenius Cheseldine (No. 39) and Frances (Tarlton) Cheseldine. Born in St. Mary's County October 18, 1799.

69. Charles Cheseldine (6)

Son of Cyrenius Cheseldine (No. 39) and Frances (Tarlton) Cheseldine. Born in St. Mary's County January 11, 1802.

70. Cyrenius Cheseldine (6)

Son of Cyrenius Cheseldine (No. 39) and Frances (Tarlton) Cheseldine. Born in St. Mary's County April 17, 1804. He married on December 21, 1829 Margaret Tippett. Her will was probated August, 1833. He does not appear in the 1840 or subsequent Census records. It is believed that he had one son and possibly other children. Children:
132.   I. Cyrenius (7) B. about 1830. D. 1857.

71. John Cheseldine (6)

Son of Cyrenius Cheseldine (No. 39) and Frances (Tarlton) Cheseldine. Born in St. Mary's County March 9, 1806.

72. Gerard Cheseldine (6)

Son of Cyrenius Cheseldine (No. 39) and Frances (Tarlton) Cheseldine. Born in St. Mary's County September 7, 1810. He married January 7, 1847, in Chaptico, MD, Rebecca V. Ellis born March 25, 1824 daughter of Maria (Tippett) Ellis and Alexandria Ellis. Gerard died January 23, 1882. Rebecca died December 13, 1898. They are buried at All Saints Episcopal Church. Children:

105.   I. James H. (7) B. 1847.
106.   II. Charles Edward (7) B. May 31, 1848. D. May 29, 1921.
107.   III. Ataway (7) B. July 13, 1849.
108.   IV. Ellen E. (7) B. 1852.
109.   V. Rebecca (7) B. 1854.
110.   VI. Sarah M. (7) B. February 10, 1857. D. 1932.
111.   VII. Seneca (7) B. 1860. D. 1930.
112.   VIII. Clara (7) B. 1861.
113.   IX. Henrietta (7) B. March 26, 1865. D. October 14, 1944.

Seventh generation begins

73. Mary L. Cheseldine (7) Cullison, Taylor

Daughter of Kenelm Cheseldine (No. 40) and Lucinda (Ferguson) Cheseldine Born in St. Mary's County in 1834. Married (1) John Cullison. After his death, Mary moved to Washington, D.C., where she married (2) Edward Taylor. They moved to Kinsley, Kansas and homesteaded. They developed a very fine farm and became moderately wealthy. Mary made annual pilgramages to St. Mary's County until her death about 1915 in Kinsley, KS. Children - 1st Marriage

132A.   I. Elizabeth (Lizzie) (8) B.
132B   II. Lucy (8) B.
        Children - 2nd Marriage
132C.   III. James (8) B.
132D.   IV. Sarah (8) B.
132E.   V. Emma (8) B.

74. Andrew Jackson Cheseldine (7)

Son of Kenelm Cheseldine (No. 40) and Lucinda (Ferguson) Cheseldine. Born in St. Mary's County February 14, 1836. He served on a gun boat during the war between the states and in 1882 was living at Collingwood on Canoe Neck Creek which he sold in that year to Josiah Beitzell and other land further up the creek, he sold to Jeremiah Gibson. He then moved back to White's Neck Creek which was part of the original Cheseldine plantation. He also owned St. Katherine's Island which was acquired by his son-in-law Charles Beitzell in 1914.

He was both a riverman and a successful farmer. He married (1) Mary J. Thompson on January 9, 1854. She died in September, 1858 and is buried at Christ Church. Married (2) Anna Maria Morgan on January 30, 1860 who was born April 15, 1841. He died May 11, 1923 and Anna Maria died November 29, 1916. Both are buried at Sacred Heart Church, Bushwood, Maryland. Children: - First Marriage

133. I. William Francis (8) B. 1858
      Children: - Second Marriage:
134. II. Mary Susan (8) B. August 13, 1862
135. III. Mary Alice (8) B. 1865
136. IV. Catherine Elizabeth (8) B. April 21, 1868.
      D. August 28, 1902.
137. V. Mary Beatrice (8) B. 1870
138. VI. Robert (8) B. January 15, 1872. D. September 29, 1896.
139. VII. Andrew Freeman (8) B. June 7, 1874. D. May 12, 1935.
140. VIII. Lelia Virginia (8) B. October 22, 1876.
      D. December 5, 1914.
141. IX. Mary Ida (8) B.1882. D. May, 1947.
142. X. Garrett Francis (8) B. May 19, 1883.

75. Ann Maria Cheseldine (7) Ellis

Daughter of Kenelm Cheseldine (No. 40) and Lucinda (Ferguson) Cheseldine. Born in St. Mary's County May, 1837. Married John Ellis April 10, 1861, by Reverend Levin. Children:

142A. I. William Nobel Ellis (8) B. January 11, 1862.
       D. September 5, 1929.

76. Sarah Elizabeth Cheseldine (7) Norris

Daughter of Kenelm Cheseldine (No. 40) and Lucinda (Ferguson) Cheseldine. Born in St. Mary's County May, 1842. Died March, 1844. Buried at All Saints Church. (Vestry records Tomakokan Church (All Saints) Vol. 2).

77. Jane Ann Cheseldine (7) Norris

Daughter of Kenelm Cheseldine (No. 40) and Lucinda (Ferguson) Cheseldine. Born in St. Mary's County on March 17, 1844. She was baptised at All Saints Church July 7, 1844. Married January 25, 1864 John Hanson Norris, a farmer, by Father John B. De Wolfe. They lived for some years at "Barton Hall" and were residing at Collingwood in 1882. Collingwood was purchased that same year by Josiah Beitzell from Andrew Jackson Cheseldine, a brother of Jane (Jennie). John died in April, 1885. Jennie survived him and died June 27, 1914.

Both are buried at Sacred Heart Church, Bushwood, MD. Jennie lived at Collingwood with her daughter Elizabeth. (Lizzie) who married Josiah E. Beitzell, for many years after the death of John Hanson. She was a great "teller of ghost stories" to the huge delight of her youngest Beitzell grandchild, Edwin.. He well remembered the many happy hours spent in Grandma's room. She was an invalid in her last years and every evening after supper was the time to play innumerable games of "seven up" or hear stories. The ghost story always began with the grandson sitting over in his favorite corner but invariably ended with him on the bed with Grandma, sure that no one had noticed his very gradual inching a little closer to Grandma as the story progressed. She always kept a store of hard candy at hand and there was always a piece for the younger grandchildren. She loved tobacco and used it freely. Children:

143.   I. Mary Elizabeth (8) B. March 6, 1865. D. August 17, 1925.
144.   II. Lucy Rebecca (8) B. October 4, 1866. D. June 3, 1930.
145.   III. Joseph Alvin (8) B. 1868. D. March 4, 1945.
146.   IV. Frances Lorraine (8) B. March 20, 1873. D. January 9, 1926.
147.   V. Jane Nettie (8) B. January 25, 1875
148.   VI. John Lee (8) B. April 11, 1877.
149.   VII. James Benjamin (8) B. September 9, 1879
150.   VIII. John Edward (8) B. December 16, 1883.

78. John Kenelm Cheseldine (7)

Son of Kenelm Cheseldine (No. 40) and Lucinda (Ferguson) Cheseldine. Born in St. Mary's County August 19, 1847. He lived at White's Neck on a part of the original family plantation. He married (1) Frances A. Bailey on November 23, 1868. She died January 20, 1882. (2) Mary Long, daughter of Richard Long and Mary J. Buckler Long, born August 1, 1863. They were married July 22, 1882 by Father Basil Pacciarini. Children - 1st Marriage:

151.   I. Mary Jane (8) B. 1869. D. young.
152.   II. Lucinda (8) B. 1871
153.   III. Rebecca (8) B. D. young
154.   IV. David (8) B. D. young.
155.   V. John W. (8) B. 1873. D. August, 1939.
156.   VI. George F. (8) B. 1875
157.   VII. Ann R. B. 1877
158.VIII. Henry D. (8) B. 1879
         Children: - 2nd Marriage
159.   IX. Mary Jane (8) B. D. young
160.   X. James Arthur (8) B. D. young
161.   XI. Mary Whittie (8) B. May 4, 1886. D January 24, 1968.
162.   XII. Mary Elizabeth (Maria) (8) B.
163.   XIII. Mary Agnes (8) D. age 4
164. XIV. Lily G. (8) B. April 7, 1893. D. October 17, 1986.
165.   XV. David Stevens (8) B. September 2, 1895. D. December 9, 1969.
166. XVI. Robert Boyd (8) B. February 28, 1897
167.XVII. Gladys May (8) B. May 24, 1900
168.XVIII.Reginald Kenelm (8) B. February 4, 1902.
169.   XIX.Wilmer (8) D. infant
170.   XX.Virginia (8) B. April 9, 1910
170A.XXI Twin boy died at birth
170B.XXI Twin boy died at birth

79. George W. Cheseldine (7)

Son of Kenelm Cheseldine (No. 40) and Lucinda Ferguson Cheseldine. Born in St. Mary's County about 1849. He married (1)

Mary Flora Morris, on December 21, 1875 by the Reverend Mr. Hammond. She was born in 1859. Married (2) Elizabeth Morris on July 23, 1833 by Father Clement S. Lancaster. Children: - First Marriage

    171.   I. Eva (8) B.
           Children: - Second Marriage
    172.   II. Ida (8) B.
    173.   III. son (8) B.

80. Mary Ellen Cheseldine (7) Ellis

Daughter of John Cheseldine (No. 41) and Ellen (Watson) Cheseldine. Born in St. Mary's County in 1830. Married John W. Ellis January 6, 1851. Children:

    173A.   I. Mary Ellen Adelaide (8) B. October 6, 1856
              D. February 16, 1914.
    173B.   II. Richard (8) B. 1858.
    173C.   III. John Bernard (8) B. 1857. D. March 26, 1895.
    173D.   IV. Thomas (8) B. 1862.
    173E.   V. Edward (8) B. 1862.

81. Mary J. Cheseldine (7)

Daughter of John Cheseldine (No. 41) and Ellen (Watson) Cheseldine. Born in St. Mary's County in 1837.

82. Ann Lucille Cheseldine (7) Russell

Daughter of John Cheseldine (No. 41) and Julia Ann (Cullison) Cheseldine. Born in St. Mary's County in 1840. Married Joseph E. Russell. Children:

    173F.   I. Edward (8) B. 1865.
    173G.   II. Priscilla (8) B.

83. John Nelson Cheseldine (7)

Son of John Cheseldine (No. 41) and Julia Ann (Cullison) Cheseldine. Born in St. Mary's County in 1844. He is listed in the 1880 Census. He was married to Ann R. Thompson on July 1, 1872

by Father Basil Pacciarini. Children:
- 174. I. Joseph Endress (8) B. 1874.
- 175. II. Thomas A. (8) B. 1876.
- 176. III. William (8) B. 1877.
- 177. IV Eleana (8) B. 1879.
- 178. V. Nelson Alphonse (8) B. March 2, 1880. D. January 8, 1952.

84. William A. Cheseldine (7)

Son of John Cheseldine (No. 41) and Julia Ann (Cullison) Cheseldine. Born in St. Mary's County July 15, 1847. Married Eleanora _____ Cheseldine. He died May 5, 1876 and he, his wife and child are buried in the churchyard at All Saints Church, Oakley, Maryland. Children:
- 178A. I. Marchel (8) B. October 30, 1874. D. October 20, 1875.

85. Susan Cheseldine (7) Tippett

Daughter of William H. Cheseldine (No. 43) and Susan E. Payne Cheseldine. Born in St. Mary's County. Married Robert B. Tippett.

86. Alfred W. Cheseldine (7)

Son of George Washington Cheseldine (No. 44) and Mary Ann _____ Cheseldine. Born in St. Mary's County.

87. Augustus D. Cheseldine (7)

Son of George Washington Cheseldine (No. 44) and Mary Ann _____ Cheseldine. Born in St. Mary's County in 1849.

88. Cora Cheseldine (7)

Daughter of George Washington Cheseldine (No. 44) and Mary Ann _____ Cheseldine. Born in St. Mary's County.

89. Addie Cheseldine (7) Smith

Daughter of George Washington Cheseldine (No. 44) and Mary Ann _____ Cheseldine. Born in St. Mary's County. Married _____ Smith. Children:

178B.   I. Evelyn Smith (8) B.

90. Mary Marcellina Cheseldine (7) Ellis

Daughter of Charles C. Cheseldine (No. 48) and Ann (Gibson) Cheseldine. Born 1831. Married John Nelson Ellis, Sr., born in 1832, St. Mary's County, MD, January 26, 1852 in St. Mary's County, MD. After Mary Marcellina died _____, John N. married Mary Jane Rowe on August 29, 1865 in St. Mary's County, MD, by Rev. Levin. Their child, John Nelson Ellis, Jr., born in 1866. John Nelson Ellis, Sr. died April, 1880.

Children: of Mary Marcellina and John Ellis

178B1.   I. Charles Alexandria (8) B. September 9, 1854. D. February 25, 1914.
178B2.   II. Jane Marie (8) B. October 24, 1860. D. after 1910.
178B3.   III. John Nelson, Jr. (8) B. 1857, D. January 31, 1896.
178B4.   IV. Thomas E. (8) B. 1858.
178B5.   V. Mary Attaway (8) B. 1858, D. June, 1877.
178B6.   VI. Susan (8) B. October 24, 1862.

91. Jane Cheseldine (7) Morgan

Daughter of Charles C. Cheseldine (No. 48) and Ann (Gibson) Cheseldine. Born in St. Mary's County in 1835. Married at 19 years old, Thomas Daniel Morgan on August 7, 1854 at Sacred Heart Roman Catholic Church, age 33, widower. Children:

178B7.   I. Ann Emily (8) B.
178B8.   II. James Columbus (8) B.
178B9.   III. Thomas Daniel (8) B.
178B10.   IV. Anna (8) B.

92. Anna Cheseldine (7)

Daughter of Charles C. Cheseldine (No. 48) and Ann Gibson Cheseldine. Born in St.Mary's County in 1838.

93. Clara E. Cheseldine (7)

Daughter of Charles C. Cheseldine (No. 48) and Ann (Gibson) Cheseldine. Born in St. Mary's County in 1839.

94. Josephine Cheseldine (7) Ellis

Daughter of Charles C. Cheseldine (No. 48) and Henrietta (Morgan) Cheseldine. Born in St. Mary's County in 1850. Married Charles Ellis on November 28, 1868 by Father John B. De Wolfe. Children:

178C.   I. Addie (8) B.
178D.   II. Susan (8) B. July 25, 1871.
178E.   III. Thomas (8) B.
178F.   IV. Eva (8) B.
178G.   V. Ernest (8) B.
178H.   VI. Randolph (8) B. D. young.

95. Thomas E. Cheseldine (7)

Son of Charles C. Cheseldine (No. 48) and Henrietta (Morgan) Cheseldine. Born in St. Mary's County in 1856. Died prior to 1870.

96. Roseanna Cheseldine (7)

Daughter of Charles C. Cheseldine (No. 48) and Henrietta (Morgan) Cheseldine. Born in St. Mary's County in 1858. Died May 9, 1885. Will probated May 2, 1885 leaving everything to her sister Josephine Ellis.

97. William C. Cheseldine (7)

Son of William C. Cheseldine (No. 51) and Eleanor (Thompson) Cheseldine. Born in St. Mary's County 1843. He was in the Civil War in Co. C of the 1st MD Cavalry, CSA. He enlisted on August 10, 1862 and was wounded at Pollar's Farm. He died on June 8, 1864, after his right leg had been amputated at the thigh.

98. Catherine Cheseldine (7)

Daughter of William C. Cheseldine (No. 51) and Eleanor (Thompson) Cheseldine. Born in St. Mary's County in 1845.

99. John F. Cheseldine (7)

Son of William C. Cheseldine (No. 51) and Eleanor (Thompson) Cheseldine. Born in St. Mary's County on 1847. Died prior to 1860.

100. Ann V. Cheseldine (7)

Daughter of William C. Cheseldine (No. 51) and Eleanor (Thompson) Cheseldine. Born in St. Mary's County in 1849. Died prior to 1860.

101. Thomas Philip Cheseldine (7)

Son of William C. Cheseldine (No. 51) and Eleanor (Thompson) Cheseldine. Born in St. Mary's County 1850. Children:
179.   I. Phillip Henry (8) B.
180.   II. William (8) B.
181.   III. Susie (8) B.
182.   IV. Ludwell (8) B. D. 1946.
183.   V. Julia (8) B.

102. Ellen Cheseldine (7)

Daughter of William C. Cheseldine (No. 51) and Eleanor (Thompson) Cheseldine. Born in St. Mary's County in 1852.

103. Mary Cheseldine (7)

Daughter of William C. Cheseldine (No. 51) and Eleanor (Thompson) Cheseldine. Born in St. Mary's County in 1852.

104. Leddy Cheseldine (7)

Son of William C. Cheseldine (No. 51) and Eleanor (Thompson) Cheseldine. Born in St. Mary's County in 1859.

105. James H. Cheseldine (7)

Son of Gerard Cheseldine (No. 72) and Rebecca V. (Ellis) Cheseldine. Born in St. Mary's County in 1847. He married (1) Susan (surname unknown) Cheseldine and (2) Louisa (Husemann) Cheseldine, born 1858. Children: - First Marriage

184.   I. Tilly (8) B.
185.   II. Ida (8) B.
186.   III. Nettie (8) B. D. June 18, 1976.
        Children: - Second Marriage
187.   IV. James H. (8) B. 1872
188.   V. Mary M. (8) B. 1874.
189.   VI. W. Marshall (8) B. 1877. D. July 22, 1954.
190.   VII. Louisa (8) B. 1880
191.   VIII. John Reed (8) B 1882. D. September 6, 1977.

106. Charles Edward Cheseldine (7)

Son of Gerard Cheseldine (No. 72) and Rebecca V. (Ellis) Cheseldine. Born in St. Mary's County May 31, 1848. He married Mary Adelaide (surname unknown) Cheseldine, born October 6, 1856, who died February 16, 1915. Charles died May 29, 1921 in St. Mary's County, MD. Children:

192.   I. Charles Benjamin Fenwick (8) B. July 27,1875.
            D. November 4, 1883. (Beacon 11/15/1883).
193.   II. Mary Magdeline (8) B. 1876. D. 1947.
194.   III. Sarah Fenwick (8) B. 1879.
195.   IV. Patty (8) B.
196.   V. Carl Costello (8) B. 1895.
197.   VI. Florence "Flotie" (8) B. 1881. D. 1952.
198.   VII. Mazie (8) B. 1887. D. 1948.
199.   VIII. Marie (Dolly) (8) B. 1892. D. 1980.

107. Ataway Cheseldine (7)

Daughter of Gerard Cheseldine (No. 72) and Rebecca V. (Ellis) Cheseldine. Born in St. Mary's County July 13, 1849. Died young.

108. Ellen E. Cheseldine (7)

Daughter of Gerard Cheseldine (No. 72) and Rebecca V. (Ellis) Cheseldine.   Born in St. Mary's County in 1852.

109. Rebecca Cheseldine (7) Ellis

Daughter of Gerard Cheseldine (No. 72) and Rebecca V. (Ellis) Cheseldine. Born in St. Mary's County in 1854. Married November 12, 1879, Bernard Ellis, by the Reverend Mr. Murphy. Children:
- 200.   I. Ada (8) B.
- 201.   II. Daisy (8) B.
- 202.   III. Minnie (8) B.
- 203.   IV. Harry (8) B. 1886. D. 1967.
- 204.   V. Fenny (8) B.

110. Sarah M. Cheseldine (7) Gibson

Daughter of Gerard Cheseldine (No. 72) and Rebecca V. (Ellis) Cheseldine. Born February 10, 1857. Married September 28, 1882, Captain John Joe Gibson. They lived most of their long and happy married life on Canoe Neck Creek in St. Mary's County. Capt. John Joe was a famous river Captain on the Potomac River and spent many years on his schooner "Sunny South" plying the river and the Chesapeake Bay, hauling wheat, tobacco, oysters and the likes to Washington, D.C. and Baltimore, Maryland. Children:
- 205.   I. William Joseph (8) B. May 8, 1884. D. January 15, 1887.
- 206.   II. Mary Ida (8) B. August 1, 1886. D. September 17, 1887.
- 207.   III. Ann Rebecca (8) B. November 17, 1888.
- 208.   IV. Joseph Edgar (8) B. July 16, 1890.

209.   V. James Sylvester (8) B.February 15, 1892.
210.   VI. George Washington (8) B. February 22, 1894.
211.   VII. Cecil Francis (8) B. June 15, 1896.
212.VIII. Sarah Elizabeth (8) B. February 23, 1898.

111. Seneca Cheseldine (7)

Son of Gerard Cheseldine (No. 72) and Rebecca V. (Ellis) Cheseldine. Born in St. Mary's County in 1860. Married, May, 1887, Nellie Norris, born 1872. They resided at White's Neck Creek. Captain Seneca was a riverman all his life. Nellie died in 1930. Seneca died 1935. They are buried at Sacred Heart Church, Bushwood, Maryland. Children:
213.   I. Carrie (8) B. September 7, 1893. D. March 19, 1967.
214.   II. Isabel (8) B. January 4, 1909. D. May 19, 1968.
215.   III. Elmer Bennett (8) B. October 1, 1897. D. April 17, 1974.

112. Clara Cheseldine (7) Hogue

Daughter of Gerard Cheseldine (No. 72) and Rebecca V. (Ellis) Cheseldine. Born in St. Mary's County in 1861. Married on February 3, 1880 to Daniel Hogue by Reverend Mr. Keeble. Daniel was born in 1852 and died in 1929. They are both buried at All Saints. Children:
216.   I. William (8) B.
217.   II. Bruce (8) B.
218.   III. Mamie (8) B.
219   IV. Bessie (8) B.

113. Henrietta Cheseldine (7) Dingee

Daughter of Gerard Cheseldine (No. 72) and Rebecca V. (Ellis) Cheseldine. Born in St. Mary's County March 26, 1865. Married James Richard Dingee on October 30, 1883 at Green Springs by Rev. J. Gant. Captain Jimmy was the son of Julia A. and Edward Dingee, in the 1880 Census of St. Mary's County, born January 22, 1857, was a waterman. James and Henrietta lived on the point in Bushwood, Maryland and moved to Washington, D.C., where all of their children were living around 1938. They lived with their youngest daughter May and her husband Buster Javins. James died January 15, 1939, and Henrietta went to live with her daughter, Carrie, at 661 Morris Place, N.E., Washington, D.C., where she died on October 14, 1944. James and Henrietta are buried side by side at All Saints, Oakley, MD. Children:

220. I. Bessie (8) B. July 28, 1884. D. June 13, 1980.
221. II. Edith May (8) B. March 10, 1886. D. November 24, 1966.
222. III. Agnes (8) B. January 1, 1888. D. December 13, 1969.
223. IV. Ida V. (8) B. June 1, 1890. D. March 15, 1962.
224. V. Carrie Levonia (8) B. May 2, 1892. D. May 21, 1969.
225. VI. James Luther (8) B. December 7, 1893. D.
226. VII. Lida (8) B. December 9, 1898 D. March 9, 1985.
227. VIII. Nell (8) B. January 30, 1901 D. January 10, 1982.
228. IX. Minnie May (8) B. May 1, 1905 D. October 16, 1982.

114. Ann S. Cheseldine (7) Knott

Daughter of Biscoe Cheseldine (No. 54) and Ann Rebecca (Blackistone) Cheseldine Born in Machodac, Westmoreland County, VA in 1858. Married William Knott. She died on June 7, 1887. Children:

228A. I. George Biscoe (8) B. November 8, 1884. D. June 7, 1887.
228B. II. Maria (8) B. August 15, 1882.

115. Rebecca Cheseldine (7)

Daughter of Biscoe Cheseldine (No. 54) and Ann Rebecca (Blackistone) Cheseldine. Born in Machodac, Westmoreland County, VA in 1859. Died September 7, 1869.

116. Maria Stuart Cheseldine (7) Sullivan

Daughter of Biscoe Cheseldine (No. 54) and Ann Rebecca

(Blackistone) Cheseldine. Born in Machodac, Westmoreland County, VA August 15, 1862. Married D. A. Sullivan. Children:

    228C.   I. Ethel Mae (8) B.
    228D.   II.
    228E.   III.
    228F.   IV.

117. Elizabeth B. Cheseldine (7) Young

Daughter of Biscoe Cheseldine (No. 54) and Ann Rebecca (Blackistone) Cheseldine. Born in Machodac, Westmoreland County, VA in 1866. Married John Young, a widower with one son, Edward.

118. Samuel Dent Cheseldine (7)

Son of Posey Cheseldine (No. 55) and Nancy (Sims) Cheseldine. Born about 1847. He married Katie_____ Cheseldine. Died September 2, 1902, at Fort Worth, Texas. He owned stores in Columbus, Ohio. Children:

    229.   I. Jennie (8)
    230.   II. Bessie (8)
    231.   III. Donald (8)
    232.   IV. Sterling (8)

119. Charles Cheseldine (7)

Son of Posey Cheseldine (No. 55) and Nancy (Sims) Cheseldine. Born April 10, 1863, at Williamsburg, Ohio. Married September 11, 1890, Elizabeth (Minnie) Minshall. Minnie was called Pet by the family. Pet's grandmother was the daughter of Thomas Jefferson's brother, Randolph. Charlie inherited the big Cheseldine home on High Street, London, Ohio. He also inherited part of his father's business and became a wealthy merchant in London. He died February 23, 1908, at the young age of 44 and is buried in London, Ohio. He evidently left Pet well off, for she lived in the Cheseldine home until she was quite old. Her friend, Urcel Miller lived there with her. Ercell had a sister, Fay. Charles took care of their finances for them. She sent their two sons, Raymond and Kenneth to Ohio Wesleyan University. Children:

233.   I. Raymond Minshall (8) B. April, 1892. D. December, 1954.
234.   II. Kenneth George (8) B. June 30, 1898. D. March 26, 1988.

120. Biscoe Kenelm (Pearl) Cheseldine (7)

Son of Posey Cheseldine (No. 55) and Izora (Sims) Cheseldine. Born November 1, 1866, at Williamsburg, Ohio. He died June 19, 1929 at Lebanon, Ohio. Married, February 14, 1888, Margaret Lawler. She was born February 22, 1868 at Machanicsburg, Ohio. She died August 23, 1938, and is buried at the Lebanon, Ohio Cemetery. Biscoe Kenelm was commonly called Pearl by all who knew him. The nickname, Pearl, probably developed because his mother would call him "her little Pearl". He was very small and thin but considered a handsome man. His wife, Maggie, was a practical nurse. They were divorced in 1920. He became the victim of a familial disease known as Huntington's Chorea. It has not been learned from which side of the family Pearl inherited the disease. He is buried in the Lebanon Cemetery close to the fence on the west side of the old section. Children:
235.   I. Izora (8) B. November 16, 1889. D. May 18, 1921.
236.   II. Anna Evelyn (8) B. October 27, 1890. D. August 1, 1961.
237.   III. Edward Kyle (Prudy) (8) B. July 26, 1892. D. November 23, 1954.
238.   IV. Harold (Chick) (8) B. November 4, 1893. D. December 23, 1954.

121. Annie (Nannie) E. Cheseldine (7) Mattingly

Daughter of William E. Cheseldine (No. 62) and Ann Elizabeth Cheseldine. Born in St. Mary's County in 1854. Married Oscar Mattingly. Children:
239.   I. Nellie (8) B. 1872.

122. Susan F. Cheseldine (7) St. Clair

Daughter of William E. Cheseldine (No. 62) and Ann Elizabeth Cheseldine. Born in St. Mary's County in 1858. Married George St. Clair. Children:

240.   I. Josephine (8) B.

123. Richard Talbert Cheseldine (7)

Son of William E. Cheseldine (No. 62) and Ann Elizabeth Cheseldine. Born in St. Mary's County May 3, 1860. Was married to Annie Rebecca Turner, (Miss Nanny), on February 8, 1885 by Father Clement S. Lancaster. His father, William E. Cheseldine, a member of Company B., 1st Maryland Infantry, U.S.A., died in camp on February 20, 1865, leaving him without a father at the age of five. Captain Dick was a riverman on the Potomac and made his living by oystering, fishing, crabbing and hauling freight to Washington, D.C. by sailboat. At one time he ran a general merchandise store. He was small, about 5'5" tall, wiry, and a very strong man. Stories were told of him tossing nail kegs, including the nails, for sport. He made his home at White's Neck Creek on a part of the original Cheseldine plantation. The house was shaded by huge poplar trees which provided a refreshing cool breeze during the hot summer months. A neighbor, George Gibson, always said it was the coolest spot around and liked to "pass" the time of day with "Capt" Dick in rocking chairs on the front porch. "Miss Nanny" was quite a story teller of ghost tales and delighted in frightening the young boys that came to call on her granddaughters. There was always a house full of friends and relatives from the "City" for dinner on Sundays during the summertime. There would be platters of fried chicken, country ham, crab cakes, soft shell crabs, and vegetables fresh from the garden. To top off these bountiful dinners would be fresh home made ice cream, using the milk and cream from their own cow, and fresh baked pies. In their latter years they made their home on C Street, NE, on Capitol Hill in Washington, DC., where "Capt." Dick died on September 6, 1947 and "Miss Nanny" died September 3, 1959. They are both buried at Sacred Heart Church, Bushwood, Maryland. Children:

241.   I. George Walter (8) B. July 4, 1886. D. August 11, 1957.

242.   II. Richard Benjamin (8) B. February 20, 1889. D. February 22, 1963.
243.   III. Etta (8) B. September 20, 1891. D. February 15, 1960.
244.   IV. Alton Grover (8) B. December 18, 1893. D. June 9, 1981.

124. Jeremiah Cheseldine (7)

Son of Elijah Cheseldine (No. 66) and Sophia (surname unknown) Cheseldine. Born in St. Mary's County in 1823.

125. Jane M. Cheseldine (7) Frass

Daughter of Elijah Cheseldine (No. 66) and Sophia (surname unknown) Cheseldine. Born in St. Mary's County in 1835. Married August 26, 1856 John M. Frass.

126. Alemedia Cheseldine (7) Gardiner

Daughter of Elijah Cheseldine (No. 66) and Sophia (surname unknown) Cheseldine. Born in St. Mary's County on July 16, 1838. Married February 15, 1866, James Gardiner in Washington, D.C.

127. Richard Henry Cheseldine (7)

Son of Richard Cheseldine (No. 67) and Ann (Weakley) Cheseldine. Born in St. Mary's County about 1826. He married (1) Ann _____ around 1870. There seems to be no issue from this marriage. He married (2) March 14, 1889, Mrs. Emily Morgan Ellis. Children:
245.   I. Everett (8) B.
246.   II. William Dent (8) B. August 23, 1887. D. December 16, 1955.
247.   III. Joseph Richard (8) B. March 29, 1891. D. March 6, 1960.

128. Elizabeth Cheseldine (7) Thompson

Daughter of Richard Cheseldine (No. 67) and Ann (Weakley) Cheseldine. Born in St. Mary's County in 1830. Married _____Thompson.

129. Mary Caroline Cheseldine (7) Arnold

Daughter of Richard Cheseldine (No. 67) and Ann (Weakley) Cheseldine. Born in St. Mary's County in 1837. Married February, 1863, Richard Arnold.

130. Jane Cheseldine (7)

Daughter of Richard Cheseldine (No. 67) and Ann (Weakley) Cheseldine. Born in St. Mary's County in 1841.

131. Grayson L. Cheseldine (7)

Son of Richard Cheseldine (No. 67) and Ann (Weakley) Cheseldine. Born in St. Mary's County in 1845.

132. Cyrenius Cheseldine (7)

Son of Cyrenius Cheseldine (No. 70) and Margaret (Tippett) Cheseldine. Born about 1830 and married Caroline (Herbert) on October 21, 1856. He died in 1857. Apparently there was no issue. Caroline married James Ellis December 6, 1858.

Eighth generation begins
132A. Elizabeth Cullison (8) Barlow

Daughter of Mary L. (Cheseldine) Cullison (No. 73) and John Cullison. Lizzie was born _____. Married J. Barlow. Children:
247A. I. Chester (9) B.

132B. Lucy Cullison (8)

Daughter of Mary L. (Cheseldine) Cullison (No. 73) and John Cullison. Born.

132C. James Taylor (8)

Son of Mary L. (Cheseldine) Cullison Taylor (No. 73) and Edward Taylor. Born_____. Married _____. Children: 247B. I. Edward (9) B.

132D. Sarah Taylor (8)

Daughter of Mary L (Cheseldine) Cullison Taylor (No. 73) and Edward Taylor. Born

132E. Emma Taylor (8)

Daughter of Mary L. (Cheseldine) Cullison Taylor (No. 73) and Edward Taylor. Born.

133. William Francis Cheseldine (8)

Son of Andrew Jackson Cheseldine (No. 74) and Mary J. (Thompson) Cheseldine. Born in 1858 and married on January 14, 1884, Alice Brookbank. He lived for a number of years on St. Katherine's Island. Children:
248.   I. William Francis, Jr. (9) B. 1881. D. 1966.
249.   II. Grace Bell (9) B.
250.   III. Andrew Jackson (9) B. 1892. D. August 25, 1949.
251.   IV. Maud Regina (9) B.

134. Mary Susan Cheseldine (8) Morgan

Daughter of Andrew Jackson Cheseldine (No. 74) and Ann Maria (Morgan) Cheseldine. Born in St. Mary's County, August 13, 1862. Married James Morgan who drowned near Lewis B. Stone's wharf on St. Clement's Bay when he was knocked overboard by the careening of his boat during a heavy gale storm. He is buried at

Sacred Heart Church Cemetery. (Reported in St. Mary's Beacon March 4, 1897.) Children:
    252.   I. Louise (9) B. D. Infancy
    253.   II. Katherine Beatrice (9) B. August 6, 1902.

135. Mary Alice Cheseldine (8) Russell

Daughter of Andrew Jackson Cheseldine (No. 74) and Ann Maria (Morgan) Cheseldine. Born in St. Mary's County 1865. Married Edward N. Russell, February 15, 1886 by Father Clemont S. Lancaster. Children:
    254.   I. Lillian Marie (9) B. March 14, 1888.
    255.   II. Annie Beatrice (9) B.
    256.   III. Edward William Garrett (9) B.
    257.   IV. Ida Pearl (9) B.
    258.   V. Annette Louise (9) B. D. March 28, 1920.
    259.   VI. Joseph Lester (9) B. March 3, 1901. D. December 5, 1972.
    260.   VII. Theresa (9) B. D. In infancy.
    261.   VIII. Garrett (9) B.

136. Catherine Elizabeth Cheseldine (8) Bailey

Daughter of Andrew Jackson Cheseldine (No. 74) and Ann Maria (Morgan) Cheseldine. Born in St. Mary's County April 21, 1868 and married James Theodore Bailey. They lived on St. Margaret's Island for many years. This was one of the original three Islands that were included in Thomas Gerard's grant of St. Clement's Manor. The compiler of these notes (Edwin W. Beitzell) remembers as a small boy visiting here. He went by motor boat from Canoe Neck Creek with his parents for week end visits and remembers the good times had playing about the island with his cousin Freddie Cheseldine, a grandson of "Capt" Theodore. She died August 28, 1902, and is buried at Sacred Heart Church, Bushwood, MD. Children:
    262.   I. James Andrew (9) B. November 3, 1887.
    263.   II. Susie Elizabeth (9) B. November 3, 1888. D. October 8, 1969.
    264.   III. Catherine Elizabeth (9) B. January 17, 1891.

265. IV. Ann Maria (9) B. Died in infancy.
266. V. Robert Pendleton (9) B. May 1, 1895.
267. VI. Samuel Mathew (9) B. November 29, 1896. D. November 13, 1980.
268. VII. Maud Roberta (9) B. D. Infancy
269. VIII. Walter Benjamin (9) B. D. Infancy

137. Mary Beatrice Cheseldine (8)

Daughter of Andrew Jackson Cheseldine (No. 74) and Ann Maria (Morgan) Cheseldine. Born in St. Mary's County in 1870.

138. Robert Cheseldine (8)

Son of Andrew Jackson Cheseldine (No. 74) and Ann Maria (Morgan) Cheseldine. Born in St. Mary's County January 15, 1872. He died during the storm of Tuesday, September 29, 1896. The pungy, Capitol, of Milestown District was swamped off Sandy Point, Potomac River. Captain Robert Cheseldine and two black men, William B. Jones and Joseph Price were drowned. He is buried at Sacred Heart in Bushwood, MD. The story of the tragedy appeared in the St. Mary's Beacon of October 8, 1896.

139. Andrew Freeman Cheseldine (8)

Son of Andrew Jackson Cheseldine (No. 74) and Ann Maria (Morgan) Cheseldine. Born in St. Mary's County June 7, 1874. He married May 17, 1898, Annie Maud Lone, born November 7, 1881. They had a very fine farm at White's Neck, which is a part of the original Cheseldine holdings. Freeman died May 12, 1935 and is buried at Sacred Heart Church Cemetery. Children:
270. I. Doris (9) B. May 26, 1900. D. June 20, 1976.
271. II. Mary Elsie (9) B. October 1, 1902. D. June 2, 1977
272. III. Andrew Freeman (9) B. March 28, 1905
273. IV. Maria (9) B.

140. Lelia Virginia Cheseldine (8) Beitzell

Daughter of Andrew Jackson Cheseldine (No. 74) and Ann

Maria (Morgan) Cheseldine. Born in St. Mary's County October 22, 1876. Married in May, 1911, Charles Henry Beitzell, born September 1872. They lived in the Imperial Valley, California for a few years after their marriage but returned to White's Neck, St. Mary's County in 1914. Lelia died July 5, 1914. (See St. Mary's Beacon 7/9/1914). Children:

    274.   I. Mary Alice (9) B. July 27, 1912.
    275.   II. baby girl (9) B. 1914. Died same year.

141. Mary Ida Cheseldine (8) Beitzell

Daughter of Andrew Jackson Cheseldine (No. 74) and Ann Maria (Morgan) Cheseldine. Born in St. Mary's County 1882. Married October 25, 1916 Charles Henry Beitzell, her brother-in-law. She was considered a wonderful wife, mother, friend and neighbor. Everyone loved her for her piety, good works, ready wit and good humor. They resided on St. Katherine's Island until the children became of school age. They then moved to the mainland and developed a fine farm at White's Neck, St. Mary's County. Mary Ida died in May, 1947. Children:

    276.   I. Lelia Virginia (9) B. October 11, 1917.
    277.   II. Grace (9) B. January 11, 1919.
    278.   III. George Lee (9) B. April 5, 1922.

142. Garrett Francis Cheseldine (8)

Son of Andrew Jackson Cheseldine (No. 74) and Ann Maria (Morgan) Cheseldine. Born in St. Mary's County May 19, 1883. Married Mary Lillian (Gass) at Sacred Heart Church on April 29, 1908 by Father Joseph Kelly at a Nuptial Mass. They resided at White's Neck on a part of the original Cheseldine holdings. Mary Lillian died April 20, 1975 and is buried at Sacred Heart Church. Children:

    279.   I. Mary Beatrice (9) B.
    280.   II. Robert Garrett (9) B. February 3, 1917.
               D. November 28, 1967.
    281.   III. James (9) B.
    282.   IV. Mabel (9) B. March 2, 1923.

142A. William Nobel Ellis (8)

Son of Ann Maria (Cheseldine) Ellis (No. 75) and John Ellis. Born January 11, 1862. Died September 5, 1929.

143. Mary Elizabeth Norris (8) Beitzell

Daughter of Jane Ann (Cheseldine) Norris (No. 77) and John Hanson Norris. Born in St. Mary's County, Maryland, March 6, 1865. She married November 21, 1888, Josiah E. Beitzell of St. Mary's County and lived at Collingwood, Abell, Maryland. After her death in 1925, Josiah married secondly, Mrs. Katy (Husemann) Anderson, June 1927, a widow with three daughters, Gladys, Lorraine and Frances. There were no children of the second marriage. Capt. Josiah died January 15, 1959.

Elizabeth (Lizzie), although she had practically no formal education, loved to read and did everything in her power to ensure that her children would be educated as well as possible. She was deeply religious and a devout Catholic and a wonderful wife and mother. All who knew her, white and colored, relatives, friends and neighbors, loved her. When there was illness among the neighbors and the Doctor was not available, a messenger was sent "to fetch Miss Lizzie". It was a principle with her that unless she could speak well of another she kept her own counsel and would not speak out unless an innocent person would be injured. "Aunt Lizzie" was missed, after her death, almost as much by her many nephews and nieces as by her own children. She faced death bravely, as she faced life, and died after nine months of intense suffering, fully conscious of the approaching end. Her last request to her youngest son, Edwin Warfield, was to read to her the prayers of the Holy Mass, as she had requested many times during her long illness. She died August 17, 1925 and is buried at Sacred Heart Church, Bushwood, Maryland. Children: - First Marriage

282A. I. Josiah Edward, Jr. (9) B. July 19, 1890.
282B. II. Mary Alice (9) B. August 7, 1891.
282C. III. Charles Benjamin (9) B. May 7, 1893.
282D. IV. Harry Alvin (9) B. September 26, 1896.
282E. V. Albert Clement (9) B. September 25, 1898.
282F. VI. Walter Bryan (9) B. June 19, 1900.
282G. VII. Edwin Warfield (9) B. June 19, 1905.

144. Lucy Rebecca Norris (8) Owens

Daughter of Jane Ann (Cheseldine) Norris (No. 77) and John Hanson Norris. Lucy Rebecca was born October 4, 1866, in St. Mary's County, MD, married July 23, 1883, by Father Clement S. Lancaster, Benjamin Isaac Owens, born December 26, 1860. Lucy died June 3, 1930. Benjamin died August 28, 1935. They resided in Abell, MD, on a part of the farm "Collingwood", St. Mary's County, in 1949, the home of their youngest daughter, Elizabeth. Children:

282H.   I. _____ (9)
282I.   II. _____ (9)
282J.   III. William Lee (9) B. September 14, 1887.
282K.   IV. Jane Ann (9) B. August 16, 1890.
282L.   V. John Joseph (9) B. February 27, 1892.
282M.   VI. Daisy Dora (9) B. July 1, 1894. D. November 12, 1895.
282N.   VII. Grover Raymond (9) B. March 8, 1896.
282O.VIII. James Benjamin (9) B. October 4, 1897.
282P.   IX. Essie May (9) B. March 1, 1900.
282Q.   X. Charles Larry Palmer (9) B. March 25, 1903.
282R.   XI. Joseph Maynard (9) B. January 3, 1908.D. October 6, 1908.
282S.   XII. Mary Elizabeth (9) B. September 9, 1910.

145. Joseph Alvin Norris (8)

Son of Jane Ann (Cheseldine) Norris (No. 77) and John Hanson Norris. Joseph Alvin, born 1868, in St. Mary's County, married September 1, 1897, Rosella Alvey. She died about 1902 and Al died March 4, 1945. He was a hard worker and the finest gardener in St. Mary's County, MD, where he lived all his life. Children:

282T.   I. John Francis (9) B. April 10, 1898.
282U.   II. Eldridge (9) B. about 1900. D. about 1916.

146. Frances Lorraine Norris (8) Thompson

Daughter of Jane Ann (Cheseldine) Norris (No. 77) and John Hanson Norris. Frances Lorraine, born March 20, 1873, St. Mary's

County, married June 23, 1888, William Edgar Thompson, born February 18, 1873. Resided on St. Patrick's Creek, St. Mary's County, MD. She died January 9, 1926. Children:

282V.   I. Grace Genevieve (9) B. April 28, 1889.
282W.   II. Ruth Lorraine (9) B. April 8, 1891.
282X.   III. Edgar Francis (9) B. January 1, 1893.
282Y.   IV. William Lee (9) B. October 11, 1898.
282Z.   V. Leonard Allen (9) B. March 20, 1903.

147. Jane Nettie Norris (8) Swann

Daughter of Jane Ann (Cheseldine) Norris (No. 77) and John Hanson Norris. Jane Nettie, born January 25, 1875, St. Mary's County, married April 4, 1899, Henry Samuel Swann, born in Maryland, September 20, 1875, who died November 21, 1934. They resided in Ryceville, MD., near Charlotte Hall, until about 1920, when they moved to Redd's Corner, Camp Springs, MD. Children:

283A.   I. Laura Virginia (9) B. June 1, 1900.
283B.   II. Annabelle (Annie Bell) (9) B. August 21, 1905.

148. John Lee Norris (8)

Son of Jane Ann (Cheseldine) Norris (No. 77) and John Hanson Norris. John Lee, born April 11, 1877, St. Mary's County, married September 26, 1896, (1) Mary Norma Knott (Marriage license reads "Marion Knotts"). She died May 29, 1920. (2) Mrs. Stuart Norris, a widow with 11 children. Children: - First Marriage

283C.   I. Alma (9) B. 1897. D. In infancy.
283D.   II. William Allen Boyd (9) B. August 19, 1899.
283E.   III. James Ralph (9) B. May 22, 1903.
283F.   IV. Bernard Elmer (9) B. July 11, 1904.
283G.   V. Mary Norma (9) B. February 20, 1908.
283H.   VI. John Walter (9) B. May 29, 1910.
283I.   VII. John Leo (9) B. December 20, 1912.
283J.   VIII. Charles Ernest (9) B. July 20, 1915.
283K.   IX. Mary Alice (9) B. September 4, 1918.

149. James Benjamin Norris (8)

Son of Jane Ann (Cheseldine) Norris (No. 77) and John Hanson Norris. James Benjamin was born September 9, 1879, at Barton Hall, St. Mary's County, MD. As a young man he went to Washington, DC, where he married, February 20, 1906, Helen Maud McClure at St. Patrick's Church. She was born in Kenosha, WI, July 7, 1887, and died in Minneapolis, MN, June 12, 1937. Moved to Chicago about 1912 and a year later to Minneapolis. Employed there by the Chicago-Northwestern Railroad, the Pence Automobile Company and in 1947, Draper Kramer Company at Fair Oaks Apartment Homes. Children:

    283L.   I. Edna Genevieve (9) B. December 6, 1907.
    283M.   II. James Stafford (9) B. July 17, 1910.
    283N.   III. John Randolph (9) B. July 2, 1919.

150. John Edward Norris (8)

Son of Jane Ann (Cheseldine) Norris (No. 77) and John Hanson Norris. John Edward, born December 16, 1883, married June 28, 1909, Bernadette Owens, a niece of Benjamin I. Owens, who married Lucy Rebecca Norris. They resided in St. Mary's County, MD, until about 1922 when they moved to Washington, DC. Children:

    283O.   I. Irving (9) B. October 1, 1910.
    283P.   II. Olive (9) B. September 7, 1912.
    283Q.   III. Jane A. (9) B. March 17, 1919.
    283R.   IV. Martha (9) B. November 27, 1923.
    283S.   V. Betty (9) B. May 1, 1932.

151. Mary Jane Cheseldine (8)

Daughter of John Kenelm Cheseldine (No. 78) and Frances A. (Bailey) Cheseldine. Born 1869. Died young.

152. Lucinda Cheseldine (8)

Daughter of John Kenelm Cheseldine (No. 78) and Frances A. (Bailey) Cheseldine. Born 1871.

153. Rebecca Cheseldine (8)

Daughter of John Kenelm Cheseldine (No. 78) and Frances A. (Bailey) Cheseldine. Born _____. Died young.

154. David Cheseldine (8)

Son of John Kenelm Cheseldine (No. 78) and Frances A. (Bailey) Cheseldine. Born _____. Died young.

155. John W. Cheseldine (8)

Son of John Kenelm Cheseldine (No. 78) and Frances A. (Bailey) Cheseldine. Born in St. Mary's County, 1873. Married Mary Magdaline (Maggie) Cheseldine. He was a boat builder on White's Neck Creek. He died August, 1939 and is buried at All Saints Church, Oakley, Maryland. Children:
283T.   I. Annie (9) B.

156. George F. Cheseldine (8)

Son of John Kenelm Cheseldine (No. 78) and Frances A. (Bailey) Cheseldine. Born in St. Mary's County, 1875. Married Sarah Fanny Cheseldine, (No. 194). Children:
284.   I. George Benjamin (9) B.
285.   II. Frederick (9) B.

157. Ann R. Cheseldine (8)

Daughter of John Kenelm Cheseldine (No. 78) and Frances A. (Bailey) Cheseldine. Born 1877.

158. Henry D. Cheseldine (8)

Son of John Kenelm Cheseldine (No. 78) and Frances A. (Bailey) Cheseldine. Born in St. Mary's County in 1879.

159. Mary Jane Cheseldine (8)

Daughter of John Kenelm Cheseldine (No. 78) and Mary (Long) Cheseldine. Born _____. Died young

160. James Arthur Cheseldine (8)

Son of John Kenelm Cheseldine (No. 78) and Mary (Long) Cheseldine. Born _____. Died young.

161. Mary Whittie Cheseldine (8) Oliver

Daughter of John Kenelm Cheseldine (No. 78) and Mary (Long) Cheseldine. Born in St. Mary's County on May 4, 1886. Died January 24, 1968. Married Vick Oliver.

162. Mary Elizabeth (Maria) Cheseldine (8) Nelson

Daughter of John Kenelm Cheseldine (No. 78) and Mary (Long) Cheseldine. Born in St. Mary's County. Married Carl Nelson.

163. Mary Agnes Cheseldine (8)

Daughter of John Kenelm Cheseldine (No. 78) and Mary (Long) Cheseldine. Born_____. Died age 4.

164. Lily G. Cheseldine (8) Eibel, DeWaard

Daughter of John Kenelm Cheseldine (No. 78) and Mary (Long) Cheseldine. Born in St. Mary's County on April 7, 1893. Married (1) Charles Eibel. (2) Leo DeWaard, born August 3, 1887. He died July 10, 1973. Lily died October 17, 1986. They are buried at All Saints Church Cemetery, Oakley, MD.

165. David Stevens Cheseldine (8)

Son of John Kenelm Cheseldine (No. 78) and Mary (Long) Cheseldine. Born in St. Mary's County September 2, 1895. Married

(1) Bertha Bailey. (2) Roberta A. Walker. He died November 9, 1969. She died March 8, 1976. They are buried at Cedar Hill Cemetery, Suitland, MD. Children:
- 286. I. Marjorie (9) B. 1920.
- 287. II. Betty Lee (9) B. 1923.

166. Robert Boyd Cheseldine (8)

Son of John Kenelm Cheseldine (No. 78) and Mary (Long) Cheseldine. Born in St. Mary's County February 28, 1897. Married Lillian Ellis. Children:
- 288. I. John Wilmer (9) B.
- 289. II. Margaret Louise (9) B.
- 290. III. Robert Boyd, Jr. (9) B.

167. Gladys May Cheseldine (8) Hall

Daughter of John Kenelm Cheseldine (No. 78) and Mary (Long) Cheseldine. Born in St. Mary's County May 24, 1900. Married John Hall.

168. Reginald Kenelm Cheseldine (8)

Son of John Kenelm Cheseldine (No. 78) and Mary (Long) Cheseldine. Born in St. Mary's County on February 4, 1903.

169. Wilmer Cheseldine (8)

Son of John Kenelm Cheseldine (No. 78) and Mary (Long) Cheseldine. Born _____. Died in infancy.

170. Virginia Cheseldine (8) Bailey

Daughter of John Kenelm Cheseldine (No. 78) and Mary (Long) Cheseldine. Born in St. Mary's County on April 9, 1910. Married Paul Bailey.

170A. Infant (8) Twin boy Cheseldine

Son of John Kenelm Cheseldine (No. 78) and Mary (Long) Cheseldine. Born _____. Died at birth.

170B. Infant (8) Twin boy Cheseldine

Son of John Kenelm Cheseldine (No. 78) and Mary (Long) Cheseldine. Born _____. Died at birth.

171. Eva Cheseldine (8) Dyson, Hall

Daughter of George W. Cheseldine (No. 79) and Mary Flora (Morris) Cheseldine. Born ____. Married (1) John Dyson and (2) _____ Hall. Children:
  290A. I.
  290B. II.

172. Ida Cheseldine (8)

Daughter of George W. Cheseldine (No. 79) and Elizabeth (Morris) Cheseldine. Born ____.

173. son Cheseldine (8)

Son of George W. Cheseldine (No. 79) and Elizabeth (Morris) Cheseldine. Born _____.

173A. Mary Ellen Ellis (8)

Daughter of Mary Ellen (Cheseldine) Ellis (No. 80) and John W. Ellis. Born October 6, 1856 in St. Mary's County, MD. Died February 16, 1914 in St. Mary's County, MD.

173B. Richard Ellis (8)

Son of Mary Ellen (Cheseldine) Ellis (No. 80) and John W. Ellis. Born 1858.

173C. Bernard Ellis (8)

Son of Mary Ellen (Cheseldine) Ellis (No. 80) and John W. Ellis. Born 1860.

173D. Thomas Ellis (8)

Son of Mary Ellen (Cheseldine) Ellis (No. 80) and John W. Ellis. Born 1862.

173E. Edward Ellis (8)

Son of Mary Ellen (Cheseldine) Ellis (No. 80) and John W. Ellis. Born 1862.

173F. Edward N. Russell (8)

Son of Ann Lucille (Cheseldine) Russell (No. 82) and Joseph E. Russell. Born 1865. Married Mary Alice Cheseldine (No. 135), February 15, 1886 by Father Clemont S. Lancaster. Children:
- 254.   I. Lillian Marie (9) B. March 14, 1888.
- 255.   II. Annie Beatrice (9) B.
- 256.   III. Edward William Garrett (9) B.
- 257.   IV. Ida Pearl (9) B.
- 258.   V. Annette Louise (9) B. D. March 28, 1920.
- 259.   VI. Joseph Lester (9) B. March 3, 1901. D. December 5, 1972.
- 260.   VII. Theresa (9) B. D. In infancy.
- 261.   VIII. Garrett (9) B.

173G. Priscilla Russell (8)

Daughter of Ann Lucille (Cheseldine) Russell (No. 82) and Joseph E. Russell. Born _____.

174. Joseph Endress Cheseldine (8)

Son of John Nelson Cheseldine (No. 83) and Ann R. (Thompson) Cheseldine. Born in St. Mary's County about 1874.

Married Mary Maud Mattingly, October 27, 1896. Buried at Sacred Heart. Children:
    291.   I. Grace (9) B. D. young.
    292.   II. Stanley (9) B. D. young.
    293.   III. W. Wallace (9) B. D. March 23, 1949.
    294.   IV. Lillian (9) B.
    295.   V. Margaret (9) B.

175. Thomas A. Cheseldine (8)

Son of John Nelson Cheseldine (No. 83) and Ann R. (Thompson) Cheseldine. Born in St. Mary's County in 1876.

176. William Cheseldine (8)

Son of John Nelson Cheseldine (No 83) and Ann R. (Thompson) Cheseldine. Born in St. Mary's County in 1877.

177. Eleana Cheseldine (8)

Daughter of John Nelson Cheseldine (No. 83) and Ann R. (Thompson) Cheseldine. Born in St. Mary's County in 1879.

178. Nelson Alphonse Cheseldine (8)

Son of John Nelson Cheseldine (No. 83) and Ann R. (Thompson) Cheseldine. Born in St. Mary's County March 2, 1880. He was know as "Capt. Fauny". He made his home at Colton's Point, MD. Married January 25, 1908, Elizabeth Mattingly who died December 23, 1949. He died January 8, 1952. They are buried at Sacred Heart. Children:
    296.   I. Everett Alphonse (9) B. April 3, 1910.

178A. Marchel Cheseldine (8)

Son of William A. Cheseldine (No. 84) and Eleanora _____ Cheseldine. Born October 30, 1874. Died October 20, 1875. Buried with his parents at All Saints Church Cemetery.

178B. Evelyn Smith (8) Dent

Daughter of Addie (Cheseldine) Smith (No. 89) and _____
Smith. Born _____. Married Warren Dent.

178B1. Charles Alexandria Ellis (8)

Son of Mary Marcellina (Cheseldine) Ellis (No. 90) and John
Nelson Ellis, Sr. Born September 9, 1854 in St. Mary's County, MD.
Died February 25, 1914 in St. Mary's County, MD.

178B2. Jane Marie Ellis (8)

Daughter of Mary Marcellina (Cheseldine) Ellis (No. 90) and
John Nelson Ellis, Sr. Born October 24, 1860. Died after 1910.

178B3. John Nelson Ellis, Jr. (8)

Son of Mary Marcellina (Cheseldine) Ellis (No. 90) and John
Nelson Ellis, Sr. Born 1857. Died January 31, 1896.

178B4. Thomas E. Ellis (8)

Son of Mary Marcellina (Cheseldine) Ellis (No. 90) and John
Nelson Ellis, Sr. Born 1858.

178B5. Mary Attaway Ellis (8)

Daughter of Mary Marcellina (Cheseldine) Ellis (No. 90) and
John Nelson Ellis, Sr. Born 1858. Died June, 1877.

178B6. Susan Ellis (8)

Daughter of Mary Marcellina (Cheseldine) Ellis (No. 90) and
John Nelson Ellis, Sr. Born October 24, 1862.

178B7. Ann Emily Morgan (8)

Daughter of Jane (Cheseldine) Morgan (No. 91) and Thomas
Daniel Morgan. Born

178B8. James Columbus Morgan (8)

Son of Jane (Cheseldine) Morgan (No. 91) and Thomas Daniel Morgan. Born

178B9. Thomas Daniel Morgan (8)

Son of Jane (Cheseldine) Morgan (No. 91) and Thomas Daniel Morgan. Born

178B10. Anna Morgan (8)

Daughter of Jane (Cheseldine) Morgan (No. 91) and Thomas Daniel Morgan. Born

178C. Addie Ellis (8) Thompson

Daughter of Josephine (Cheseldine) Ellis (No. 94) and Charles Ellis. Born _____. Married Otho Thompson.

178D. Susan Ellis (8) Beitzell

Daughter of Josephine (Cheseldine) Ellis (No. 94) and Charles Ellis. Born July 25, 1871. Married July 5, 1899, George Lee Beitzell. Children:
- 296A.   I. Masie (9) B. August 4, 1900.
- 296B.   II. Josephine (9) B. July 8, 1904.
- 296C.   III. Leonard (9) B. December 13, 1908. Died young.
- 296D.   IV. Marguerite (9) B. July 11, 1913.

178E. Thomas Ellis (8)

Son of Josephine (Cheseldine) Ellis (No. 94) and Charles Ellis. Born _____. Married Ella _____. Children:
- 296E.   I. Gilbert (9) B.
- 296F.   II. Delmas (9) B.

178F. Eva Ellis (8) Morris

Daughter of Josephine (Cheseldine) Ellis (No. 94) and Charles Ellis. Born ____. Married Foster Morris. Children:

296G.　I. Earl (9) B.
296H.　II. Ernest (9) B.
296I.　III. Dora (9) B.

178G. Ernest Ellis (8)

Son of Josephine Cheseldine Ellis (No 94) and Charles Ellis. Born _____. Married Esther Morris.

178H. Randolph Ellis (8)

Son of Josephine (Cheseldine) Ellis (No. 94) and Charles Ellis Born _____. Died young.

179. Phillip Henry Cheseldine (8)

Son of Thomas Philip Cheseldine (No 101) and _____. Born ____. Children:

297.　I. Elmer Henry (9) B. ___.
298.　II. Grace May (9) B. ____.

180. William Cheseldine (8)

Son of Thomas Philip Cheseldine (No. 101) and _____. Born _____.

181. Susie Cheseldine (8) Pumphrey

Daughter of Thomas Philip Cheseldine (No. 101) and _____. Born _____.M. _____Pumphrey.

182. Ludwell Cheseldine (8)

Son of Thomas Philip Cheseldine (No. 101) and _____. Born ____. Died 1946.

77

183. Julia Cheseldine (8) Barbour

Daughter of Thomas Philip Cheseldine (No. 101) and _____. Born _____. Married _____Barbour.

184. Tilly Cheseldine (8) Chauncey

Daughter of James H. Cheseldine (No. 105) and Susan (surname unknown) Cheseldine. Born _____. Married _____Chauncey. In 1954 she lived at 4514 Conn. Ave., NW, Washington, DC.

185. Ida Cheseldine (8) Johnson

Daughter of James H. Cheseldine (No. 105) and Susan (surname unknown) Cheseldine. Born _____. Married _____Johnson.

186. Nettie Cheseldine (8) Carter

Daughter of James H. Cheseldine (No. 105) and Susan (surname unknown) Cheseldine. Born _____. Married _____Carter. In 1954 she lived at 4514 Conn. Ave., NW, Washington, DC. Died June 18, 1976.

187. James H. Cheseldine (8)

Son of James H. Cheseldine (No. 105) and Louisa (Husemann) Cheseldine. Born 1872.

188. Mary M. Cheseldine (8)

Daughter of James H. Cheseldine (No. 105) and Louisa (Husemann) Cheseldine. Born 1874.

189. W. Marshall Cheseldine (8)

Son of James H. Cheseldine (No. 105) and Louisa (Husemann) Cheseldine. Born at River Springs in St. Mary's County, 1877. He made his home in Washington, DC. He graduated from the Washington College of Law, now a part of American University. He did post graduate work at George Washington University in the field of railroad transportation and became an authority in that field. He was admitted to practice before the U.S. Supreme Court. He began his career with the Interstate Commerce Commission on March 7, 1910 and retired on May 31, 1948. He returned on a temporary appointment from November 1950 to April 1951. He died July 22, 1954 at age 76.

NOTE: Obituary from 1954

W. M. Cheseldine, ICC Employee for 38 Years, Dies

W. M. Cheseldine, 76, a retired Interstate Commerce Commission examiner, died today after a heart attack at his home, 4801 Connecticut Avenue, N.W. (Washington, D.C.). He was an authority on railroad transportation. Mr. Cheseldine began his career with the commission as a junior clerk on March 7, 1910. He retired May 31, 1948, but returned to the ICC as an examiner on a temporary appointment from November, 1950 to April, 1955. A native of River Springs, St. Mary's County, MD, Mr. Cheseldine was graduated from the Washington College of Law, now a part of American University. He later took post graduate work at George Washington University in the field of railroad transportation.

(As of 1954) Mr. Cheseldine, a surviving brother, John Reed Cheseldine, 2720 Wisconsin Avenue, N.W., and a nephew, James Corbin Cheseldine, 4376 North Pershing Drive, Arlington (VA), all passed the District bar examination simultaneously in the 1920's. The three were later admitted to practice before the Supreme Court.

Mr. Cheseldine also is survived by two sisters, Mrs. Tillie C. Chauncey, and Mrs. Nettie C. Carter, both of 4514 Connecticut Avenue, N.W.

Funeral arrangements have not been completed.

190. Louisa Cheseldine (8)

Daughter of James H. Cheseldine (No 105) and Louisa (Husemann) Cheseldine. Born 1880.

191. John Reed Cheseldine (8)

Son of James H. Cheseldine (No. 105) and Louisa (Husemann) Cheseldine. Born in St. Mary's County about 1882. He was an attorney for the Internal Revenue Service for more than 30 years. Married_____. In 1954 listed at 2720 Wisconsin Ave., NW, Washington, DC. Died September 6, 1977. Buried in Arlington Cemetery. Children:

    299.   I. James Corbin (8) B. D. August 31, 1977.

192. Charles Benjamin Fenwick Cheseldine (8)

Son of Charles Edward Cheseldine (No. 106) and Mary Adelaide (surname unknown) Cheseldine. Born July 27, 1875. Died November 4, 1883. Buried at All Saints Oakley, MD.

193. Mary Magdaline Cheseldine (8)

Daughter of Charles Edward Cheseldine (No. 106) and Mary Adelaide (surname unknown) Cheseldine. Born in 1876. Married John Cheseldine. Died 1947. Buried at All Saints, Oakley, MD.

194. Sarah Fenwick Cheseldine (8)

Daughter of Charles Edward Cheseldine (No. 106) and Mary Adelaide (surname unknown) Cheseldine. Born 1879. Married George Cheseldine (No.156) born 1875. Children:

    284.   I. George Benjamin (9) B.
    285.   II. Frederick (9) B.

195. Patty Cheseldine (8)

Daughter of Charles Edward Cheseldine (No. 106) and Mary Adelaide (surname unknown) Cheseldine. Born _____.

196. Carl Costello Cheseldine (8)

Son of Charles Edward Cheseldine (No 106) and Mary Adelaide (surname unknown) Cheseldine. Born in St. Mary's County

1895.   Married Maud Owens.   Died 1975.   Buried at All Saints, Oakley, MD. Children:

      300.   I. Mary Adelaide (9) B. August 3, 1920.

      301.   II. Carl Costello, Jr. (9) B. August 3, 1930. D. 1981.

197. Florence (Flotie) Cheseldine (8) Quade

Daughter of Charles Edward Cheseldine (No. 106) and Mary Adelaide (surname unknown) Cheseldine. Born 1881. Married Bruce Quade. Died 1952. Buried at All Saints, Oakley, MD.

198. Mazie R. Cheseldine (8) Bailey

Daughter of Charles Edward Cheseldine (No. 106) and Mary Adelaide (surname unknown) Cheseldine. Born 1887. Married Joseph (Fenny) Bailey. Died 1948. Buried at Sacred Heart.

199. Marie (Dolly) Cheseldine (8) Oliver, Long

Daughter of Charles Edward Cheseldine (No. 106) and Mary Adelaide (surname unknown) Cheseldine. Born 1892. Married (1) Raymond Oliver and (2) Phillip Long. Died 1980. Buried at St. Joseph's, Morganza, MD.

200. Ada Ellis (8) Smith

Daughter of Rebecca (Cheseldine) Ellis (No. 109) and Bernard Ellis. Born ____. Married Will Smith.

201. Daisy Ellis (8) Oliver

Daughter of Rebecca (Cheseldine) Ellis (No. 109) and Bernard Ellis. Born_____. Married Wood Oliver.

202. Minnie Ellis (8) Smith

Daughter of Rebecca (Cheseldine) Ellis (No. 109) and Bernard Ellis. Born _____. Married Walter Smith.

203. Harry Ellis (8)

Son of Rebecca (Cheseldine) Ellis (No. 109) and Bernard Ellis. Born 1886. Married Nellie Owens, born 1899, died 1980. Died 1967 Buried at All Saints.

204. Fenny Ellis (8)

Son of Rebecca (Cheseldine) Ellis (No. 109) and Bernard Ellis. Born _____.

205. William Joseph Gibson (8)

Son of Sarah M. (Cheseldine) Gibson (No. 110) and Captain John Joe Gibson. Born May 8, 1884. Died January 15, 1887.

206. Mary Ida Gibson (8)

Daughter of Sarah M. (Cheseldine) Gibson (No. 110) and Captain John Joe Gibson. Born August 1, 1886. Died September 17, 1887.

207. Ann Rebecca Gibson (8)

Daughter of Sarah M. (Cheseldine) Gibson (No. 110) and Captain John Joe Gibson. Born November 17, 1888.

208. Joseph Edgar Gibson (8)

Son of Sarah M. (Cheseldine) Gibson (No. 110) and Captain John Joe Gibson. Born July 16, 1890. Married Eva Thompson. Children:

301A.   I. William Thomas (9) B. October 28, 1914. D. August 4, 1917.
301B.   II. Mary Annie (9) B.
301C.   III. John Edgar (9) B.
301D.   IV. Margaret Adelaide (9) B.

209. James Sylvester Gibson (8)

Son of Sarah M. (Cheseldine) Gibson (No. 110) and Captain John Joe Gibson. Born February 15, 1892. Married Violet Perry. Children:

301E	I.	James Relmond (9) B. July 25, 1917.
301F.	II.	Gordon Perry (9) B.
301G.	III.	James Everett (9) B.

210. George Washington Gibson (8)

Son of Sarah M. (Cheseldine) Gibson (No 110) and Captain John Joe Gibson. Born February 22, 1894. Married Bessie Owens. Children:

301H	I.	Elizabeth (9) B.
301I.	II.	George Roland (9) B.
301J.	III.	John Wallace (9) B.
301K	IV.	Bernice (9) B.
301L.	V.	Eleanor (9) B.
301M.	VI.	Joseph (9) B.

211. Cecil Francis Gibson (8)

Son of Sarah M. (Cheseldine) Gibson (No. 110) and Captain John Joe Gibson. Born June 15, 1896. Married Elizabeth Shuett. Children:

301N.	I.	Leah Elizabeth (9) B.
301O.	II.	Mary Louise (9) B.
301P.	III.	Sarah Ann (9) B. D. In infancy.
301Q.	IV.	Cecil F., Jr. (9) B.

212. Sarah Elizabeth Gibson (8) Wyant

Daughter of Sarah M. (Cheseldine) Gibson (No. 110) and Captain John Joe Gibson. Born February 23, 1898. Married George Wyant. Children:

301R.	I.	Robert Louis (9) B. April 22, 1930.
301S.	II.	James Dewey (9) B. July 18, 1933.
301T.	III.	George Charles (9) B. March 4, 1935.

213. Carrie Cheseldine (8) Dixon

Daughter of Seneca Cheseldine (No 111) and Nellie (Norris) Cheseldine. Born September 7, 1893. Married Edgar Dixon. Died March 19, 1967.

214. Isabel Cheseldine (8)

Daughter of Seneca Cheseldine (No. 111) and Nellie (Norris) Cheseldine. Born January 4, 1909. Did not marry. Died May 19, 1968.

215. Elmer Bennett Cheseldine (8)

Son of Seneca Cheseldine (No. 111) and Nellie (Norris) Cheseldine. Born at River Springs, St. Mary's County, October 1, 1897. Married Hope Wheeler August 7, 1950. He worked as an upholsterer for the U. S. Senate for 30 years. He died at his home in Camp Springs, MD, April 17, 1974. He is buried at Sacred Heart Church, Bushwood, MD. No issue.

216. William Hogue (8)

Son of Clara (Cheseldine) Hogue (No. 112) and Daniel Hogue. Born_____.

217. Bruce Hogue (8)

Son of Clara (Cheseldine) Hogue (No. 112) and Daniel Hogue. Born _____.

218. Mamie Hogue (8)

Daughter of Clara (Cheseldine) Hogue (No. 112) and Daniel Hogue. Born _____.

219. Bessie Hogue (8)

Daughter of Clara (Cheseldine) Hogue (No. 112) and Daniel Hogue. Born _____.

220. Bessie Dingee (8) Carney, Smith

Daughter of Henrietta (Cheseldine) Dingee (No. 113) and James Richard Dingee. Born July 28, 1884 in St. Mary's County, MD. Married (1) _____ Carney and (2) George Smith. They resided in Washington, DC. Bessie died June 13, 1980. There were no children.

221. Edith May Dingee (8) Meushaw

Daughter of Henrietta (Cheseldine) Dingee (No. 113) and James Richard Dingee. Born March 10, 1886 in St. Mary's County. Married William Thomas Meushaw, born August 25, 1882, in Baltimore, MD. Edith died November 24, 1966 and Willie died February 12, 1954. Children:
  301U. I. Bessie Sedonia (9) B.
  301U1. II. Helen (9) B.
  301U2. III. John (9) B.
  301U3. IV. Marie (9) B.
  301U4. V. Melba (9) B.
  301U5. VI. Catherine (9) B.
  301U6. VII. Harold (9) B.

222. Agnes Dingee (8) Cullens.

Daughter of Henrietta (Cheseldine) Dingee (No. 113) and James Richard Dingee. Born January 1, 1888 in St. Mary's County. Married Aubrey Cullens. "Mary Agnes" Cullens died December 13, 1969. Children:
  301U7. I. Wallace (9) B.
  301U8. II. Richard (9) B.
  301U9. III. William (9) B. Lives in New Carrolton, MD.

223. Ida V. Dingee (8) Turner

Daughter of Henrietta (Cheseldine) Dingee (No. 113) and James Richard Dingee. Born June 1, 1890 in St. Mary's County. Married Harry Turner. Resided in S.E. Washington, DC. Ida died March 15, 1962 and Harry died September 4, 1964. Children:
  301V. I. James L. (9) B. D. April 30, 1962.

301W.   II. Virginia (9) B. .D.
301X.   III. Henrietta (9) B. .D.
301Y.   IV. Betty (9) B. D.
301Z.   V. Raymond (9) B. D.

224. Carrie Levonia Dingee (8) Yates

Daughter of Henrietta (Cheseldine) Dingee (No. 113) and James Richard Dingee. Born May 2, 1892 in St. Mary's County. Married Warren A. Yates, June 23, 1910, in St. Mary's County, MD. After the birth of their fifth child, Carrie and her children left Bushwood, MD, around 1922, and moved to Washington, DC. Carrie raised her youngest children with the help of the oldest children working at young ages. Carrie's parents, James and Henrietta Dingee moved to Washington in 1938. James died January 15, 1939, and Henrietta died October 14, 1944. They are buried at All Saints, Oakley, MD.

Carrie and her younger sisters were fun loving and laughter was a big part of her family. She was a wonderful, daughter, sister, mother and grandmother. Carrie died May 21, 1969 at the age of 77 and is buried at Fort Lincoln Cemetery, Washington, DC. Warren, born 1884, died September 1, 1953, and is buried at Cobb Island, MD. Children:

302A   I. Olive Levonia (9) B. November 17, 1911. D. December 13, 1974.
302B.   II. Thomas Irvin (9) B. September 3, 1914. D. March 23, 1986.
302C.   III. Ralph Augustus (9) B. October 16, 1917. D. June 6, 1992.
302D.   IV. Martha Mae (9) B. May 17, 1919. D. July 3, 1992.
302E.   V. Katherine Jane (9) B. November 14, 1921. D. January 7, 1994.

225. James Luther Dingee (8)

Only son of Henrietta (Cheseldine) Dingee (No. 113) and James Richard Dingee. Born December 7, 1893 in St. Mary's County. Married Gertie Knott. They had no children, but raised the children of

Luthers' sister, Lida, who had married Lee Knott, brother of Gertie. They lived in Washington, DC.

226. Lida Dingee (8) Knott

Daughter of Henrietta (Cheseldine) Dingee (No. 113) and James Richard Dingee. Born December 9, 1898 in St. Mary's County. Married Lee Knott, brother of Gertie who married Lida's brother Luther. Lida and Lee divorced and Luther and Gertie raised their childen. They lived in Washington, DC. Lida died March 9, 1985. Children:

302F	I. Joseph Donald (9) B.1916. D. October 12, 1986.
302G.	II. Dorothy (9) B. 1919/1920.

227. Nell Dingee (8) Simpson, Newman

Daughter of Henrietta (Cheseldine) Dingee (No. 113) and James Richard Dingee. Born January 30, 1901 in St. Mary's County. Married (1) Frank S. Simpson, died February 12, 1982, and (2) Nathan Harry Newman. They lived in Washington, DC. Nell died January 10, 1982. Children: - First Marriage

302H	I. John Francis Simpson (9) B.September 14, 1922. D. April 17, 1996.

228. Minnie May Dingee (8) Javins

Daughter of Henrietta (Cheseldine) Dingee (No. 113) and James Richard Dingee. Born May 1, 1905. Married John V. "Buster" Javins. The lived in Washington, DC. Buster died March 10, 1964. May died October 16, 1982. There were no children.

228A. George Biscoe Knott (8)

Son of Ann S. (Cheseldine) Knott (No. 114) and William Knott. Born November 8, 1884. Married November 5, 1916, Julia Hannah Husemann, born November 16, 1887. Died June 7, 1887. Children:

302I.	I. Biscoe (9) B. February 16, 1918.
302J.	II. Jane Elizabeth (9) B. July 31, 1920.

228B. Maria Knott (8) Palmer

Daughter of Ann S. (Cheseldine) Knott (No. 114) and William Knott. Born August 15, 1882. Married Charles Larry Palmer. Children:

302K.   I. Windsor (9) B. September 4, 19__.
302L.   II. Lielia (9) B. 19__.

228C. Ethel Mae Sullivan (8) Walsh

Daughter of Mary Stuart (Cheseldine) Sullivan (No. 116) and D. A. Sullivan. Born _____. Married F. B. Walsh.

228D. _____ Sullivan (8)

Child of Mary Stuart (Cheseldine) Sullivan (No. 116) and D. A. Sullivan. Born _____.

228E. _____ Sullivan (8)

Child of Mary Stuart (Cheseldine) Sullivan (No. 116) and D. A. Sullivan. Born _____.

228F. _____ Sullivan (8)

Child of Mary Stuart (Cheseldine) Sullivan (No. 116) and D. A. Sullivan. Born _____.

229. Jennie Cheseldine (8)

Daughter of Samuel Dent Cheseldine (No. 118) and Katie _____ Cheseldine. Born _____.

230. Bessie Cheseldine (8)

Daughter of Samuel Dent Cheseldine (No. 118) and Katie _____ Cheseldine. Born _____.

231. Donald Cheseldine (8)

Son of Samuel Dent Cheseldine (No. 118) and Katie _____ Cheseldine. Born _____.

232. Sterling Cheseldine (8)

Son of Samuel Dent Cheseldine (No. 118) and Katie _____ Cheseldine. Born _____.

233. Raymond Minshall Cheseldine (8)

Son of Charles Cheseldine (No. 119) and Minnie Minshall. Born April, 1892 in London, Madison, OH. Married (1) Dorothy Canfield of California, and (2) Estelle _____. Raymond died December 1954 in Fullerton, CA. A native of London, Ohio, Raymond received a Bachelor of Arts Degree from Ohio Wesleyan in 1914. He served as a Captain with the 16th Infantry of the famed Rainbow Division in World War I. Following the war he was the publisher and editor of the London, Ohio Press. In 1924 he returned to active duty as a Lieutenant Colonel with the Militia Bureau. He returned to civilian life in 1929 and became a business analyst for the Standard Statistice Company in New York. In 1933 he joined the staff of the banking and industrial committee of the Federal Reserve Board. He also served as Executive Secretary for Economic Recovery. After the outbreak of World War II, he served as an assistant in the Industrial Division, Office of the Chief of Ordnance. In 1945 he was promoted to Colonel and went to Germany as an Economic Advisor to the American Military Gov. under General Lucius Clay. In 1947 he was made an executive assistant to the Undersecretary of the Army. He retired in 1951 and moved to California. He was a 32nd degree Mason and is buried in Arlington, VA.. Children: - First Marriage

302.   I. Dorothy Elizabeth (9) B. 1916. D. January, 1991.
303.   II. Sue (9) B. 1920.
304.   III. Charles Canfield (Tommy) (9) B. September 1921. D. February 9, 1967.
    Children: - Second Marriage
305.   IV. Raymond Minshall, Jr. (Skip) (9). B. 1929.

234. Kenneth George Cheseldine (8)

Son of Charles Cheseldine (No. 119) and Minnie Minshall. Born June 30, 1898. Kenneth was a lieutenant in the Rainbow Division. Prior to starting his import/export business in Seattle, he ran the London, Ohio Press along with his brother Raymond.

He married Rebecca Hughes of Columbus, Ohio, on June 30, 1920.

Kenneth was a terrific grandfather and a great storyteller. He told a story about himself and Raymond when they were young boys. Raymond and friends were playing a game. Raymond drew a square in the dirt and told Kenneth that it was the jail and Kenneth was the jailer. Raymond gave him a croquette mallet and told him to hit anyone who tried to escape over the head. Well, one boy tried and Kenneth knocked him out! My grandfather said that the boy's mother had him out pounding the ground with the mallet to see how hard he could hit. He also talked a lot about his Boston terrier, Colonel. He and Raymond had a spider monkey for a pet when they were boys.

Kenneth cared for his mother, Minnie Minshall and her friend Ercell Miller, for many years. When Ercell finally went into a full care facility, Minnie moved in with Kenneth and Becky.

Kenneth and Becky were married 67 years. When Minnie became too sick to stay at home, Kenneth moved into the same room with her at the convalescent hospital. Kenneth died March 26, 1988 and Rebecca Hughes Cheseldine died July 09, 1988. Children:

    306.   I. Barbara Elizabeth (9) B. July 20, 1921.

235. Izora Cheseldine (8) Oswald

Daughter of Biscoe Kenelm Cheseldine (No. 120) and Margaret Lawler. Born in London, Ohio, on November 16, 1889. Married Ernest Oswald about 1915. She was remembered as a very sweet person, loved by all who knew her. She died on May 18, 1921 of tuberculosis when she was 32 years old. She is buried at Lebanon, OH. Children:

    307.   I. Kenneth (9) B.
    308.   II. Betty (9) B.

236. Anna Evelyn Cheseldine (8) Fraser

Daughter of Biscoe Kenelm Cheseldine (No. 120) and Margaret Lawler. Born in London, Ohio on October 27, 1890. Married on August 3, 1911, Charles Thomas Fraser, known as "Chalk". Anna Evelyn died August. 1961. Chalk was born in 1892, in Lebanon, OH. After leaving school he was a barber. As a young man he was very interested in politics. He worked and supported the Republican Party. It was at a party in Cincinnati for William Howard Taft that he met Anna Cheseldine. They were introduced by Dutch Oswald who was married to Izora Cheseldine, Anna's sister. Anna used to say he was the best dressed fellow in Lebanon. He maintained his interest in all aspects of government and politics until the very end of his life. He was quite an athlete in his youth, playing both football and baseball. He didn't miss one opening game for the Cincinnati Reds until later in life when he couldn't get around well. He owned his own barbershop until 1917 when he became very ill. He had a tape worm but no one knew what was wrong with him. He became so run down that he contracted tuberculosis which destroyed most of his lung tissue. He was sent to Arizona to recuperate for a year, and returned to Ohio to spend another year in a sanatorium. The tuberculosis became inactive but he developed allergies, had asthma and emphysema. He died of emphysema May 9, 1976.

Anna went to Business College in Cincinnati, OH, after she graduated from high school. She worked as a bookkeeper for Moses Hyman in his Lebanon store. Anna is remembered as enjoying the better things in life. She entertained large groups of ladies for bridge at the Golden Lamb Hotel. She wore lovely clothes. She was a wonderful housekeeper and a great cook. She is lovingly remembered for her angel food cake and strawberry shortcake. She made her own biscuit shortcake. The family loved her potato salad and fruit salad which she made with her own mayonnaise. Sunday dinner was a great favorite with breaded veal cutlets, mashed potatoes, creamed peas, fruit salad and her special cake for dessert. She was strict with her children, just like her father was with his. She taught them to hold their heads high and to look everyone in the eye, to have pride and the ambition to be successful in life. Children:

    309.   I. Maxine Charlotte (9) B. October 10, 1912.
    310.   II. Jeanette Fraser (9) B. November 17, 1913.
    311.   III. Peggy Lee (9) B. March 9, 1925.

237. Edward Kyle (Prudy) Cheseldine (8)

Son of Biscoe Kenelm Cheseldine (No. 120) and Izora (Sims) Cheseldine. Born July 26, 1892 in South Charleston, Ohio. Married Neva Snook. Prudy worked at the Cincinnati Milling Machine Company all of his life. Neva was a seamstress and worked for the Smith Kassen's Department Store in the alterations department. Prudy and Neva were great party-goers. They loved having people around. He was a great fan of the Cincinnati Reds. His sense of humor was keen and he was very funny. He made people laugh easily. When Sunday night was over he became very serious, got up very early, worked hard all day, and went to bed shortly after he ate dinner at night. Prudy, Neva and their children were small people. Prudy may have been over five feet tall, but Neva and the children were not over five feet. They were dark complexioned, handsome people, father, mother and the girls.

Both girls graduated from high school, then got jobs as secretaries. The oldest girl, Kathleen, hung herself when she was in her late twenties. Prudy and Neva never got over this. Prudy died a few years later, November 23, 1954, and was cremated. Neva searched many religions for answers to Kathleen's death. Martha married and had a son. Both women had unpleasant lives. They went to Florida to live. Neva was institutionalized, and for the rest of her life she was in and out of the Florida State Hospital. Martha was shot, but not killed. Children:

312.   I. Kathleen (9) B. D. around 1952.
313.   II. Martha (9) B.

238. Harold (Chick) Cheseldine (8)

Son of Biscoe Kenelm Cheseldine (No. 120) and Izora Sims Cheseldine. Born November 4, 1893 at South Charleston, Ohio. Married Elsie James of South Lebanon, Ohio. His nickname was "Chick". He was a Western and Southern Life Insurance salesman. He walked with such a staggering gate, and his body was in perpetual motion. This began in his late 40's. Elsie finally had him committed to the State Hospital in Cincinnati. Another patient killed him by landing a blow on his head. Harold died December 23, 1954. He is buried in the Lebanon Cemetery next to his mother. Chick inherited the disease,

Huntington's Corea, from his father. Both of his children had the disease. Jane died in the Dayton State Hospital in her early 40's. Dick and his wife lived in Montgomery, AL. Children:

    313A.   I. Jane (9) B.
    313B.   II. Dick (9) B.

239. Nellie Mattingly (8)

Daughter of Annie E. Cheseldine (No. 121) and Oscar Mattingly. Born 1872.

240. Josephine St. Clair (8)

Daughter of Susan F. Cheseldine St. Clair (No. 122) and George St. Clair. Born

241. George Walter Cheseldine (8)

Son of Richard Talbert Cheseldine (No. 123) and Annie Rebecca (Turner) Cheseldine. Born in St. Mary's County July 4, 1886. Married (1) May 2, 1905, Susie Elizabeth Bailey, born November 3, 1888. He married (2) Elsie Knapp, from Baltimore, MD. He designed, built and made his home at River Springs on St. Katherine's Sound. He was an exceptional craftsman who designed and built his own boats. His nephew, Alton F. Cheseldine, has a half-model of a boat he built for Alton G. Cheseldine, when he became an inspector for the Maryland Conservation Department in 1936. This boat was extremely fast for its day. He constructed a steam box in order to bend the wood to fit the shape he wanted and took great pride in fitting each board so that it was very difficult, if not impossible, to locate the seams after the final sanding was done. He had his own forge for making the metal parts he needed. He built his own marine railway to haul his boats out of the water for painting and repairs.

Walter was also a very fine gunsmith, having made, in the days of the big gun market duck hunting, his own duck gun. The gun was made from a 10 foot steel tube obtained in Philadelphia. The bore was 1 1/2 inches and the wall of the barrel was 1 inch thick. He reamed the barrel 18 times by hand, using an expansion reamer and then polished the inside with emery cloth. The stock was made by hand from a

Black Walnut tree that had been blown down in a hurricane. A lock and hammer from an old Springfield rifle was utilized to complete the gun. The finished barrel was 7 feet 6 inches in length and the bore 1 and 9/16 inches. The measuring charge was a steer's horn of black powder and 1 and 1/2 pounds of single FG shot. Single strands of wad rope wound up was used for wadding, one before the shot and one after. The gun rest on the punt was made from the same piece of walnut as the stock and was covered with elk skin. The big gun was mounted on the punt with the muzzle pointed over the bow so that the whole gunning skiff was aimed at the wild fowl rather than just the gun. It was not uncommon to kill 15 to 20 geese or 40 to 50 ducks with a single shot. Walter's largest kill occurred on a New Year's night when he killed 72 canvasbacks with one shot. Both the gun and punt are on display at the Potomac River Museum at Colton's Point, MD.

He was also, undoubtedly, the premier fishing guide on the Potomac River. He usually trolled around Tall Timbers on the lower Potomac River. His skill while circling the "Rock Pile" there, where he would catch a rock fish on every trip around, was proverbial. Fishing became his occupation on the day he caught a 60 pound red drum. In the early 1940's, he captained a fishing party which made a record trolling catch of 1,090 pounds of rock fish in one day. He could literally smell a school of trout and insisted that he could locate them because of the slick on the water and the watermelon odor emitted by the trout.

R. G. Williams, of the Baltimore Sun, said in an article, when he died, "Captain Walter was truly the fishingest gentleman". Walter was a member of the Thomas Shryock Masonic Lodge 223, The Tall Cedars Lodge and a charter patron of the Julia Hall Chapter 107, Eastern Star, in Hollywood, MD. George Walter died on August 11, 1957. Elsie died on February 6, 1995. Both are buried at All Saints, Church, Oakley, MD. Children: - First Marriage

314.   I. George Frederick (9) B. February 12, 1906. D. January 15, 1996.

Children: - Second Marriage

315.   II. Geraldine Lois (9) B. June 15, 1921

242. Richard Benjamin Cheseldine (8)

Son of Richard Talbert Cheseldine (No. 123) and Annie Rebecca (Turner) Cheseldine. Born in St. Mary's County February 20,

1889. "Capt. Jack" was a life long waterman. He married Agnes Gwinette (Nettie) Bowles. They made their home at Avenue, MD. He died February 22, 1963. She died December 15, 1970. They are buried at Sacred Heart Church, Bushwood, MD. Children:

   316.   I. Joseph Clement (9) B. July 16, 1916.
   317.   II. Linda (9) B. February, 1920.
   318.   III. Audrey (9) B. June, 1926.
   319.   IV. John Melvin (9) B. July, 1928.
   320.   V. Eleanor Marie (9) B. May 29, 1930.

243. Etta Beatrice Cheseldine (8) Rice, West, Mahoney

Daughter of Richard Talbert Cheseldine (No. 123) and Annie Rebecca (Turner) Cheseldine. Born in St. Mary's County September 20, 1891. Married (1) Richard Claxton Rice. Claxton worked in the building trades. He was a master bricklayer and was widely known for his exceptional skill. In his earlier years he owned a country store. He died on March 19, 1956 and is buried at Sacred Heart Church Cemetery, Bushwood, MD. Etta married (2) Franklin Delano West. Frank was a second cousin to President Franklin Delano Roosevelt, for whom he was named. He died_____. Etta married (3) Robert Mahoney . There was no issue from the third marriage. He died _____. She died February 15, 1960 and is buried at Fort Lincoln Cemetery, Bladensburg, MD. Children: - First Marriage

   321.   I. Sophie Rebecca (9) B. March 20, 1908.
   322.   II. Richard (Bennie) (9) B. May 12, 1912. D. August 5, 1979.
   323.   III. Mary Beatrice (Bea) (9) B. August 14, 1913. D. March 31, 1982.
   324.   IV. George Grover (Tabby) (9) B. February 18, 1916. D. April 26, 1964.
               Children: - Second Marriage
   325.   V. Caroline Leviathan (9). B. December 13, 1921. D. May 17, 1989.
   326.   VI. Benjamin Franklin (Kenny) (9) B. December 12, 1923. D. August 5, 1989.
   327.   VII. Grace Sinclair (9) B. February 2, 1924. D. July 21, 1993.

328.   VIII. William Russell (9) B. May 5, 1925. D. June 6, 1930.

329.   IX. Elizabeth Rittenhouse (9) B. June 21, 1927.

330.   X. Nalley Francis (9) B. June 21, 1927. D. August 28, 1928.

244. Alton Grover Cheseldine (8)

Son of Richard Talbert Cheseldine (No. 123) and Annie Rebecca (Turner) Cheseldine. Born in St. Mary's County, December 18, 1893. Married October 15, 1918, Ida Blanche Waltemeyer from Baltimore, MD, born March 4, 1897. He entered the U. S. Army at Baltimore, MD, November 3, 1917. Received basic training at Camp Meade, MD, where, upon completion, he shipped to France on the S. S. Leviathan, which, before the war, had been a luxury liner. He served with the American Expeditionary Force - France, from July 8, 1918 to June 7, 1919. He was assigned to Company E, 313th Infantry, 79th Division. He saw action in four battles, in Verdun and the Meuse Argonne sectors. (1) from 9/13/1918 to 9/25/1918 (2) from 9/26/1918 to 9/30/1918 (3) from 10/8/1918 to 10/30/1918 (4) from 11/8/1918 to 11/11/1918. During the battle of the Meuse Argonne his company came under a mustard gas attack where he was injured by this attack. Upon discharge, he and his wife Ida made their home at White's Neck, St. Mary's County, later moving to St. Katherine's Island, where he continued the life of a waterman. When people talk about the "Land of Pleasant Living" this is what they are talking about. The house was a large two story building that had a wrap around porch. This was a perfect place for a young boy to ride his tricycle. There was a water tower, which was off limits to the children, where one could look out all over the area. At that time it was about 65 acres, mostly open, with a few cedars on the east end. The island was full of wild game: rabbit, duck, geese and quail. The waters surrounding the Island were full of crabs, oysters, clams, turtles and all kinds of fish.

The land was fertile and grew the best of vegetables, which were "canned" for winter use. On the southeast end of the island was about a quarter of an acre field of asparagus. There were peaches, apples, pears, plums and grapes. The fields were full of blackberries and huckleberries, and as was the custom in those days a cow, lots of chickens and several hogs. Flour and sugar were bought by the barrel, salt by hundred pound bags. So, truly, they had everything that was needed right on the island.

At night, about midnight, the steamboats, on their runs between Norfolk, VA and Washington, DC, would pass the island. As they passed they would blow their steam whistles. What a beautiful sound! Sadly, as it became more difficult for the children to get to school in the winter due to the ice on the sound, mother and dad decided to move back to the mainland. Some of the happiest days of their son, Fred's, life were spent on the island.

About 1936 Alton joined the Maryland Conservation Department, now known as the Maryland Marine Police. He was the captain of the patrol boat, "Kent of Annapolis", a 65 foot boat equipped with a .50 cal. machine gun mounted on the bow. Fred, his son, recalls the many happy days spent on the "Kent" as his father patrolled the Potomac from Point Lookout to Alexandria, VA. He is still amazed as to how his father was able to navigate the river in rain, snow, and fog so thick you could not see 50 feet in front of the boat. Fred recalls one day when the fog was really thick and his father was on the way to Pope's Creek. The first mate was on the bow as a lookout. As they neared the creek they could hear a Coast Guard tender driving piles for a buoy that had been moved by the ice. Fred's dad slowed the boat, and, as they got close, he leaned out the window and called to the tender and asked if he was on course for Pope's Creek wharf. The reply came back "Captain, if you continue as you are, you will knock the wharf down". Amazing! This navigating was done with a compass and a clock. Alton held this position until World War II, when he joined the defense effort helping to build defense buildings at Fort Belvoir and the Patuxent River Naval Air Station. Alton was a member of the Masonic Lodge and the Eastern Star. Alton died June 9, 1981. Ida died July 13, 1974. Ida was a member of the Eastern Star. They both are buried at All Saints Church, Oakley, MD. They are lovingly remembered and greatly missed. Children:

331.   I. Dorothy Leviathan (9) B. August 10, 1920.
332.   II. Eileen Estella (9) B. August 7, 1922.
333.   III. Alton Frederick (9) B. October 6, 1928.

(See #247 for #334 - #336)

245. Everett Cheseldine (8)

Son of Richard Henry Cheseldine (No. 127) and Mrs. Emily Morgan Ellis Cheseldine. Born

246. William Dent Cheseldine (8)

Son of Richard Henry Cheseldine (No. 127) and Mrs. Emily (Morgan) Ellis Cheseldine. Born in St. Mary's County, August 23, 1887 (or 1888). Died December 16, 1955, at age 67 in Washington, DC. Buried at Cedar Hill Cemetery, Suitland, MD. Married Mary Madeline Lewis of Clinton, MD, on October 23, 1911 at St. Patrick's Catholic Church, Washington, DC, by Father William Carroll. William Dent was always called "Dent". His wife, Mary Madeline Lewis Cheseldine, was born March 9, 1891 in Surratsville, now known as Clinton, MD. Her parents were John Boyd Lewis and Lucy Ellen Harrison Lewis, both of Shiloh Post Office, King George County, Virginia. Mary's parents had a farm in Clinton, MD, near the Surrat house. They had eleven children. Mary Madeline died November 26, 1972, and is buried in Cedar Hill Cemetery, Suitland, MD. Children:

337. I. Mary Madeline (9) B. September 20, 1911. D. January 1, 1988.
338. II. Edna Helena (9) B. January 30, 1913.
339. III. Joseph Wilmer (9) B. April 16, 1916. D. September 19, 1983.
340. IV. Elizabeth Evelyn (9) B. November 14, 1919. D. December 2, 1946.
341. V. Thomas Brent (9) B. October 15, 1922.
342. VI. Theresa Nora (9) B. February 23, 1926.

247. Joseph Richard Cheseldine (8)

Son of Richard Henry Cheseldine (No. 127) and Mrs. Emily (Morgan) Ellis Cheseldine. Born March 29, 1891 in Abell, MD. Died March 6, 1960. Married (1) Lea Bertie _____ born 1875. Died January 9, 1929, buried Cedar Hill Cemetery, Suitland, MD No issue from this marriage. (2) Mary Amelia Mattingly, born July 19, 1903 at Leonardtown, MD. Died October 25, 1987 at Suitland, MD. Buried at St. Joseph's Cemetery, Morganza, MD. Children:-Second

Marriage:
334.   I. Harry Joseph (9) B. November 29, 1926.
335.   II. Bernard Eugene (9) B. December 12, 1931.
336.   III. Joseph Richard, Jr. (9) B. September 16, 1935.
Ninth generation begins
247A. Chester Barlow (9)

Son of Elizabeth (Cullison) Barlow (No.132A) and J. Barlow.
Educated at Leonardtown, MD.

247B. Edward Taylor (9)

Son of James Taylor (No. 132C) and _____. B.

248. William Francis Cheseldine, Jr. (9)

Son of William Francis Cheseldine (No. 133) and Alice
(Brookbank) Cheseldine. Born in 1881. Died 1966. Married Laura
Scott. He is buried at All Faith Episcopal Church. Children:
343.   I. Mary Gladys (10) B.
344.   II. Pearl Frances (10) B.
345.   III. Marion (10) B.

249. Grace Bell Cheseldine (9) Poling

Daughter of William Francis Cheseldine (No. 133) and Alice
(Brookbank) Cheseldine. Born ____. Married Wilson Poling from
West Virginia. Children:
346.   I. Andrew Cheseldine (10) B.
347.   II. Osborn (10) B.
348.   III. Dorothy (10) B.

250. Andrew Jackson Cheseldine (9)

Son of William Francis Cheseldine (No. 133) and Alice
(Brookbank) Cheseldine. Born 1892. Married (1) Marie Carrie
(Carricato) Cheseldine from Kentucky. Married (2) Mary A. (surname
unknown) Cheseldine. Andrew Jackson died August 25, 1949 in
Washington, DC. Buried at Louisville, KY.

251. Maud Regina Cheseldine (9) Dodd

Daughter of William Francis Cheseldine (No. 133) and Alice (Brookbank) Cheseldine. Married _____Dodd. Children:
349.   I. Alice (10) B.

252. Louise Morgan (9)

Daughter of Mary Susan (Cheseldine) Morgan (No. 134) and James Morgan. Born _____. Died in infancy.

253. Katherine Beatrice Morgan (9) Gibson

Daughter of Mary Susan (Cheseldine) Morgan (No. 134) and James Morgan. Born August 6, 1902. Married December 25, 1917, William Thomas (Buddy) Gibson, who died August 13, 1935.Children:
349A.   I. Mary Susan (10) B. December 4, 1918.
349B.   II. Ann Louise (10) B. May 9, 1920.
349C.   III. Andrew Jackson (10) B. September 8, 1921.
349D.   IV. Catherine Veronica (10) B. June 13, 1924.
349E.   V. George Bernard (10) B. September 10, 1930.
349F.   VI. Helen Reta (10) B. July 31, 1932.
349G.   VII. Mary Clare (10) B. October 13, 1935.

254. Lillian Marie Russell (9) St. Clair

Daughter of Mary Alice (Cheseldine) Russell (No. 135) and Edward N. Russell. Born March 14, 1888. Married Joseph St. Clair. Children:
349H.   I. Joseph Earl (10) B.

255. Annie Beatrice Russell (9) Compton

Daughter of Mary Alice (Cheseldine) Russell (No. 135) and Edward N. Russell. Born _____. Married August 10, 1914, Milton Edwin Compton. Children:
349I.   I. Milton Edwin, Jr. (10) B. July 21, 1921.

256. Edward William Garrett Russell (9)

Son of Mary Alice (Cheseldine) Russell (No. 135) and Edward
N. Russell. Born _____. Married Ruth Gibson. Children:
349J. I. Milton Joseph (10) B.
349K. II. Christian (10) B.
349L. III. Martha (10) B.
349M. IV. Edward William Garrett, Jr. (10) B.
349N. V. Shirley (10) B.

257. Ida Pearl Russell (9) Gibson

Daughter of Mary Alice (Cheseldine) Russell (No. 135) and
Edward N. Russell. Born _____. Married Garner Gibson. Children:
349O. I. Mary Lillian (10) B. June 19, 1921.
349P. II. Dorothy Nellie (10) B. August 12, 1924.
349Q. III. Mary Alice (10) B. June 21, 1929.

258. Annette Louise Russell (9) Froesch

Daughter of Mary Alice (Cheseldine) Russell (No. 135) and
Edward N. Russell. Born _____. Married Charles Froesch. Died
March 28, 1920.

259. Joseph Lester Russell (9)

Son of Mary Alice (Cheseldine) Russell (No. 135) and Edward
N. Russell. Born March 3, 1901. Married Mary Gibson. Died
December 5, 1972. Children:
349R. I. Mary Helen (10) B.

260. Theresa Russell (9)

Daughter of Mary Alice (Cheseldine) Russell (No. 135) and
Edward N. Russell. Born _____. Died in infancy.

261. Garrett Russell (9)

Son of Mary Alice (Cheseldine) Russell (No. 135) and Edward N. Russell. Born _____. Married Elsie Long. Children:
349S.   I. Betty Jane (10) B. April 18, 1931.
349T.   II. Eleanor (10) B.
349U.   III. Barbara Ann (10) B.

262. James Andrew Bailey (9)

Son of Catherine Elizabeth (Cheseldine) Bailey (No. 136) and James Theodore Bailey. Born November 3, 1887. Dominican Brother, Cincinnati, Ohio.

263. Susie Elizabeth Bailey (9) Cheseldine

Daughter of Catherine Elizabeth (Cheseldine) Bailey (No. 136) and James Theodore Bailey. Born November 3, 1888. Married May 2, 1905, George Walter Cheseldine. Died October 8, 1969. Children:
349V.   I. George Frederick (10) B. February 12, 1906.

264. Catherine Elizabeth Bailey (9)

Daughter of Catherine Elizabeth (Cheseldine) Bailey (No. 136) and James Theodore Bailey. Born January 17, 1891. Dominican Sister at Mt. St. Mary's, Newburgh, NY.

265. Ann Maria Bailey (9)

Daughter of Catherine Elizabeth (Cheseldine) Bailey (No. 136) and James Theodore Bailey. Born. Died in infancy.

266. Robert Pendleton Bailey (9)

Son of Catherine Elizabeth (Cheseldine) Bailey (No. 136) and James Theodore Bailey. Born May 1, 1895. Married June 26, 1931, Pearl Culler from Frederick, MD. Children:
349W.   I. James Theodore (10) B. June 19, 1933.

349X.	II. Philip Roger (10) B. July 8, 1934.
349Y.	III. Lulu Kate (10) B. July 9, 1934.
350.	IV. Alice Estelle (10) B. November 26, 1936.
350A.	V. Janice Mae (10) B. February 9, 1938.
350B.	VI. Susie Elizabeth (10) B. December 3, 1939.
350C.	VII. Robert Pendleton, Jr. (10) B. January 15, 1941.
350D.	VIII. Kenneth Andrew (10) B. May 14, 1942.
350E.	IX. John Talbert (10) B. April 10, 1945.

267. Samuel Mathew Bailey (9)

Son of Catherine Elizabeth (Cheseldine) Bailey (No. 136) and James Theodore Bailey. Born November 29, 1896. Married Thelma Migonette Cullins on January 3, 1920. Died November 13, 1980. Children:

350F.	I. Eleanor Beatrice (Beezie) (10) B. July 12, 1922. D. January 3, 1992.
350G.	II. Thelma Lucille (10) B. March 26, 1926.
350H.	III. Catherine Marie (Kitty) (10) B. December 10, 1928.
350I.	IV. Samuel Mathew, Jr. (Bo) (10) B. July 19,1931
350J.	V. William Edward (10) B. March 11, 1936.
350K.	VI. Bernard Anthony (10) B. February 8, 1939.

268. Maud Roberta Bailey (9)

Daughter of Catherine Elizabeth (Cheseldine) Bailey (No. 136) and James Theodore Bailey. Born _____. Died in infancy.

269. Walter Benjamin Bailey (9)

Son of Catherine Elizabeth (Cheseldine) Bailey (No. 136) and James Theodore Bailey. Born _____. Died in infancy.

270. Doris Cheseldine (9) Gibson

Daughter of Andrew Freeman Cheseldine (No. 139) and Annie Maud (Lone) Cheseldine. Born May 26, 1900. Married August 17, 1920, Charles Henry Gibson, born June 8, 1896. They lived on a part of "Collingwood", St. Mary's County. She died June 20, 1976 and is buried at Sacred Heart Church. Children:

350L.   I. Charles Freeman (10) B. July 11, 1921.
351.   II. Joseph Henry (10) B. June 23, 1926.
352.   III. James Anthony (10) B. May 3, 1931.
353.   IV. Shirly Marie (10) B. April 18, 1933.
354.   V. Margaret Ann (10) B. March 15, 1935.
355.   VI. Thelma Beatrice (10) B. June 18, 1939.

271. Mary Elsie Cheseldine (9) Beitzell

Daughter of Andrew Freeman Cheseldine (No. 139) and Annie Maud (Lone) Cheseldine. Born October 1, 1902. Married August 8, 1922, her cousin, Walter Bryan Beitzell, born June 19, 1900. They lived on a part of Collingwood, St. Mary's County, but later on moved to Washington, DC. She died June 2, 1977. They are buried at Sacred Heart Church, Bushwood, MD. Children:

356.   I. Mary Ann (10) B. February 26, 1926.
357.   II. Andrew Walter (10) B. August 4, 1928.
358.   III. Joseph Francis (10) B. August 30, 1932.
359.   IV. William Benjamin (10) B. February 9, 1939.

272. Andrew Freeman Cheseldine (9)

Son of Andrew Freeman Cheseldine (No. 139) and Annie Maud (Lone) Cheseldine. Born in St. Mary's County on March 28, 1905. Married November, 1923, Annie Cheseldine, his cousin, daughter of John and Maggie Cheseldine. Children:

360.   I. John William (10) B. May 25, 1925.
361.   II. Robert Lee (10) B. November 21, 1926.

273. Maria Cheseldine (9)

Daughter of Andrew Freeman Cheseldine (No. 139) and Annie Maud (Lone) Cheseldine. Born _____.

274. Mary Alice Beitzell (9) McWilliams

Daughter of Lelia Virginia (Cheseldine) Beitzell (No. 140) and

Charles Henry Beitzell. Born July 27, 1912. Married George McWilliams, Jr. They resided at Clements, MD. Children:

361A.	I.	George (10) B. October 8, 1934.
361B.	II.	Mary Alice (10) B. December 13, 1935.
361C.	III.	Ida Claudia (10) B. September 8, 1938.
361D.	IV.	James Joseph (10) B. February 7, 1941.
361E.	V.	Charles Henry (10) B. February 17, 1942
361F.	VI.	Rose Marie (10) B. December 14, 1942.
361G.	VII.	Andrew Jackson (10) B. January 6, 1945.
361H.	VIII.	William Patrick (10) B. January 4, 1947.

275. baby girl Beitzell (9)

Daughter of Lelia Virginia (Cheseldine) Beitzell (No 140) and Charles Henry Beitzell. Born 1914. Died same year.

276. Lelia Virginia Beitzell (9)

Daughter of Mary Ida (Cheseldine) Beitzell (No. 141) and Charles Henry Beitzell. Born October 11, 1917.

277. Grace Beitzell (9)

Daughter of Mary Ida (Cheseldine) Beitzell (No. 141) and Charles Henry Beitzell. Born January 11, 1919.

278. George Lee Beitzell (9)

Son of Mary Ida (Cheseldine) Beitzell (No. 141) and Charles Henry Beitzell. Born April 5, 1922. Married September 20, 1947, Frances Martha Battenfield, in Washington, DC. George took over the operation of his father's farm, "Hard Bargain", where they made their home. Children:

361I.	I.	Charles Henry, II (10) B. August 4, 1948.

279. Mary Beatrice Cheseldine (9) Mattingly

Daughter of Garrett Francis Cheseldine (No. 142) and Mary Lillian (Gass). Born _____. Married Moakley Mattingly.

Children:
361J.   I. James (10) B.
361K.   II. Alfred (10) B.
361L.   III. Robert (10) B.
362.   IV. Beatrice (10) B.

280. Robert Garrett Cheseldine, Sr. (9)

Son of Garrett Francis Cheseldine (No. 142) and Mary Lillian (Gass). Born in St. Mary's County on February 3, 1917. Married Mary Pilkerton. He died November 28, 1967. Children:
363.   I. Susie (10) B.
364.   II. Lorraine (10) B.
365.   III. Garrett, Jr. (10) B.
366.   IV. Leonard (10) B.

281. James George Cheseldine (9)

Son of Garrett Francis Cheseldine (No.142) and Mary Lillian (Gass). Born in Bushwood, St. Mary's County October 21, 1916. Christened November 25, 1916 at Holy Angels Church, Avenue, MD. Married Ruby Hewitt, born March 4, 1924 in Leonardtown, MD, daughter of Madeline (Long) Hewitt and Hiram Hewitt, at St. Aloysius Church, Leonardtown, MD. No issue.

282. Mabel Loretta Cheseldine (9) Hayden

Daughter of Garrett Francis Cheseldine (No. 142) and Mary Lillian (Gass). Born in St. Mary's County. Married John Joseph Hayden, born August 16, 1918, Drayden, St. Mary's County, MD, at Holy Angels Church, Avenue, MD, son of Bertha Adelaide (Sheehan) and Joseph Ignatius Hayden. Children:
367.   I. Charles Bernard (10) B. September 17, 1943.
368.   II. James Richard (10) B.

282A. Josiah Edward Beitzell, Jr. (9)

Son of Mary Elizabeth (Norris) Beitzell (No. 143) and Josiah E. Beitzell Born July 19, 1890. Married May 30, 1916 Constance

Lowe of Allegan, Michigan, born January 22, 1892. Joe, after leaving St. Mary's County as a young man, worked a few years in Washington, DC and then joined his uncle, Charles Beitzell in California. He married there and farmed in the Imperial Valley until 1921 when he returned to St. Mary's County. After about 2 years the call of the west was too much for the family and with Connie and Jim, their son, born 1917, they returned to Upland, California, where he was employed by the large irrigation company there until retirement. Children:

368A.	I. James Edward III (10) B. March 22, 1917.	
368B	II. David Lowe (10) B. June 13, 1924.	
368C.	III. Mary Elizabeth (10) B. June 9, 1926.	
368D	IV. Charles Henry (10) B. March 4, 1929.	

282B. Mary Alice Beitzell (9) Husemann

Daughter of Mary Elizabeth (Norris) Beitzell (No. 143) and Josiah E. Beitzell. Born August 7, 1891. Married March 4, 1919, Charles William Husemann, born February 13, 1890, son of William and Jennie Husemann of St. Patrick's Creek, St. Mary's County. Alice was educated at St. Mary's Academy, Leonardtown, MD, and taught school in the 7th District for several years before her marriage. Charlie was a riverman through and through and no housewife's kitchen was in any better shape than his boat. Except for a short sojourn in the Army in World War I, Charlie spent all of his life on the Potomac River. He died August 24, 1950. Children:

368E.	I. William Joseph (10) B. November 12, 1920.	
368F.	II. Charles Ross (10) B. August 15, 1922.	
368G.	III. Harry Benjamin (10) B. October 24, 1924.	
368H.	IV. Elizabeth Jane (10) B. August 9, 1928	

282C. Charles Benjamin Beitzell (9)

Son of Mary Elizabeth (Norris) Beitzell (No 143) and Josiah E. Beitzell. Born May 7, 1893. Married May 3, 1916, Janie Marie (Louise) Miller, born March 8, 1894, daughter of William Arthur and Ida Elizabeth Miller (nee Cox) of Washington, DC. Charlie came to Washington, DC as a young man and worked for his uncle, A. E. Beitzell, who was engaged in the wholesale liquor business until prohibition. At that time "A. E." sold the business to Charlie and two associates who converted it to a wholesale soft drink business. Charlie had a successful business career. He had a modest summer home on part of Collingwood but maintained his residence in Washington, DC. Children:

    368I.   I. Janie Louise (10) B. May 29, 1917.
    368J.   II. Elizabeth Hart (10) B. July 28, 1919.
    368K.   III. Rose Mary (Marie) (10) B. January 27, 1923.

282D. Harry Alvin Beitzell (9)

Son of Mary Elizabeth (Norris) Beitzell (No. 143) and Josiah E. Beitzell. Born September 26, 1896. Married September 16, 1924, Julia A. Sullivan, born February 2, 1901, of Washington, DC. Harry served in World War I. (No. 4628676) Corpl Co. A. Convalescent Demobilization Group Headquarters Department from September 2, 1918 to May 20, 1919. He was employed by the American Federation of Labor, in Washington, DC, after his Army service. Educated at Leonard Hall, Leonardtown, MD. Active in work of the Holy Comforter Church. He died May 31, 1959 and is buried at Arlington National Cemetery, Arlington, VA. Children:

    368L.   I. Mary Jeanne (10) B. December 25, 1926.
    368M.   II. Raymond Harry (10) B. January 2, 1931.

282E. Albert Clement Beitzell (9)

Son of Mary Elizabeth (Norris) Beitzell (No. 143) and Josiah E. Beitzell. Born September 25, 1898. Married August 17, 1921 Rosalie Arnold, born White Plains, St. Mary's County, daughter of Richard and Regina Arnold. Clem was a riverman on the Potomac all his life and did some carpenter work on the side. Rosie and Clem were confirmed St. Mary's Countians and resided on a portion of Collingwood. Clem died January 31, 1976. Children:

    368N.   I. Richard Elwood (10) B. January 18, 1923.
    368O.   II. James Bernard (10) B. November 13, 1929.

282F. Walter Bryan Beitzell (9)

Son of Mary Elizabeth (Norris) Beitzell (No. 143) and Josiah E. Beitzell. Born June 19, 1900. Married August 8, 1922, Mary Elsie

Cheseldine (his second cousin) born October 1, 1902, daughter of Freeman and Annie Maud Cheseldine (nee Long) of White's Neck, St. Mary's County, MD. Walter attended Leonard Hall High School and was a waterman on the Potomac until about 1943 when the family moved to Washington, DC. Walter died in Washington July 31, 1961 and is buried in Sacred Heart Cemetery, Bushwood, MD. Children:

368P.	I. Mary Ann (Anna) (10) B. February 26, 1926.	
368Q.	II. Andrew Walter (10) B. August 4, 1928.	
368R.	III. Joseph Francis (10) B. August 30, 1932. D. May 2, 1953.	
368S.	IV. William Benjamin (10) B. February 19, 1939.	

282G. Edwin Warfield Beitzell (9)

This is the original writer of our history. Mr. Beitzell wrote the first part in 1949, and updated before his death.

Son of Mary Elizabeth (Norris) Beitzell (No. 143) and Josiah E. Beitzell. Edwin Warfield Beitzell was born June 19, 1905. Married July 21, 1928 Josephine Isabel Kinney, born August 29, 1908, in Cooperstown, NY, daughter of Jay P. and Minnie Kinney (nee Olive) of Washington, DC and Springfield Center, NY. Josephine (Jo) was raised in Washington, DC and graduated from Central High School in 1926. She worked briefly at the Smithsonian Institution before her marriage in 1928. In 1950, Jo began work at Woodward & Lothrop, a famed Washington department store. She retired in 1966. Jo was instrumental in involving her husband and children in an amateur theatrical group, The Masquers of Roosevelt Center, and upon retirement when she moved to St. Mary's County, she was a docent at Sotterly Plantation. She was also an active member of the Women's Club and The St. Mary's County Historical Society. After a long illness, she died at the St. Mary's Nursing Center in Leonardtown on July 5, 1997 at the age of 88.

Edwin was educated in the public schools of St. Mary's County and by the Xaverian Brothers at Leonard Hall High School, Leonardtown, MD, and graduated in 1924. He left St. Mary's County to enter Georgetown University, graduating in 1928. He also received a degree from Benjamin Franklin University, Washington, DC in 1937. He was employed by the Chesapeake and Potomac Telephone

Company from 1925 until his retirement in 1966.

Edwin was active in the alumni affairs of Georgetown University for many years. He was a charter member of the Georgetown Club of Metropolitan Washington and served as President in 1952. He received their distinguished service award in 1953 and served six years as treasurer of their scholarship fund which he was instrumental in founding in 1954. He also served two years as Secretary of the G. U. Alumni Association and was a member of the Alumni Senate. In 1964, on the 175th anniversary of the founding of Georgetown University, he was awarded the John Carroll medal for his services to the University and the community. He was active on the Education, American Ideals and the River and Harbor Committee of the Washington Board of Trade, where he was a member for 25 years. He served also as an officer and director of the Washington Travelers Aid Society for 10 years.

NOTE: The following is taken from an obituary that appeared in The Chronicles of St. Mary's - the monthly bulletin of St. Mary's County Historical Society, Vol. 33, No. 1, January, 1985.

"Edwin Beitzell died 13 November, 1984, at St. Mary's County Hospital, Leonardtown, after a stroke. He was born 19 June 1905 in St. Mary's County, the son of Josiah Edward "Joe" Beitzell and Mary Elizabeth "Lizzie" Norris Beitzell.

"Edwin attended Oakley School in the 7th District and moved to Washington in 1924 to attend Georgetown University. He worked for the C. & P. Telephone Company as Staff Supervisor - Personnel from 1925 to his retirement in 1966 when he returned to St. Mary's County to his home on Canoe Neck Creek near Abell, MD.

Mr. Beitzell's interest in Southern Maryland history began in his boyhood when he attended the St. Francis Xavier Catholic Church at Newtown Neck, the oldest Catholic Church in English speaking North America.

"Mr. Beitzell was the author of four books: "The Jesuit Missions of St. Mary's County Maryland", "Life on the Potomac River", "Point Lookout Prison Camp for Confederates", and "Calendar of Events St. Mary's County in the American Revolution".

"He researched and wrote several genealogies, among which are genealogies of the Beitzell, Gerard/Cheseldine, Husemann and Kinney families. He also wrote many local history articles for publications, including Maryland Historical Magazine, Georgetown

110

Alumni Magazine, The Catholic Standard, and The Chronicles of St. Mary's - the official monthly of St. Mary's County Historical Society, of which he was Editor from 1956 to 1983.

"Organizations of which Mr. Beitzell was an active member include the 7th District Optimists, Maryland Bicentennial Commission, St. Clement's Island/Potomac River Museum and the Sons of the Confederate Veterans. Honors given Edwin include the Father Andrew White, S. J.Award from the Catholic Historical Society and an honorary Doctorate from St. Mary's College of Maryland.

"Mr. Beitzell is survived by his wife of 56 years, Josephine Kinney Beitzell of Abell, MD; a son, Edwin Warfield Beitzell, Jr. of Los Angeles, a daughter, Jean B. Quinnette of Arlington, VA, and four grand-children: John, Kathryn, Joseph and Charles Quinnette. One sister, Alice B. Husemann, also survives.

"The funeral mass for Mr. Beitzell was offered at Holy Angeles Church, Avenue, by Rev. Aloysius E. O'Connor. Eulogies were delivered by Father O'Connor and by Bishop Thomas Lyon. Interment was in Sacred Heart Catholic Church Cemetery, Bushwood, MD.

"An Edwin W. Beitzell Memorial Publication Fund has been established at St. Mary's County Historical Society to honor his memory and to promote a labor to which Edwin Beitzell devoted his lifetime - the recording and sharing of St. Mary's County History."

NOTE: Due to the encouragement, support and generosity of Mr. Beitzell, who always made sure that Alton Fred Cheseldine received a copy of any material Edwin came across relating to the Cheseldine family, Fred attempted to continue the research and Edwin's manuscript on the genealogy of the family updated. Edwin was very proud of his ancestry and was always so glad to have others know what he knew.

Fred has supplied the current Editors with a great deal of information from his files to help make this edition of Edwin Beitzell's book about the Cheseldine and Gerard families as complete and accurate as possible, for which the present Editors are grateful.

Children of Edwin Warfield and Josephine Isabel Kinney Beitzell are:

368T.   I. Edwin Warfield Beitzell, Jr. (10) B. April 27, 1929. D. July 13, 1988.

368U.   II. Jean Isabel Beitzell (10) B. June 3, 1934.

282H. _____ Owens (9)

First child of Lucy Rebecca (Norris) Owens and Benjamin Isaac Owens.

282I. _____ Owens (9)

Second child of Lucy Rebecca (Norris) Owens and Benjamin Isaac Owens.

282J. William Lee Owens (9)

Son of Lucy Rebecca (Norris) Owens (No. 144) and Benjamin Isaac Owens. Born September 14, 1887, married February 21, 1909, Katherine Dove Russell, born August 25, 1889. They resided in Abell, MD, on a part of Collingwood. Children:

369.   I. Mary Irma (10) B. March 6, 1911.
370.   II. William Anthony (10) B. January 7, 1914.
371.   III. Annie Rebecca (10) B. October 3, 1917.
372.   IV. James Ignatius (10) B. February 9, 1921.
373.   V. Lois Ruth (10) B. August 7, 1923.

282K. Jane Ann Owens (9) Woodburn

Daughter of Lucy Rebecca (Norris) Owens (No. 144) and Benjamin Isaac Owens. Born August 16, 1890. Married February 5, 1911, in St. Mary's County, Joseph Lancaster Woodburn. Resided in Washington, DC. Children:

374.   I. Edwin (10) B. May 3, 1912.
375.   II. Mary Alice (10) B. August 6, 1913.

282L. John Joseph Owens (9)

Son of Lucy Rebecca (Norris) Owens (No. 144) and Benjamin Isaac Owens. Born February 27, 1892. Married September 3, 1921, Elizabeth (Morgan). Resided in Washington, DC. Children:

376.   I. Alice Regina (10) B. April 29, 1923.

282M. Daisy Dora Owens (9)

Daughter of Lucy Rebecca (Norris) Owens (No. 144) and Benjamin Isaac Owens. Born July 1, 1894. Died November 12, 1895.

282N. Grover Raymond Owens (9)

Son of Lucy Rebecca (Norris) Owens (No. 144) and Benjamin Isaac Owens. Born March 8, 1896. Married, March 17, 1917, Gertrude Owens (his cousin). Resided in Washington, DC. Children:

377.   I. John (10) B. July 20, 1918.
378.   II. Benjamin (10) B. January 20, 1920.
379.   III. Walter (10) B. November, 1922. D. 1933.
380.   IV. Bernita (10) B. June 30, 1925.
381.   V. Shirley (10) B. March 14, 1928.
382.   VI. Vivian (10) B. January 31, 1934.
383.   VII. Robert Walter (10) B. June 30, 1937.

282O. James Benjamin Owens (9)

Son of Lucy Rebecca (Norris) Owens (No. 144) and Benjamin Isaac Owens. Born October 4, 1897. Married October 6, 1918, Martha Ellen Mattingly, born April 13, 1902. Resided in Abell, MD, on a part of Collingwood. Children:

384.   I. Mary Lucille (10) B. October 19, 1919.
385.   II. Joseph Walter (10) B. October 6, 1923.
386.   III. Teresa (10) B. April 2, 1929.

282P. Essie May Owens (9) Gibson

Daughter of Lucy Rebecca (Norris) Owens (No. 144) and Benjamin Isaac Owens. Born March 1, 1900. Married October 23, 1922, Thomas Laurie Gibson. Resided in St. Mary's County, MD. Children:

387.   I. Thomas Laurie (10) B. February 7, 1924.
388.   II. James Henry (10) B. June 30, 1925.
389.   III. Francis De Sales (10) B. June 28, 1927.
390.   IV. Mary Elizabeth (10) B. November 8, 1930.

391. V. Helen Cecelia (10) B. April 1, 1933.
392. VI. May Rosaline (10) B. July 27, 1934.
393. VII. Sophia Bernadette (10) B. May 9, 1937.
394. VIII. Aloysius McGuire (10) B. November 6, 1938.
395. IX. Joseph Walter (10) B. May 22, 1940.

282Q. Charles Larry Palmer Owens (9)

Son of Lucy Rebecca (Norris) Owens (No. 144) and Benjamin Isaac Owens. Born March 25, 1903. Married January 1, 1927, Esther Lorraine Lawrence. They resided in Abell, MD, on a part of Collingwood. Children:
396. I. Melba Marie (10) B. September 28, 1927.
397. II. Mary Louise (Lou) (10) B. February 26, 1935.

282R. Joseph Maynard Owens (9)

Son of Lucy Rebecca (Norris) Owens (No. 144) and Benjamin Isaac Owens. Born January 3, 1908. Died October 6, 1908.

282S. Mary Elizabeth Owens (9) Mattingly

Daughter of Lucy Rebecca (Norris) Owens (No. 144) and Benjamin Isaac Owens. Born September 9, 1910. Married January 2, 1933, James W. Mattingly. They resided in Abell, MD, in her mother's old home at Collingwood. Children:
398. I. James Donald (10) B. March 22, 1935.
399. II. Michael Wayne (10) B. September 26, 1937.

282T. John Francis Norris (9)

Son of Joseph Alvin Norris (No. 145) and Rosella (Alvey) Norris. Born April 10, 1898. Married (1) December 7, 1918, in Washington, DC, Madeline Devine, born in Germantown, MD, 1900, and (2) Catherine Hardt. Children - First Marriage
400. I. Ruene Marcella (10) B. October 1, 1919.

282U. Eldridge Norris (9)

Son of Joseph Alvin Norris (No. 145) and Rosella (Alvey) Norris. Born about 1900. He was swept overboard from the schooner of Captain John Joseph Gibson, and drowned in the Potomac River, in a night storm, when about 16 years of age. Died about 1916.

282V. Grace Genevieve Thompson (9) Lawrence

Daughter of Frances Lorraine (Norris) Thompson (No. 146) and William Edgar Thompson. Born April 28, 1889. Married March 29, 1910, Joseph Francis Lawrence, born August 20, 1887. Resided in Abell, MD, on a part of Collingwood. Children:

401.	I. Francis De Sales (10) B. January 18, 1911.	
402.	II. Charles (10) B. 1912. Died around 1920.	
403.	III. Margaret Rose (10) B. May 18, 1917.	
404.	IV. Frances Ruth (10) B. March 1, 1919.	
405.	V. Mary Emily (10) B. May 22, 1922.	
406.	VI. Barbara Ellen (10) B. September 18, 1924.	

282W. Ruth Lorraine Thompson (9)

Daughter of Frances Lorraine (Norris) Thompson (No. 146) and William Edgar Thompson. Born April 8, 1891. Is a Nun, Sister Frances Louise, in a convent at Nazareth, KY.

282X. Edgar Francis Thompson (9)

Son of Frances Lorraine (Norris) Thompson (No. 146) and William Edgar Thompson. Born January 1, 1893. Married (1) May 9, 1914, Annie May Miller and (2) August 21, 1931, Elsie Marie Witherspoon. There are no children.

282Y. William Lee Thompson (9)

Son of Frances Lorraine (Norris) Thompson (No. 146) and William Edgar Thompson. Born October 11, 1898. Married January 16, 1924, Lola Ames of Riverton, NJ, who died at their home in Washington, DC, in 1947. Children:

407. I. William Ames (10) B. March 5, 1927.
408. II. Frances Eleanor (10) B. 1929.
409. III. Donald (10) B. 1934.

282Z. Leonard Allen Thompson (9)

Son of Frances Lorraine (Norris) Thompson (No. 146) and William Edgar Thompson. Born March 20, 1903. Married November 25, 1924, Mary Edith Mattingly, born August 21, 1901, daughter of William Mattingly. Reside on St. Patrick's Creek, St. Mary's County, MD. Children:
410. I. Mary Frances (10) B. September 9, 1926.
411. II. Joseph Harvey (10) B. August 3, 1931.

283A. Laura Virginia Swann (9) Biggs

Daughter of Jane Nettie (Norris) Swann (No. 147) and Henry Samuel Swann. Born June 1, 1900. Married at Alexandria, VA, in 1922, William Warren Biggs. They resided in Camp Springs, MD. Children:
412. I. Constance (10) B. April 5, 1923.
413. II. William Warren, Jr. (10) B. September 23, 1924.

283B. Annabelle (Annie Bell) Swann (9) Biggs

Daughter of Jane Nettie (Norris) Swann (No. 147) and Henry Samuel Swann. Born August 21, 1905. Married June 10, 1925, Thomas George Biggs, a cousin of William Warren Biggs. They resided in Camp Springs, MD. Children:
414. I. Dorothy Irma (10) B. March 19, 1926.
415. II. Robert George (10) B. December 14, 1935.

283C. Alma Norris (9)

Daughter of John Lee Norris (No. 148) and Mary Norma (Knott) Norris. Born 1897. Died in infancy.

283D. William Allen Boyd Norris (9)

Son of John Lee Norris (No. 148) and Mary Norma (Knott) Norris. Born August 19, 1899. Married April 4, 1920, Washington, DC, Ella Gates. Resided in Ardmore, MD. No children.

283E. James Ralph Norris (9)

Son of John Lee Norris (No. 148) and Mary Norma (Knott) Norris. Born May 22, 1903. Married December 27, 1925, Washington, DC, Elsie Clatterbuck, born Warrenton, VA. Resided in Washington, DC. Children:
416.   I. James Ralph (10) B. April 29, 1927.
417.   II. Shirley Mae (10) B. January 16, 1930.

283F. Bernard Elmer Norris (9)

Son of John Lee Norris (No. 148) and Mary Norma (Knott) Norris. Born July 11, 1904. Married December 25, 1923, Mary Evangeline Bailey. Resided in River Springs, MD. Children:
418.   I. Joseph Leonard (10) B. November 18, 1927.
419.   II. Rosemary (10) B. April 20, 1932.

283G. Mary Norma Norris (9) Wible, Dudley

Daughter of John Lee Norris (No. 148) and Mary Norma (Knott) Norris. Born February 20, 1908. Married September 5, 1922, (1) Allan Wible and (2) Henry J. Dudley. Children: - First Marriage
420.   I. Allan (10) B. September 2, 1923.
421.   II. Robert (10) B. September 27, 1924.

283H. John Walter Norris (9)

Son of John Lee Norris (No. 148) and Mary Norma (Knott) Norris. Born May 29, 1910. Married December 31, 1932, Christine Meininger. Resided in Washington, DC. Children:
422.   I. Joan (10) B. November 28, 1941.
423.   II. Janet (10) B. February 10, 1945.

283I. John Leo Norris (9)

Son of John Lee Norris (No. 148) and Mary Norma (Knott) Norris. Born December 20, 1912. Married March 26, 1933, Lydia Rauch. They resided in Oxon Hill, MD. Children:
- 424.   I. John Leo, III, (10) B. July 17, 1939.
- 425.   II. Sharon Irene (10) B. November 7, 1943.

283J. Charles Ernest Norris (9)

Son of John Lee Norris (No. 148) and Mary Norma (Knott) Norris. Born July 20, 1915. Married October 9, 1937, Lydia Ballard. They resided in Washington, DC. He served in World War II in Japan. Children:
- 426.   I. Charles Ernest, Jr. (10) B. January 16, 1939.

283K. Mary Alice Norris (9) German

Daughter of John Lee Norris (No. 148) and Mary Norma (Knott) Norris. Born September 4, 1918. Married June 9, 1937, Raymond C. German. They resided in Bethesda, MD. Children:
- 427.   I. Raymond C., Jr. (10) B. February 25, 1938.
- 428.   II. Kenneth Lee (10) B. June 17, 1939.
- 429.   III. Judith Ann (10) B. September 9, 1942.
- 430.   IV. Robert Norris (10) B. May 6, 1944.

283L. Edna Genevieve Norris (9) Rasmussen

Daughter of James Benjamin Norris (No. 149) and Helen Maud (McClure). Born December 6, 1907, in Washington, DC. Graduated from St. Margaret's Academy, Minneapolis. Oppheum Circuit Entertainer and Premier Danseuse with Earl Carroll's Vanities in New York. Married Halvar Peter Rasmussen in 1927 in Philadelphia, PA, who was born 1900 in Minneapolis. Halvar was employed by King Features Syndicate and is the creator of the "Aggie Mack" cartoon strip. They resided in Kew Gardens, NY. Children:
- 431.   I. Halvar Peter, Jr. (10) B. 1928.

283M. James Stafford Norris (9)

Son of James Benjamin Norris (No. 149) and Helen Maud (McClure). Born July 17, 1910, in Washington, DC. Attended West High School, Minneapolis. Married in Minneapolis in 1936. Stafford served in the Army during World War II, connected with the Air Force. Overseas in England, and awarded the Bronze Star when serving with the 78th Division near Aachen, Germany. Resided in Minneapolis. Children:

432.	I. Darlene (10) B. 1937.
433.	II. Joyce (10) B. 1939.
434.	III. Mary (10) B. 1940.

283N. John Randolph Norris (9)

Son of James Benjamin Norris (No. 149) and Helen Maud (McClure). Born July 2, 1919, in Minneapolis. Graduated from West High School, Minneapolis. Entertainer on Orpheum Circuit. Publisher of weekly periodical. During World War II, served with the First U.S. Army in Europe, from Omaha Beach to Berlin. Married September 6, 1940, Ruth Hibelink, in Pender, NE. She also was an entertainer and they appeared as a dance team under billing of Randolph and Hillary. They resided in Minneapolis. Children:

435.	I. Jay Randolph (10) B. November 3, 1942.
436.	II. Stephanie Lynn (10) B. October 22, 1946.

283O. Irving Norris (9)

Son of John Edward Norris (No. 150) and Bernadette (Owens) Norris. Born October 1, 1910. Married 1934, (1) Louise Hold, who died and (2) 1935, Peggy Donovan. Served 2 1/2 years during World War II. They resided in Arlington, VA. There are no children.

283P. Olive Norris (9) Herman

Daughter of John Edward Norris (No. 150) and Bernadette (Owens) Norris. Born September 7, 1912. Married, 1935, Oscar Herman. They resided in Washington, DC. Children:

437. I. Mary (10) B. February 10, 1942.
438. II. Ann (10) B. August 27, 1943.
439. III. Bernadette Lee (10) B. February 8, 1946.

283Q. Jane A. Norris (9) Ricardi

Daughter of John Edward Norris (No. 150) and Bernadette (Owens) Norris. Born March 17, 1919. Married, 1937, Anthony Ricardi. They resided in Washington, DC. Children:
440. I. Patricia (10) B. September 4, 1941.
441. II. Ralph (10) B. January 21, 1943.

283R. Martha Norris (9) Dunnigan

Daughter of John Edward Norris (No. 150) and Bernadette (Owens) Norris. Born November 27, 1923. Married September 7, 1946, Robert Dunnigan. They resided in Washington, DC.

283S. Betty Norris (9)

Daughter of John Edward Norris (No. 150) and Bernadette (Owens) Norris. Born May 1, 1932.

283T. Annie Cheseldine (9)

Daughter of John W. Cheseldine (No. 155) and Mary Magdaline (Maggie) Cheseldine. Born _____. Married November, 1923, Andrew Freeman Cheseldine, her cousin, born March 28, 1905. Children:
442. I. John William (10) B. May 25, 1925.
443. II. Robert Lee (10) B. November 21, 1926.

284. George Benjamin Cheseldine (9)

Son of George F. Cheseldine (No. 156) and Sarah Fanny Cheseldine (No. 194). Born in St. Mary's County.

285. Frederick Cheseldine (9)

Son of George F. Cheseldine (No. 156) and Sarah Fanny Cheseldine (No. 194). Born in St.Mary's County.

286. Marjorie Cheseldine (9) Nail, Hirst

Daughter of David Stevenson Cheseldine (No. 165) and _____. Born 1920. Married (1) Harold V. Nail, and (2) Warren Hirst.. Children: - First Marriage-Nail
444.   I. William David (10) B. November 21, 1942.
445.   II. Winnie Fay (10) B. June 2, 1944.
446.   III. Michael David (10) B. November 21, 1965.
447.   IV. Jeffrey Allen (10) B. July 31, 1971.
Children: - Second Marriage-Hirst
448.   V. Brenda Lee (10) B. 1952.
449.   VI. Linda Ann (10) B. 1954.
450.   VII. Darlene Marie (10) B. 1958.
451.   VIII. Dawn Louise (10) B. 1963.

287. Betty Lee Cheseldine (9) Mellon

Daughter of David Stevenson Cheseldine (No. 165) and _____. Born 1923. Married Richard Mellon in 1944. Children:
452.   I. Richard Paul (10) B. 1945.
453.   II. James Stephen (10) B. 1948.
454.   III. David Michael (10) B. 1955.

288. John Wilmer Cheseldine (9)

Son of Robert Boyd Cheseldine (No. 166) and Lillian (Ellis) born in St. Mary's County. Married _____ Grimes. Children:
455.   I. Judith Lee (10) B.

289. Margaret Louise Cheseldine (9) Lacy

Daughter of Robert Boyd Cheseldine (No. 166) and Lillian (Ellis). Born _____. Married John Lacy. Children:
456.   I. Susan (10) B.
457.   II. Linda (10) B.

290. Robert Boyd Cheseldine, Jr. (9)

Son of Robert Boyd Cheseldine (No. 166) and Lillian (Ellis)
Born in St. Mary's County.

291. Grace Cheseldine (9)

Daughter of Joseph Endress Cheseldine (No. 174) and Mary
Maud (Mattingly) Cheseldine. Born _____. Died young.

292. Stanley Cheseldine (9)

Son of Joseph Endress Cheseldine (No. 174) and Mary Maud
(Mattingly) Cheseldine. Born _____. Died young.

293. W. Wallace Cheseldine (9)

Son of Joseph Endress Cheseldine (No. 174) and Mary Maud
(Mattingly) Cheseldine. Born in St. Mary's County _____.
Married Flora A. _____. Died March 23, 1949. Children:
    458.   I. Mary E. (10)
    459.   II. Lillian (10)
    460.   III. Robert (10)
    461.   IV. Ronald (10)
    462.   V. Stanley (10)
    463.   VI. Carla (10)
    464.   VII. James (10)

294. Lillian Cheseldine (9) Hancock

Daughter of Joseph Endress Cheseldine (No. 174) and Mary
Maud (Mattingly) Cheseldine. Born _____. Married
_____Hancock.

295. Margaret Cheseldine (9) Irvin

Daughter of Joseph Endress Cheseldine (No. 174) and Mary
Maud (Mattingly) Cheseldine. Born _____. Married
_____ Irvin.

296. Everett Alphonse Cheseldine (9)

Son of Nelson Alphonse Cheseldine (No. 178) and Elizabeth (Mattingly) Cheseldine. Born April 3, 1910. Married Margaret Mullen, December 2, 1939. Children:
    465.   I. Everett Alphonsus, Jr. (10) B. January 22, 1942.

296A. Masie Beitzell (9) LeBarron

Daughter of Susan (Ellis) Beitzell (No. 178D) and George Lee Beitzell. Born August 4, 1900. Married Freemond LeBarron, January 26, 1945.

296B. Josephine Beitzell (9)

Daughter of Susan (Ellis) Beitzell (No. 178D) and George Lee Beitzell. Born July 8, 1904.

296C. Leonard Beitzell (9)

Son of Susan (Ellis) Beitzell (No. 178D) and George Lee Beitzell. Born December 13, 1908. Died in childhood.

296D. Marguerite Beitzell (9) Hanck

Daughter of Susan (Ellis) Beitzell (No. 178D) and George Lee Beitzell. Born July 11, 1913. Married Henery M. Hanck, October 20, 1939.

296E. Gilbert Ellis (9)

Son of Thomas Ellis (No. 178E) and Ella (surname unknown) Ellis. Born

296F. Delmas Ellis (9)
Child of Thomas Ellis (No. 178E) and Ella (surname unknown) Ellis. Born

296G. Earl Morris (9)

Son of Eva (Ellis) Morris (No. 178F) and Foster Morris. Born

296H. Ernest Morris (9)

Son of Eva (Ellis) Morris (No. 178F) and Foster Morris. Born

296I. Dora Morris (9)

Daughter of Eva (Ellis) Morris (No. 178F) and Foster Morris.
Born

297. Elmer Henry Cheseldine (9)

Son of Phillip Henry Cheseldine (No. 179) and
_____ Cheseldine. Born _____. Married Elizabeth
Kepplinger. She died March 18, 1971. Children:
466.   I. Elmer Henry, Jr. (10) B.
467.   II. Donald Richard (10) B.
468.   III. Rosemary (10) B.

298. Grace May Cheseldine (9)

Daughter of Phillip Henry Cheseldine (No. 179) and
_____ .Born _____ .

299. James Corbin Cheseldine (9)

Son of John Reed Cheseldine (No. 191) and _____ .
Born _____. Married Minnie A. _____. In 1954 lived at
North Pershing Drive, Arlington, VA. Died August 31, 1977.
Children:
469.   I. Mary (10) B.

300. Mary Adelaide Cheseldine (9) Clements

Daughter of Carl Costello Cheseldine (No. 196) and Maud
(Owens) Cheseldine. Born August 3, 1920. Married on March 23,

1940, Samuel Burch Clements, Jr. He was born April 17, 1920. He served in the Navy in WWII and died October 2, 1996. He is buried at All Saints Cemetery, Oakley, MD. Children:

470.   I. Samuel Burch, (10) B. January 18, 1945.
471.   II. Carl Cheseldine Clements (10) He was the son of Robert Cheseldine, Mary's brother. but was adopted and raised by Mary and Sam Clements.

301. Carl Costello Cheseldine, Jr. (9)

Son of Carl Costello Cheseldine (No. 196) and Maud (Owens) Cheseldine. Born August 3, 1930. Served in the U. S. Army as a Corporal in the Korean War. Died 1981 and is buried at All Saints Church, Oakley, MD.

301A. William Thomas Gibson (9)

Son of Joseph Edgar Gibson (No. 208) and Eva (Thompson) Gibson. Born October 28, 1914. Died August 4, 1917.

301B. Mary Annie Gibson (9)

Daughter of Joseph Edgar Gibson (No. 208) and Eva (Thompson) Gibson. Born.

301C. John Edgar Gibson (9)

Son of Joseph Edgar Gibson (No. 208) and Eva (Thompson) Gibson. Born
301D. Margaret Adelaide Gibson (9)

Daughter of Joseph Edgar Gibson (No. 208) and Eva (Thompson) Gibson. Born

301E. James Relmond Gibson (9)

Son of James Sylvester Gibson (No. 209) and Violet (Perry) Gibson. Born July 25, 1917.

301F. Gordon Perry Gibson (9)

Son of James Sylvester Gibson (No. 209) and Violet (Perry) Gibson. Born

301G. James Everett Gibson (9)

Son of James Sylvester Gibson (No. 209) and Violet (Perry) Gibson. Born

301H. Elizabeth Gibson (9)

Daughter of George Washington Gibson (No. 210) and Bessie (Owens) Gibson. Born

301I. George Roland Gibson (9)

Son of George Washington Gibson (No. 210) and Bessie (Owens) Gibson. Born

301J. John Wallace Gibson (9)

Son of George Washington Gibson (No. 210) and Bessie (Owens) Cheseldine. Born

301K. Bernice Gibson (9)

Daughter of George Washington Gibson (No. 210) and Bessie (Owens) Gibson. Born

301L. Eleanor Gibson (9)

Daughter of George Washington Gibson (No. 210) and Bessie (Owens) Gibson. Born.

301M. Joseph Gibson (9)

Son of George Washington Gibson (No. 210) and Bessie (Owens) Gibson. Born

301N. Leah Elizabeth Gibson (9)

Daughter of Cecil Francis Gibson (No. 211) and Elizabeth (Shuett) Gibson. Born

301O. Mary Louise Gibson (9)

Daughter of Cecil Francis Gibson (No. 211) and Elizabeth (Shuett) Gibson. Born

301P. Sarah Ann Gibson (9)

Daughter of Cecil Francis Gibson (No. 211) and Elizabeth (Shuett) Gibson. Born _____ Died in infancy.

301Q. Cecil Francis Gibson, Jr. (9)

Son of Cecil Francis Gibson (No. 211) and Elizabeth (Shuett) Gibson. Born

301R. Robert Louis Wyant (9)

Son of Sarah Elizabeth (Gibson) Wyant (No. 212) and George Wyant. Born April 22, 1930.

301S. James Dewey Wyant (9)

Son of Sarah Elizabeth (Gibson) Wyant (No. 212) and George Wyant. Born July 18, 1933.

301T. George Charles Wyant (9)

Son of Sarah Elizabeth (Gibson) Wyant (No. 212) and George Wyant. Born March 4, 1935.

301U. Bessie Sedonia Meushaw (9)

Daughter of Edith May (Dingee) Meushaw (No. 221) and William Thomas Meushaw. Bessie was named for her aunt, Bessie Dingee Carney Smith (No. 220). Born _____. Children:

301U1. Helen Meushaw (9) McCumber

Daughter of Edith May (Dingee) Meushaw (No. 221) and William Thomas Meushaw. Born August 3, 1905.

301U2. John Meushaw (9)

Son of Edith May (Dingee) Meushaw (No. 221) and William Thomas Meushaw. Born

301U3. Marie Meushaw (9) Lee

Daughter of Edith May (Dingee) Meushaw (No. 221) and William Thomas Meushaw. Born_____. Married _____ Lee.

301U4. Melba Meushaw (9)
Daughter of Edith May (Dingee) Meushaw (No. 221) and William Thomas Meushaw. Born

301U5. Catherine Meushaw (9)

Daughter of Edith May (Dingee) Meushaw (No. 221) and William Thomas Meushaw. Born

301U6. Harold Meushaw (9)

Son of Edith May (Dingee) Meushaw (No. 221) and William Thomas Meushaw. Born _____. Children:
- 471A.   I. Wallace (10) B.
- 471B.   II. Richard (10) B.
- 471C.   III. William (10) B.

301U7. Wallace Cullens (9)

Son of Agnes (Dingee) Cullens (No. 222) and Aubrey Cullens. Born

301U8. Richard Cullens (9)

Born

Son of Agnes (Dingee) Cullens (No. 222) and Aubrey Cullens.

301U9. William Cullens (9)

Born

Son of Agnes (Dingee) Cullens (No. 222) and Aubrey Cullens.

301V. James L. Turner (9)

Born_____. Died April 30, 1962.

Son of Ida V. (Dingee) Turner (No. 223) and Harry Turner.

301W. Virginia Turner (9)

Daughter of Ida V. (Dingee) Turner (No. 223) and Harry Turner. Born _____.

301X. Henrietta Turner (9)

Daughter of Ida V. (Dingee) Turner (No. 223) and Harry Turner. Born _____.

301Y. Betty Turner (9)

Daughter of Ida V. (Dingee) Turner (No. 223) and Harry Turner. Born _____.

301Z. Raymond Turner (9)

Born _____. As of 1998, lives in Silver Spring, MD.

Son of Ida V. (Dingee) Turner (No. 223) and Harry Turner.

302. Dorothy Elizabeth Cheseldine (9) Garver

Daughter of Raymond Minshall Cheseldine (No. 233) and Dorothy (Canfield) Cheseldine. Born about 1916, in Columbus, OH.

129

Married R. H. Garver. Dorothy died in January, 1991 in California. Children:

474.   I. Dorothy (10) B.
473.   II. Raymond C. (10) B.
474.   III. Earl Charles (Squeak) (10) B .

302A. Olive Levonia Yates (9) Cryer, Wortz

Daughter of Carrie Levonia (Dingee) Yates (No. 224) and Warren A. Yates. Born November 7, 1911, in St. Mary's County, MD, and lived in Bushwood until her late teens, when her family moved to Washington, DC. Olive, 16, married (1) William Francis Cryer, 23, on June 20, 1928. Olive, "Lee", lived at 813 L. Street, NW. Washington, DC at the time of their marriage. One daughter was born, Margaret Patricia. Lee and Francis separated October 18, 1938 and later divorced. Francis drowned in a boating accident on the Potomac River. Lee married (2) Charles Wortz, who died May 13, 1958. No issue from the second marriage. Lee died December 13, 1974, at her daughter Pat's home in Virginia and is buried with her mother, Carrie at Fort Lincoln Cemetery, Washington, DC. Children: First Marriage

475.   I. Margaret Patricia Cryer (10) B. April 29, 1931.

302B. Thomas Irvin Yates (9)

Son of Carrie Levonia (Dingee) Yates (No. 224) and Warren A. Yates. Born September 3, 1914, in St. Mary's County, MD, and moved to Washington, DC, with his mother, brother and sisters, around 1922.

Tom eloped with Mary Helena Morgan on June 7, 1934 and they remarried in church July 16, 1934. They were loving, devoted parents to their children and were wonderful loving grandparents. Tom was the life of the party. He loved the water and lived to fish. He enjoyed playing cards, writing poetry, singing songs and playing the harmonica and organ. He did indeed leave a loving legacy.

Tom, Jr. recalled a day when his Dad took him to visit his Uncle Milton and Aunt Martha (No. 302D) and Tom, Sr., Tom, Jr. and Milton went to the airport where Milton, an aeronautical engineer, worked, and picked up some airplane paint. They took the paint back to Miltons' house and painted Tom Sr.'s old car with the airplane paint.

Tom, Jr. recalled his Dad saying many times, over the years, "I can't believe I painted my car with airplane paint!"

Tom retired after 37 years with Bergmann's Laundry as the Virginia Plant Manager. They resided in Upper Marlboro, MD. Tom died March 23, 1986. Mary died May 19, 1988. Children:

476.   I. Thomas Irvin, Jr. (10) B. October 1, 1938.
477.   II. Carol Ann (10) B. June 2, 1942.
478.   III. Elaine Kay (10) B. January 15, 1946.

302C. Ralph Augustus "Gus" Yates (9)

Son of Carrie Levonia (Dingee) Yates (No. 224) and Warren A. Yates. Born October 16, 1917, in St. Mary's County, MD, but his birth was not registered until October 26, 1917.

Gus married Florence Kaye Everett, born December 5, 1919, Washington, DC, on December 24, 1937 with his sister, Martha (No. 302D) and her husband, Milton, standing for them at their wedding.

Florence is the daughter of James Franklin Everett, a pharmacist, born September 18, 1882, died in 1951, and Florence Christine Kaye, born January 4, 1889, died November 3, 1966. Gus died June 6, 1992. Flo lives in Annapolis, MD. Children:

479.   I. Sandra Kaye (10) B. February 16, 1939.
480.   II. Bonnie Jean (10) B. November 2, 1944.
481.   III. Ralph Everett (10) B. September 20, 1953.

302D. Martha Mae Yates (9) Baggett

Daughter of Carrie Levonia (Dingee) Yates (No. 224) and Warren A. Yates. Born May 17, 1919, in St. Mary's County, MD, lived in Bushwood until around 1922, then moved to Washington, DC. with her mother, brothers and sisters. Martha, 18, of 719 Sixth Street, N. W., Washington, DC. married Milton Baggett, 23, who was born in Salemburg, NC, June 13, 1914, of 232 11th Street, S. W.,Washington, DC, on September 1, 1937. Milton was a college graduate, and an aeronautical engineer, working for Fairchild Aircraft and the Army, as a civilian. Martha was an office manager for Elman Labels in Silver Spring, MD, for almost 30 years.

Martha and Milton separated, but never divorced. Martha was a wonderful loving mother. She worked hard, always loved her children and gave them more than she could afford.

In the last years of her life, Martha and her sister Jane shared a house in Odenton, MD. Milton died March 11, 1969, in Washington, DC. Martha died July 3, 1992, at Greater Laurel Hospital, Laurel, MD, at the age of 73. At her wishes, Martha was cremated and her ashes were strewn in the Chesapeake Bay. Children:

482. I. Beverly Jeanne (10) B. May 11, 1939.
483. II. Larry Eugene (10) B. August 1, 1947.

302E. Katherine Jane Yates (9) Richard

Daughter of Carrie Levonia (Dingee) Yates (No. 224) and Warren A. Yates. Born November 14, 1921, in St. Mary's County, MD, lived in Bushwood, MD, for the first year of her life, then moved to Washington, DC, with her family.

Jane married Edward Richard from Providence, RI, who was a Marine, and lived in Rhode Island for a while. When Rich was sent overseas, Jane moved to Washington, DC, with her sons, Fred and Jerry. Their daughter Debra was born when the boys were in high school. Jane and her sister, Martha shared an apartment for most of Debbie's younger years. In early 1992, Jane and Martha moved to a house in Odenton, MD. While Martha was in the hospital and after her death, Jane lived with her daughter Deb Richard in Bowie, MD. Jane died January 7, 1994, was cremated, and her ashes are buried in Waldorf, Maryland. Children:

484. I. Fred Douglas (10) B. May 5, 1945.
485. II. Gerald Thomas (10) B. October 4, 1947. D. January 24, 1988.
486. III. Debra Jayne (10) B. November 2, 1963.

302F. Joseph Donald Knott (9)

Son of Lida (Dingee) Knott (No. 226) and Lee Knott.

302G. Dorothy Knott (9) Goode

Daughter of Lida (Dingee) Knott (No. 226) and Lee Knott. Born. Married Walter Goode. Children:

486A.   I. Penny (10)
486B.   II. Joyce (10)
486C.   III. Skip (10)

302H. John Francis Simpson (9)

Son of Nell Elizabeth (Dingee) Simpson Newman (No. 227) and Frank S. Simpson. Born September 14, 1922 in Sibley Hospital, Washington, DC. Married Gloria Jean Simmers, born August 14, 1925 in Thompson #2, PA. Francis died April 17, 1996 in St. Lukes Hospital, New York City, NY. Children:

486D.   I. John Francis, Jr. (10) B. December 30, 1944.
486E.   II. Donald Alan (10) B. November 6, 1947.
486F.   III. James Richard (10) B. April 19, 1951.
486G.   IV. David Wayne (10) B. March 4, 1957.
486H.   V. Michael Kevin (10) B. April 1, 1965.

302I. Biscoe Knott (9)

Son of George Biscoe Knott (No.228A) and Julia Hannah Huseman. Born February 16, 1918. Married July 26, 1941 Fern Darly Miller. Children:

486I.   I. Fern Darly (10) B. January 18, 1948.

302J. Jane Elizabeth Knott (9) Long

Daughter of George Biscoe Knott (No. 228A) and Julia Hannah Huseman. Born July 31, 1920. Married March 21, 1941 Otis F. Long. Children:

486J.   I. John Biscoe (10) B. December 31, 1942.

302K. Windsor Palmer (9)

Son of Maria (Knott) Palmer (No. 228B) and Charles Larry Palmer. Born September 4, 19__. Married Mary Alice Drury. Children:

486K.   I. Larry Bailey Palmer (10) B.
486L.   II. Angela Palmer (10) B.
486M.   III. Mary Windsor Palmer (10) B.

133

302L. Lielia Palmer (9) Pogue

Daughter of Maria (Knott) Palmer (No. 228B) and Charles Larry Palmer. Born_____. Married Billingsley Garner Pogue. Children:

    486N.   I. Billingsley Garner Pogue, Jr. (10) B.

303. Sue Cheseldine (9) Huntington

Daughter of Raymond Minshall Cheseldine (No. 253) and Dorothy (Canfield) Cheseldine. Born about 1920 in London, OH. Married John D. Huntington on June 11, 1939. Children:

    487.   I. John Spencer (10) B.
    488.   II. Sue Canfield (10) B.
    489.   III. Elizabeth (10) B.
    490.   IV. J. Wallace (10) B.
    491.   V. Jeanne (10) B.
    492.   VI. Priscilla (10) B.

304. Charles Canfield (Tommy) Cheseldine (9)

Son of Raymond Minshall Cheseldine (No. 233) and Dorothy (Canfield) Cheseldine. Tommy was born September 3, 1921 in Columbus, OH. Married Laura Dodd in 1952. He was a Professor at Haile Selassie University. Died on February 9, 1967 in Ethiopia. Children:

    493.   I. Dianne Hillsamer Cheseldine (10) B. December 3, 1944 in Indiana. She is the daughter of Laura and her first husband, David Hillsamer. She was adopted by Charles upon his marriage to Laura in 1952.

305. Raymond "Skip" Minshall Cheseldine, Jr. (9)

Son of Raymond Minshall Cheseldine (No. 233) and Estelle (surname unknown) Cheseldine. Born about 1929. Skip married_____. In 1998 he was living in Chicago, IL. Children:

    494.   I. Cary (10) B.
    495.   II. Kim (10) B.

306. Barbara Elizabeth Cheseldine (9) Jones

Daughter of Kenneth George Cheseldine (No. 234) and Rebecca (Hughes) Cheseldine. Born July 20, 1921 at Columbus, OH, but grew up in Seattle, WA. Barbara and Roland Morris Jones were high school sweethearts and were married October 19, 1938. Barbara has always been active in the Episcopal Church. She is accomplished at needlepoint. One of her projects was a new seat cover for a chair that belonged to Posey Cheseldine. She now resides in Santa Rosa, CA. Roland worked for Carnation Milk Co. and Dillingham Corp. He died July 24, 1988 shortly before their 50th wedding anniversary.
Children:

496.	I. Barbara Sue (10) B. September 17, 1942.
497.	II. Catherine Elizabeth (10) B. October 19, 1946.
498.	III. Owen Williams (10) B. October 28, 1949.

307. Kenneth Oswald (9)

Son of Izora (Cheseldine) Oswald (No. 235) and Ernest Oswald. Born _____.

308. Betty Oswald (9)

Daughter of Izora (Cheseldine) Oswald (No. 235) and Ernest Oswald. Born _____.

309. Maxine Charlotte Fraser (9) Lesan

Daughter of Anna Evelyn (Cheseldine) Fraser (No. 236) and Charles Thomas Fraser. Born October 10, 1912. Married Robert Carlton Lesan about 1937.

310. Jeanette Fraser (9) Carter

Daughter of Anna Evelyn (Cheseldine) Fraser (No. 236) and Charles Thomas Fraser. Born November 17, 1913. Married Frank Carter about 1937.

311. Peggy Lee Fraser (9) Rufner

Daughter of Anna Evelyn (Cheseldine) Fraser (No. 236) and Charles Thomas Fraser. Born in Lebanon, OH, on March 9, 1925. Upon graduation from Lebanon High School, she applied to Miami Valley Hospital School of Nursing in Dayton, OH. She was accepted and entered at the end of August in 1943. In September of 1957 Peggy took a position in the Kettering School where she spent the next 22 years. After working as a staff nurse for a few years she was promoted to Supervisor of Health Services. She retired from that position in March 1981. She became the Executive Director of the National Association of School Nurses, having served as President Elect and President. She remained as Executive Director until 1986. Peggy married Donald Hoyt Rufner on May 18, 1946. Children:

    499.   I. Richard Kevin (10)
    500.   II. Deborah Kay (10)

312. Kathleen Cheseldine (9)

Daughter of Edward Kyle (Prudy) Cheseldine (No. 237) and Neva (Snook) Cheseldine. Born _____.

313. Martha Cheseldine (9)

Daughter of Edward Kyle (Prudy) Cheseldine (No. 237) and Neva (Snook) Cheseldine. Born _____.

313A. Jane Cheseldine (9)

Daughter of Harold "Chick" Cheseldine (No. 238) and Elsie (James) Cheseldine. Born_____. Died in the Dayton OH State Hospital in her early forties

313B. Dick Cheseldine (9)

Son of Harold "Chick" Cheseldine (No. 238) and Elsie (James) Cheseldine. Born _____. Dick and his wife lived in Montgomery, AL.

314. George Frederick Cheseldine (9)

Son of George Walter Cheseldine (No. 241) and Susie Elizabeth (Bailey) Cheseldine. Born in Washington, DC, on February 24, 1906. He was baptized on June 14, 1906 in St. Peter's Church, Washington, DC. Married on November 6, 1926, Mary Hilda Pilkerton. As a young man he held a variety of jobs, including oystering and delivering seafood to Washington, DC and Baltimore, MD. Fred for many years was associated with the Exide Batteries in Washington, DC. Later on he had his own battery business in Arlington, VA. Hilda was a manager in the Budget and Finance Department of the C & P Telephone Company, in Washington, DC, where she worked for over 40 years. She retired on April 24, 1967. After her retirement, she worked part-time for Kopel's Marina, in Colton's Point, MD. Hilda was active in church and community affairs. She was a member of All Saints Episcopal Church, Avenue, MD, where she served as treasurer for many years. She also served as treasurer of the St. Mary's County Historical Society. They maintained an apartment in Washington, but spent the weekends at their lovely home on St. Patrick's Creek in St. Mary's County or on their very comfortable cruiser plying the water ways of Maryland and Virginia. Capt. Fred was a charter member of the Seventh District Optimist Club in Bushwood, MD and an active participant in the annual ceremonies for the Blessing of the Fleet at St. Clement's Island. Hilda died on April 24, 1986 of a massive heart attack at the age of 80. Fred died January 15, 1996 after a long struggle with Alzheimer's disease at the age of 89. They are buried at Sacred Heart Church Cemetery, Bushwood, MD. Children:

    501.   I. Bertrand Frederick (10) B. October 21, 1936.
    502.   II. Mary Thomas (10) B. June 8, 1940.

315. Geraldine Lois Cheseldine (9) Savage

Daughter of George Walter Cheseldine (No. 241) and Elsie (Knapp) Cheseldine. Born June 15, 1921. Married April 4, 1944, Clifford Daniel Savage from Iowa, born July 22, 1921. He died January 16, 1997. Children:

    503.   I. Lois Ann (10) B. November, 1946.
    504.   II. Daniel C. (10) B. November 22, 1948
    505.   III. Mary Jane (10) B. July 19, 1952.

316. Joseph Clement Cheseldine (9)

Son of Richard Benjamin Cheseldine (No. 242) and Agnes Gwinette "Nettie" (Bowles) Cheseldine. Born in St. Mary's County, MD, on July 16, 1916. Married on September 16, 1940, Mary Marguerite Hayden, born on May 21, 1921 at Leonardtown, MD. "Captain" Clem was a life long waterman. He began his love affair with the water at the age of 10, when his father gave him a twelve foot rowboat complete with window curtains for sails. By the time he was sixteen years of age the water was such a part of his life that he quit school to work full time on the river.

In the beginning of his career, it was normal for him to bring in a hundred bushels of oysters by the end of a days work. However, by the time he retired the catch was down to just four bushels a day. Population growth, pollution, and over harvesting having made the river in-hospitable for the oyster to reproduce and thrive.

On days when, due to bad weather, it was not possible to go out on the river, and during the "off" season, "Capt." Clem would be busy making crab pots. When the oyster season was over and the crab season started, he would be found on the water again, harvesting the famous Chesapeake Blue Crab.

When a slight stroke prevented him from oystering, he needed something to occupy his time. Being experienced working with wood, having built his own boats, he turned to carving the figures he had seen all his life while working on the water. From blocks of wood, cedar stumps, and pieces of tree limbs, he began to whittle, shape, sand and paint sea-gulls, ducks and other birds. These beautiful works of art he does not sell, but prefers to give as gifts to friends and family.

His work shop is also a "port" to a fleet of sailing vessels. All of which he has carved, shaped, rigged and painted, so realistic, they look ready to set sail for long ago ports of call along the Chesapeake. Should they ever set sail, they would easily find their "Home Port" on return. A Lighthouse he built, complete with light, sits in his front yard to guide them home. Marguerite, his wife of over 56 years, jokes that on some foggy night they are going to end up with ships in their yard.

He was an active member of his community, belonging to the Men's Club of Holy Angels Church, working at Bingo for the school, and working with the Optimist Club of the Seventh District. He was a fan of, and enjoys attending the NASCAR Auto Races and Hydroplane Boat Races.

They made their home at White's Neck, in St. Mary's County, MD, on a part of the original Cheseldine holdings. Children:

506.   I. John William (10) B. November 6, 1942.
507.   II. Mary Agnes Henderson (10) B. August 4, 1944.
508.   III. Rose Marie (10) B. June 2, 1948.

317. Linda Cheseldine (9) Knott

Daughter of Richard Benjamin Cheseldine (No. 242) and Agnes Gwinette "Nettie" (Bowles) Cheseldine. Born February 1920. Married ____ Bryan Knott. Children:

509.   I. Andrew (10) B.
510.   II. Samuel (10) B.
511.   III. Son (10) B.
512.   IV. Daughter (10) B.

318. Audrey Cheseldine (9) Miller, Embrey

Daughter of Richard Benjamin Cheseldine (No. 242) and Agnes Gwinette "Nettie" (Bowles) Cheseldine. Born June, 1926. Married (1) James Miller and (2) ____ Embrey. Children: First Marriage.

513.   I. James Miller (10) B.

319. John Melvin Cheseldine (9)

Son of Richard Benjamin Cheseldine (No. 242) and Agnes Gwinette "Nettie" (Bowles) Cheseldine. Born July, 1928. Married

320. Eleanor Marie Cheseldine (9) Graves

Daughter of Richard Benjamin Cheseldine (No. 242) and Agnes Gwinette "Nettie" (Bowles) Cheseldine. Born in St. Mary's County, May 29, 1930. Married Joseph Melvin Graves, born January 27, 1927. Joseph Melvin works in the building trades as a carpenter. He served in the U.S. Army as a Staff Sgt. and was stationed in Germany. His interests include boating, crabbing, fishing and oystering. Children:

514.   I. Joseph Daniel (10) B. June 23, 1949.
515.   II. Francis Wayne (10) B. August 5, 1950.
516.   III. Glen David (10) B. October 7, 1959.

321. Sophie Rebecca Rice (9) Gibson

Daughter of Etta Beatrice (Cheseldine) Rice West Mahoney (243) and Richard Claxton Rice. Born March 20, 1908. Married Sidney Lawrence Gibson on November 21, 1925. Sidney was a boat builder and worked in the building trades. He was a master carpenter known for his skill in the cabinet and finishing work. As a young man he was also an excellent ice skater. He died on August 31, 1983 and is buried at Sacred Heart Cemetery, Bushwood, MD. Sophie was a flamboyant character. During the Prohibition years, when she was just seventeen, she ran bootleg whiskey. The only girl in the county with a new Ford. Upon moving to Washington, DC, she was in the numbers and racing business for forty years. Needless to say she had many friends in the gambling world. Children:
517.   I. Mary Jane (10) B. June 1, 1927.
518.   II. Charlotte Rebecca (10) B. January 19, 1931.
519.   III. Sidney Ann (10) B. November 2, 1944.
520.   IV. Alan Douglas (10) B. June 16, 1947.

322. Richard (Bennie) Rice (9)

Son of Etta Beatrice (Cheseldine) Rice West Mahoney (243) and Richard Claxton Rice. Born May 12, 1912. Married Margaret Florence Laughford, a lovely lady, on _____. Bennie fought in WWII and the Korean War. Died August 5, 1979, and is buried at Cheltenham, MD. Children:
521.   I. Florence (10) B.

323. Mary Beatrice Rice (9) Smith, Hanback

Daughter of Etta Beatrice (Cheseldine) Rice West Mahoney (No. 243) and Richard Claxton Rice. Born August 14, 1913. Married (1) Lawrence Smith, (2) Leroy Hanback. Bea died March 31, 1982. Children: - First Marriage
522.   I. Rachel Rebecca Smith (10) B.

Children: - Second Marriage
523. II. Virginia Lee Hanback (10) B.
524. III. Evelyn Hanback (10) B.

324. George Grover (Tabby) Rice (9)

Son of Etta Beatrice (Cheseldine) Rice West Mahoney (No. 243) and Richard Claxton Rice. Born February 18, 1916. Married Ruth Lopez. Tabby was blind. Unfortunately during a robbery he was beaten to death. He died April 26, 1964. He is buried at Fort Lincoln Cemetery, Bladensburg, MD.

325. Caroline Leviathan West (9) Fisk, Hopkins

Daughter of Etta Beatrice (Cheseldine) Rice West Mahoney (No. 243) and Franklin Delano West. Born December 13, 1921. Married (1) Paul Fisk, (2) Howard Hopkins. Caroline died on May 17, 1989. Children: - First Marriage
525. I. Carol Fisk (10) B.
526. II. Robert Fisk (10) B.
527. III. James Fisk (10) B.
       Children: - Second Marriage
528. IV. Peggy Hopkins (10) B.
529. V. Bonnie Hopkins (10) B.
530. VI. Glenn Hopkins (10) B.

326. Benjamin Franklin (Kenny) West (9)

Son of Etta Beatrice (Cheseldine) Rice West Mahoney (No. 243) and Franklin Delano West. Born December 12, 1923. He served in WWII. Died August 5, 1989. No issue.

327. Grace Sinclair West (9) _____

Daughter of Etta Beatrice (Cheseldine) Rice West Mahoney (No. 243) and Franklin Delano West. Born February 2, 1924. Died July 21, 1993. Children:
531. I. Thomas (10) B.
532. II. Nancy (10) B.

328. William Russell West (9)

Son of Etta Beatrice (Cheseldine) Rice West Mahoney (No. 243) and Franklin Delano West. Born May 5, 1925. He was hit and killed by a motorcycle policeman on June 6, 1930.

329. Elizabeth Rittenhouse West (9) Thomas

Daughter of Etta Beatrice (Cheseldine) Rice West Mahoney (No. 243) and Franklin Delano West. Born June 21, 1927 with her twin, Nalley Francis. Married Daniel Thomas. Children:

533.　　　I. Mary Jane (10) B.

330. Nalley Francis West (9)

Son of Etta Beatrice (Cheseldine) Rice West Mahoney (No. 243) and Franklin Delano West. Born June 21, 1927 with his twin, Elizabeth Rittenhouse. Died August 1928 at 14 months of age.

331. Dorothy Leviathan Cheseldine (9) Mattingly, Sweeney

Daughter of Alton Grover Cheseldine (No. 244) and Ida Blanche (Waltermeyer) Cheseldine. Born in St. Mary's County on August 10, 1920. Married (1) October 13, 1940, William Frances Mattingly, of Abell, MD, born January 13, 1915. He died November 12, 1964, and is buried at Sacred Heart Church Cemetery, Bushwood, MD. Children: - First Marriage

534.　　　I. Alton Francis Mattingly (10) B. August 6, 1941.
　　　　　　　D. June 23, 1964.

Married (2) August 6, 1960, Samuel Sweeney, of Pine Grove, MD, born March 18, 1922. They made their home in Lothian, MD. No issue.

332. Eileen Estella Cheseldine (9) Wible, McDonald

Daughter of Alton Grover Cheseldine (No. 244) and Ida Blanche (Waltermeyer) Cheseldine. Born in St. Mary's County, August 7, 1922. Married (1) September, 1942, Ramey Wible, of

Capitol Hill, MD. No issue. (2) July 14, 1946, Thomas A. McDonald, of Washington, DC. They made their home in Texas. Children:
535.   I. Thomas A. McDonald, Jr. (10) B. August 9, 1951.

333. Alton Frederick Cheseldine (9)

Son of Alton Grover Cheseldine (No. 244) and Ida Blanche (Waltermeyer) Cheseldine. Born October 6, 1928. Married November 27, 1953, Carol Jean Jourdon from Coshocton, OH, born September 25, 1936. Fred attended the Charlotte Hall Military Academy, at Charlotte Hall, MD, class of 1946. He was employed by the Acacia Mutual Life Insurance Company at their home office, in Washington, DC, on June 25, 1946, as the company photographer. He left in 1951 to serve in the U. S. Air Force. Upon discharge he returned to Acacia where he went to work in the Printing Department. It was at Acacia he met his wife Carol. He thought she had the most beautiful eyes he had ever seen. A friend arranged a luncheon date which soon led to a date at the altar. In 1964, after working in all areas of the department, he was promoted to Manager. He was promoted again in 1978 as an appointed Officer in charge of the Printing, Purchasing, Transcribing and Supply Departments. He retired December 31, 1989, having served for 43 years. Fred's interests included music, having managed a 17 piece band during the fifties, boating, fishing, trap shooting, woodworking and being a "Gymnastics Dad" for his daughter Tricia. Carol spent endless hours chauffeuring Tricia to her coach six days a week to practice for four to six hours a day. The gym was thirty-two miles from their home, which meant they didn't see very much of each other. Tricia got to see a lot of the U.S. and England.

After retiring, Fred renewed his interest in genealogy, and began updating the work of Edwin Beitzell on the Cheseldine Family History. Carol and Fred make their home in Temple Hills, MD. Children:
536.   I. Linda Diane (10) B. April 24, 1959.
537.   II. Patricia Gayle (10) B. August 21, 1973.

334. Harry Joseph Cheseldine (9)

Son of Joseph Richard Cheseldine (No. 247) and Mary Amelia

(Mattingly) Cheseldine. Born November 29, 1926. Married Althea Celeste Schmidt, born June 16, 1927. Children:

    538.   I. Michael Richard (10) B. July 17, 1949.
    539.   II. Brenda Theresa (10) B. May 15, 1951.
    540.   III. Susan Lynn (10) B. December 14, 1955.

335. Bernard Eugene Cheseldine (9)

Son of Joseph Richard Cheseldine (No. 247) and Mary Amelia (Mattingly) Cheseldine. Born December 12, 1931. Married Bertha _____, born February 21, 1922, Jackson, Michigan. No children born of this marriage. One stepson, Benjamin White Eagle, born July 19, 1949.

336. Joseph Richard Cheseldine, Jr. (9)

Son of Joseph Richard Cheseldine (No 247) and Mary Amelia (Mattingly) Cheseldine. Born September 16, 1935. Married November 19, 1960, Marianne McBride, born September 18, 1941 in Portsmouth, VA, christened October, 1941, St. Paul's Catholic Church, Portsmouth, Va. Marianne's parents were Paul Thomas and Inez Matilda (Simmons) McBride. Children:

    541.   I. Joseph Richard, III, (10) B. December 2, 1961.
    542.   II. Bridget Marie (10) B. March 26, 1964.
    543.   III. Katie Ann (10) B. July 2, 1967.

337. Mary Madeline Cheseldine (9) Florence

Daughter of William Dent Cheseldine (No. 246) and Mary Madeline (Lewis) Cheseldine. Born in Washington, DC, September 20, 1911, and baptized St. Dominic's Church. She graduated from St. Dominic's School and continued her education by taking private and other courses over the years.

Being the oldest child, Madeline worked and also helped her mother raise the younger children. The Depression came, jobs were hard to come by but she and her sister, Edna, did obtain work at Green's 5 & 10 cent Store located at 7th and D Streets, NW, Washington, DC. Part of their income went to the family. She then obtained a position with the Home Owners Loan Corporation (HOLC) set up by the U. S. Government. When that office closed down Madeline went to work for the Potomac Electric Power Company in Washington, DC - there she met her husband to be.

Milburn Bowen Florence of Washington, DC was both a creative and commercial artist. He worked for the Electric Institute as designer of advertising, display and promotion.

"Brick", as Milburn was called, because of his rusty color thick hair, was selected to design a War Bond which toured the U. S. during World War II. His artistry won top award from the Department of Defense and he received an award from the White House.

Madeline was a beautiful petite young lady - her dark hair and blue-green eyes sparkled as she and her many admirers danced at the old "Glen Echo Park Pavillion" - "The Swanee Club", Chesapeake Beach Pavillion, Lotus Club, etc. Brick was one of her gratest admirers too and he was quite a dancer. When they danced together it was as if their feet never touched the floor. They had lots of fun.

Madeline loved the legitimate theatre. Each summer her vacation was spent with her brother at his summer theatres. Brick also enjoyed himself each year with Madeline and Tommy Brent.

Madeline and Milburn Bowen Florence married August 3, 1931 at Chestertown, MD. Church ceremony at St. Dominic's Catholic Church, 6th and E Streets, SW, Washington, DC in 1931.

Milburn "Brick" died May 31, 1971 and Madeline died January 1, 1988. Both are buried in Cedar Hill Cemetery, Suitland, MD. There was no issue from this marriage.

338. Edna Helena Cheseldine (9) Sesso

Daughter of William Dent Cheseldine (No. 246) and Mary Madeline (Lewis) Cheseldine. Born in Washington, DC, on January 30, 1913. She was baptized at St. Dominic's Catholic Church and attended St. Dominic's School.

Edna and her sister Madeline were very close. Both worked and helped to support the family. The Depression came, jobs were hard to obtain - but Edna did get a job at Greens 5 & 10 cent Store located at 7th and D Streets, NW, Washington, DC. She later obtained an office position.

Edna was a beautiful girl but a little on the shy side. She and her sister, Madeline, had many of the same friends - they went to the

145

same parties and dances with the same groups. Everyone loved Edna. She was a kind, gentle lady, and pretty as a picture.

Edna's entire life was dedicated to her family, her mother and family, participation in school activities, helping the nuns, helping the less fortunate and always doing for others. She was an excellent cook, seamstress, crocheting and knitting were her favorite hobbies. She always held the family holiday celebrations, remembered by all, at her home.

She met Anthony Sesso at one of the dances. They were married in Baltimore, MD, with a church ceremony at St. Peter's Catholic Church in SE, Washington, DC.

Tony was born in SE Washington, DC. He was the son of Mary (Petrella) and Nicholas Sesso - both from Naples, Italy - buried in St. Mary's Cemetery (off North Capitol Streets, Washington, DC). Tony followed his father in the business of barbering. In later years he owned a Billiard Parlor. He had one brother, Michael.

Edna was a very religious person. At this writing she is 86 years of age and living in the Villa Rosa Nursing Home, Md, with Alzheimers Disease. Children:

544.   I. Joyce Marie (10) B. April 25, 1935.
545.   II. Jean Frances (10) B. July 21, 1942.
545A.   III. Patricia Sesso (10) B.

339. Joseph Wilmer Cheseldine (9)

Son of William Dent Cheseldine (No. 246) and Mary Madeline (Lewis) Cheseldine. Born April 16, 1916 at Clinton, MD, baptized at St. John's Catholic Church, Clinton, MD. Married Blanche (Dolly) Ellen Schriver on March 4, 1939, at Perryville, MD. Church ceremony at St. Dominic's Catholic Church, 6th & E Street, S.W., Washington, DC. Joseph graduated from St. Dominic's Catholic School, Washington, DC. Joe, as he was always called, was a very popular handsome young man. He was a leader. There was always a group of young men following him, wherever he went. He loved automobiles, boxing and girls.

He held positions with the Old Capital Traction Company, (then Capital Transit Co.). He was a plumber after leaving school. He left the trade to go on the railroad to work. He was an engineer for the Pennsylvania and Conrail Railroad for 40 years before he retired after a stroke. Joseph died September 19, 1983 in Waldorf, MD and is buried at Cedar Hill Cemetery, Suitland, MD. Blanche (Dolly) died April 2, 1991 in Waldorf, MD, and is buried at Cedar Hill Cemetery, Suitland, MD. Children:

546.   I. Joseph Edward (10) B. January 27, 1940.
547.   II. John Dominic (Jackie) (10) B. July 20, 1941.
548.   III. Dennis Patrick (10) B. April 2, 1953.

340. Elizabeth Evelyn Cheseldine (9)

Daughter of William Dent Cheseldine (No. 246) and Mary Madeline (Lewis) Cheseldine. Born November 14, 1919, in Washington, DC.

Evelyn was baptized in St. Dominic's Church and attended its adjacent school in Southwest, and later, Eastern High School in Southeast Washington. Very popular with both girls and boys, she had many friends. Sundays, they attended church together, after which they would gather at Judd's Drug Store at corner of 7th and F Streets, SW for a "cherry coke". All dressed up, some of the couples would walk to the nearby museums where it was warm and friendly.

After finishing school, Evelyn was employed by the Washington Credit Union. An unusually beautiful girl, she was chosen by both business and civic group leaders to represent the Nation's Capitol in a major Beauty Pageant in Washington, including sitting on a throne on a float in a parade down Pennsylvania Avenue.

At eighteen, Evelyn became seriously ill with multiple sclerosis and other complications and underwent several operations that made the rest of her life difficult. However, she worked four years in the office of one of her physicians, Doctor Robert Groh, and was engaged to a young colonel in the Air Force. But the illness continued and she died December 2, 1946 at Washington, DC. Evelyn is buried at Cedar Hill Cemetery, Suitland, Md, where other members of her family rest.

341. Thomas Brent Cheseldine (9)

Thomas Brent Cheseldine was born at 602 Eleventh St., S.W., Washington, DC on October 15, 1922, the son of William Dent Cheseldine (No. 246) and Mary Madeline (Lewis) Cheseldine. He later

147

resided with the family at 494 and 487 Eye St., SW and 721 F St. SW, in Washington. He attended St. Dominic's School and Church at 6th and F St., SW; Hine Jr. High School and graduated from Eastern High School in SE.

He first held office jobs with the Roslyn Steel & Cement Co. in Georgetown and the British Air Commission on Massachusetts Avenue. He was interested in theatre and acted at this time with the Mayotha Stock Company, Blackfriars Guild and the Crossroads Barn Theatre at Bailey 's Cross Roads in Arlington, VA.

In June, 1941, at the age of eighteen, he went to New York City to seek a career in the theatre. His first job was as an usher in the famous New Amsterdam Theatre which was showing films and has recently been restored as a stage house by the Disney Corporation. Odd jobs he had included; assistant to Oscar Homolka when he starred on Broadway in "The Innocent Voyage" and "I Remember Mama"; assistant to authors Ruth L. Yorck and John Latouche; a super at the old original Metropolitan Opera House and later with the New York City Opera; worked as an extra in films, including "Stage Door Canteen" (scene with Harpo Marx near end of film); assistant manager of the Genius Club, a theatrical private club; co-producer of No. 1 Charles Street in Greenwich Village, one of the first off-Broadway cabaret theatres in Manhattan.

As an actor he played juveniles on Billy Bryant's Showboat on the Ohio and Kanawha rivers (one of the last real showboats operating); the Princess Stock Co. touring Missouri and Arkansas; Greenbush Theatre, Nyack, NY, Milford, PA, Surry, Maine.

He was producer of summer stock in several theatres including locations at Milford, PA; Rochester, NH; Morristown, NJ; Great Barrington, MA; McLean, VA; Ocean City, MD; Falls Church, VA; and Matunuck, RI where he was producer of Theatre-by-the-Sea for 22 years. All the above were theatres where he produced all of his shows from scratch; none of them were touring package houses.

When he went into show business, Thomas was known as Tommy Brent.

Tommy was a top-notch press agent and publicity director, at times, at other theatres, including: Greenbush Theatre, Nyack, NY; Surry Theatre in Maine; Daytona Beach, Fl; Barnesville, PA; Virginia Beach, VA; Allenberry Playhouse, PA; North Shore Music Theatre, MA; Charlotte Music Theatre, NC; Sombrero Playhouse, Phoenix,

AZ; Laguna Beach, CA; Alley Theatre, Houston, TX; Arena Stage, Buffalo, NY; Tappan Zee Playhouse, Nyack, NY; Carousel Theatre, Framingham, MA; Gateway Playhouse, LI, NY; Mineola Playhouse, NY.

Tommy has been press agent for more than 100 top stars in their appearances at various theatres and was press agent for the Beatles when they gave their final tour and played in Boston in the 60's. He handled stars who played at Blinstrubs in Boston; was P.A. for the Opera Company of Boston; and in 1990 produced in Boston as a new play, "First Night", which ran for 26 weeks there.

Earlier in his career, he was press agent for Andre Gide's play, "The Immoralist" which was the first production at the then new Bouwrie Lane Theatre in NYC, and was assistant-director on a film, "Young Man in a Straw Hat", shot at various star summer theatres on the east coast.

As of 1998, Thomas lives in Matunuck, RI, near the Theatre-by-the-Sea where he produced for 22 years, with monthly trips to his apartment in NYC. He is currently working on archives of his past for the Lincoln Center of Performing Arts, Billy Rose Collection in NYC.

342. Theresa Nora Cheseldine (9) Saylor

Daughter of William Dent Cheseldine (No. 246) and Mary Madeline (Lewis) Cheseldine. Born February 23, 1926, at Washington, DC. She attended Parochial Schools - St. Dominic's and Immaculate Conception Academy in Washington, DC. She continued her education attending Temple Business School in Washington, DC.

Theresa was employed by the District of Columbia Criminal Court and then transferred to the U. S. Federal Government becoming an Administrative Secretary and Program Assistant in international health for the U. S. Surgeon General of the U. S. Public Health Service. After 30 years of government service she retired in 1981.

On February 22, 1944, she married Nevin King Saylor at St. Dominic's Catholic Church in Washington, DC. They reside in Lower Marlboro, Calvert County, MD. Her interest have always been her family, her interesting positions with the U.S. government, genealogy, church activities, historical society involvement, helping the less fortunate, and enjoying the pleasures of her grandchildren and great grandchildren.

Nevin King Saylor was born in Union Bridge, MD, on September 29, 1924. His parents were Stanley and Clara Boone Saylor of Union Bridge, MD. His grandparents were Martin Luther and Sophia Maude Reck Saylor. Nevin is of German descent, whose ancestors entered the port of Philadelphia, PA, in the early 1700's. His great great grandmother, Catherine Mary Donsife, arrived in Pennsylvania in 1820. The name Saylor entered on the port of entry records varied: Seyler, Seiler, Saler, Sailer. A large number of Saylors settled in Woodsboro, MD. The 1790 Pennsylvania census listed Seylor and Saylors. There were several Seilers from Switzerland.

Nevin's parents moved to Washington, DC, when he was six months old. He attended public schools in Washington, DC and Oxon Hill, MD. He worked for the U. S. Post Office and then having taught himself photography and processing, he was employed by the U. S. Signal Corps located in the Pentagon in Washington, DC. He served in the Pacific in World War II, being stationed in the Philippines at the 4th General Hospital. He was honorably discharged in 1946. He was employed by the Hecht Company (now May Company) in Washington, DC, for 32 years, retiring in 1981.

Nevin is a most talented individual. His hobbies include engineering, designing and building 18th century furniture. He excels in building 18th century tall case clocks with inlaid pieces. He will not sell any of his pieces but hopes his daughters and grandchildren will appreciate them when he leaves this world. He has restored their present residence "King Fields" - an 18th century house which is listed in the Maryland Historic Trust Inventory of Historic Places in Calvert County. He is also a talented artist. Children:

549. I. Joan Theresa (10) B. November 13, 1944.
550. II. Evelyn Marie (10) B. December 22, 1948.

Tenth generation begins

343. Mary Gladys Cheseldine (10) Payne

Daughter of William Francis Cheseldine, Jr. (No. 248) and Laura (Scott) Cheseldine. Born _____. Married Roland Payne from Virginia.

344. Pearl Frances Cheseldine (10) Breckenridge

Daughter of William Francis Cheseldine, Jr. (No. 248) and

Laura (Scott) Cheseldine. Born _____. Married C. V. Breckenridge from Virginia.

345. Marion Cheseldine (10)

Son of William Francis Cheseldine, Jr. (No. 248) and Laura (Scott) Cheseldine. Born _____.

346. Andrew Cheseldine Poling (10)

Son of Grace Bell Cheseldine Poling (No. 249) and Wilson Poling. Born _____.

347. Osborn Poling (10)

Son of Grace Bell Cheseldine Poling (No. 249) and Wilson Poling. Born _____.

348. Dorothy Poling (10)

Daughter of Grace Bell Cheseldine Poling (No. 249) and Wilson Poling. Born _____.

349. Alice Dodd (10)

Daughter of Maud Regina (Cheseldine) Dodd (No. 251) and _____ Dodd. Born _____.

349A. Mary Susan Theresa Gibson (10) Bailey

Daughter of Katherine Beatrice (Morgan) Gibson (No. 253) and William Thomas "Buddy" Gibson. Born December 4, 1918. Married on June 17, 1941 Joseph David Bailey, born June 11, 1908. Children:
550A.   I. Ann Elizabeth (11) B. November 20, 1942.

349B. Ann Louise Gibson (10) Bruse

Daughter of Katherine Beatrice (Morgan) Gibson (No. 253)

and William Thomas "Buddy" Gibson. Born May 9, 1920. Married James Bruse May 9, 1945. Children:
550B. I. Sue Ann (11) B. January 29, 1948.

349C. Andrew Jackson Gibson (10)

Son of Katherine Beatrice (Morgan) Gibson (No. 253) and William Thomas "Buddy" Gibson. Born September 8, 1921. Married Mildred Downs June, 1944. Children:
550C. I. Andrew Jackson, Jr. (11) B. August 15, 1945.
550D. II. Sherry Madeline (11) B. July 1947.

349D. Catherine Veronica Gibson (10) Tippett

Daughter of Katherine Beatrice (Morgan) Gibson (No. 253) and William Thomas "Buddy" Gibson. Born June 13, 1924. Married Garnet Archie Tippett February 12, 1945. Children:
550E. I. James Thomas (11) B. September 9, 1946.
550F. II. Bernard Archie (11) B. September 7, 1949.
550G. III. Mary Clare (11) B. December 2, 1955.
550H. IV. Barbara Kay (11) B. July 26, 1957.

349E. George Bernard Gibson (10)

Son of Katherine Beatrice (Morgan) Gibson (No. 253) and William Thomas "Buddy" Gibson. Born September 10, 1930.

349F. Helen Reta Gibson (10)

Daughter of Katherine Beatrice (Morgan) Gibson (No. 253) and William Thomas "Buddy" Gibson. Born July 31, 1932.

349G. Mary Clare Gibson (10)

Daughter of Katherine Beatrice (Morgan) Gibson (No. 253) and William Thomas "Buddy" Gibson. Born October 13, 1935.

349H. Joseph Earl St. Clair (10)

Son of Lillian Marie (Russell) St. Clair (No. 254) and Joseph St. Clair. Born _____.

349I. Milton Edwin Compton, Jr. (10)

Son of Annie Beatrice (Russell) Compton (No. 255) and Milton Edwin Compton. Born July 21, 1921.

349J. Milton Joseph Russell (10)

Son of Edward William Garrett Russell (No. 256) and Ruth (Gibson). Born _____.

349K. Christian Russell (10)

Son of Edward William Garrett Russell (No. 256) and Ruth (Gibson). Born _____.

349L. Martha Russell (10)

Daughter of Edward William Garrett Russell (No. 256) and Ruth (Gibson). Born _____.

349M. Edward William Garrett Russell, Jr. (10)

Son of Edward William Garrett Russell (No. 256) and Ruth (Gibson). Born _____.

349N. Shirley Russell (10)

Daughter of Edward William Garrett Russell (No. 256) and Ruth (Gibson). Born _____.

349O. Mary Lillian Gibson (10) Morgan

Daughter of Ida Pearl (Russell) Gibson (No. 257) and Garner Gibson. Born June 19, 1921. Married Eugene Morgan, Jr. Children:

550I.   I. Eugene III (11) B.

550J.   II. Judith Ann (11) B.

349P. Dorothy Nellie Gibson (10)

Daughter of Ida Pearl (Russell) Gibson (No. 257) and Garner Gibson. Born August 12, 1924.

349Q. Mary Alice Gibson (10)

Daughter of Ida Pearl (Russell) Gibson (No. 257) and Garner Gibson. Born June 21, 1929.

349R. Mary Helen Russell (10)

Daughter of Joseph Lester Russell (No. 259) and Mary (Gibson) Russell. Born _____.

349S. Betty Jane Russell (10)

Daughter of Garrett Russell (No. 261) and Elsie (Long) Russell. Born April 18, 1931.

349T. Eleanor Russell (10)

Daughter of Garrett Russell (No. 261) and Elsie (Long) Russell. Born _____.

349U. Barbara Ann Russell (10)

Daughter of Garrett Russell (No. 261) and Elsie (Long) Russell. Born _____.

349V. George Frederick Cheseldine (10)

Son of Susie Elizabeth (Bailey) Cheseldine (No. 263) and George Walter Cheseldine. Born February 12, 1906.

349W. James Theodore Bailey (10)

Son of Robert Pendleton Bailey (No. 266) and Pearl (Culler) Bailey. Born June 19, 1933.

349X. Philip Roger Bailey (10)

Son of Robert Pendleton Bailey (No. 266) and Pearl (Culler) Bailey. Born July 8, 1934.

349Y. Lulu Kate Bailey (10)

Daughter of Robert Pendleton Bailey (No. 266) and Pearl (Culler) Bailey. Born July 9, 1934.

350. Alice Estelle Bailey (10)

Daughter of Robert Pendleton Bailey (No. 266) and Pearl (Culler) Bailey. Born November 26, 1936.

350A. Janice Mae Bailey (10)

Daughter of Robert Pendleton Bailey (No. 266) and Pearl (Culler) Bailey. Born February 9, 1938.

350B. Susie Elizabeth Bailey (10)

Daughter of Robert Pendleton Bailey (No. 266) and Pearl (Culler) Bailey. Born December 3, 1939.

350C. Robert Pendleton Bailey, Jr. (10)

Son of Robert Pendleton Bailey (No. 266) and Pearl (Culler) Bailey. Born January 15, 1941.

350D. Kenneth Andrew Bailey (10)

Son of Robert Pendleton Bailey (No. 266) and Pearl Culler Bailey. Born May 14, 1942.

350E. John Talbert Bailey (10)

Son of Robert Pendleton Bailey (No. 266) and Pearl (Culler) Bailey. Born April 10, 1945.

350F. Eleanor Beatrice Bailey (10) Tippett

Daughter of Samuel Mathew Bailey (No. 267) and Thelma Migonette (Cullins) Bailey. Born July 12, 1922. Married Dennis Tippett on November 30, 1940. (Beezie) died January 3, 1992 and is buried at Sacred Heart Church Cemetery. Children:

550K.	I. Richard (11) B. January 19, 1942.
550L	II. David (11) B. September 5, 1943.

350G. Thelma Lucille Bailey (10) Farr

Daughter of Samuel Mathew Bailey (No. 267) and Thelma Migonette (Cullins) Bailey. Born March 26, 1926. Married Joseph Farr on November 18, 1944. Children:

550M.	I. Carol Ann (11) B. August 1, 1945.
550N.	II. Joseph (11) B. August 26, 1946.

350H. Catherine Marie Bailey (10)

Daughter of Samuel Mathew "Bo" Bailey (No. 267) and Thelma Migonette (Cullins) Bailey. Born December 10, 1928. "Kitty" married Francis Gwynn Swann, Jr. on July 21, 1951. Children:

550O.	I. Nancy Lee (11) B. June 22, 1952
550P.	II. Francis Allan (11) B. March 19, 1957.

350I. Samuel Mathew Bailey, Jr. (10)

Son of Samuel Mathew "Bo" Bailey (No. 267) and Thelma Migonette (Cullins) Bailey. Born July 19, 1931. Married (1) Joan Marie Coale on February 7, 1953. She died July 7, 1977. (2) Louanne Adams Cosimano on April 28, 1978. Children:-First Marriage:

550Q.	I. Fay Marie (11) B. August 25, 1954.
550R.	II. Samuel Mathew III (11) B. June 3, 1957.

550S.   III. Mark Andrew (11) B. June 28, 1960.

550T.   IV. Beverly Sue (11) B. June 12, 1962.

350J. William Edward Bailey (10)

Son of Samuel Mathew "Bo" Bailey (No. 267) and Thelma Migonette (Cullins) Bailey. Born March 11, 1936. Married Patricia Ann Blair on July 26, 1958. Children:

550U.   I. Donna Lee (11) B. October 26, 1959.

550V.   II. William Edward Jr. (11) B. September 16, 1963.

550W.   III. Jacqueline (11) B. January 1, 1966.

350K. Bernard Anthony Bailey (10)

Son of Samuel Mathew Bailey (No. 267) and Thelma Migonette (Cullins) Bailey. Born February 8, 1939. Married (1) Judith Lee Herbert on May 19, 1957. Divorced on December 10, 1973. (2) Shirley Delores Hintze (Burch) on December 31, 1981. Children: - First Marriage:

550X.   I. Bernard Anthony Jr. (11) B. January 31, 1958.

350L. Charles Freeman Gibson (10)

Son of Doris (Cheseldine) Gibson (No. 270) and Charles Henry Gibson. Born July 11, 1921. Married June 14, 1947 Grace Jackson "Bebe" Morris Gibson.

351. Joseph Henry Gibson (10)

Son of Doris (Cheseldine) Gibson (No. 270) and Charles Henry Gibson. Born June 23, 1926.

352. James Anthony Gibson (10)

Son of Doris (Cheseldine) Gibson (No. 270) and Charles Henry Gibson. Born May 3, 1931.

353. Shirly Marie Gibson (10)

Daughter of Doris (Cheseldine) Gibson (No. 270) and Charles Henry Gibson. Born April 18, 1933.

354. Margaret Ann Gibson (10)

Daughter of Doris (Cheseldine) Gibson (No. 270) and Charles Henry Gibson. Born March 15, 1935.

355. Thelma Beatrice Gibson (10)

Daughter of Doris (Cheseldine) Gibson (No. 270) and Charles Henry Gibson. Born June 18, 1939.

356. Mary Ann Beitzell (10)

Daughter of Mary Elsie (Cheseldine) Beitzell (No. 271) and Walter Bryan Beitzell. Born February 26, 1926.

357. Andrew Walter Beitzell (10)

Son of Mary Elsie (Cheseldine) Beitzell (No. 271) and Walter Bryan Beitzell. Born August 4, 1928.

358. Joseph Francis Beitzell (10)

Son of Mary Elsie (Cheseldine) Beitzell (No. 271) and Walter Bryan Beitzell. Born August 30, 1932.

359. William Benjamin Beitzell (10)

Son of Mary Elsie (Cheseldine) Beitzell (No. 271) and Walter Bryan Beitzell. Born February 19, 1939.

360. John William Cheseldine (10)

Son of Andrew Freeman Cheseldine (No. 272) and Annie Cheseldine, daughter of John and Maggie Cheseldine. Born May 25,

1925. Married Dorothy Cullins. Children:
  551. I. John Kenelm (11) B.
  552. II. Jerry Wayne (11) B.

361. Robert Lee Cheseldine (10)

Son of Andrew Freeman Cheseldine (No. 272) and Annie Cheseldine, daughter of John and Maggie Cheseldine. Born November 21, 1926. Married Lucille Sterling. Children:
  553. I. Robert Lee, Jr., (11) B.
  554. II. Dewberry Ann (11) B.
  555. III. Steve (11) B.
  556. IV. Beth (11) B.
  557. V. Ben (11) B.

361A. George McWilliams (10)

Son of Mary Alice (Beitzell) McWilliams (No. 274) and George McWilliams, Jr. Born October 8, 1934.

361B. Mary Alice McWilliams (10)

Daughter of Mary Alice (Beitzell) McWilliams (No. 274) and George McWilliams, Jr. Born December 13, 1935.

361C. Ida Claudia McWilliams (10)

Daughter of Mary Alice (Beitzell) McWilliams (No. 274) and George McWilliams, Jr. Born September 8, 1938.

361D. James Joseph McWilliams (10)

Son of Mary Alice (Beitzell) McWilliams (No. 274) and George McWilliams, Jr. Born February 7, 1941.

361E. Charles Henry McWilliams (10)

Son of Mary Alice (Beitzell) McWilliams (No. 274) and George McWilliams, Jr. Born February 17, 1942.

361F. Rose Marie McWilliams (10)

Daughter of Mary Alice (Beitzell) McWilliams (No. 274) and George McWilliams, Jr. Born December 14, 1942.

361G. Andrew Jackson McWilliams (10)

Son of Mary Alice (Beitzell) McWilliams (No. 274) and George McWilliams, Jr. Born January 6, 1945.

361H. William Patrick McWilliams (10)

Son of Mary Alice (Beitzell) McWilliams (No. 274) and George McWilliams, Jr. Born January 4, 1947.

361I. Charles Henry Beitzell, Jr. (10)

Son of George Lee Beitzell (No. 278) and Frances Martha (Battenfield) Beitzell. Born August 4, 1948.

361J. James Mattingly (10)

Son of Mary Beatrice (Cheseldine) Mattingly (No. 279) and Moakley Mattingly. Born _____.

361K. Alfred Mattingly (10)

Son of Mary Beatrice (Cheseldine) Mattingly (No. 279) and Moakley Mattingly. Born _____.

361L. Robert Mattingly (10)

Son of Mary Beatrice (Cheseldine) Mattingly (No. 279) and Moakley Mattingly. Born _____.

362. Beatrice Mattingly (10)

Daughter of Mary Beatrice (Cheseldine) Mattingly (No. 279) and Moakley Mattingly. Born _____.

363. Susie Cheseldine (10)

Daughter of Robert Garrett Cheseldine, Sr. (No. 280) and Mary (Pilkerton) Cheseldine. Born   . Married   Nelson.

364. Lorraine Cheseldine (10)

Daughter of Robert Garrett Cheseldine, Sr. (No. 280) and Mary (Pilkerton) Cheseldine. Born

365. Garrett Cheseldine, Jr. (10)

Son of Robert Garrett Cheseldine, Sr. (No. 280) and Mary (Pilkerton) Cheseldine. Born

366. Leonard Cheseldine (10)

Son of Robert Garrett Cheseldine, Sr. (No. 280) and Mary (Pilkerton) Cheseldine. Born

367. Charles Hayden (10)

Son of Mabel Loretta (Cheseldine) Hayden (No. 282) and John Hayden. Born September 17, 1943. Married Patricia (Schmalgemeyer) Hayden.

368. Richard Hayden (10)

Son of Mabel Loretta (Cheseldine) Hayden (No. 282) and John Hayden. Born October 18, 1944. Married Mary Gertrude (Weiland) Hayden.

368A. James Edward Beitzell, III (10)

Son of Josiah Edward Beitzell, Jr. (No. 282A) and Constance (Lowe). Born March 22, 1917. Volunteer in World War II in November, 1942, Master Sergeant, overseas in Algiers, then Naples and took part in the drive from Rome to the Appenninies and then the Po Valley drive to Gritza, near the Jugo-Slavia border. Demobilized October, 1945. Jim celebrated his 25th Anniversary with the Southern California Edison Company July 1966.

368B. David Lowe Beitzell (10)

Son of Josiah Edward Beitzell, Jr. (No. 282A) and Constance (Lowe). Born June 13, 1924. Served in World War II, going in February, 1943. Saw service at Kiska, Aleutians then returned to Seattle, WA, for further training and in January, 1944, overseas to Naples. In the Appennines and Po Valley drives and was at Capperetto, Italy, near Austria at end of war. Was mustered out December 1945. His division, the 10th Mt. had 51% casualties and 15% killed in action.

On December 4, 1949, he married Ruth Reichers who was the sister of his partner in the operation of a Chevron Standard Oil Station.

368C. Mary Elizabeth Beitzell (10) Conway

Daughter of Josiah Edward Beitzell, Jr. (No. 282A) and Constance (Lowe). Born June 9, 1926. Married January, 1967, Donald Conway of Upland, California employed by the Orange Products of Ontario, California.

368D. Charles Henry Beitzell (10)

Son of Josiah Edward Beitzell, Jr. (No. 282A) and Constance (Lowe). Born March 4, 1929. In October, 1947 in U. S. Army serving in Tokyo, Japan. Became a Staff Sergeant and served in Korea throughout the war. Reenlisted for a second 3 years and mustered out in 1954, after which he took a job with the Southern California Edison Company.

368E. William Joseph Husemann (10)

Son of Mary Alice (Beitzell) Husemann (No. 282B) and Charles William Husemann. Born November 12, 1920 in Palmer's, MD. Married March 17, 1945, Ann Elizabeth Downs, daughter of Clifford Downs, of St. Mary's County, MD, where they live. Served in World War II, from November 9, 1944 to July 31, 1946. Stationed at Camp Meade, MD, Camp Blanding, FL, overseas March, 1945, France, Belgium and Germany. Employed by the Gulf Company. Children:

557A.   I. William Joseph, Jr. (11) B. April 29, 1947.
557B.   II. Walter Daniel (11) B. January 24, 1952.
557C.   III. Donald Allan (11) B. February 4, 1958.

368F. Charles Ross Husemann (10)

Son of Mary Alice (Beitzell) Husemann (No. 282B) and Charles William Husemann. Born August 15, 1922 in Palmers, MD. Married August 22, 1943, Elizabeth Irene Lacy of St. Mary's County, MD. They lived on a small portion of Collingwood. Ross was employed as a bricklayer. Children:

557D.   I. Charles Albert (11) B. March 27, 1944.
557E.   II. Charlene Ann (11) B. March 29, 1945.
557F.   III. Richard Benjamin (11) B. January 29, 1947.
557G.   IV. Michael Ross (11) B. January 10, 1950.
557H.   V. Francis Joseph (11) B. July 23, 1957.
557I.   VI. Jeffrey Lynn (11) B. March 21, 1962.

368G. Harry Benjamin Husemann (10)

Son of Mary Alice Beitzell Husemann (No. 282B) and Charles William Husemann. Born October 24, 1924 in Palmer's, MD. Served in World War II, from March 31, 1943 to January 19, 1946. Trained at Camp Edwards and Honolulu, P.I. Saw action throughout the Leyte and Okinawa campaigns.

On July 10, 1949, married Virginia Clarke. They resided on the Patuxent River where Harry was a waterman. Children:

557J.   I. Karen Ann (11) B. September 20, 1953.
557K.   II. Harry Benjamin, Jr. (11) B. November 11, 1958.

368H. Elizabeth Jane Husemann (10) Downs

Daughter of Mary Alice Beitzell Husemann (No. 282B) and Charles William Husemann. Born August 9, 1928, Collingwood. Married September 6, 1947, James Milton Downs, son of Clifford Downs, St. Mary's County, MD. James (Buddy) was employed by the Surburban Plumbing & Heating Company, of Colton's Point, MD. Children:

557L. I. James Milton (11) B. September 26, 1948.
Graduated Chopticon High School in 1966.
557M. II. Sharon Elizabeth (11) B. June 26, 1950. Student
at Chopticon High School in 1966.
557N. III. Charles David (11) B. February 6, 1960.

368I. Janie Louise Beitzell (10) Smith

Daughter of Charles Benjamin Beitzell (No. 282C) and Janie
Marie (Louise) Miller. Born May 29, 1917. Married November 13,
1936, Kemp Beyer Smith, who was in the excavating business in
Washington, DC. Children:
557O. I. Daniel Kemp (11) B. April 30, 1942.
557P. II. Linda Louise Smith (11) B. September 18, 1944.
557Q. III. Melenia Allyn (11) B. July 18, 1949.
557R. IV. Christina Ellen (11) B. August 16, 1957.

368J. Elizabeth Hart Beitzell (10) Zeleski

Daughter of Charles Benjamin Beitzell (No. 282C) and Janie
Marie (Louise) Miller. Born July 28, 1919. Married January 14,
1945, Leo Francis Zeleski. They lived at Fairhaven, MD, and
Washington, DC. Children:
557S. I. Charles Leo (11) B. June 17, 1948.
557T. II. Carol Ann (11) B. January 2, 1950.

368K. Rose Mary (Marie) Beitzell (10) Mayer

Daughter of Charles Benjamin Beitzell (No. 282C) and Janie
Marie (Louise) Miller. Born January 27, 1923. Married Raymond
Ellis Mayer, Jr., September 6, 1952. They resided at 1210
Brookhaven Drive, Silver Spring, MD. Children:
557U. I. Susan Kathleen (11) B. February 12, 1955.
557V. II. Robert Craig (11) B. May 23, 1961.

368L. Mary Jeanne Beitzell (10) Jusino

Daughter of Harry Alvin Beitzell (No. 282D) and Julia A.
Sullivan. Born December 25, 1926. Graduated from Catholic

University June, 1947, with a degree in Aeronautical Engineering at the age of 20. Married March 4, 1950, Gilberto R. Jusino of Bayamon, Puerto Rico, who was a medical student at the time. They lived in Mexico for 5 years while Bert finished his medical studies. Jeanne was an Aerospace Engineer at the Naval Ordnance Laboratory, White Oak, MD. Children:

557W.	I. Joseph (11) B. December 2, 1950.
557X.	II. David (11) B. August 17, 1952.
557Y.	III. Bertito (11) B. November 15, 1953.
557Z.	IV. John (11) B. February 11, 1956.
558.	V. Mark (11) B. October 14, 1962.

368M. Raymond Harry Beitzell (10)

Son of Harry Alvin Beitzell (No. 282D) and Julia A. Sullivan. Born January 2, 1931. Attended Holy Comforter School 1936 to 1944, Gonzaga High School 1944 to 1948, Maryland University 1948 to 1950. Military service: September 1950 to June 1952, 169th Military Police Battalion, Rank Staff Sergeant. He was employed at the Chesapeake and Potomac Telephone Company, Washington, DC, after his Army discharge. Married Barbara Hubbard, April 24, 1954. Children:

558A.	I. Raymond Harry, Jr. (11) B. January 20, 1955.
558B.	II. Julia Ann (11) B. January 29, 1956.
558C.	III. Joseph (11) B. June 29, 1957.
558D.	IV. Paul (11) B. July 17, 1959.
558E.	V. Madeline Patricia (11) B. May 12, 1961.
558F.	VI. Mary Constance (11) B. February 14, 1963.
558G.	VII. John (11) B. September 23, 1964.
558H.	VIII. Andrew (11) B. July 21, 1966.

368N. Richard Elwood Beitzell (10)

Son of Albert Clement Beitzell (No. 282E) and Rosalie Arnold. Born January 18, 1923. Educated George Washington and Georgetown Universities. Employed by The Chesapeake and Potomac Telephone Company for several years. Resided in Washington, DC. Saw considerable action in World War II in the European Theatre. Corpl., Battery B, 71st A.F.A., BN. Has worked for the Federal

Credit Union for 10 years and held position of Assistant Treasurer in 1965.

368O. James Bernard Beitzell (10)

Son of Albert Clement Beitzell (No. 282E) and Rosalie Arnold. Born November 13, 1929. Was in the Korean War and upon return reassumed his position with the Chesapeake and Potomac Telephone Company of MD, working out of Leonardtown. On March 2, 1956, married Rose Elva Brown and they resided in a nice home on Canoe Neck Creek. Children:

    558I.   I. Brenda Lee (11) B. March 9, 1958.
    558J.   II. James Bernard, Jr. (11) B. August 21, 1959.
    558K.   III. Mark Gerard (11) B. September 18, 1963.
    558L.   IV. Stephen Eric (11) B.

368P. Mary Ann (Anna) Beitzell (10) Guinard

Daughter of Walter Bryan Beitzell (No. 282F) and Mary Elsie (Cheseldine). Born February 26, 1926. Married Norman W. Guinard, June 20, 1953, who was employed as a physicist at the Naval Research Laboratory in Washington, DC. They resided in Alexandria, VA. Children:

    558M.   I. Frances Ann (11) B. September 28, 1954.
    558N.   II. Barbara Ellen (11) B. April 10, 1956.
    558O.   III. William Joseph (11) B. May 19, 1958.

368Q. Andrew Walter Beitzell (10)

Son of Walter Bryan Beitzell (No. 282F) and Mary Elsie (Cheseldine). Born August 4, 1928. Served with the U.S. Marine Corp. Married Lois Joanne Alson, August 13, 1956. Andrew was Office Manager for H. B. Lantzsch in Fairfax, VA.in 1966. Children:

    558P.   I. Andrew Joseph (11) B. July 2, 1958.
    558Q.   II. Douglas Wayne (11) B. May 11, 1962.

368R. Joseph Francis Beitzell (10)

Son of Walter Bryan Beitzell (No. 282F) and Mary Elsie (Cheseldine). Born August 30, 1932. Died May 2, 1953, while serving in the U. S. Navy. He was only 21 years old. Buried in Arlington National Cemetery, Arlington, VA.

368S. William Benjamin Beitzell (10)

Son of Walter Bryan Beitzell (No. 282F) and Mary Elsie (Cheseldine). Born February 19, 1939. Married Regina Gail McFadden, March 8, 1957. Benjamin was Senior Accountant for Bowles Engineering Corp. in Silver Spring, MD, where he had his home. Children:

558R.   I. Debra Marie (11) B. January 22, 1958.
558S.   II. Teresa Lynn (11) B. December 28, 1958.
558T.   III. William Benjamin (11) B. December 25, 1960.
558U.   IV. Laura Jean (11) B. May 3, 1963.
558V.   V. Christopher Allen (11) B. May 29, 1965.

368T. Edwin Warfield Beitzell, Jr. (10)

Son of Edwin Warfield Beitzell, Jr. (No. 282G) and Josephine Isabel (Kinney) Beitzell. Born April 27, 1929. Edwin was awarded a scholarship to the University of Pennsylvania but instead attended Yale University, George Washington and American Universities and the Corcoran School of Art. He worked for the Washington Post and the Phillips Art Gallery in Washington, DC. In the summer of 1966, he moved to Hollywood, CA. He was a professional artist and was painting full time.

During the early 1960s, he produced a series of oil paintings on historic houses in St. Mary's County, his inspiration based on his father's interest and work on family and Maryland history.

Edwin, Jr. died of lung cancer on July 13, 1988. Prior to Edwin Jr.'s death, he tried to recover as many of those works as possible and left them in the care of his sister who hopes in the next few years to find a venue to exhibit them.

368U. Jean Isabel Beitzell (10) Quinnette

Daughter of Edwin Warfield Beitzell (No. 282G) and Josephine Isabel Kinney. Born June 3, 1934. Graduated from Holy Cross Academy in Washington, DC. Worked for the National Broadcasting Company, Inc. in Washington, DC and San Francisco, CA. Entered the Congregation of the Holy Cross but returned to private life. On October 7, 1961, she married Richard R. Quinnette, son of Raymond and Kathryn Quinnette (nee Daley) of De Pere, Wisconsin. Dick was a Producer-Director of NBC. They were divorced in 1977.

Jean returned to work at the Smithsonian Institution in 1973. She spent over 20 years in the film unit as an associate producer of art documentaries and as special assistant to the director of that office. She retired in 1994, moving back to her home town of Washington, DC. Jean also maintains her parents home, Gerard's Cove, in Abell, MD, as a gathering place for the children and grandchildren. Children:

558W.   I. John Jay (11) B. June 4, 1962.
558X.   II. Kathryn Marya (11) B. June 22, 1963.
558Y.   III. Joseph Richard (11) B. November 15, 1964.
558Z.   IV. Charles Daley (11) B. April 10, 1966.

369. Mary Irma Owens (10)

Daughter of William Lee Owens (No. 282J) and Katherine Dove (Russell) Owens. Born March 6, 1911.

370. William Anthony Owens (10)

Son of William Lee Owens (No. 282J) and Katherine Dove (Russell) Owens. Born January 7, 1914.

371. Annie Rebecca Owens (10)

Daughter of William Lee Owens (No. 282J) and Katherine Dove (Russell) Owens. Born October 3, 1917.

372. James Ignatius Owens (10)

Son of William Lee Owens (No. 282J) and Katherine Dove (Russell) Owens. Born February 9, 1921.

373. Lois Ruth Owens (10)

Daughter of William Lee Owens (No. 282J) and Katherine Dove (Russell) Owens. Born August 7, 1923.

374. Edwin Woodburn (10)

Son of Jane Ann (Owens) Woodburn (No. 282K) and Joseph Lancaster Woodburn. Born May 3, 1912.

375. Mary Alice Woodburn (10)

Daughter of Jane Ann (Owens) Woodburn (No. 282K) and Joseph Lancaster Woodburn. Born August 6, 1913.

376. Alice Regina Owens (10) Basile

Daughter of John Joseph Owens (No. 282L) and Elizabeth (Morgan) Owens. Born April 29, 1923 in Washington, DC. Attended Holy Comforter School, graduated from St. Cecelia's Academy in 1941. Class of 39 girls. Alice and her schoolmates have had reunions every five years, and had a special weekend celebration for their 50th reunion. They now get together every year, with their husbands to celebrate.

Alice met Alfonso Mario Basile, first generation from Italy, who attended Eastern High School. Al was born in Vandergrift, PA, December 17, 1921, son of Antoinette (DePaolis) and Amedeo Basile. Al and Alice went together for five years, engaged for two and a half years while Al was in the U. S. Air Force overseas.

Alice and Al were married at Holy Comforter Church July 26, 1945. Alice has spent the past 26 years researching her family. She has spent many hours in the Courthouses of Maryland and Virginia, since her grandfather on her father's side was born in King George County, VA. Children:

169

558Z1.　I. Ralph John (11) B. July 25, 1950.
558Z2.　II. Paul Anthony (11) B. October 28, 1952.
558Z3.　III. John Joseph (11) B. August 26, 1954.

377. John Owens (10)

Son of Grover Raymond Owens (No. 282N) and Gertrude Owens, his cousin. Born July 20, 1918.

378. Benjamin Owens (10)

Son of Grover Raymond Owens (No. 282N) and Gertrude Owens, his cousin. Born January 20, 1920.

379. Walter Owens (10)

Son of Grover Raymond Owens (No. 282N) and Gertrude Owens, his cousin. Born November, 1922. Died 1933. Drowned in the Potomac River.

380. Bernita Owens (10)

Daughter of Grover Raymond Owens (No. 282N) and Gertrude Owens. Born June 30, 1925.

381. Shirley Owens (10)

Daughter of Grover Raymond Owens (No. 282N) and Gertrude Owens. Born March 14, 1928.

382. Vivian Owens (10)

Daughter of Grover Raymond Owens (No. 282N) and Gertrude Owens. Born January 31, 1934.

383. Robert Walter Owens (10)

Son of Grover Raymond Owens (No. 282N) and Gertrude Owens. Born June 30, 1937.

384. Mary Lucille Owens (10)

Daughter of James Benjamin Owens (No. 282O) and Martha Ellen (Mattingly) Owens. Born October 19, 1919.

385. Joseph Walter Owens (10)

Son of James Benjamin Owens (No. 282O) and Martha Ellen (Mattingly) Owens. Born October 6, 1923.

386. Teresa Owens (10)

Daughter of James Benjamin Owens (No. 282O) and Martha Ellen (Mattingly) Owens. Born April 2, 1929.

387. Thomas Laurie Gibson (10)

Son of Essie May Owens Gibson (No. 282P) and Thomas Laurie Gibson. Born February 7, 1924.

388. James Henry Gibson (10)

Son of Essie May Owens Gibson (No. 282P) and Thomas Laurie Gibson. Born June 30, 1925.

389. Francis De Sales Gibson (10)

Son of Essie May Owens Gibson (No 282P) and Thomas Laurie Gibson. Born June 28, 1927.

390. Mary Elizabeth Gibson (10)

Daughter of Essie May Owens Gibson (No. 282P) and Thomas Laurie Gibson. Born November 8, 1930.

391. Helen Cecelia Gibson (10) Hewitt

Daughter of Essie May Owens Gibson (No. 282P) and Thomas Laurie Gibson. Born April 1, 1933 in Bushwood, St. Mary's County,

MD, christened April 30, 1933 at Sacred Heart Church, Bushwood. Married November 27, 1952 William Benjamin Hewitt, Sr., Sacred Heart Church, Bushwood, born February 4, 1926 at Medley's Neck, Leonardtown, MD. William is the son of Madeline Roe Long Hewitt and Hiram Hewitt. Children:

558Z4.	I. Rose Ellen (11) B. November 1, 1953.
558Z5.	II. William Benjamin, Jr. (11) B. November 9,1955.
558Z6.	III. Barton Anthony (11) B. August 23, 1958.
558Z7.	IV. Michael Patrick (11) B. July 30, 1960.
558Z8.	V. Laurie Ann (11) B. July 23, 1961.
558Z9.	VI. Mark Christopher (11) B. February 8, 1963.
558Z10.	VII. Mary Beth (11) B. January 19, 1966.
558Z11.	VIII. Joanne Patricia (11) B. March 3, 1967.
558Z12.	IX. Donald Allen (11) B. September 5, 1971

392. May Rosaline Gibson (10)

Daughter of Essie May (Owens) Gibson (No. 282P) and Thomas Laurie Gibson. Born July 27, 1934.

393. Sophia Bernadette Gibson (10)

Daughter of Essie May (Owens) Gibson (No 282P) and Thomas Laurie Gibson. Born May 9, 1937.

394. Aloysius McGuire Gibson (10)

Son of Essie May (Owens) Gibson (No 282P) and Thomas Laurie Gibson. Born November 6, 1938.

395. Joseph Walter Gibson (10)

Son of Essie May (Owens) Gibson (No. 282P) and Thomas Laurie Gibson. Born May 22, 1940.

396. Melba Marie Owens (10)

Daughter of Charles Larry Palmer Owens (NO. 282Q) and Esther Lorraine Lawrence Owens. Born September 28, 1927.

397. Mary Louise Owens (10)

Daughter of Charles Larry Palmer Owens (No. 282Q) and Esther Lorraine Lawrence Owens. Born February 26, 1935. (Lou).

398. James Donald Mattingly (10)

Son of Mary Elizabeth Owens Mattingly (No. 282S) and James W. Mattingly. Born March 22, 1935.

399. Michael Wayne Mattingly (10)

Son of Mary Elizabeth (Owens) Mattingly (No. 282S) and James W. Mattingly. Born September 26, 1937.

400. Ruene Marcella Norris (10) Drew, Russell

Daughter of John Francis Norris (No. 282T) and Madeline (Devine) Norris. Born October 1, 1919. Married (1) August 20, 1937, Charles Preston Drew and (2) July 5, 1945, James Lawrence Russell. They resided in Washington, DC. Children: First Marriage

559.	I. Ruene Marie Drew (11) B. April 26, 1938.
559A.	II. Dolores Juanita Drew (11) B. December 26, 1940.

401. Francis De Sales Lawrence (10)

Son of Grace Genevieve (Thompson) Lawrence (No. 282V) and Joseph Francis Lawrence. Born January 18, 1911. Married July 2, 1934, Mary Elizabeth Bailey, born June 6, 1913. Children:

559B.	I. James Francis (11) B. September 14, 1936.
559C.	II. Rose Francis (11) B. August 20, 1938.
559D.	III. Charles Emory (11) B. October 14, 1940.
559E.	IV. William De Sales (11) B. March 6, 1944.
559F.	V. George Eliot (11) B. October 26, 1945.
559G.	VI. Barbara Ann (11) B. September 12, 1947.

402. Charles Lawrence (10)

Son of Grace Genevieve (Thompson) Lawrence (No. 282V) and Joseph Francis Lawrence. Born 1912. Died when about 8 years of age.

403. Margaret Rose Lawrence (10) Downs

Daughter of Grace Genevieve (Thompson) Lawrence (No. 282V) and Joseph Francis Lawrence. Born May 18, 1917. Married December 29, 1935, Andrew Wallace Downs. Children:
559H.   I. Grace Ann Downs (11) B. July 5, 1938.
559I.   II. Melanie Andrea Downs (11) B. April 18, 1943.

404. Frances Ruth Lawrence (10) Warder Quinn

Daughter of Grace Genevieve (Thompson) Lawrence (No. 282V) and Joseph Francis Lawrence. Born March 1, 1919. Married (1) Joseph Ernest Warder and (2) David Quinn. Children: - First Marriage.
559J.   I. Joseph Reid (11) B. May, 1939.
559K.   II. Eugenia Seline (11) B. December, 1941.

405. Mary Emily Lawrence (10) Thompson

Daughter of Grace Genevieve (Thompson) Lawrence (No 282V) and Joseph Francis Lawrence. Born May 22, 1922. Married February, 1940, William Bishop Thompson. Children:
559L.   I. William Lawrence Thompson (11) B. October, 1941.

406. Barbara Ellen Lawrence (10) Fissell

Daughter of Grace Genevieve (Thompson) Lawrence (No. 282V) and Joseph Francis Lawrence. Born September 18, 1924. Married September 22, 1944, Walter Fissell. Children:
559M.   I. Steven Lawrence Fissell (11) B. August, 1947.

407. William Ames Thompson (10)

Son of William Lee Thompson (No. 282Y) and Lola (Ames) Lawrence. Born March 5, 1927.

408. Frances Eleanor Thompson (10)

Daughter of William Lee Thompson (No. 282Y) and Lola (Ames) Lawrence. Born 1929.

409. Donald Thompson (10)

Son of William Lee Thompson (No. 282Y) and Lola (Ames) Lawrence. Born 1934.

410. Mary Frances Thompson (10)

Daughter of Leonard Allen Thompson (No. 282Z) and Mary Edith (Mattingly) Thompson. Born September 19, 1926.

411. Joseph Harvey Thompson (10)

Son of Leonard Allen Thompson (No. 282Z) and Mary Edith (Mattingly) Thompson. Born August 3, 1931.

412. Constance Biggs (10)

Daughter of Laura Virginia (Swann) Biggs (No. 283A) and William Warren Biggs. Born April 5, 1923.

413. William Warren Biggs, Jr. (10)

Son of Laura Virginia (Swann) Biggs (No. 283A) and William Warren Biggs. Born September 23, 1924.

414. Dorothy Irma Biggs (10) Bush

Daughter of Annabelle "Annie Bell" (Swann) Biggs (No. 283B) and Thomas George Biggs. Born March 19, 1926. Married

October 23, 1943, Darrell Bush. They resided in Camp Springs, MD. Children:

    559N.   I. Linda Ann Bush (11) B. May 2, 1935.

415. Robert George Biggs (10)

Son of Annabelle "Annie Bell" (Swann) Gibbs (No. 283B) and Thomas George Biggs. Born December 14, 1935.

416. James Ralph Norris, Jr. (10)

Son of James Ralph Norris (No. 283E) and Elsie (Clatterbuck) Norris. Born April 29, 1927.

417. Shirley Mae Norris (10)

Daughter of James Ralph Norris (No. 283E) and Elsie (Clatterbuck) Norris. Born January 16, 1930.

418. Joseph Leonard Norris (10)

Son of Bernard Elmer Norris (No. 283F) and Mary Evangeline (Bailey) Norris. Born November 18, 1927.

419. Rosemary Norris (10)

Daughter of Bernard Elmer Norris (No. 283F) and Mary Evangeline (Bailey) Norris. Born April 20, 1932.

420. Allan Wible (10)

Son of Mary Norma (Norris) Wible Dudley (No. 283G) and Allan Wible. Born September 2, 1923. Married December 15, 1944, Rita Johnson. They resided at Clement, MD. Children:

    559O.   I. Sandra Wible (11) B. August, 1945.
    559P.   II. Garry Wible (11) B. March 15, 1947.

421. Robert Wible (10)

Son of Mary Norma (Norris) Wible Dudley (No. 283G) and Allan Wible. Born September 27, 1924.

422. Joan Norris (10)

Daughter of John Walter Norris (No. 283H) and Christine (Meininger) Norris. Born November 28, 1941.

423. Janet Norris (10)

Daughter of John Walter Norris (No. 283H) and Christine (Meininger) Norris. Born February 10, 1945.

424. John Leo Norris, III (10)

Son of John Leo Norris (No. 283I) and Lydia (Rauch) Norris. Born July 17, 1939.

425. Sharon Irene Norris (10)

Daughter of John Leo Norris (No. 283I) and Lydia (Rauch) Norris. Born November 7, 1943.

426. Charles Ernest Norris, Jr. (10)

Son of Charles Ernest Norris (No. 283J) and Lydia (Ballard) Norris. Born January 16, 1939.

427. Raymond C. German, Jr. (10)

Son of Mary Alice (Norris) German (No. 283K) and Raymond C. German. Born February 25, 1938.

428. Kenneth Lee German (10)

Son of Mary Alice (Norris) German (No. 283K) and Raymond C. German. Born June 17, 1939.

429. Judith Ann German (10)

Daughter of Mary Alice (Norris) German (No. 283K) and Raymond German. Born September 9, 1942.

430. Robert Norris German (10)

Son of Mary Alice (Norris) German (No. 283K) and Raymond German Born May 6, 1944.

431. Halvar Peter Rasmussen, Jr. (10)

Son of Edna Genevieve (Norris) Rasmuseen (No. 283L) and Halvar Peter Rasmussen. Born 1928 in Cincinnati, OH. Was in the US Army, stationed in Japan.

432. Darlene Norris (10)

Daughter of James Stafford Norris (No. 283M) and _____. Born 1937.

433. Joyce Norris (10)

Daughter of James Stafford Norris (No. 283M) and _____. Born 1939.

434. Mary Norris (10)

Daughter of James Stafford Norris (No. 283M) and _____. Born 1940.

435. Jay Randolph Norris (10)

Son of John Randolph Norris (No. 283N) and Ruth (Hibelink) Norris. Born November 3, 1942 in Minneapolis, MN.

436. Stephanie Lynn Norris (10)

Daughter of John Randolph Norris (No. 283N) and Ruth (Hibelink) Norris. Born October 22, 1946 in Minneapolis, MN.

437. Mary Herman (10)

Daughter of Olive (Norris) Herman (No. 283P) and Oscar Herman. Born February 10, 1942.

438. Ann Herman (10)

Daughter of Olive (Norris) Herman (No. 283P) and Oscar Herman. Born August 27, 1943.

439. Bernadette Lee Herman (10)

Daughter of Olive (Norris) Herman (No. 283P) and Oscar Herman. Born February 8, 1946.

440. Patricia Ricardi (10)

Daughter of Jane A. (Norris) Ricardi (No. 283Q) and Anthony Ricardi. Born September 14, 1941.

441. Ralph Ricardi (10)

Son of Jane A. (Norris) Ricardi (No. 283Q) and Anthony Ricardi. Born January 21, 1943.

442. John William Cheseldine (10)

Son of Annie Cheseldine (No. 283T) and Andrew Freeman Cheseldine, her cousin. Born May 25, 1925.

443. Robert Lee Cheseldine (10)

Son of Annie Cheseldine (No. 283T) and Andrew Freeman Cheseldine, her cousin. Born November 21, 1926.

444. William David Nail (10)

Son of Marjorie (Cheseldine) Nail Hirst (No. 286) and Harold V. Nail. Born November 21, 1942.

445. Winnie Fay Nail (10)

Daughter of Marjorie (Cheseldine) Nail Hirst (No. 286) and Harold V. Nail. Born June 2, 1944.

446. Michael David Nail (10)

Son of Marjorie (Cheseldine) Nail Hirst (No. 286) and Harold V. Nail. Born November 21, 1965.

447. Jeffrey Allen Nail (10)

Son of Marjorie (Cheseldine) Nail Hirst (No. 286) and Harold V. Nail. Born July 31, 1971.

448. Brenda Lee Hirst (10)

Daughter of Marjorie (Cheseldine) Nail Hirst (No. 286) and Harold V. Nail. Born 1952.

449. Linda Ann Hirst (10)

Daughter of Marjorie (Cheseldine) Nail Hirst (No. 286) and Warren Hirst. Born 1954.

450. Darlene Marie Hirst (10)

Daughter of Marjorie (Cheseldine) Nail Hirst (No. 286) and Warren Hirst. Born 1958.

451. Dawn Louise Hirst (10)

Daughter of Marjorie (Cheseldine) Nail Hirst (No. 286) and Warren Hirst. Born 1963.

452. Richard Paul Mellon (10)

Son of Betty Lee (Cheseldine) Mellon (No. 287) and Richard Mellon. Born 1945. Married Julie Clove in 1968.

453. James Stephen Mellon (10)

Son of Betty Lee (Cheseldine) Mellon (No. 287) and Richard Mellon. Born 1948. Married _____. Children:
    559.   I. James Stephen Mellon, Jr. (11) B. 1974.

454. David Michael Mellon (10)

Son of Betty Lee (Cheseldine) Mellon (No. 287) and Richard Mellon. Born 1955.

455. Judith Lee Cheseldine (10) Van Horn

Daughter of John Wilmer Cheseldine (No. 288) and _____ (Grimes) Cheseldine. Born _____. Married _____ Van Horn. Children:
    560.   I. Daniel Van Horn (11) B.

456. Susan Lacy (10)

Daughter of Margaret Louise (Cheseldine) Lacy (No. 289) and John Lacy. Born

457. Linda Lacy (10)

Daughter of Margaret Louise (Cheseldine) Lacy (No. 289) and John Lacy. Born

458. Mary E. Cheseldine (10)

Daughter of W. Wallace Cheseldine (No. 293) and Flora A. (surname unknown) Cheseldine. Born

459. Lillian Cheseldine (10)

Daughter of W. Wallace Cheseldine (No. 293) and Flora A. (surname unknown) Cheseldine. Born

460. Robert Cheseldine (10)

Son of W. Wallace Cheseldine (No. 293) and Flora A. (surname unknown) Cheseldine. Born

461. Ronald Cheseldine (10)

Son of W. Wallace Cheseldine (No. 293) and Flora A. (surname unknown) Cheseldine. Born

462. Stanley Cheseldine (10)

Son of W. Wallace Cheseldine (No. 293) and Flora A. (surname unknown) Cheseldine. Born

463. Carla Cheseldine (10)

Daughter of W. Wallace Cheseldine (No. 293) and Flora A. (surname unknown) Cheseldine. Born

464. James Cheseldine (10)

Son of W. Wallace Cheseldine (No. 293) and Flora A. (surname unknown) Cheseldine. Born

465. Everett Alphonse Cheseldine, Jr. (10)

Son of Everett Alphonse Cheseldine (No. 296) and Margaret (Mullen) Cheseldine. Born January 22, 1942. Married October 22, 1966, Wendy Marie Mark. Children:

    560A.   I. Everett Alphonsus, III (11) B. September 5, 1967.
    560B.   II. Wendy Margaret (11) B. January 1, 1971.

466. Elmer Henry Cheseldine, Jr. (10)

Son of Elmer Henry Cheseldine (No. 297) and Elizabeth (Kepplinger) Cheseldine. Born _____. Elizabeth died March 18, 1971.

467. Donald Richard Cheseldine (10)

Son of Elmer Henry Cheseldine (No. 297) and Elizabeth (Kepplinger) Cheseldine. Born

468. Rosemary Cheseldine (10)

Daughter of Elmer Henry Cheseldine (No. 297) and Elizabeth (Kepplinger) Cheseldine. Born

469. Mary Cheseldine (10) Mazure

Daughter of James Corbin Cheseldine (No. 299) and Minnie A. (surname unknown) Cheseldine. Born _____. Married Joseph Mazure. They resided in Utica, MI.

470. Samuel Burch Clements (10)

Son of Mary Adelaide (Cheseldine) Clements (No. 300) and Samuel Burch Clements, Jr. Born January 18, 1945.

471. Carl Cheseldine Clements (10)

Carl was the son of Robert Cheseldine, Mary Adelaide Cheseldine Clements brother, but was adopted and raised by Mary and Samuel Burch Clements. Born

471A. Wallace Meushaw (10)

Son of Harold Meushaw (No. 301U6) and _____.
Born

471B. Richard Meushaw (10)

Son of Harold Meushaw (No. 301U6) and _____.
Born

471C. William Meushaw (10)

Son of Harold Meushaw (No. 301U6) and _____.
Born

472. Dorothy Garver (10)

Daughter of Dorothy Elizabeth (Cheseldine) Garver (No. 302) and R. H. Garver. Born

473. Raymond Garver (10)

Son of Dorothy Elizabeth (Cheseldine) Garver (No. 302) and R. H. Garver. Born

474. Earl Charles (Squeak) Garver (10)

Son of Dorothy Elizabeth (Cheseldine) Garver (No. 302) and R. H. Garver. Born

475. Margaret Patricia Cryer (10) Redmond, Spence

Daughter of Olive Levonia (Yates) Cryer Wortz (No. 302A) and William Francis Cryer. Born April 29, 1931 in Washington, DC. Pat, being the first grandchild of Carrie Yates, was seen in almost all of the old family photographs with many relatives around her and was surely lovingly spoiled by all. Her mother and father were divorced, then her father died, and times were tough for Pat and her mother. Married (1) Dean Redmond. Divorced. Married (2) Thomas Duncan Spence, born January 25, 1931 in Hawaii, November 19, 1951 in Virginia. Pat and Tom were a match made in heaven, and were so in love for all their married life, they were the envy of everyone.

Pat was a top bowler for the WIBC in the 60's and 70's, making the front cover of Southern Bowler Magazine in February. 1965. She loved bowling, homemaking and raising her family. Tom retired from the Navy as a Chief Petty Officer in 1966 and went into the computer technology field with IBM. Their favorite place to live was Virginia in the Tidewater region. In 1971, she and Tom shared the blessed gift of having a son, Andy. In 1978, Tom was transferred to Orlando, FL. Daughters Terry and Lynn joined the venture with Pat, Tom and Andy. There were no happier moments in Pats life than the time of raising their son and being presented with their first grandchild, Mandy, daughter of Lynn.

Pat's home was honored by Better Homes. She loved decorating, sewing and gardening.

Andy died on October 9, 1989.

Pat and Tom renewed their love in 1991 by traveling to the very spot they met, at Glen Echo Amuesement Park (now a Museum) in Washington, DC. Pat described their final years as "the love affair of her life". Tom died on May 15, 1997. Pat sold her home in Lake Mary, FL and traveled between Cari's home in Houston, TX and Lynn and Terry's in Sanford and Hollywood, FL. She loved the Casino scene, and the traveling between her daughter's homes. She was an Internet nerd and always found some of the most unusual sites to forward to everyone. She was extremely politically inclined and posted to the Internet boards daily. Pat was a brilliant woman. Upon her death on April 6, 1999, dozens of condolences were forwarded from her Internet friends to the family. She planned to move back to Florida in the fall of 1999, hoping to bring Cari and her two sons, Alex and Mark with her.

On August 7, 1999 joined by the ashes of her husband and son, Pat's ashes were scattered off Hollywood Beach in Florida.

Children - First Marriage:

560C.   I. Terry Darlene (11) B. September 4, 1950.

Children: - Second Marriage

560D.   II. Tommye Dawn (11) B. August 3, 1952.

560E.   III. Patricia Lynn (11) B. March 25, 1957.

560F.   IV. Cari Leigh (11) B. April 28, 1960.

560G.   V. Andrew Duncan (11) B. December 2, 1971 D. October 9, 1989.

476. Thomas Irvin Yates, Jr. (10)

Son of Thomas Irvin Yates (No. 302B) and Mary Helena (Morgan) Yates. Born October 1, 1938. One daughter, Noella Jean Tartaglino Cipriano.

560H.   I. Noella Jean Tartaglino Cipriano (11) B. June 15, 1956.

Married Ava Nell (Noble) Yates, February 1, 1957. Children:

560I.   II. Thomas Irvin, III. (11) B. November 17, 1957.

560J.   III. Michael Leonard (11) B. October 27, 1960.

560K.   III. John Warren (11) B. March 11, 1962.

560L .   IV. Pamela (11) B._____. D._____.

477. Carol Ann Yates (10) Kimble

Daughter of Thomas Irvin Yates (No. 302B) and Mary Helena (Morgan) Yates. Born June 2, 1942, in Washington, DC. Married Galen Robert Kimble, September 7, 1962. Galen and Carol live in Edgewater, MD. Children:

560M.   I. Carrie Lynn (11) B. March 27, 1965.

560N.   II. Catherine Marie (11) B. March 3, 1967.

560O.   III. Kevin Robert (11) B. July 25, 1969.

478. Elaine Kay Yates (10) Cartwright

Daughter of Thomas Irvin Yates (No. 302B) and Mary Helena (Morgan) Yates. Born January 15, 1946, Sibley Hospital, Washington, DC. Graduated Suitland Senior High School, Suitland, MD, June, 1964. Started work in July, 1964 with the Bureau of Aeronautics, Department of the Navy as a Secretary Stenographer. Continued working with the Department of the Navy and retired as a Management Analyst in August, 1993. Always loved children and went to work as a substitute teacher in local school for physically and mentally challenged students between the ages of 5 and 21 years old. Has resided in Maryland since 1950. Married Robert Scott Cartwright, July 2, 1978. Raised two stepchildren; Patricia Ann Cartwright, born February 17, 1966, unmarried, and Robert Scott Cartwright, Jr., born September 24, 1969, unmarried. Elaine and Bob live in Upper Marlboro, MD.

479. Sandra Kaye Yates (10) Willie

Daughter of Ralph A. Yates (No. 302C) and Florence Kaye (Everett) Yates. Born February 16, 1939. Married George Willis Willie. Children:

560P.	I. Christine Kaye (11) B. October 13, 1959.
560Q.	II. Kathleen Kaye (11) B. April 18, 1962.
560R.	III. George Spencer (11) B. July 6, 1968.

480. Bonnie Jean Yates (10) Grant, Kershaw

Daughter of Ralph A. Yates (No. 302C) and Florence Kaye (Everett) Yates. Born November 2, 1944. Married (1) Robert R. Grant. Divorced. Married (2) Victor Kershaw, born September 30, 1951, February 16, 1974. Bonnie and Vic reside in Florida. Children: First Marriage:

560S.	I. Robert Darrin (11) B. December 11, 1964.
560T.	II. Lori Paige (11) B. June 24, 1968.
	Children: - Second Marriage
560U.	III. Victor Scott (11) B. February 19, 1977.

481. Ralph Everett Yates (10)

Son of Ralph A. Yates (No. 302C) and Florence Kaye (Everett) Yates. Born September 20, 1953, in Takoma Park, MD. Married (1) Elizabeth Yanchulis Yates, May 11, 1974, and (2) Tina Thompson Yates January 1, 1991. Divorced August, 1997. Ralph resides in Shadyside, MD. Children: - First Marriage:
    560V.   I. Timothy Augustus (11) B. November 10, 1974.
    560W.   II. Tyler Charles Yates (11) B. December 26, 1977.
                  D. December 21, 1991.

482. Beverly Jeanne Baggett (10) Renner Wild

Daughter of Martha Mae (Yates) Baggett (No. 302D) and Milton Baggett. Born May 11, 1939 .in Washington, DC. Married (1) James Daniel Renner, born February 28, 1932, June 28, 1958. Divorced. Jim died August 6, 1992, age 60, in Florida. Married (2) Gerard Wild, born March 23, 1945 in Philadelphia, PA, January 8, 1982. Beverly was a Purchasing Manager for Choice Hotels/Manor Care, in Silver Spring, MD, 1971 to 1991, and has been a Buyer/Travel Coordinator with SFA, Inc., a government contractor, for 5 years.

Beverly studied art for three years, as a teenager, and after not painting for thirty years, began painting once again in 1991, and had her first show a year later. She is one of the founders of the Guild of Bowie Artists, in Bowie, MD, was their treasurer for four years, and has shown her artwork in Bowie and Annapolis, MD. Beverly has written a children's book, is currently working on the illustrations, loves to embroider, read, and makes hand made "Ready or Not" dolls. She was the recording secretary for Prince George's County Genealogy Society for one year, and through the Society met Tommy Brent (Cheseldine), this books co-author.

Jerry was in the US Army Europe 1962 to 1965. He studied electronics and electricity in Boston, MA and Philadelphia, PA. Jerry has worked in the construction, steel, newspaper, and aerospace industries. Currently working at NASA, he is involved with Cobe, and the Hubble space telescope and recently transported "Host" from Greenbelt, MD to Cape Kennedy to go into space with John Glenn.

Jerry has studied martial arts since 1972, and holds Black Belts in Tae Kwon Do, Kempo, and Gung/Fu. Jerry and Bev raised his two children from his first marriage. Renee Dawn, born September 28, 1970, is divorced and has a daughter, Shelby Nicole, born August 2, 1993. Jerry, Jr., born June 27, 1975, has a daughter, Julianna, born July 13, 1994. Bev and Jerry have lived in Bowie, MD for twenty years. No children from this marriage. Children: - First Marriage

560X.   I. Kelly Ann (11) B. March 7, 1960.
560Y.   II. James Darryl (11) B. October 12, 1965.

483. Larry Eugene Baggett (10)

Son of Martha Mae Yates Baggett (No. 302D) and Milton Baggett. Born August 1, 1947, at 3:20 AM at the Pittman Hospital in Fayetteville, NC. Larry grew up in Washington, DC and graduated from Anacostia High School in 1965. On July 25, 1965, he started working for the C & P Telephone Company.

On January 28, 1967, he married Alice Ann Davies, born August 18, 1948 in Harrisburg, Virginia. The name on her birth certificate was Elizabeth Vivian Davies until November of 1966 when her mother went to Richmond and had it corrected to read Alice Ann Davies. Alice was the middle of three children born to Elizabeth Vivian (Lewis) and Burton Talieson Davies. Both Elizabeth and Burton were from Wilkes-barrie, PA. The other children were Joan Elizabeth Davies, married to Fred Douglas Richard (No. 484), and Burton Talieson Davies, born September 9, 1950 at Doctors Hospital, Washington, DC, deceased on July 30, 1970 in Suitland, MD.

Larry joined the U.S. Army on October 28, 1966. Their first son, Mark David was born at Andrews Air Force Base on March 27, 1968. A couple of days later Larry was in Mannheim, Germany. Alice and Mark followed Larry to Germany. Larry received an Honorable Discharge on October 8, 1969.

Joyce Lynn was born in LaPlata, MD November 1, 1972 and Richard Alan was born in LaPlata, MD on November 12, 1973. On March 28, 1974, the Baggett family moved to St. Charles in Waldorf, MD. During the first eight years Alice and Larry were married they had three children and lost five children during the early (3 to 4 months) part of Alices' pregnancy.

Larry has been with the telephone company for 34 years. He is currently an instructor in a training lab. Alice worked at Sears for 7 years.

When his sister Bev became interested in genealogy, she was excited and hoped it would interest Larry also. It took a while, but soon, Larry and spent many days at National Archives, the Morman Temple Research Library, the Hall of Records in Annapolis, and your basic "cemetery hopping". Later Alice joined them. Children:

560Z.	I. Mark David (11) B. March 27, 1968.
560Z1.	II. Joyce Lynn (11) B. November 1, 1972.
560Z2.	III. Richard Alan (11) B. November 12, 1973.

484. Fred Dougla Richard (10)

Son of Katherine Jane (Yates) Richard (No. 302E) and Edward Richard. Born May 5, 1945. Married Joan Davies Richard born September 22, 1947 on October 23, 1965. Joan is the sister of Alice Davies married to Larry Baggett (NO. 483). Fred and Joan live in St. Charles, Waldorf, MD. Children:

560Z3.	I. Brian Douglas (11) B. October 31, 1968.
560Z4.	II. Robin Renee (11) B. May 25, 1974.

485. Gerald Thomas Richard (10)

Son of Katherine Jane (Yates) Richard (No. 302E) and Edward Richard. Born October 4, 1947. Married (1) Francine (Malakatis) Richard. Divorced. Married (2) Susan Hess Cardwell Richard, who had two children, Shane and Christina. Jerry died January 24, 1988, in Santa Domingo, the Dominican Republic. He was a partner in a small telephone company, and he and his partner were installing telephones in the Embassy of the Dominican Republic. On a day off while surveying a water spout in the rocks, a wave washed Jerry's partner into the ocean. Jerry tried to rescue his partner and they both drowned. Children: - First Marriage

560Z5.	I. Gerald Thomas (11) B. . Jay was adopted by his stepfather, is now Jay Dove. Jay lives in New Orleans, LA.

560Z6.   II. Jason Keith (11) B.
                Jason was adopted by his stepfather and is now
                Jason Keith Dove. Jason lives in New
                Orleans, LA.
                Children: - Second Marriage
560Z7.   III. Heather Renee (11) B. January 5, 1978 in
                Camp Springs, MD.

486. Debra Jayne Richard (10)

Daughter of Katherine Jayne (Yates) Richard (No. 302E) and Edward Richard. Born November 2, 1963. Debbie has lived in Bowie, MD for eight years, with Terri Roberson. They have a beautiful cape cod home and both Terri and Debbie love gardening. Debbie is an accomplished photographer who has won many Maryland State competitions.

486A. Penny Goode (10)

Daughter of Dorothy (Knott) Goode (No. 302G) and Walter Goode. Born _____.

486B. Joyce Goode (10)

Daughter of Dorothy (Knott) Goode (No. 302G) and Walter Goode. Born _____.

486C. Skip Goode (10)

Son of Dorothy (Knott) Goode (No. 302G) and Walter Goode. Born _____.

486D. John "Jack" Francis Simpson, Jr. (10)

Son of John Francis Simpson (No. 302H) and Gloria Jean (Simmons) Simpson. Born December 30. 1944 in Rockingham Memorial Hospital, Harrisonburg, VA. Married Carol Ann Hutchison, born December 21, 1947 in Sibley Hospital, Washington, DC. Children:

560Z8.   I. Dennis Craig, Sr. (11) B. November 17, 1966.
560Z9.   II. Christina Jean (11) B. May 20, 1968.

486E. Donald Alan Simpson (10)

Son of John Francis Simpson (No. 302H) and Gloria Jean (Simmons) Simpson. Born November 6, 1947 in Sibley Hospital, Washington, DC. Married Patricia Marie McCann, born March 6, 1948 in Illinois. Children:

560Z10.   I. Deborah Lynn (11) B. June 11, 1971.
560Z11.   II. Jason Daniel (11) B. September 16, 1973.

486F. James Richard Simpson (10)

Son of John Francis Simpson (No. 302H) and Gloria Jean (Simmons) Simpson. Born April 19, 1951 in Sibley Hospital, Washington, DC. Married (1) Diane Davic, divorced. Married (2) Linda Rice, divorced. No children from either marriage.

486G. David Wayne Simpson (10)

Son of John Francis Simpson (No. 302H) and Gloria Jean (Simmons) Simpson. Born March 4, 1957 in Garfield, Washington, DC. Married Cheryl Moore, divorced. No children.

486H. Michael Kevin Simpson (10)

Son of John Francis Simpson (No. 302H) and Gloria Jean (Simmons) Simpson. Born April 1, 1965 in Washington Hospital Center, Washington, DC. Married Lisa Ann Merry, born May 14, 1965. Children:

560Z12.   I. Michael Kevin, Jr. (11) B. March 29, 1987.
560Z13.   II. Brandon Kurtis (11) B. March 5, 1991.
560Z14.   III. Kathleen Merry (11) B. May 25, 1992.

486I. Fern Darly Knott (10)

Daughter of Biscoe Knott (No. 302I) and Fern Darly Miller. Born January 18, 1948.

486J. John Biscoe Long (10)

Son of Jane Elizabeth Knott Long (No. 302J) and Otis F. Long. Born December 31, 1942.

486K. Larry Bailey Palmer (10)

Son of Windsor Palmer (No. 302K) and Mary Alice Drury. Born _____.

486L. Angela Palmer (10)

Daughter of Windsor Palmer (No. 302K) and Mary Alice Drury. Born _____.

486M. Mary Windsor Palmer (10)

Daughter of Windsor Palmer (No. 302K) and Mary Alice Drury. Born _____.

486N. Billingsley Garner Pogue, Jr. (10)

Son of Lielia Palmer Pogue (No. 302L) and Billingsley Garner Pogue. Born _____.

487. John Spencer Huntington (10)

Son of Sue (Cheseldine) Huntington (No. 303) and John D. Huntington.

488. Sue Canfield Huntington (10)

Daughter of Sue (Cheseldine) Huntington (No. 303) and John D. Huntington.

489. Elizabeth Huntington (10)

Daughter of Sue (Cheseldine) Huntington (No. 303) and John D. Huntington.

490. J. Wallace Huntington (10)

Son of Sue (Cheseldine) Huntington (No. 303) and John D. Huntington.

491. Jeanne Huntington (10)

Daughter of Sue (Cheseldine) Huntington (No. 303) and John D. Huntington.

492. Priscilla Huntington (10)

Daughter of Sue (Cheseldine) Huntington (No. 303) and John D. Huntington.

493. Dianne Hillsamer Cheseldine (10)

Daughter of Laura (Dodd) Cheseldine and David Hillsamer, Diane's first husband. Dianne was adopted by Charles Canfield (Tommy) Cheseldine (No. 304). Born December 3, 1944, in Indiana.

494. Cary Cheseldine (10)

Child of Raymond M (Skip) Cheseldine, Jr., (No. 305) and _____ Cheseldine.

495. Kim Cheseldine (10)

Daughter of Raymond M. (Skip) Cheseldine, Jr., (No. 305) and _____ Cheseldine.

496. Barbara Sue Jones (10) Giubbini Phillips

Daughter of Barbara Elizabeth (Cheseldine) Jones (No. 306) and Roland Morris Jones. Born September 17, 1942 in San Antonio, TX. Christened April 11, 1943 at Church of the Nativity, Maysville, KY. Married (1) Robert Giubbini, February 15, 1962, and had two children. Divorced. Married (2) John Walter Phillips born February 11, 1937 in Salinas, CA., on September 28, 1974. Barbara and John

now live in Fremont, CA. Children - 1st Marriage:
>   560Z15.   I. Mark Robert (11) B. February 11, 1966
>   560Z16.   II. Kristin Elizabeth (11) B. February 16,1968.

497. Catherine Elizabeth Jones (10)

Daughter of Barbara Elizabeth (Cheseldine) Jones (No. 306) and Roland Morris Jones. Born October 9, 1946 in Burlingame, San Mateo, CA. Married William Monaco, June 29, 1968. Divorced 1978. Cathy now lives in Phoenix, AZ. Children:
>   560Z17.   I. Gretchen Elizabeth Monaco (11) B. February 26, 1973.
>   560Z18.   II. Regina Maureen Monaco (11) B. March 2, 1975.

498. Owen Williams Jones (10)

Son of Barbara Elizabeth (Cheseldine) Jones (No. 306) and Roland Morris Jones. Born October 28, 1949. Owen lives in Fremont, CA.

499. Richard Kevin Rufner (10)

Son of Peggy Lee (Fraser) Rufner (No. 311) and Donald Hoyt Rufner.

500. Deborah Kay Rufner (10)

Daughter of Peggy Lee (Fraser) Rufner (No. 311) and Donald Hoyt Rufner.

501. Bertrand Frederick Cheseldine (10)

Son of George Frederick Cheseldine (No. 314) and Mary Hilda (Pilkerton) Cheseldine. Born October 21, 1936. Married (1) Marian Smith, September 27, 1958 and (2) Agnes Bonnette (Bonnie) Cox, March 2, 1962. Children: First Marriage:

561.   I. Charles Frederick (11) B. August 25, 1960. (Adopted February 1966, by Curtis J. Will, Atlantic, Iowa, who married Marian Smith Cheseldine). He died November 27, 1979.

Children: Second Marriage:

562.   II. Joseph Frederick (11) B. December 27, 1967.

563.   III. Saundra Bonnette (11) B. July 3, 1969.

502. Mary Thomas Cheseldine (10) Bragg, Robbins, Taylor

Daughter of George Frederick Cheseldine (No. 314) and Mary Hilda (Pilkerton) Cheseldine. Born June 8, 1940. Married (1) William Pierce Bragg, Jr. and (2) Bertrand B. Robbins, Jr., on April 19, 1963. Mary married (3) David E. Taylor, Jr., about 1971 in Washington, DC. No children born to third marriage. She died by drowning, August 4, 1976, and is buried at Sacred Heart Church. Children: First Marriage:

564.   I. William Pierce Bragg (11) B. October 28, 1957.

565.   II. Allan James Bragg (11) B. June 27, 1959.

Children: Second Marriage:

566.   III. Christi Sue Robbins (11) B. August 20, 1964.

503. Lois Ann Savage (10) Bowman, Tennent

Daughter of Geraldine Lois (Cheseldine) Savage (No. 315) and Clifford Daniel Savage. Born November, 11, 1946. Married (1) Jeffrey M. Bowman, before 1972, and (2) John Tennent from Portland, OR, on February 21, 1986. Children: First Marriage:

567.   I. Michael E. Bowman (11) B. November 14, 1972.

568.   II. Brian E. Bowman (11) B. October 30, 1977.

504. Daniel C. Savage (10)

Son of Geraldine Lois (Cheseldine) Savage (No. 315) and Clifford Daniel Savage. Born November 22, 1948. Married April 5, 1980, Marsha Gay Ross. Children:

569.   I. Megan Ann (11) B. June 5, 1980

570.   II. Jason Daniel (11) B. June 5, 1980

505. Mary Jane Savage (10) Thomas

Daughter of Geraldine Lois (Cheseldine) Savage (No. 315) and Clifford Daniel Savage. Born July 19, 1952. Married Herbert Thomas.

506. John William Cheseldine (10)

Son of Joseph Clement Cheseldine (No. 316) and Mary Marguerite (Hayden) Cheseldine. Born November 6, 1942 at Leonardtown, MD. Married Patricia Ann Irby, born March 26, 1943. Children:

571.   I. John William , Jr. (11) B. August 2, 1962.
572.   II. Jeffrey Scott (11) B.
573.   III. Joseph Gary (11) B. October 1, 1964.

507. Mary Agnes Henderson Cheseldine (10) Anderson

Daughter of Joseph Clement Cheseldine (No. 316) and Mary Marguerite (Hayden) Cheseldine. Born August 4, 1944. Married January 1, 1963, Jenning William Anderson. Divorced. She attended school at St. Mary's Academy, Leonardtown, MD, and worked as a legal secretary, St. Mary's County States Attorney Office, Leonardtown, MD. She made her home at Wildwood, California, MD. Children:

574.   I. Donna Lee (11) B. October 23, 1964.
575.   II. Richard Dale (11) B. January 26, 1967.
576.   III. Denise Elizabeth (11) B. October 20, 1969.
577.   IV. Julie Gwenette (11) B. June 13, 1976.

508. Rose Marie Cheseldine (10) Davis

Daughter of Joseph Clement Cheseldine (No. 316) and Mary Marguerite (Hayden) Cheseldine. Born June 2, 1948. She attended St. Mary's Academy at Leonardtown, MD. Married her high school sweetheart, Charles Daniel Davis, Jr. on September 10, 1966. She was employed in the accounting department of the St. Mary's County Public School System. Both she and her husband were active

197

members of their community, having devoted over 27 years each of volunteer service to their local Volunteer Fire Department. Rose has been a member since 1971 of the Ladies Auxiliary, Hollywood Volunteer Fire Department and Past President (1995) of the Southern Maryland Volunteer Fireman's Association. They made their home at Hollywood, MD. Children:

578.   I. Heather Lynn (11) B. October 7, 1973.

509. Andrew Knott (10)

Son of Linda (Cheseldine) Knott (No. 317) and Bryan Knott.

510. Samuel Knott (10)

Son of Linda (Cheseldine) Knott (No. 317) and Bryan Knott.

511. son Knott (10)

Son of Linda (Cheseldine) Knott (No. 317) and Bryan Knott.

512. daughter Knott (10)

Daughter of Linda (Cheseldine) Knott (No. 317) and Bryan Knott.

513. James Miller (10)

Son of Audrey (Cheseldine) Miller Embrey (No. 318) and _____ Miller.

514. Joseph Daniel Graves (10)

Son of Eleanor Marie (Cheseldine) Graves (No. 320) and Joseph Melvin Graves. Born in Leonardtown, MD June 23, 1948. Married Anita Faye Morgan.

515. Francis Wayne Graves (10)

Son of Eleanor Marie (Cheseldine) Graves (No. 320) and

Joseph Melvin Graves. Born in Leonardtown, MD August 5, 1950. Married Patricia Ann Thompson.

516. Glen David Graves (10)

Son of Eleanor Marie (Cheseldine) Graves (No. 320) and Joseph Melvin Graves. Born in Leonardtown, MD October 7, 1959. Married Tina Patricia Lawrence.

517. Mary Jane Gibson (10)

Daughter of Sophie Rebecca (Rice) Gibson (No. 321) and Sidney Lawrence Gibson. Born June 1, 1927. She died February 8, 1937 of head injuries sustained in a fall and is buried at Sacred Heart Cemetery, Bushwood, MD.

518. Charlotte Rebecca Gibson (10) Branson

Daughter of Sophie Rebecca (Rice) Gibson (No. 321) and Sidney Lawrence Gibson. Born January 19, 1931. Married Ernest Daniel Branson on June 2, 1951. Children:

578A.	I. Daniel Patrick (11) B. May 6, 1952.
578B.	II. David Lawrence (11) B. March 19, 1954. D. September 1, 1982.
578C.	III. Dorian Lee (11) B. February 15, 1956.
578D.	IV. Sharon Ann (11) B. October 18, 1957.
578E.	V. Steven Perry (11) B. October 18, 1960.
578F.	VI. Raquel Marie (11) B. March 29, 1969.

519. Sidney Ann Gibson (10) Saitia

Daughter of Sophie Rebecca (Rice) Gibson (No. 321) and Sidney Lawrence Gibson. Born November 2, 1944. Married James Michel Saitia on October 13, 1962. Children:

578G.	I. Angelina Marie (11) B. February 28, 1982.

520. Alan Douglas Gibson (10)

Son of Sophie Rebecca (Rice) Gibson (No. 321) and Sidney

Lawrence Gibson. Born June 16, 1947. Married (1) Elizabeth Ann Bowaster on June 28, 1971. (2) Janet Rae French on January 26, 1974. No issue.

521. Florence Rice (10)

Daughter of Richard (Bennie) Rice (No. 322) and Margaret Florence (Laughford) Rice.

522. Rachel Rebecca Smith (10)

Daughter of Mary Beatrice (Rice) Smith Hanback (No. 323) and Lawrence Smith.

523. Virginia Lee Hanback (10)

Daughter of Mary Beatrice (Rice) Smith Hanback (No. 323) and Leroy Hanback.

524. Evelyn Hanback (10)

Daughter of Mary Beatrice (Rice) Smith Hanback (No. 323) and Leroy Hanback.

525. Carol Fisk (10)

Daughter of Caroline Leviathan (West) Fisk Hopkins (No. 325) and Paul Fisk.

526. Robert Fisk (10)

Son of Caroline Leviathan (West) Fisk Hopkins (No. 325) and Paul Fisk.

527. James Fisk (10)

Son of Caroline Leviathan (West) Fisk Hopkins (No. 325) and Paul Fisk.

528. Peggy Hopkins (10)

Daughter of Caroline Leviathan (West) Fisk Hopkins (No. 325) and Howard Hopkins.

529. Bonnie Hopkins (10)

Daughter of Caroline Leviathan (West) Fisk Hopkins (No. 325) and Howard Hopkins.

530. Glenn Hopkins (10)

Son of Caroline Leviathan (West) Fisk Hopkins (No. 325) and Howard Hopkins.

531. Thomas West (10)

Son of Grace (Sinclair) West (No 327) and ____ West.

532. Nancy West (10)

Daughter of Grace (Sinclair) West (No. 327) and ___ West.

533. Mary Jane Thomas (10)

Daughter of Elizabeth Rittenhouse (West) Thomas (No. 329) and Daniel Thomas.

534. Alton Francis Mattingly (10)

Son of Dorothy Leviathan (Cheseldine) Mattingly Sweeny (No. 331) and William Francis Mattingly. Born August 6, 1941. Married April 25, 1964 Margaret Fowler Mattingly. Died June 23, 1964. Children:
579.   I. Scott (11) B. March 5, 1965.

535. Thomas A. McDonald, Jr. (10)

Son of Eileen Estella (Cheseldine) Wible McDonald (No. 332) and Thomas A. McDonald. Born August 9, 1951.

536. Linda Diane Cheseldine (10) Stanley, Glenn

Daughter of Alton Frederick Cheseldine (No. 333) and Carol Jean (Jourdan) Cheseldine. Born April 24, 1959. Married (1) August 21, 1976, Gary Stanley from Indiana, and (2) July 21, 1984, Timothy Glenn from Temple Hills, MD. They make their home in Waldorf, MD. Children: - First Marriage

580.   I. Sommer Ann Stanley (11) B. July 22, 1980. Adopted by Timothy Glenn.

537. Patricia Gayle Cheseldine (10) Murry

Daughter of Alton Frederick Cheseldine (No. 333) and Carol Jean (Jourdan) Cheseldine. Born August 21, 1973. Married October 19, 1996, Brian William Murry, born Frankfort, Germany, May 5, 1962.

538. Michael Richard Cheseldine (10)

Son of Harry Joseph Cheseldine (No. 334) and Althea Celeste (Schmidt) Cheseldine. Born July 17, 1949. No children.

539. Brenda Theresa Cheseldine (10) Basile

Daughter of Harry Joseph Cheseldine (No. 334) and Althea Celeste (Schmidt) Cheseldine. Born May 15, 1951. Married Robert Basile. Children:

580A.   I. Brian (11) B. _____ in Albuquerque, NM.
580B.   II. Andrea (11) B. _____ in Albuquerque, NM.

540. Susan Lynn Cheseldine (10) Street

Daughter of Harry Joseph Cheseldine (No. 334) and Althea Celeste (Schmidt) Cheseldine. Born December 14, 1955. Married Kent Street. Children:

580C.   I. Kyle (11) B. March 18, 1987.
580D.   II. Zachery (11) B. March 16, 1989.

541. Joseph Richard Cheseldine III (10)

Son of Joseph Richard Cheseldine, Jr. (No. 336) and Marianne (McBride) Cheseldine. Born December 2, 1961 in Cheverly, MD. Married Susan Elizabeth Trexler born February 9, 1959, June 24, 1989, St. Columbia Church, Oxon Hill, MD, whose parents were Morgan Joseph Trexler and Dorothy Gertrude (Tippett) Trexler. Children:

    581.   I. Kathleen Amanda (11) B. July 15, 1993.

542. Bridget Marie Cheseldine (10) Cavey

Daughter of Joseph Richard Cheseldine, Jr. (No. 336) and Marianne (McBride) Cheseldine. Born March 26, 1964, Cheverly, MD. Married February 12, 1994, Keith Daryl Cavey, St. Janes Church, Pasadena, MD. Children:

    582.   I. Sean Patrick (11) B. September 6, 1994.

543. Katie Ann Cheseldine (10) Hartman, Turner

Daughter of Joseph Richard Cheseldine, Jr. (No. 336) and Marianne (McBride) Cheseldine. Born July 2, 1967, Cheverly, MD. Married (1) Robert Hartman, May 10, 1987, whose parents were Robert Jerome Hartman and Jacqueline Ann Hering, Enterprise, MD. Divorced. Married (2) Herman Michael Turner whose parents were Herman Whaley Turner and Billie Rae (Dix) Turner, September 13, 1997, in Newark, MD. Children:-First Marriage:

    583.   I. Robert Jerome Hartman V (11) B. September 8, 1988.
            Children: - Second Marriage
    583A1. II. William Joseph Turner (11) B. October 5, 1998.

544. Joyce Marie Sesso (10) Buswell

Daughter of Edna Helena (Cheseldine) Sesso (No. 338) and Anthony Sesso. Born April 25, 1935 in Washington, DC. Attended St. Theresa's Catholic School, Washington, DC where she played basketball in the Catholic Youth Organization (CYO) in the Washington area. She was selected for the All Star League in 1948.

Joyce attended parochial high school, Immaculate Conception Academy, Washington, DC where she received the "Secretarial Award" at the graduation ceremony. She attended the University of Maryland from 1953 to 1955. She was married on September 15, 1956 to William Edmund Buswell of Ansonia, CT at St. Theresa's Catholic Church in Washington, DC.

Joyce worked as a secretary for the Justice Department and Department of the Army at the Pentagon before she entered the University of Maryland. She worked in the Office of the Executive Director of the Foreign Claims Settlement Commission from 1955 to 1958. After staying home and raising her children for 18 years, Joyce went back to the work force. In 1977 she was employed at NASA/Goddard Space Flight Center in Greenbelt, MD. She is a member of Professional Secretaries International, a professional organization for secretaries that sets the guidelines for all secretaries throughout the world. She was the Membership/Program Coordinator for the Prince George's chapter and she represented and voted for the chapter at many conventions throughout the United States. She is an executive secretary for the International Projects Program Manager. She provides administration support for the project which took her throughout Europe (Argentina, France, Germany, Italy, Switzerland and The Netherlands).

William Edmund Buswell was the son of William Albert Buswell and Mary Margaret (Cronin) Buswell of Ansonia, CT. Birthdate: June 3, 1932. William's father was of English descent (Edmund Buswell and Elizabeth Walsh) and his mother was Irish (Timothy Joseph Cronin and Margaret Mary Flynn). They were married in 1894 in County Limerick, Ireland and came to America in 1896. William attended Ansonia High School and played football, baseball and basketball for the high school team. He graduated in 1950. He attended prep school and then enlisted in the Navy in 1951 and was a Dental Technician at Paris Island, SC. William played basketball in the Navy and at the University of Maryland in 1953. He was honorably discharged in 1953. William worked as a sales representative for Metropolitan Life Insurance Company, International Business Machines (IBM), and Cushwa Building Supplies. He and Joyce established their own steam carpet cleaning business (Belcroft Enterprises). William passed away August 3, 1989. He is buried in the Cheltenham Veterans Cemetery in Crownsville, MD. Children:

583A2.   I. Edmund Anthony (11) B. June 12, 1957.
583B.   II. Karen Helena (11) B. August 29, 1958.
583C.   III. Elizabeth Evelyn (11) B. December 25, 1961.
583D.   IV. Maureen Louise (11) B. November 5, 1965.

545. Jean Frances Sesso (10) Hinson

Daughter of Edna Helena (Cheseldine) Sesso (No. 338) and Anthony Sesso. Born July 21, 1942 in Washington, DC. Married Bruce Elton Hinson, November 18, 1961 at St. Teresa's Catholic Church, Anacostia. Washington, DC. She attended parochial schools - St. Teresa's and Immaculate Conception Academy in Washington, DC.

She was employed by the Department of Health, Education and Welfare as an Executive Assistant to the Director of Water Pollution.

In June 1963, she resigned from her job to stay home and take care of their first child, Cheryl Helene. Bruce opened their first optical store in 1968 in New Carrollton, MD.

They expanded their optical business to six stores around the DC metropolitan area. With retirement approaching, they decided to downsize to two stores - one in Annandale, VA - the other in Temple Hills, MD, which they currently operate.

Jean stayed home for twenty-three years and raised four children. She became involved in the optical businesses in 1986 and currently manages McGinnis Opticians in Temple Hills, MD. Bruce is President and Jean is Vice President of the Guild of Prescription Opticians of Washington, DC. Jean is First Vice President of the Prevention of Blindness Society of Washington, DC and helps promote its annual charity gala event. She has been Secretary of the Marlow Heights Merchants Association for ten years. Jean is also very involved with the Central Fairfax Chanber of Commerce and the local Christian Women's Group.

Jean enjoys volunteer work for various organizations, supervising fundraising efforts, such as an annual luncheon in Emmitsburg for the elderly nuns who taught her in high school, shopping and traveling for pleasure.

Bruce Elton Hinson was born in Washington, DC on August 15, 1941, son of George Elton Hinson and Helen Margaret (Hastings) Hinson, both born in Virginia and both buried at Montross, VA.

Bruce attended Anacostia High School, Washington, DC, then worked for Kinsman Optical Co. before going into the U. S. Army for two years. After service, in 1968, he opened his first optical shop business which quickly grew to six stores. Children:

    583E.   I. Cheryl Helene (11) B. June 29, 1963.
    583F.   II. Debra Lyn (11) B. October 23, 1964.
    583G.   III. Bruce Elton, Jr. (11) B. June 23, 1968.
    583H.   IV. Keith Anthony (11) B. December 13, 1969.

545A. Patricia Sesso (10)

Daughter of Edna (Cheseldine) Sesso (No. 338) and _____ Finnegan. Born Wash., DC; lived at St. Ann's Convent; adopted by Anthony Sesso; Attended school and worked in DC. Later moved to Miami, FL. Patricia had two children; Kathleen Ann Sesso, born Wash., DC, Dec. 26, 1950 (given to adoption). Also Scott David Sesso, Born June 27, 1961. Scott was in the Navy and later lived in Vero Beach, FL.

546. Joseph Edward Cheseldine (10)

Son of Joseph Wilmer Cheseldine (No. 339) and Blanch "Dolly" Ellen (Schriver) Cheseldine. Born January 27, 1940, at Washington, DC. Married Wilda Crossley Brann on February 16, 1958 at Mt. Calvary Catholic Church, District Heights, MD. Served in the U. S. Marines 1957-1959. He attended Anacostia High School from 1955-1958. He played football and ran track for Anacostia High School. Joseph had a trade in the Sheet Metal Local 102, Washington, DC for 12 years. He is self employed at Cheseldine's Sports and Lettering and has been in business since 1972 in Waldorf, MD. He also owns Rascals Saloon and has been in business since 1980 in Waldorf, MD. Joseph has been actively involved in youth sports since 1962, including coaching St. Francis Xavier Catholic School from 1962 - 1966. He was instrumental in starting the John Unitas Football League for youth in Charles County, MD in 1969. He coached the St. Charles Rams from 1969-1975, winning three championships. Joseph was inducted into the Washington, DC Boxing Hall of Fame in November 1991 as an amateur boxer with a record of 68 wins, 4 losses.

Wilda was born in Washington, DC to Wesley Crossley Brann and Frances Lorena Wood Brann, both of Virginia. Wilda attended Anacostia High School from 1955-1958. She worked as a legal secretary from 1960-1981. From 1981-1995 she worked as a real estate agent in the Waldorf, MD area. They currently (1999) reside in Newburg, MD. Children:

584.   I. Joseph (Joey) Edward, Jr. (11) B. September 21, 1958.

585.   II. Jay Michael (11) B. December 16, 1960.

547. John Dominic (Jackie) Cheseldine (10)

Son of Joseph Wilmer Cheseldine (No. 339) and Blanch "Dolly" Ellen (Schriver) Cheseldine. Born July 20, 1943, Washington, DC. Attended St. Dominic's grade school and then St. Teresa's grade school, in SE, Washington, DC. Graduated from Anacostia High School, June 1962. Worked for the District of Columbia Government from September 1962 thru June, 1979. Since 1980, manager of GNT, Inc. in Waldorf, MD. High successful baseball coach in Washington, DC CYO, McNamara High School, Forrestville, MD, and Semi-Pro leagues in Charles County and currently assistant coach at Ryken High School in Leonardtown, MD. President of the Charles St. Mary's Baseball league for the past five years.

Married (1) Judith Lynn Coogan, September 12, 1964 at Washington, DC. and (2) Theresa Anne Knight, March 17, 1984, at Waldorf, MD.

Theresa was born August 31, 1955. Graduated from Wakefield High School, Arlington, Va, June, 1973. Flight attendant for Braniff Airlines, Dallas, TX from 1977 - 1983. Has been employed with AT&T in Washington, DC as a Program Manager for 15 years. Theresa is very active in the children's activities including teacher of Religious Education (CCD) at Our Lady Help of Christians Church in Waldorf, MD. Children:-First Marriage:

586.   I. John Dominic (Nick), Jr. (11) B. December 6, 1967

587.   II. Erin Marie (11) B. June 15, 1972.

    Children:-Second Marriage:

588.   III. Madeline Danielle (11) B. October 13, 1985.

589.   IV. Colleen Elizabeth (11) B. April 27, 1989.

590.   V. Allison (11) B.October 9, 1990.

207

548. Dennis Patrick Cheseldine (10)

Son of Joseph Wilmer Cheseldine (No. 339) and Blanch "Dolly" Ellen (Schriver) Cheseldine. Born April 2, 1953, at Washington, DC. Dennis attended St. Francis Xavier Parochial School in SE, Washington, DC, and McNamara Parochial High School in MD.

Dennis married (1) Deborah Frances (Mattingly) Cheseldine on May 12, 1979 at St. Ignatius Catholic Church, Chapel Point, MD. No issue from this marriage.

On July 1, 1991 Dennis married (2) Gail Ann Melvin Underwood Cheseldine in Annapolis, MD. No issue from this marriage, however Gail has three children from a previous marriage - Robert Underwood, James Michael Underwood and Brandy Michele Underwood.

Dennis is employed as a sheet metal mechanic at the House Office Building in Washington, DC. His hobbies are golf and fishing.

549. Joan Theresa Saylor (10) Donnelly

Daughter of Theresa Nora (Cheseldine) Saylor (No.342) and Nevin Saylor. Born in Washington, DC November 13, 1944. She attended Parochial Schools - Our Lady Queen of Peace and Immaculate Conception Academy in Washington, DC. She continued her education attending Strayer Junior College in Washington, DC. She was a Cheer Leader on the Varsity basketball team.

Joan was employed by the Bureau of Customs, Department of the Treasury. She transferred to the Department of the Navy holding the position of Secretary to the Chief of Operations of the Bureau of Public Printing. Her next position was as Personal Secretary to the Assistant Judge Advocate General, Department of the Navy.

She apparently takes after her father since she is a most talented lady. Her talents lie in an artistic vein. She enjoys floral designing. She keeps busy caring for her family and her grandson Christopher, and when possible travelling with her husband. She lives in Fairfax, VA.

On June 4, 1966 she married Gary Wayne Donnelly at St. Philip's Catholic Church, Camp Springs, MD. Gary was born March

18, 1944 in San Diego, CA. He attended Parochial and public schools in San Diego and Chula Vista, CA. He continued his education at the University of Maryland. He joined the U. S. Marine Corps in 1962 being honorably discharged in 1967.

He has held positions of Legislative Aide to a U. S. Member of Congress; Lobbyist/Association Management with the National Limestone Institute and National Crushed Stone Association. In 1986 until 1990 he was employed as Senior Vice President of the Building Owners and Managers Association International; and his present position is President and CEO of the National Lumber and Building Material Dealers Association.

He is a direct descendent of Daniel Donnelly who was born in Dublin in 1788 and became the boxing champion of Ireland. In a 34 round fight in England he beat Tom Oliver. He was knighted in a tavern near Crawley Commons by the then Prince Regent and inducted into Ring Magazine's Hall of Fame in 1960. In "The Hideout", in Kilcullen County Kildare, the right arm of Sir Dan Donnelly hangs. Children:

590A.	I. Eric Nevin Donnelly (11) B. November 21, 1967. D. March 30, 1996.
590B.	II. Mark Orville Donnelly (11) B. May 12, 1971.
590C.	III. Michele Theresa Donnelly (11) B. October 7, 1975.

550. Evelyn Marie Saylor (10) Bostic

Daughter of Theresa Nora (Cheseldine) Saylor (No. 342) and Nevin Saylor. Born December 22, 1948 in Washington, DC. She attended Parochial Schools _ Our Lady of Peace in Washington, DC and LaReine High School in Suitland MD. Marie was employed by the Naval Overseas Employment Office, Department of the Navy. She transferred to the Department of Health, Education and Welfare becoming Secretary to the Director of Physical Security, Office of Internal Security.

Marie keeps busy taking care of her family, working part-time for a physician, attending antique shows, doing counted cross stitch pieces and enjoying her grandchild - Elizabeth - 6 years old. She makes her home in Lower Marlboro in Calvert County, MD.

In 1967 she married John Michael Bostic at St. Philip's

Catholic Church, Camp Springs, MD. Mike was born in Washington, DC October 22, 1947 son of Delores Louise Morris of Washington, DC and Cecil Bostic of Clarksburg, Virginia. He attended public schools in Prince Georges County. He continued his education for a time at Maryland University. He was employed as a refrigeration and air conditioning technician at the Naval Research Laboratory. He joined the Hecht Company in Washington DC in 1969 and at the present time he is the Chief Engineer covering all engineering employees employed by May Company in Washington, DC, Maryland, Virginia. His hobbies are baseball, football, coaching, golf, antique cars. Children:

590D.   I. Sean Paul Bostic (11) B. April 7, 1968.
590E.   II. Scott Michael Bostic (11) B. July 26, 1973.

Eleventh generation begins

550A. Ann Elizabeth Bailey (11) Guy

Daughter of Mary Susan Theresa (Gibson) Bailey (No. 349A) and Joseph David Bailey. Born November 20, 1942. Married William Guy October, 1958.

550B. Sue Ann Bruse (11)

Daughter of Ann Louise (Gibson) Bruse (No. 349B) and James Bruse. Born January 29, 1948.

550C. Andrew Jackson Gibson, Jr. (11)

Son of Andrew Jackson Gibson (No. 349C) and Mildred Downs. Born August 15, 1945.

550D. Sherry Madeline Gibson (11)

Daughter of Andrew Jackson Gibson (No. 349C) and Mildred Downs. Born July, 1947.

550E. James Thomas Tippett (11)

Son of Catherine Veronica (Gibson) Tippett (No. 349D) and Garnett Archie Tippett. Born September 9, 1946.

550F. Bernard Archie Tippett (11)

Son of Catherine Veronica (Gibson) Tippett (No. 349D) and Garnett Archie Tippett. Born September 7, 1949.

550G. Mary Clare Tippett (11) Hayden

Daughter of Catherine Veronica (Gibson) Tippett (No. 349D) and Garnett Archie Tippett. Born December 2, 1955. Married James Rholand Hayden, Jr., March 12, 1976.

550H. Barbara Kay Tippett (11)

Daughter of Catherine Veronica (Gibson) Tippett (No. 349D) and Garnett Archie Tippett. Born July 26, 1957.

550I. Eugene Morgan III (11)

Son of Mary Lillian (Gibson) Morgan (No. 349O) and Eugene Morgan, Jr. Born

550J. Judith Ann Morgan (11)

Daughter of Mary Lillian (Gibson) Morgan (No. 349O) and Eugene Morgan, Jr. Born

550K. Richard Tippett (11)

Son of Eleanor Beatrice "Beezie" (Mathews) Tippett (No.350F) and Dennis Tippett. Born January 19, 1942.

550L. David Tippett (11)

Son of Eleanor Beatrice "Beezie" (Mathews) Tippett (No. 350F) and Dennis Tippett. Born September 5, 1943.

550M. Carol Ann Farr (11)

Daughter of Thelma Lucille (Mathews) Farr (No. 350G) and Joseph Farr. Born August 1, 1945.

550N. Joseph Farr (11)

Son of Thelma Lucille (Mathews) Farr (No. 350G) and Joseph Farr. Born August 26, 1946.

550O. Nancy Lee Swann (11)

Daughter of Catherine Marie "Kitty" (Mathews) Swann (No. 350H) and Francis Gwynn Swann, Jr. Born June 22, 1952.

550P. Francis Allan Swann (11)

Son of Catherine Marie "Kitty" (Mathews) Swann (No. 350H) and Francis Gwynn Swann, Jr. Born March 19, 1957.

550Q. Fay Marie Bailey (11)

Daughter of Samuel Mathew Bailey, Jr. (No.350I) and Joan Marie (Coale) Bailey. Born August 25, 1954.

550R. Samuel Mathew Bailey III (11)

Son of Samuel Mathew Bailey, Jr. (No. 350I) and Joan Marie (Coale) Bailey. Born June 3, 1957.

550S. Mark Andrew Bailey (11)

Son of Samuel Mathew Bailey, Jr. (No. 350I) and Joan Marie (Coale) Bailey. Born June 28, 1960.

550T. Beverly Sue Bailey (11)

Daughter of Samuel Mathew Bailey, Jr. (No. 350I) and Joan Marie (Coale) Bailey. Born June 12, 1962.

550U. Donna Lee Bailey (11)

Daughter of William Edward Bailey (No. 350J) and Patricia Ann (Blair) Bailey. Born October 26, 1959.

550V. William Edward Bailey, Jr. (11)

Son of William Edward Bailey (No. 350J) and Patricia Ann (Blair) Bailey. Born September 16, 1963.

550W. Jacqueline Bailey (11)

Daughter of William Edward Bailey (No. 350J) and Patricia Ann (Blair) Bailey. Born January 1, 1966.

550X. Bernard Anthony Bailey, Jr. (11)

Son of Bernard Anthony Bailey (No. 350K) and Judith Lee (Herbert). Born January 31, 1958.

551. John Kenelm Cheseldine (11)

Son of John William Cheseldine (No. 360) and Dorothy (Cullins) Cheseldine. Born

552. Jerry Wayne Cheseldine (11)

Son of John William Cheseldine (No. 360) and Dorothy (Cullins) Cheseldine. Born

553. Robert Lee Cheseldine, Jr. (11)

Son of Robert Lee Cheseldine (No. 361) and Lucille (Sterling) Cheseldine. Born

554. Dewberry Ann Cheseldine (11)

Daughter of Robert Lee Cheseldine (No. 361) and Lucille (Sterling) Cheseldine. Born

555. Steve Cheseldine (11)

Son of Robert Lee Cheseldine (No. 361) and Lucille (Sterling) Cheseldine. Born

556. Beth Cheseldine (11)

Daughter of Robert Lee Cheseldine (No. 361) and Lucille (Sterling) Cheseldine. Born

557 Ben Cheseldine (11)

Son of Robert Lee Cheseldine (No. 361) and Lucille (Sterling) Cheseldine. Born

557A. William Joseph Husemann, Jr. (11)

Son of William Joseph Husemann (No. 368E) and Ann Elizabeth (Downs) Husemann. Born April 29, 1947. Served in the US Army in 1966.

557B. Walter Daniel Husemann (11)

Son of William Joseph Husemann (No. 368E) and Ann Elizabeth (Downs) Husemann. Born January 24, 1952. Was a student at Ryken High School in 1966.

557C. Donald Allan Husemann (11)

Son of William Joseph Husemann (No. 368E) and Ann Elizabeth (Downs) Husemann. Born February 4, 1958.

557D. Charles Albert Husemann (11)

Son of Charles Ross Huseman (No. 368F) and Elizabeth Irene (Lacy) Husemann. Born March 27, 1944. Was employed by the Southern Maryland Electric Company in 1966.

557E. Charlene Ann Husemann (11)

Daughter of Charles Ross Husemann (No. 368F) and Elizabeth Irene (Lacy) Husemann. Born March 29, 1945. Was employed as a teacher's aid at Holy Angels School in 1966.

557F. Richard Benjamin Husemann (11)

Son of Charles Ross Husemann (No. 368F) and Elizabeth Irene (Lacy) Husemann. Born January 10, 1950. Was attending Chapticon High School in 1966.

557G. Michael Ross Husemann (11)

Son of Charles Ross Husemann (No. 368F) and Elizabeth Irene (Lacy) Husemann. Born January 10, 1950. Was attending Chapticon High School in 1966.

557H. Francis Joseph Husemann (11)

Son of Charles Ross Husemann (No. 368F) and Elizabeth Irene (Lacy) Husemann. Born July 23, 1957.

557I. Jeffrey Lynn Husemann (11)

Son of Charles Ross Husemann (No. 368F) and Elizabeth Irene (Lacy) Husemann. Born March 21, 1962.

557J. Karen Ann Husemann (11)

Daughter of Harry Benjamin Husemann (No. 368G) and Virginia (Clarke) Husemann. Born September 20, 1953.

557K. Harry Benjamin Husemann, Jr. (11)

Son of Harry Benjamin Husemann (No. 368G) and Virginia (Clarke) Husemann. Born November 11, 1958.

557L. James Milton Downs (11)

Son of Elizabeth Jane (Husemann) Downs (No. 368H) and James Milton Downs. Born September 26, 1948. Was a student at Chopticon High School in 1966.

557M. Sharon Elizabeth Downs (11)

Daughter of Elizabeth Jane (Husemann) Downs (No. 368H) and James Milton Downs. Born June 26, 1950. Was a student at Chopticon High School in 1966.

557N. Charles David Downs (11)

Son of Elizabeth Jane (Husemann) Downs (No. 368H) and James Milton Downs. Born February 6, 1960.

557O. Daniel Kemp Smith (11)

Son of Janie Louise (Beitzell) Smith (No. 368I) and Kemp Beyer Smith. Born April 30, 1942. Married Diane Lee (Storey) Smith. After completing his service as a navigator with grade of Lt. in the US Army Air Force in September, 1966, Danny accepted a position with the Univac Corp. They resided at 1023 Carson Street, Silver Spring, MD. Children:
590F.   I. Donna Lynn (12) B. March 30, 1965.

557P. Linda Louise Smith (11)

Daughter of Janie Louise (Beitzell) Smith (No. 368I) and Kemp Beyer Smith. Born September 18, 1944.

557Q. Melenia Allyn Smith (11)

Child of Janie Louise (Beitzell) Smith (No. 368I) and Kemp Beyer Smith. Born July 18, 1949.

557R. Christina Ellen Smith (11)

Daughter of Janie Louise (Beitzell) Smith (No.368I) and Kemp Beyer Smith. Born August 16, 1957.

557S. Charles Leo Zeleski (11)

Son of Elizabeth Hart (Beitzell) Zeleski (No. 368J) and Leo Francis Zeleski. Born June 17, 1948. Attended University of Cinn. in 1966.

557T. Carol Ann Zeleski (11)

Daughter of Elizabeth Hart (Beitzell) Zeleski (No. 368J) and Leo Francis Zeleski. Born January 2, 1950.

557U. Susan Kathleen Mayer (11)

Daughter of Rose Mary "Marie" (Beitzell) Mayer (No. 368K) and Raymond Ellis Mayer, Jr. Born February 12, 1953.

557V. Robert Craig Mayer (11)

Son of Rose Mary "Marie" (Beitzell) Jusino (No. 368K) and Raymond Ellis Mayer, Jr. Born May 23, 1961.

557W. Joseph Jusino (11)

Son of Mary Jeanne (Beitzell) Jusino (No. 368L) and Gilberto R. Jusino. Born December 2, 1950.

557X. David Jusino (11)

Son of Mary Jeanne (Beitzell) Jusino (No. 368L) and Gilberto R. Jusino. Born August 17, 1952.

557Y. Bertito Jusino (11)

Son of Mary Jeanne (Beitzell) Jusino (No. 368L) and Gilberto R. Jusino. Born November 15, 1953.

557Z. John Jusino (11)

Son of Mary Jeanne (Beitzell) Jusino (No. 368L) and Gilberto R. Jusino. Born February 11, 1956.

558. Mark Jusino (11)

Son of Mary Jeanne (Beitzell) Jusino (No. 368L) and Gilberto R. Jusino. Born October 14, 1962.

558A. Raymond Harry Beitzell, Jr. (11)

Son of Raymond Harry Beitzell (No. 368M) and Barbara (Hubbard) Beitzell. Born January 20, 1955.

558B. Julia Ann Beitzell (11)

Daughter of Raymond Harry Beitzell (No. 368M) and Barbara (Hubbard) Beitzell. Born January 29, 1956.

558C. Joseph Beitzell (11)

Son of Raymond Harry Beitzell (No. 368M) and Barbara (Hubbard) Beitzell. Born June 29, 1957.

558D. Paul Beitzell (11)

Son of Raymond Harry Beitzell (No. 368M) and Barbara (Hubbard) Beitzell. Born July 17, 1959.

558E. Madeline Patricia Beitzell (11)

Daughter of Raymond Harry Beitzell (No. 368M) and Barbara (Hubbard) Beitzell. Born May 12, 1961.

558F. Mary Constance Beitzell (11)

Daughter of Raymond Harry Beitzell (No. 368M) and Barbara (Hubbard) Beitzell. Born February 4, 1963.

558G. John Beitzell (11)

Son of Raymond Harry Beitzell (No. 368M) and Barbara (Hubbard) Beitzell. Born September 23, 1964.

558H. Andrew Beitzell (11)

Son of Raymond Harry Beitzell (No. 368M) and Barbara (Hubbard) Beitzell. Born July 21, 1966.

558I. Brenda Lee Beitzell (11)

Daughter of James Bernard Beitzell (No. 368O) and Rose Elva (Brown) Beitzell. Born March 9, 1958.

558J. James Bernard Beitzell, Jr. (11)

Son of James Bernard Beitzell (No. 368O) and Rose Elva (Brown) Beitzell. Born August 21, 1959.

558K. Mark Gerard Beitzell (11)

Son of James Bernard Beitzell (No. 368O) and Rose Elva (Brown) Beitzell. Born September 18, 1963.

558L. Stephen Eric Beitzell (11)

Son of James Bernard Beitzell (No. 368O) and Rose Elva (Brown) Beitzell. Born _____. Married Janice Marie (Keister) Beitzell. Janice was a native of College Park, MD, a graduate of Laurel High School and attended the University of Maryland. She was first married to Meredith Baugher; second to Stephen Eric Beitzell. Janice died September 24, 1998. Funeral mass at St. Augustine Catholic Church, Elkridge, MD. Buried: Meadowridge Memorial Park. She left a son from her first marriage, Daniel Baugher. Children - Second Marriage:
590G.   I. Samantha Rose (12) B. February, 1998.

558M. Frances Ann Guinard (11)

Daughter of Mary Ann "Anna" (Beitzell) Guinard (No. 368P) and Norman W. Guinard. Born September 28, 1954.

558N. Barbara Ellen Guinard (11)

Daughter of Mary Ann "Anna" (Beitzell) Guinard (No. 368P) and Norman W. Guinard. Born April 10, 1956.

558O. William Joseph Guinard (11)

Son of Mary Ann "Anna" (Beitzell) Guinard (No. 368P) and Norman W. Guinard. Born May 19, 1958.

558P. Andrew Joseph Beitzell (11)

Son of Andrew Walter Beitzell (No. 368Q) and Lois Joanne (Alson) Beitzell. Born July 2, 1958.

558Q. Douglas Wayne Beitzell (11)

Son of Andrew Walter Beitzell (No. 368Q) and Lois Joanne (Alson) Beitzell. Born May 11, 1962.

558R. Debra Marie Beitzell (11)

Daughter of William Benjamin Beitzell (No. 368S) and Regina Gail (McFadden) Beitzell. Born January 22, 1958.

558S. Teresa Lynn Beitzell (11)

Daughter of William Benjamin Beitzell (No. 368S) and Regina Gail (McFadden) Beitzell. Born December 28, 1958.

558T. William Benjamin Beitzell, Jr. (11)

Son of William Benjamin Beitzell (No. 368S) and Regina Gail (McFadden) Beitzell. Born December 25, 1960.

558U. Laura Jean Beitzell (11)

Daughter of William Benjamin Beitzell (No. 368S) and Regina Gail (McFadden) Beitzell. Born May 3, 1963.

558V. Christopher Allen Beitzell (11)

Son of William Benjamin Beitzell (No. 368S) and Regina Gail (McFadden) Beitzell. Born May 29, 1965.

558W. John Jay Quinnette (11)

Son of Jean Isabel (Beitzell) Quinnette (No. 368U) and Richard R. Quinnette. Born June 4, 1962. John graduated from Yorktown High School in Arlington, VA, and attended Northern Virginia Community College before becoming a television news cameraman. He has been employed in the DC bureau of CNN since 1985. His assignments have included the White House, Pentagon, State Department, Capitol Hill and many other government agencies, and he accompanied President Reagan on his first trip to the then U.S.S.R.

John married Tara Merkel, born May 31, 1966 in Chicago, IL, on September 18, 1999 at St. Francis Xavier Church on Newtown Neck (where his grandfather and all his family worshipped when Edwin Warfield Beitzell, Sr. was a boy and which inspired his first historical research and writing). Tara is the daughter of Charles A. Merkel (his father was from family named Klose but took his adopted father's name) and Wilma C. (Kazin) Merkel. Tara graduated from Indiana University with a BA in Journalism, worked for several years for CNN, and is currently the Director of Human Resources for Pathnet, a telecommunications company based in Washington.

John and Tara reside in Arlington, VA.

558X. Kathryn Marya Quinnette (11) Laslie

Daughter of Jean Isabel (Beitzell) Quinnette (No. 368U) and Richard R. Quinnette. Born June 22, 1963. Kate graduated from Virginia Commonwealth University/Medical College of Virginia with a degree in Occupational Therapy, worked for a year at Eureka General Hospital in CA before returning to her native Virginia. She then worked as an OT in several northern Virginia hospitals, rehabing a retired Supreme Court Justice among many others, before joining the Fairfax County School System in 1997 to work with disabled children. On September 27, 1997, she married Charles Brent Laslie, born June

3, 1957, son of Charles B. Laslie and Audrey Jane (Lentz) Laslie. Charlie earned his Masters in Social Work from Virginia Commonwealth University and is an administrator for Family Advocacy Services (Therapeutic Foster Care for Teenagers).

Kate, Charlie and Lauryn live in Woodridge, VA.

590H.   I. Lauryn Elisabeth (12) B. October 1, 1999.

558Y. Joseph Richard Quinnette (11)

Son of Jean Isabel (Beitzell) Quinnette (No. 368U) and Richard R. Quinnette. Born November 15, 1964. Joe graduated from Yorktown High School in Arlington, VA and immediately began work in the heating and air conditioning field with Combustioneer and later Capital Boiler Works. He joined the staff at the Pentagon in 1998 where he is a maintenance mechanic.

Joe married Erin Margaret McClanahan, born April 12, 1962, on April 3, 1993, in St. Mary's County, where they lived for a few years before relocating to Fairfax, VA. Erin is the daughter of Demmy Davis McClanahan and Margaret Ann (Nunn) McClanahan. Erin was a loan researcher for Sallie Mae until she decided to stay at home with their children in 1998. Children:

590I.   I. Kathryn Nicole (12) B. March 20, 1995.

590J.   II. Richard Raymond (12) B. October 1, 1997.

558Z. Charles Daley Quinnette (11)

Son of Jean Isabel (Beitzell) Quinnette (No. 368U) and Richard R. Quinnette. Born April 10, 1966. Charlie graduated from Elon College in North Carolina with a degree in Business and after several years with John Hancock Insurance, he is now in the mortgage and refinancing field with Continental Mortgage & Investment Corporation in Arlington, VA.

Charlie married Melinda Katherine Stewart, born July 6, 1966, on May 13, 1989, in Richmond, VA. Mindy, the daughter of Henry and Katherine Stewart is a graduate of the University of Richmond, and works at Fairfax Hospital where she is a registrar for the Women's and Children's Center. Children:

590K.   I. Katherine Elise (12) B. October 26, 1989.

590L.   II. Emma Nicole (12) Born August 20, 1992.

558Z1. Ralph John Basile (11)

Son of Alice Regina (Owens) Basile (No. 376) and Alfonso Mario Basile. Born July 25, 1950 in Georgetown University Hospital, Washington, DC. Attended Bishop O'Connell High School, Virginia Tech University and George Mason University Law School. Ralph is a principal in "Basile, Baumann, Prost and Associates, Inc." Public/Private Development Advisors in Annapolis, MD.

On September 8, 1973 he married Deborah Gail Painter at Virginia Tech Chapel at Blacksburg, VA. They live in Annapolis, MD. Children:

    591A.   I. Courtenay Allyson (12) B. March 3, 1981.
    591B.   II. Todd Christopher (12) B. May 20, 1984.

558Z2. Paul Anthony Basile (11)

Son of Alice Regina (Owens) Basile (No. 376) and Alfonso Mario Basile. Born October 21, 1952 in Georgetown University Hospital, Washington, DC. Attended Bishop O'Connell High School, Mount St. Mary's College, Emmittsburg, MD. Paul is the Regional Sales Manager of Diamond Brands, Inc.

On October 10, 1982 he married Jill Ann Banghardt at St. Bonaventure Church, Patterson, NJ. They live in Herndon, VA. Children:

    591C.   I. Joseph Alfonso (12) B. July 8, 1982.
    591D.   II. David Paul (12) B. July 8, 1982.

558Z3. John Joseph Basile (11)

Son of Alice Regina (Owens) Basile (No. 376) and Alfonso Mario Basile. Born August 26, 1954 in Georgetown University Hospital, Washington, DC. Attended Bishop O'Connell High School, University of Virginia College, Charlottesville, VA, Medical College of Virginia, Richmond, VA, Bowman Gray Baptist Hospital College, Winston-Salem, NC. Dr. John Joseph Basile was certified by the American Board of Urology in February, 1988.

On March 27, 1982 he married Nedra Rae Linder at the Richmond Country Club in a Catholic and Jewish ceremony. They reside in Potomac, MD. Children:

591E.   I. Katherine Linder (12) B. December 18, 1983.
591F.   II. Joshua John (12) B. September 3, 1985.

558Z4. Rose Ellen Hewitt (11)

Daughter of Helen Cecelia (Gibson) Hewitt (No. 391) and William Benjamin Hewitt, Sr. Born November 1, 1953.

558Z5. William Benjamin Hewit, Jr. (11)

Son of Helen Cecelia (Gibson) Hewitt (No. 391) and William Benjamin Hewitt, Sr. Born November 9, 1955.

558Z6. Barton Anthony Hewitt (11)

Son of Helen Cecelia (Gibson) Hewitt (No. 391) and William Benjamin Hewitt, Sr. Born August 23, 1958.

558Z7. Michael Patrick Hewitt (11)

Son of Helen Cecelia (Gibson) Hewitt (No. 391) and William Benjamin Hewitt, Sr. Born July 30, 1960.

558Z8. Laurie Ann Hewitt (11)

Daughter of Helen Cecelia (Gibson) Hewitt (No. 391) and William Benjamin Hewitt, Sr. Born July 23, 1961.

558Z9. Mark Christopher Hewitt (11)

Son of Helen Cecelia (Gibson) Hewitt (No. 391) and William Benjamin Hewitt, Sr. Born February 8, 1963.

558Z10. Mary Beth Hewitt (11)

Daughter of Helen Cecelia (Gibson) Hewitt (No. 391) and William Benjamin Hewitt, Sr. Born January 19, 1966.

558Z11. Joanne Patricia Hewitt (11)

Daughter of Helen Cecelia (Gibson) Hewitt (No. 391) and William Benjamin Hewitt, Sr. Born March 3, 1967.

558Z12. Donald Allen Hewitt (11)

Son of Helen Cecelia (Gibson) Hewitt (No. 391) and William Benjamin Hewitt, Sr. Born September 5, 1971.

558Z13. Ruene Marie Drew (11)

Daughter of Ruene Marcella (Norris) Drew Russell (No. 400) and Charles Preston Drew. Born April 26, 1938.

558Z14. Dolores Juanita Drew (11)

Daughter of Ruene Marcella (Norris) Drew Russell (No. 400) and Charles Preston Drew. Born December 26, 1940.

558Z15. James Francis Lawrence (11)

Son of Francis De Sales Lawrence (No. 401) and Mary Elizabeth (Bailey) Lawrence. Born September 14, 1936.

558Z16. Rose Francis Lawrence (11)

Daughter of Francis De Sales Lawrence (No. 401) and Mary Elizabeth (Bailey) Lawrence. Born August 20, 1938.

558Z17. Charles Emory Lawrence (11)

Son of Francis De Sales Lawrence (No. 401) and Mary Elizabeth (Bailey) Lawrence. Born October 14, 1940.

558Z18. William De Sales Lawrence (11)

Son of Francis De Sales Lawrence (No. 401) and Mary Elizabeth (Bailey) Lawrence. Born March 6, 1944.

558Z19. George Eliot Lawrence (11)

Son of Francis De Sales Lawrence (No. 401) and Mary Elizabeth (Bailey) Lawrence. Born October 26, 1945.

558Z20. Barbara Ann Lawrence (11)

Daughter of Francis De Sales Lawrence (No. 401) and Mary Elizabeth (Bailey) Lawrence. Born September 12, 1947.

558Z21. Grace Ann Downs (11)

Daughter of Margaret Rose (Lawrence) Downs (No. 403) and Andrew Wallace Downs. Born July 5, 1938.

558Z22. Melanie Andrea Downs (11)

Daughter of Margaret Rose (Lawrence) Downs (No. 403) and Andrew Wallace Downs. Born April 18, 1943.

558Z23. Joseph Reid Warder (11)

Son of Frances Ruth (Lawrence) Warder Quinn (No. 404) and Joseph Ernest Warder. Born May, 1939.

558Z24. Eugenia Seline Warder (11)

Daughter of Frances Ruth (Lawrence) Warder Quinn (No. 404) and Joseph Ernest Warder. Born December, 1941.

558Z25. William Lawrence Thompson (11)

Son of Mary Emily (Lawrence) Thompson (No. 405) and William Bishop Thompson. Born October, 1941.

558Z26. Steven Lawrence Fissell (11)

Son of Barbara Ellen (Lawrence) Fissell (No. 406) and Walter Fissell. Born August, 1947.

558Z27. Linda Ann Bush (11)

Daughter of Dorothy Irma (Biggs) Bush (No. 414) and Darrell Bush. Born May 2, 1935.

558Z28. Sandra Wible (11)

Daughter of Allan Wible (No. 420) and Rita (Johnson) Wible. Born August, 1945.

558Z29. Garry Wible (11)

Son of Allan Wible (No. 420) and Rita (Johnson) Wible. Born March 15, 1947.

559. James Stephen Mellon, Jr. (11)

Son of James Stephen Mellon (No. 453) and _____ Born about 1974.

560. Daniel Van Horn (11)

Son of Judith Lee (Cheseldine) Van Horn (No. 455) and _____ Van Horn. Born

560A. Everett Alphonse Cheseldine, III (11)

Son of Everett Alphonse Cheseldine, Jr. (No. 296) and Wendy Marie (Mark) Cheseldine. Born September 5, 1967.

560B. Wendy Margaret Cheseldine (11)

Daughter of Everett Alphonse Cheseldine, Jr. (No. 296) and Wendy Marie (Mark) Cheseldine. Born January 1, 1971.

560C. Terry Darlene Redmond (11) Bast

Daughter of Margaret Patricia (Cryer) Redmond Spence (No. 475) and Dean Redmond. Born September 4, 1950 in Washington,

DC. Married Paul S. Bast in 1978, a widower with five children. All five children are married, and Terry and Paul have five granddaughters. Terry and Paul own and run their own small business. Terry's hobbies are gardening, fishing, boating, arts and crafts, and home-making. No children born of this marriage.

560D. Tommye Dawn Spence (11)

Daughter of Margaret Patricia (Cryer) Redmond Spence (No. 475) and Thomas Spence. Born August 3, 1952. Retired from the Navy. Tommye is an attorney and lives in Mountainview, CA.

560E. Patricia Lynn Spence (11) Miles, Funge

Daughter of Margaret Patricia (Cryer) Redmond Spence (No. 475) and Thomas Spence. Born March 25, 1957. Married Charles C. Miles, July 19, 1981. Divorced. Married in 1998, Michael Funge, an Irish immigrant. Lives in Sanford, FL. Children - First Marriage:
591G.   I. Amanda Lynn (12) B. May 3, 1979.
591H.   II. Jocelyn Elizabeth (12) B. October 11, 1984.

560F. Cari Leigh Spence (11) Carter

Daughter of Margaret Patricia (Cryer) Redmond Spence (No. 475) and Thomas Spence. Born April 28, 1960. Married Charles "Les" Carter, May 21, 1977. Lives in Pearland, TX. Children:
591I.   I. Charles Alexander (12) B. January 19, 1989
591J.   II. Mark Andrew (12) B. June 18, 1991.

560G. Andrew Duncan Spence (11)

Son of Margaret Patricia (Cryer) Redmond Spence (No. 475) and Thomas Spence. Born December 2, 1971, died October 9, 1989.

560H. Noella Jean Tartaglino Cipriano (11)

Daughter of Thomas Irvin Yates, Jr. (No. 476) and _____. Born June 15, 1956. Married (1) Hans Peter Proske August 24, 1974. Divorced. Married Steven Charles Simone November 6, 1982. No children.

Children: - First Marriage
591K.   I. Joseph Michael (12) B. June 6, 1975.
591K1.   II. Lisamarie (12) B. June 4, 1979. D. January 7,
             1980.

560I. Thomas Irvin Yates, III (11)

Son of Thomas Irvin Yates, Jr. (No. 476) and Ava Nell
(Noble) Yates. Born November 17, 1957, Little Rock Baptist
Hospital, Little Rock, AR. Married Lauren Rice, born September 24,
1955, on August 31, 1980. They had a park wedding in Montgomery,
AL. Children:
591L.   I. Devin Elisabeth (12) B. February 11, 1984.
591M.   II. Logan Thomas (12) B. April 18, 1989.

560J. Michael Leonard Yates (11)

Son of Thomas Irvin Yates, Jr. (No. 476) and Ava Nell
(Noble) Yates. Born October 27, 1960, Mildenhall Air Force Base,
Mildenhall, England. Married Joellyn Brendle, born December 25,
1959, September 18, 1982. They were married in Frazier United
Methodist Church, Montgomery, AL. Children:
591N.   I. Brantley Dawn (12) B. September 10, 1985.
591O.   II. Michael Carson (12) B. October 26, 1988.

560K. John Warren Yates (11)

Son of Thomas Irvin Yates, Jr. (No. 476) and Ava Nell
(Noble) Yates. Born March 11, 1962, Mildenhall Air Force Base,
Mildenhall, England. Married (1) Terri Hudgens for 1 1/2 years.
Divorced. Children:
591P.   I. John Warren (12) B. August 13, 1989.
Married (2) Scarlett Lanier Hibbard, born July 1, 1963, who
has two sons from her first marriage, John Hibbard, Jr. and Tylor
Hibbard, on December 3, 1993. They were married in a wedding
chapel in Gatlinburg, TN. Reside in Wallsboro, AL. Children:
591Q.   II. Emily Elizabeth (12) B. December 23, 1994.

560L. Pamela Ann Yates (11)

Daughter of Thomas Irvin Yates, Jr. (No. 476) and Ava Nell (Noble) Yates. Born .June 21, 1963, Amarillo Air Force Base, Amarillo, TX. Died January 16, 1964.

560M. Carrie Lynn Kimble (11) Parvis

Daughter of Carol Ann (Yates) Kimble (No. 477) and Galen Kimble. Born March 27, 1965. Married Raymond Keith Parvis. Children:
591R.   I. Jennifer Rae (12) B. December 6, 1987.
591S.   II. Joshua Raymond (12) B. September 17, 1990.

560N. Catherine Marie Kimble (11) Biceuskis

Daughter of Carol Ann (Yates) Kimble (No. 477) and Galen Kimble. Born March 3, 1967. Married Andris Janis Biceuskis, March 18, 1988. Children:
591T.   I. Ashleigh Elizabethe' (12) B. September 7, 1989.
591U.   II. Megan Anna (12) B. May 29, 1992.

560O. Kevin Robert Kimble (11)

Son of Carol Ann (Yates) Kimble (No. 477) and Galen Kimble. Born July 25, 1969. Married Rebecca Kent Bush, August 28, 1993. Children:
591V.   I. Jacob Robert (12) B. January 3, 1995.
591W.   II. Matthew Kent (12) B. March 14, 1997.

560P. Christine Kaye Willie (11)

Daughter of Sandra Kaye (Yates) Willie (No. 479) and George Willis Willie. Born October 13, 1959. Married February 16, 1978.
591W1   I. Kevin (12) B. 1985.
591W2.   II. Ashley (12) B. 1991.

560Q. Kathleen Kaye Willie (11)

Daughter of Sandra Kaye (Yates) Willie (No. 479) and George Willis Willie. Born April 18, 1962. Married
591W3.   I. Megan (12) B.

560R. George Spencer Willie (11)

Son of Sandra Kaye (Yates) Willie (No. 479) and George Willis Willie. Born July 6, 1968. Married Christie Rivers June 6, 1998. George and Christie live in Columbia, MD.

560S. Robert Darrin Grant (11)

Son of Bonnie Jean (Yates) Grant Kershaw (No. 480) and Robert L. Grant. Born December 11, 1964 in Takoma Park, MD.

560T. Lori Paige Grant (11) Emmert

Daughter of Bonnie Jean (Yates) Grant Kershaw (No. 480) and Robert L. Grant. Born June 24, 1968, in Takoma Park, MD. Married James Emmert, November, 1987. Lori & Jimmy live in Shadyside, MD. Children:
591X.   I. James David, Jr. (12) B. September 22, 1994
            D. September 26, 1994.
591Y.   II. daughter

560U. Victor Scott Kershaw (11)

Son of Bonnie Jean (Yates) Grant Kershaw (No. 480) and A. Victor Kershaw. Born February 19, 1977 in Takoma Park, MD. Lives in Islamorada, FL.

560V. Timothy Augustus Yates (11)

Son of Ralph Everett Yates (No. 481) and Elizabeth (Yanchulis) Yates. Born November 10, 1974.

560W. Tyler Charles Yates (11)

Son of Ralph Everett Yates (No. 481) and Elizabeth (Yanchulis) Yates. Born December 26, 1977, died December 21, 1991.

560X. Kelly Ann Renner (11) Stilwell

Daughter of Beverly Jeanne (Baggett) Renner Wild (No. 482) and James Daniel Renner. Born March 7, 1960 in Providence Hospital, Washington, DC.

Married Timothy David Stilwell on October 10, 1992 at St. Edward's Catholic Church, Bowie, MD. Tim was born September 6, 1958 in Wilmington, DE, the son of John and Dorothy Stilwell of LaPlata, MD.

Tim is in the merchant services business and Kelly is a free lance writer and stay at home Mom.

Kelly and Tim are very active in the Hunt Valley Church. Tim is a musician, and he sings and plays in the music group. Kelly teaches Sunday School and both of them attend Bible study classes. Their oldest daughter, Taylor, loves Sunday School.

Kelly, Tim, Taylor and Jessica currently reside in Hunt Valley, MD, but have selected a piece of property in Monkton, MD to have their dream home built in a few years. Children:

592.   I. Taylor Jeanne (12) B. September 11, 1996.
592A.   II. Jessica Lauryn (12) B. July 28, 1999

560Y. James Darryl Renner (11)

Son of Beverly Jeanne (Baggett) Renner Wild (No. 482) and James Daniel Renner. Born October 12, 1965 in Washington, DC. Darryl graduated from Bowie High School and has worked for Jones Communications, now Comcast, for 9 years as a Project Coordinator, working with contractors in placing cable lines in new developments.

Darryl has played drums for over 25 years and occasionally plays at clubs or parties. He loves golf and softball. Darryl resides in Lothian, MD and is unmarried.

560Z. Mark David Baggett (11)

Son of Larry Eugene Baggett (No. 483) and Alice (Davies) Baggett. Born March 27, 1968 in Camp Springs, MD. Mark and his mother went to Mannheim, Germany to be with his father shortly afterward. Mark graduated from La Plata High School in 1986, and he went into the Army the same year. While stationed at Ft. Gordon, GA, he met Heather Clayton the daughter of Frank and Winifred Clayton from Cincinnati, OH. Mark and Heather were married on June 20, 1992. Mark graduated from Augusta College. Heather, born April 22, 1967, graduated from Ohio State University and was a school teacher before the children were born. Mark is the LAN Administrator at the Nutrasweet factory in Georgia, and he and Heather live in Evans, GA. Children:

592B.   I. Luke Chandler (12) B. April 5, 1996.
592C.   II. Danielle Nicole (12) B. October 1, 1998.

560Z1. Joyce Lynn Baggett (11) Embrey

Daughter of Larry Eugene Baggett (No. 483) and Alice (Davies) Baggett. Born November 1, 1972, in La Plata, MD. Joyce graduated from La Plata High School, Charles County Community College and Salisbury State University. Joyce married Clark Morgan Embrey, born December 23, 1967, on September 28, 1996 in La Plata, MD. Joyce manages the Limited II in St. Charles Town Center. Clark is a firefighter with the DC Fire Department. Joyce and Clark live in St. Mary's County, MD.

592D.   I. Matthew Clark (12) B. October 16, 1999.

560Z2. Richard Alan Baggett (11)

Son of Larry Eugene Baggett (No. 483) and Alice (Davies) Baggett. Born November 12, 1973 in La Plata, MD. Married Dawn Marie Seidman/Adams Baggett, born October 25, 1976 in La Plata, MD, on October 28, 1995. Richard owns a franchise with Colors on Parade. Richard and Dawn have recently purchased their first home and will be moving before Thanksgiving, 1999. Children:

592E.   I. Burton Alan (12) B. June 19, 1998.

560Z3. Brian Douglas Richard (11)

Son of Fred Douglas Richard (No. 484) and Joan (Davies) Richard. Born October 31, 1968 in La Plata, MD. Brian grew up in St. Charles, Waldorf, MD. Married Terri Curtin. Divorced. Brian currently lives in Oklahoma. Children:

592F.   I. Kayla Marie (12) B. September 13, 1992.

560Z4. Robin Renee Richard (11) Curtis

Daughter of Fred Douglas Richard (No. 484) and Joan (Davies) Richard. Born May 25, 1974 in La Plata, MD. Robin grew up in St. Charles, Waldorf, MD.

Married Joseph Kevin Curtis October 25, 1997 in LaPlata, MD. Kevin and Robin live in Silver Spring, MD.

560Z5. Gerald Thomas Richard Dove (11)

Son of Gerald Thomas Richard (No. 485) and Francine (Malakatis) Richard Dove. Born _____. Jay was adopted by his stepfather and is now Dove. Jay lives in New Orleans, LA.

560Z6. Jason Keith Richard Dove (11)

Son of Gerald Thomas Richard (No. 485) and Francine (Malakatis) Richard Dove. Born _____. Jason was also adopted by his stepfather and is now Dove. Jason is in the military.

560Z7. Heather Rene Richard (11) Khoury

Daughter of Gerald Thomas Richard (No. 485) and Susan (Hess) Cardwell Richard. Born January 5, 1978. Married Issa N. Khoury, born January 16, 1968 in Upper Marlboro, MD. Heather and Issa live in Lanham, MD. Children:

592G.   I. Travis James (12) B. February 10, 1998.
592G1.   II. Hayley Nicole (12) B. June 24, 1999.

560Z8. Dennis Craig Simpson, Sr. (11)

Son of John "Jack" Francis Simpson, Jr. (No. 486D) and Carol Ann (Hutchison) Simpson. Born November 17, 1966. Married Susan Marie (Bowling) Simpson. Children:

592H. I. Dennis Craig, Jr. (12) B. January 10, 1990.
592I. II. Cody Gaston (12) B. December 30, 1993.

560Z9. Christina Jean Simpson (11)

Daughter of John "Jack" Francis Simpson, Jr. (No. 486D) and Carol Ann (Hutchison) Simpson. Born May 20, 1968. Children:

592J. I. Kevin Andrew Catterton (12) B. April 3, 1993.

560Z10. Deborah Lynn Simpson (11)

Daughter of Donald Alan Simpson (No. 486E) and Patricia Marie (McCann) Simpson. Born June 11, 1971. Children:

592K. I. Ryan Marquess Simpson (12) B. July 1, 1991.

560Z11. Jason Daniel Simpson (11)

Son of Donald Alan Simpson (No. 486E) and Patricia Marie (McCann) Simpson. Born September 16, 1973.

560Z12. Michael Kevin Simpson, Jr. (11)

Son of Michael Kevin Simpson (No. 486H) and Lisa Ann (Merry) Simpson. Born March 29, 1987.

560Z13. Brandon Kurtis Simpson (11)

Son of Michael Kevin Simpson (No. 486H) and Lisa Ann (Merry) Simpson. Born March 5, 1991.

560Z14. Kathleen Merry Simpson (11)

Daughter of Michael Kevin Simpson (No. 486H) and Lisa Ann (Merry) Simpson. Born May 25, 1992.

560Z15. Mark Robert Guibbini (11)

Son of Barbara Sue (Jones) Guibbini Phillips (No. 496) and Robert Guibbini. Born February 11, 1966. Married Christine Agens Linder on October 23, 1993. Children:

592K1.   I. Kaitlyn Christine (12) B. March 27, 1997.

560Z16. Kristin Elizabeth Guibbini (11) Buckley

Daughter of Barbara Sue (Jones) Guibbini Phillips (No. 496) and Robert Guibbini. Born February 16, 1968. Married William L. Buckley on August 3, 1985. Divorced. Children:

592K2.   I. Megan Rebecca Elizabeth (12) B. June 16, 1985.
592K3.   II. Kendra Elizabeth Irene (12) B.May 30, 1987.
592K4.   III. Lauren Barbara Elizabeth (12) B. June 30, 1991.

560Z17. Gretchen Elizabeth Monaco (11)

Daughter of Catherine Elizabeth (Jones) (No. 497) and William Monaco. Born February 26, 1973.

560Z18. Regina Maureen Monaco (11)

Daughter of Catherine Elizabeth (Jones) (No. 497) and William Monaco. Born March 2, 1975.

561. Charles Frederick Cheseldine (11)

Son of Bertrand Frederick Cheseldine (No. 501) and Marian (Smith) Cheseldine. Born August 25, 1960, adopted February, 1966 by Curtis J. Will, Atlantic, Iowa, who married Marian Smith Cheseldine. Charles died November 27, 1979.

562. Joseph Frederick Cheseldine (11)

Son of Bertrand Frederick Cheseldine (No. 501) and Agnes Bonnette "Bonnie" (Cox) Cheseldine. Born December 27, 1967.

563. Saundra Bonnette Cheseldine (11)

Daughter of Bertrand Frederick Cheseldine (No. 501) and Agnes Bonnette "Bonnie" (Cox) Cheseldine. Born July 3, 1969.

564. William Pierce Bragg, Jr. (11)

Son of Mary Thomas (Cheseldine) Bragg Robbins (No. 502) and William Pierce Bragg. Born October 28, 1957.

565. Allan James Bragg (11)

Son of Mary Thomas (Cheseldine) Bragg Robbins (No. 502) and William Pierce Bargg. Born June 27, 1959.

566. Christi Sue Robbins (11)

Daughter of Mary Thomas (Cheseldine) Bragg Robbins (No. 502) and Bertand B. Robbins. Born August 20, 1964.

567. Michael E. Bowman (11)

Son of Lois Ann (Savage) Bowman (No. 503) and Jeffrey Bowman. Born November 14, 1972.

568. Brian M. Bowman (11)

Son of Lois Ann (Savage) Bowman (No. 503) and Jeffrey Bowman. Born October 30, 1977.

569. Megan Ann Savage (11)

Daughter of Daniel C. Savage (No. 504) and Marsha Gay (Ross) Savage. Born June 5, 1980.

570. Jason Daniel Savage (11)

Son of Daniel C. Savage (No. 504) and Marsha Gay (Ross) Savage. Born June 5, 1980.

571. John William Cheseldine, Jr. (11)

Son of John William Cheseldine (No. 506) and Patricia Ann (Irby) Cheseldine. Born August 3, 1962.

572. Jeffrey Scott Cheseldine (11)

Son of John William Cheseldine (No. 506) and Patricia Ann (Irby) Cheseldine. Born

573. Joseph Gary Cheseldine (11)

Son of John William Cheseldine (No. 506) and Patricia Ann (Irby) Cheseldine. Born October 1, 1964.

574. Donna Lee Anderson (11) Gardner

Daughter of Mary Agnes Henderson (Cheseldine) Anderson (No. 507) and Jenning William Anderson. Born October 23, 1964 at Leonardtown, MD. Married October 11, 1997, Tom Gardner.

575. Richard Dale Anderson (11)

Son of Mary Agnes Henderson (Cheseldine) Anderson (No. 507) and Jenning William Anderson. Born January 26, 1967 at Leonardtown, MD. Married August 25, 1990, Michelle Rendina.

576. Denise Elizabeth Anderson (11) Shymansky

Daughter of Mary Agnes Henderson (Cheseldine) Anderson (No. 507) and Jenning William Anderson. Born October 20, 1969 at Leonardtown, MD. Married   Shymansky. Divorced.

577. Julie Gwenette Anderson (11)

Daughter of Mary Agnes Henderson (Cheseldine) Anderson (No. 507) and Jenning William Anderson. Born June 13, 1976.

578. Heather Lynn Davis (11)

Daughter of Rose Marie (Cheseldine) Anderson (No. 508) and Charles Daniel Davis, Jr. Born October 7, 1973.

578A. Daniel Patrick Branson (11)

Son of Charlotte Rebecca (Gibson) Branson (No. 518) and Ernest Daniel Branson. Born May 6, 1952.

578B. David Lawrence Branson (11)

Son of Charlotte Rebecca (Gibson) Branson (No. 518) and Ernest Daniel Branson. Born March 19, 1954. He was an Army officer. Died September 1, 1982.

578C. Dorian Lee Branson (11)

Child of Charlotte Rebecca (Gibson) Branson (No. 518) and Ernest Daniel Branson. Born February 15, 1956.

578D. Sharon Ann Branson (11)

Daughter of Charlotte Rebecca (Gibson) Branson (No. 518) and Ernest Daniel Branson. Born October 18, 1957.

578E. Stephen Perry Branson (11)

Son of Charlotte Rebecca (Gibson) Branson (No. 518) and Ernest Daniel Branson. Born October 18, 1960.

578F. Raquel Marie Branson (11)

Daughter of Charlotte Rebecca (Gibson) Branson (No. 518) and Ernest Daniel Branson. Born March 29, 1969.

579. Scott Mattingly (11)

Son of Alton Francis Mattingly (No. 534) and Margaret (Fowler) Mattingly. Born March 5, 1965. Married (1) Karie Scott and (2) Vickie Carter.
Children – First Marriage:
592L.   I. Andy (12) B.
Children – Second Marriage
592M.   II. Jessica (12) B. June 2, 1997.

580. Sommer Ann Stanley Glenn (11)

Daughter of Linda Diane (Cheseldine) Stanley (No. 536 and Gary Stanley. Born July 22, 1980. Sommer was adopted by her mothers second husband, Timothy Glenn from Temple Hills, MD.

580A. boy Cheseldine (11)

Son of Brenda (Cheseldine)   (No. 539) and
     . Born

580B. girl Cheseldine (11)

Daughter of Brenda (Cheseldine)   (No. 539)
and   . Born

580C. boy Cheseldine (11)

Son of Lynn (Cheseldine)   (No. 540) and

     . Born

581. Kathleen Amanda Cheseldine (11)

Daughter of Joseph Richard Cheseldine, III (No. 541) and Susan Elizabeth (Trexler) Cheseldine. Born July 15, 1993 in Clinton, MD.

582. Sean Patrick Cavey (11)

Son of Bridget Marie (Cheseldine) Cavey (No. 542) and Keith Daryl Cavey. Born September 6, 1994 in Annapolis, MD.

583. Robert Jerome Hartman V (11)

Son of Katie Ann (Cheseldine) Hartman Turner (No. 543) and Robert Jerome Hartman, IV. Born September 8, 1988 in Fort Rucker, Al.

583A1. William Joseph Turner (11)

Son of Katie Ann (Cheseldine) Hartman Turner (No. 543) and Herman Michael Turner. Born October 5, 1998.

583A2. Edmund Anthony Buswell (11)

Son of Joyce Marie (Sesso) Buswell (No. 544) and William Edmund Buswell. Born in Washington, DC on June 12, 1957 at Providence Hospital. Edmund attended Buckingham Elementary, Bowie, MD and Arundel Senior High in Gambrills, MD where he played on the varsity football team as center and graduated in 1975.

Married Dayna Lindauere of Rockville, MD, born July 28, 1964, on October 28, 1989. They were married at St. Elizabeth Seton Church in Crofton, MD. Dayna is the daughter of Gene Woods Lindauere of Pittsburgh, PA and Elizabeth Mae Hinkle of McKeesport, PA. Dayna worked for Eye Lab Co. until 1985 and then worked in a restaurant chain in all capacities until she and Ed were married in 1989. Dayna runs a Day Care Center out of her home in Denton. She is wonderful with children and is a wonderful cook.
Children:

592N.	I. Jacqueline Nicole (12) B. December 10, 1991.
593.	II. William Edmund (12) B. September 5, 1993.

583B. Karen Helena Buswell (11) Stowell

Daughter of Joyce Marie (Sesso) Buswell (No. 544) and William Edmund Buswell. Born in Washington, DC on August 29, 1958 at Providence Hospital. Karen attended Buckingham Elementary, Bowie, MD and Arundel Senior High School in Gambrills, MD. Karen swam for the Crofton Swim and Tennis Club until she graduated from high school in 1976. Her best stroke was butterfly and freestyle.

Married October 1, 1983, Stephen Clifford Stowell of Wilmington, DE, born September 20, 1958, Bellows Fall, VT. They were married at St. Elizabeth Seton Church in Crofton, MD.

Stephen had a son from a previous marriage, Steven Elias Stowell, born April 2, 1978 in Newark, DE. Steven graduated from Howard High School in Columbia, MD in 1996. He is a full time student at the University of Maryland Baltimore Campus (UMBC). He is majoring in Business. Steven works in the evening for United Parcel Service (UPS). His hobbies are soccer, football and computers.

Karen worked as a secretary at NASA/Goddard Space Flight Center in Greenbelt, MD from 1977 through 1981, the Ocean Data Systems (ODSI) in Rockville, MD until 1984 when she joined Lester H. Goldberg Law Offices in Chevy Chase until 1988. In 1989 Karen was employed as the Office Manager/legal secretary for the law offices of Karen L. Bonnin.

Stephen Clifford Stowell is the son of Elias Clifford Stowell of Burlington, VT and Audrey Mae Jensen of Dairy, NH. He attended Caesar Rodney High School in DE and graduated in 1976. Steve has worked in sales for Geico Insurance Company and TruGreen Corp. Landscaping until 1994. He then was employed by TruGreen/ChemLawn Corp. as their Commercial Sale Representative until the present time. Children:

594.   I. Nicholas William (12) B. June 25, 1989.
595.   II. Matthew Casey (12) B. December 8, 1997.

583C. Elizabeth Evelyn Buswell (11) Maddox

Daughter of Joyce Marie (Sesso) Buswell (No. 544) and William Edmund Buswell. Born in Providence Hospital, Washington, DC on December 25, 1961.

Evelyn attended Buckingham Elementary, Bowie, MD and Arundel Senior High School in Gambrills, MD and graduated in 1979. She attended the University of Maryland, College Park, MD, receiving her B.A. in Law Enforcement and Criminal Justice in 1983. Evelyn swam from the time she was seven years old until present (1999). She swam for the Crofton Swim and Tennis Club and won first place in every meet. She held the record for the swim team for breast stroke and free style. She continued to swim for the University of Maryland the four years she attended Maryland and up to the present she swims the Masters program.

After graduating from college Evelyn was employed at the Environmental Protection Agency as a Security Specialist implementing security in government agencies throughout the country. In 1985 Evelyn became a Montgomery County Police Officer and is now with the Motorcycle Traffic Squad. She is extremely talented in interior decorating and needlepoint.

Married Daniel Theodore Maddox, son of Edmund Jerome Maddox of Washington, DC and Nadine (Etzler) Maddox of Glen Echo, MD. Daniel was born April 8, 1956. He attended Wheaton High School and ran on the track team. After graduation he attended Montgomery College majoring in criminal justice. He became a Montgomery County Police Officer in 1982 and is now on the MD SWAT Team. Each year Daniel runs in the Police Marathon in Washington, DC. He is currently continuing his education at Montgomery College studying physical therapy. Evelyn and Daniel reside on Gue Road, Damascus, MD.

583D. Maureen Louise Buswell (11) Sminkey

Daughter of Joyce Marie (Sesso) Buswell (No. 544) and William Edmund Buswell. Born November 5, 1965 at Prince George's Hospital, Cheverly, MD.

Attended Arthur Slade Regional School (parochial) and Arundel Senior High School in Gambrills, MD, graduating in 1983. Maureen swam for the Crofton Athletic Council. Maureen worked at the National Council Architectural Registration Board in Washington, DC from 1984 to 1987. She worked for Swales Aerospace from 1987 to 1988 and NOVA Label in Cheverly, MD from 1988 to 1989.

Married December 10, 1988 John Sminkey of Crofton, MD at St. Paul's Lutheran Church, Gambrills, MD. In 1993 they renewed their vows at Sacred Heart Catholic Church in Bowie, MD.

Maureen has been working for Balloon Wizards since 1989. She does professional decorating with balloons for weddings, banquets and other events. She also works as a subcontractor for Clown Capers performing at children's birthday parties and picnics as a professional clown.

John is the son of Donald Clark Sminkey of Cherry Hill, NJ and Tamah Marie (Kern) of Collingswood, NJ. Born February 12, 1960, John attended St. Pius X Parochial School in Bowie, MD and Bowie High School, where he graduated in 1978. John is employed by Canteen Vending and is the shop steward. He is also a Trustee on the Board for his Local Teamster's Union. Children:

596.   I. John Anthony (12) B. April 21, 1989
597.   II. Jamie Marie (12) B. February 20, 1991.
598.   III. Jenna Marie (12) B. October 14, 1996.

583E. Cheryl Helene Hinson (11) Sabat

Daughter of Jean Frances (Sesso) Hinson (No. 545) and Bruce Elton Hinson, Sr. Born in Washington, DC on June 29, 1963. She attended parochial school at LaReine High School in Suitland, MD where she graduated Salutatorian. She later graduated *magna cum laude* from the University of Maryland in 1985 with a B. S. degree in Computer Science.

For over eight years Cheryl was a Senior Software Engineer and Engineering Supervisor for E-Systems, a defense contractor in Northern VA. She is currently a Software Development Manager for BTG, a defense contractor in Fairfax, VA. Her work involves system design and software development for highly classified government projects for the Air Force, Navy, etc. Her hobbies include playing volleyball, skiing in Tahoe, attending craft fairs and watching science fiction movies.

On September 2, 1990, she married Jeffry Brennan Sabat at St. John the Evangelist Catholic Church in Clinton, MD. Jeff was born on October 1, 1964 in Washington, DC. Son of Nancy Audioun and Donald Sabat of Long Island, NY. He attended parochial school at Bishop McNamara High School in Forestville, MD. He graduated from University of Maryland in 1986 with a B. S. degree in Computer Science.

Jeff is a commercial software developer who currently works for pmpro, Inc. in Washington, DC. He has designed and developed a variety of multi-media products - games and entertainment disks such as "Jumanji" and "Time Life 35mm Photography", public kiosks for advertising and product information, and an interactive in-room "City Guide" for hotel guests in many Washington, DC and Chicago, IL hotels. Jeff received a special multi-media award for his accomplishment on the "Time Life" project. His hobbies include playing volleyball, skiing in Tahoe, watching science fiction movies, snorkeling and diving. They reside in Fairfax, VA. Children:

    598A.   I. Christina Helene (12) B. November 20, 1998.

583F. Debra Lyn Hinson (11) Joyner

Daughter of Jean Frances (Sesso) Hinson (No. 545) and Bruce Elton Hinson, Sr. Born in Washington, DC on October 23, 1964. She attended parochial school - LaReine High School in Suitland, MD. She also attended the National Institute of Real Estate and became a certified real estate agent. She majored in paralegal studies from the National Institute of Paralegal Training. Debra's first job was at the Naval Investigative Services HQ - Special Agents Division. She left that position and was employed at the U.S. House of Representatives, Committee on Banking, Finance Urban Affairs. Later she worked at a law firm working on various proactive areas. She worked for a real estate developer in the Dulles area where she was the Assistant Director of Marketing and Systems Administrator. Debra recently worked for the Managing Partner at Wiley, Rein & Fielding. Dick Wiley was a former Chairman of the Federal Communications Commission. She also worked for the former President of the American Advertising Federation, Howard Bell. Mr. Bell was inducted into the advertising industry's "Hall of Fame" alongside Walter Cronkite.

Debra is a member of several professional associations and frequently attends self improvement seminars. She is also a volunteer for Prevention of Blindness and helps in fundraising efforts for other charities. Debra enjoys softball, tennis, road rallies, gardening, snorkeling and traveling.

On September 4, 1993, she married Gary Michael Joyner at St. Mary's Catholic Church in Fairfax, VA. Gary was born on October 5, 1953 in Washington, DC. Gary's parents were Marian Biafore and Joseph Joyner. Gary attended parochial and public school - St. Bernadette's and Montgomery Blair High School in Silver Spring, MD. Gary is a department manager at Safeway in Arlington, VA. Gary enjoys gardening, cooking, researching stocks, golfing and fishing. They reside in Fairfax City, Va. Children:

599.   I. Gary Michael (12) B. September 11, 1996.

583G. Bruce Elton Hinson, Jr. (11)

Son of Jean Frances (Sesso) Hinson (No. 545) and Bruce Elton Hinson, Sr. Born in Washington, DC June 23, 1968. He attended parochial and public schools - Bishop McNamara in Forestville, MD and Robinson High School in Fairfax, VA. He continued his education at James Mason University where he graduated with a Bachelor of Business Administration in May, 1990.

For over seven years, Bruce has worked for the Gillette Company in a variety of sales positions. His most recent position is Key Account Manager in the Baltimore/Washington, DC market. His responsibilities include increasing both market share and sales of Gillette products. Bruce has been recognized as a top performer in the company and attended "Winners Circle" twice. Bruce's hobbies are golfing, skiing, reading, history and traveling.

He married Stacy Alison Butler on May 28, 1994 in Hagerstown, MD. Stacy's parents are Janice Wanamaker Butler and David John Butler. She attended public school in Maryland. She continued her education and graduated *cum laude* from Wake Forest University in May 1991 with a B. S. degree in Biology.

For eight years, Stacy has worked as an Environmental Scientist for ICF Kaiser Engineers. She has been responsible for data management and risk assessment for several large and military environmental impact studies. Since the birth of their daughter, Stacy has worked part time so she could stay at home with Brittney. Her hobbies include gardening, swimming, and making family scrap books. Bruce and Stacy are active members of Cornerstone Chapel in Leesburg. They both volunteer as leaders in several children's ministries. Children:

600.   I. Brittney Elizabeth (12) B. December 20, 1996.

583H. Keith Anthony Hinson (11)

Son of Jean Frances (Sesso) Hinson (No. 545) and Bruce Elton Hinson, Sr. Born in Washington, DC on December 13, 1969. He attended parochial and public school - Bishop McNamara High School in Forestville, MD and Robinson High School in Fairfax, VA. Keith continued his education at Bryant Community College. He is a licensed optician in the State of Virginia. He passed this difficult exam the first time. Optical stores in Virginia do not require licenses. Because Keith took the initiative to take the exam and become a licensed optician, he has increased business at Bracken Opticians. Many consumers are educated and want a licensed optician to assist in their eye wear needs.

Keith is the manager of family optical business in Annandale, Va. He has worked for the business for twelve years and has been extremely beneficial in the successful operation of the business.

247

His hobbies include watching football, gun collecting, hunting, archery, fishing and restoring "classic cars".

584. Joseph (Joey) Edward Cheseldine, Jr. (11)

Son of Joseph Edward Cheseldine (No. 546) and Wilda Crossley (Brann) Cheseldine. Born September 21, 1958 at Washington, DC, baptized at St. Dominic's Catholic Church. Married Teresa Marie Redding on May 21, 1983 at St. Mary's Catholic Church, Bryantown, MD. Joseph, Jr. graduated from Thomas Stone High School in 1976. He was a member of the Honor Society of Thomas Stone High School and was listed in The Who's Who Among American High School Students 1976. Joseph, Jr. was given the award of Athlete of the Year 1976 from Thomas Stone High School. He made the All American State Football team in 1976. Joseph played football, baseball and ran track. He made all conference in football and baseball during this time. He attended Salisbury State College from 1976 through 1978 and played football for them and was on their diving team. Joseph, Jr. is in business with his father in Cheseldine's Sport and Lettering, Waldorf, MD.

Teresa Marie Redding Cheseldine born in Wash. DC, attended St. Mary's Academy High School in Leonardtown, MD graduating in 1979. They currently reside in Issue, MD. Children:

601.   I. Melissa Ann (12) B. March 13, 1985.
602.   II. Megan Violet (12) B. September 30, 1987.

585. Jay Michael Cheseldine (11)

Son of Joseph Edward Cheseldine (No. 546) and Wilda Crossley (Brann) Cheseldine. Born December 16, 1960 at Washington, DC. Married Monica Lee Siderio Cheseldine, February 28, 1992 at St. Mary's Catholic Church, Bryantown, MD. No issue from this marriage. Jay graduated from Thomas Stone High School in 1978. He played football and baseball for Thomas Stone. Jay made all conference in both sports. Jay attended Frostburg State College from 1978 to 1982, graduating with a major in Political Science. He played Rugby for the Frostburg Rugby Team. He has been working as a mortgage banker since graduating. Children:

248

603.   I. Daniel Michael (Danny) (12) B. April 7, 1984.
           Mother - Marilyn Conner

586. John Dominic (Nick) Cheseldine, Jr. (11)

Son of John Dominic Cheseldine (No. 547) and Judith Lynn (Cogan) Cheseldine. Born December 1, 1967 at Washington, DC. Attended Dr. Samuel Mudd grade school, Waldorf, MD and John Hanson middle school. Graduated from Thomas Stone High School in Waldorf, MD, June, 1985. Enlisted in the US Navy September, 1985, served until December, 1989. Went to work for Bozick Distributors in Waldorf, MD where he progressed to Draft Account Manager. Currently he is studying Radio/TV production in Baltimore, MD.

587. Erin Marie Cheseldine (11)

Daughter of John Dominic Cheseldine (No. 547) and Judith Lynn (Cogan) Cheseldine. Born June 15, 1972 at Washington, DC. Graduated from McDonough High School in Pomfret, MD, June, 1989. Attended Charles County Community College, worked in Ocean City, MD for five years in the restaurant business. Currently employed by Fairfax County Hospital, working with autistic children. She also attends Northern Virginia Community College.

588. Madeline Danielle Cheseldine (11)

Daughter of John Dominic Cheseldine (No. 547) and Theresa Anne (Knight) Cheseldine. Born October 13, 1985 at Washington, DC. Currently is in the eighth grade at John Hanson Middle School, Waldorf, MD. She has been involved in ballet and basketball. but her interest now is in art. She enjoys sketching and would like to get into animated graphics.

589. Colleen Elizabeth Cheseldine (11)

Daughter of John Dominic Cheseldine (No. 547) and Theresa Anne (Knight) Cheseldine. Born April 27, 1989, Washington, DC. Attends T. C. Martin Elementary in Bryantown. MD, in the fourth grade. Colleen is a competitive gymnast with Hilite Gymnastics and has won several awards to date.

590. Allison Michelle Cheseldine (11)

Daughter of John Dominic Cheseldine (No. 547) and Theresa Anne (Knight) Cheseldine. Born October 9, 1990, Washington, DC. Attends T.C. Martin Elementary in Bryantown, MD, in the third grade. She participates in the Odyssey of the Minds competition and has studied Tap/Jazz for the past four years.

590A. Eric Nevin Donnelly (11)

Son of Joan Theresa (Saylor) Donnelly (No. 549) and Gary Wayne Donnelly. Born November 21, 1967 at Providence Hospital, Washington, DC. He attended St. John's Catholic School and Church in Clinton, MD - the same parish his maternal great and great-great grandparents attended. He attended Bishop McNamara High School and Surratsville Public High School.

Eric was employed by several large construction companies and also pursued his desire to become an auto mechanic. Eric adored his children, Christopher and Heather, and spent as much time as possible with them.

Eric never knew a stranger....he was always the first to lend a hand to help. He died unexpectedly March 30, 1996. He is greatly missed. Buried in Fairfax Memorial Park, Fairfax, VA. Children:

604.   I. Christopher Nevin (12) B. June 15, 1988.
605.   II. Heather Lynn (12) B. October 29, 1989.

590B. Mark Orville Donnelly (11)

Son of Joan Theresa (Saylor) Donnelly (No. 549) and Gary Wayne Donnelly. Born May 12, 1971 at Washington, DC. He attended St. John's Catholic School in Clinton, MD and when his family moved to Virginia, Chantilly High School. At St. John's, Mark played in the school band and he was selected to play the drums at a function at the White House, but always shying away from the spotlight, he decided not to do so.

After attending school in Virginia, Mark enrolled in TESST Computer and Electronic Institute, earning a degree in electronics. He enjoys electrical work and is now employed by a large company in Virginia as a supervisor.

His hobbies include automobiles, golf, weight lifting and archery. At this writing, unmarried.

590C. Michele Theresa Donnelly (11)

Daughter of Joan Theresa (Saylor) Donnelly (No. 549) and Gary Wayne Donnelly. Born October 7, 1975 at Holy Cross Hospital, MD. She attended St. John's Parochial School in Clinton, MD where she excelled in her academic studies and held several classroom offices. When her family moved to Clifton, VA she attended two years at Union Mill Elementary School, and then attended Paul The VI High Parochial School in Fairfax, VA. She ran track, was a cheer leader, member of the Key Club, volley ball team, and plays the piano. She was on the Honor Roll and was involved in many other extracurricular activities. She graduated June, 1993.

Michele then selected Radford University in Radford, VA as the school she wanted to attend. The second year she transferred to George Mason University in Fairfax, graduating June, 1997. She is currently applying to Graduate Schools to obtain her Masters in Journalism. She has written interviews and articles for several newspapers.

590D. Sean Paul Bostic (11)

Son of Evelyn Marie (Saylor) Bostic (No. 550) and John Michael Bostic. Born April 7, 1968 at Providence Hospital, Washington, DC.

He attended grade school at St. Phillip the Apostle School in Camp Springs, MD and high school at Bishop McNamara High School, graduating in 1986. He also attended the Frostburg University in Frostburg, MD.

Sean became interested in electrical work and completed his apprenticeship with Local 26 International Brotherhood Electrical Workers Union.

His hobbies are fishing and hunting.

Sean married Laura Skillin of Calvert County, MD on April 26, 1990 in Prince George's County, MD. They divorced in 1992. Children:

606.   I. Elizabeth Ann (12) B. September 24, 1991.

590E. Scott Michael Bostic (11)

Son of Evelyn Marie (Saylor) Bostic (No. 550) and John Michael Bostic. Born July 26, 1973 at Washington, DC. He attended St. Phillip's Catholic School in Camp Springs, MD and Northern High School in Calvert County, MD. He has completed three years at St. Mary's College in St. Mary's County, MD, majoring in English. He plans to return to the college next semester.

At this writing he is quite involved with computer science. He is talented - playing the guitar, singing, writing poems, etc.

He resides in Lexington Park, MD, close to the college.

12th Generation begins

590F. Donna Lynn Smith (12)

Daughter of Daniel Kemp Smith (No. 557O) and Diane Lee Storey. Born March 30, 1965.

590G. Samantha Rose Beitzell (12)

Daughter of Stephen Eric Beitzell (No. 558L) and the late Janice Marie (Keister) Beitzell. Born February, 1998, her mother died September 24, 1998.

590H. Lauryn Elisabeth Laslie (12)

Daughter of Kathryn Marya (Quinnette) Laslie (No. 558X) and Charles Brent Laslie. Born October 1, 1999, 6 pounds, 12 ounces, at Fairfax Hospital on the second birthday of her cousin Richard Raymond Quinette (No. 558Y).

590I. Kathryn Nicole Quinnette (12)

Daughter of Joseph Richard Quinnette (No. 558Y) and Erin Margaret (McClanahan) Quinnette. Born March 20, 1995.

590J. Richard Raymond Quinnette (12)

Son of Joseph Richard Quinnette (No. 558Y) and Erin Margaret (McClanahan) Quinnette. Born October 1, 1997.

590K. Katherine Elise Quinnette (12)

Daughter of Charles Daley Quinnette (No. 558Z) and Melinda Katherine (Stewart) Quinnette. Born October 26, 1989.

590L. Emma Nicole Quinnette (12)

Daughter of Charles Daley Quinnette (No. 558Z) and Melinda Katherine (Stewart) Quinnette. Born August 20, 1992.

591A. Courtenay Allyson Basile (12)

Daughter of Ralph John Basile (No. 558Z1) and Deborah Gail (Painter) Basile. Born March 3, 1981 in Anne Arundel Hospital, Annapolis, MD.

591B. Todd Christopher Basile (12)

Son of Ralph John Basile (No. 558Z1) and Deborah Gail (Painter) Basile. Born May 20, 1984 in Anne Arundel Hospital, Annapolis, MD.

591C. Joseph Alfonso Basile (12)

Son of Paul Anthony Basile (No. 558Z2) and Jill Ann (Banghardt) Basile. Born July 8, 1982 in Fairfax Inova Hospital, Falls Church, Va. Identical twin.

591D. David Paul Basile (12)

Son of Paul Anthony Basile (No. 558Z2) and Jill Ann (Banghardt) Basile. Born July 8, 1982 in Fairfax Inova Hospital, Falls Church, VA. Identical twin.

591E. Katherine Linder Basile (12)

Daughter of Dr. John Joseph Basile (No. 558Z3) and Nedra Rae (Linder) Basile. Born December 18, 1983 in Winston-Salem, NC.

591F. Joshua John Basile (12)

Son of Dr. John Joseph Basile (No. 558Z3) and Nedra Rae (Linder) Basile. Born September 3, 1985 in Winston-Salem. NC.

591G. Amanda Lynn Miles (12)

Daughter of Patricia Lynn (Spence) Miles Funge (No. 560E) and Charles C. Miles. Born May 3, 1979.

591H. Jocelyn Elizabeth Miles (12)

Daughter of Patricia Lynn (Spence) Miles Funge (No. 560E) and Charles C. Miles. Born October 11, 1984.

591I. Charles Alexander Carter (12)

Son of Cari Leigh (Spence) Carter (No. 560F) and Charles "Les" Carter. Born January 19, 1989.

591J. Mark Andrew Carter (12)

Son of Cari Leigh (Spence) Carter (No. 560F) and Charles "Les" Carter. Born June 18, 1991.

591K. Joseph Michael Proske (12)

Son of Noella Jean Tartaglino Cipriano Proske (No. 560H) and Hans Peter Proske. Born June 6, 1975.

591K1. Lisamarie Proske (12)

Daughter of Noella Jean Tartaglino Cipriano Proske (No. 560H) and Hans Peter Proske. Born June 4, 1979. Died January 7, 1980.

591L. Devin Elisabeth Yates (12)

Daughter of Thomas Irvin Yates, III (No. 560I) and Lauren (Rice) Yates. Born February 11, 1984.

591M. Logan Thomas Yates (12)

Son of Thomas Irvin Yates, III (No. 560I) and Lauren (Rice) Yates. Born April 18, 1989.

591N. Brantley Dawn Yates (12)

Daughter of Michael Leonard Yates (No. 560J) and Joellyn (Brendle) Yates. Born September 10, 1985.

591O. Michael Carson Yates (12)

Son of Michael Leonard Yates (No. 560J) and Joellyn (Brendle) Yates. Born October 26, 1988.

591P. John Warren Yates (12)

Son of John Warren Yates (No. 560K) and Terri (Hudgens) Yates. Born August 13, 1989.

591Q. Emily Elizabeth Yates (12)

Daughter of John Warren Yates (No. 560K) and Scarlett Lanier (Hibbard) Yates. Born December 22, 1994.

591R. Jennifer Rae Parvis (12)

Daughter of Carrie Lynn (Kimble) Parvis (No. 560M) and Raymond Keith Parvis. Born December 6, 1987.

591S. Joshua Raymond Parvis (12)

Son of Carrie Lynn (Kimble) Parvis (No. 560M) and Raymond Keith Parvis. Born September 17, 1990.

591T. Ashleigh Elizabethe' Biceuskis (12)

Daughter of Catherine Marie (Kimble) Biceuskis (No. 560N) and Andris Biceuskis. Born September 7, 1989.

591U. Megan Anna Biceuskis (12)

Daughter of Catherine Marie (Kimble) Biceuskis (No. 560N) and Andris Biceuskis. Born May 29, 1992.

591V. Jacob Robert Kimble (12)

Son of Kevin Robert Kimble (No. 560O) and Rebecca Kent (Bush) Kimble. Born January 3, 1995.

591W. Matthew Kent Kimble (12)

Son of Kevin Robert Kimble (No. 560O) and Rebecca Kent (Bush) Kimble. Born March 14, 1997.

591X. James David Emmert, Jr. (12)

Son of Lori Paige (Grant) Emmert (No. 560T) and James Emmert. Born September 22, 1994. Died September 26, 1994.

591Y. daughter Emmert (12)

Daughter of Lori Paige (Grant) Emmert (No. 560T) and James Emmert. Born

592. Taylor Jeanne Stilwell (12)

Daughter of Kelly Ann (Renner) Stilwell (No. 560X) and Timothy David Stilwell. Born September 11, 1996 at Greater Baltimore Medical Center, Baltimore, MD.

Taylor has many interests at the young age of three. She loves books, singing, playing dress up and beanie babies. Taylor currently attends gymnastic and ballet classes, and wants to take riding lessons. She attends pre-school two mornings a week.

592A. Jessica Lauryn Stilwell (12)

Daughter of Kelly Ann (Renner) Stilwell (No. 560X) and Timothy David Stilwell. Born July 28, 1999 at Greater Baltimore Medical Center, Baltimore, MD.

After Jessica was born, Taylor was brought to the hospital by Beth, one of her nanny's since her birth, to see her new baby sister. Taylor was so excited she had tears in her eyes. The first thing she did was sing "Happy Birthday to Jessica".

592B. Luke Chandler Baggett (12)

Son of Mark David Baggett (No. 560Z) and Heather (Clayton) Baggett. Born April 5, 1996.

592C. Danielle Nicole Baggett (12)

Daughter of Mark David Baggett (No. 560Z) and Heather (Clayton) Baggett. Born October 1, 1998.

592D. Matthew Clark Embrey (12)

Son of Joyce Lynn (Baggett) Embrey (No. 560Z1) and Clark Morgan Embrey. Matthew was born October 16, 1999, at 6:48 AM at Southern Maryland Hospital, Clinton, MD, weighing in at 9 pounds 15 ounces, and 22 inches long.

592E. Burton Alan Baggett (12)

Son of Richard Alan Baggett (No. 560Z2) and Dawn Marie (Seidman/Adams) Baggett. Born June 19, 1998.

592F. Kayla Marie Richard (12)

Daughter of Brian Douglas Richard (No. 560Z3) and Terri (Curtin) Richard. Born September 13, 1992.

592G. Travis James Khoury (12)

Son of Heather Rene (Richard) Khoury (No. 560Z7) and Issa N. Khoury. Born February 10, 1998.

592G1. Hayley Nicole Khoury (12)

Daughter of Heather Rene (Richard) Khoury (No. 560Z7) and Issa N. Khoury. Born June 24, 1999.

592H. Dennis Craig Simpson, Jr. (12)

Son of Dennis Craig Simpson (No. 560Z8) and Susan Marie (Bowling) Simpson. Born January 10, 1990.

592I. Cody Gaston Simpson (12)

Son of Dennis Craig Simpson (No. 560Z8) and Susan Marie (Bowling) Simpson. Born December 30, 1993.

592J. Kevin Andrew Catterton (12)

Son of Christina Jean Simpson (No.560Z9) and _____. Born April 3, 1993.

592K. Ryan Marquess Simpson (12)

Son of Deborah Lynn Simpson (No. 560Z10) and _____. Born July 1, 1991.

593. Jacqueline Nicole Buswell (12)

Daughter of Edmund Anthony Buswell (No. 583A2) and Dayna Jo (Lindauere) Buswell. Born December 10, 1991 in Eastern Memorial Hospital. Jackie attends Wesleyan Christian School in Denton, MD. She plays T-ball, indoor soccer and swimming.

593A. William Edmund Buswell (12)

Son of Edmund Anthony Buswell (No. 583A2) and Dayna Jo (Lindauere) Buswell. Born September 5, 1993 in Eastern Memorial Hospital. Billy attends Wesleyan Christian School in Denton, MD. He loves to go hunting, walking in the woods with his father and plays T-ball and swims.

594. Nicholas William Stowell (12)

Son of Karen Helena (Buswell) Stowell (No. 583B) and Stephen Clifford Stowell. Born June 25, 1989 in Olney, MD. He attends Waterslanding Elementary and is in the 4th grade. Nicholas loves all sports but particularly football and soccer which he plays for the Damascus team. He is also very artistic.

595. Matthew Casey Stowell (12)

Son of Karen Helena (Buswell) Stowell (No. 583B) and Stephen Clifford Stowell. Born December 8, 1997 in Gaithersburg, MD.

596. John Anthony Sminkey (12)

Son of Maureen Louise (Buswell) Sminkey (No.583D) and John Anthony Sminkey. Born April 21, 1989 at Arundel Medical Center, Annapolis, MD. Jack attends Crofton Woods Elementary School in Crofton, MD. He has played bass-violin for 2 years for Crofton Woods and really enjoys playing. His other interests are street hockey, basketball and swimming.

597. Jamie Marie Sminkey (12)

Daughter of Maureen Louise (Buswell) Sminkey (No. 583D) and John Anthony Sminkey. Born February 20, 1991 at Arundel Medical Center, Annapolis, MD. Jamie attends Crofton Woods Elementary School in Crofton, MD. Jamie excels in swimming like Mom. She swims in summer for the Bowie Swim and Bath Club and winter for Annapolis Swim Club and does very well. Jamie is very artistic and loves to do crafts. Writing and drawing are her favorites.

598. Jenna Marie Sminkey (12)

Daughter of Maureen Louise (Buswell) Sminkey (No. 583D) and John Anthony Sminkey, Born October 14, 1996 at Rebecca Clatonoff Pavilion, Annapolis, MD.

598A. Christina Helene Sabat (12)

Daughter of Cheryl Helene (Hinson) Sabat (No. 583E) and Jeffry Brennan Sabat. Born November 20, 1998 in Fairfax, VA.

599. Gary Michael Joyner, Jr. (12)

Son of Debra Lyn (Hinson) Joyner (No. 583F) and Gary Joyner. Born September 11, 1996. in Fairfax, Va.

600. Brittney Elizabeth Hinson (12)

Daughter of Bruce Elton Hinson, Jr. (No. 583G) and Stacy Alison (Butler) Hinson. Born December 20, 1996 in Denville, NJ.

601. Melissa Ann Cheseldine (12)

Daughter of Joseph Edward Cheseldine, Jr. (No.584) and Teresa Marie (Redding) Cheseldine. Born March 13, 1985.

602. Megan Violet Cheseldine (12)

Daughter of Joseph Edward Cheseldine, Jr. (No. 584) and Teresa Marie (Redding) Cheseldine. Born September 30, 1988.

603. Daniel Michael (Danny) Cheseldine (12)

Son of Jay Michael Cheseldine (No. 585) and Marilyn Conner. Born April 7, 1984 in Clinton, MD. Baptized at St. Mary's Catholic Church, Bryantown, MD.

604. Christopher Nevin Donnelly (12)

Son of Eric Nevin Donnelly (No. 590A) and Tracy Kesner. Born June 15, 1988 at Manassas, VA, resides with his grandparents, Joan and Gary Donnelly. At this writing Christopher is 10 1/2 years of age. He attends Union Mill Elementary School in Clifton, VA. He's a good student, very active in sports - especially hockey - leading his team to win the 1998 League Championship. He's an all around American boy - loves school, sports and video games.

605. Heather Lynn Donnelly (12)

Daughter of Eric Nevin Donnelly (No. 590A) and Tracy Kesner. Born October 29, 1989 at Fairfax, Va. She resides with her mother in Strasburg, VA and attends Hook Elementary School - loves pets and gymnastics. She is a good student and has a distinct talent for art.

606. Elizabeth Ann Bostic (12)

Daughter of Sean Paul Bostic (No. 590D) and Laura (Skillin) Bostic of Calvert County. Born September 24, 1991 in Calvert County, MD.

Elizabeth is a very bright intelligent child. She attends Mt. Harmony Public School in Calvert County, MD. Her grades are excellent and she loves school.

She spends weekends with her father, and her grandparents, Marie and Paul Bostic. Sean enjoys teaching her and sharing his hobbies with her, and I might add she enjoys every minute of it. She is exposed to many facets of every day life - wild life - boating - camping, etc. He takes time to explain wild life to her - plants, flowers, different kinds of sea animals, visiting Baltimore Aquarium many times. He is patient with Elizabeth and the child learns quickly.

Gerard Family

GERARD.

EN DIEU EST MON ESPERANCE

Arms of Thomas Gerard

Shield	Argent – (Silver), A Saltire (X) Gules (Red)
Mantling	Gules (Red) and Argent (Silver)
Crest	On a wreath, of the Colors, Argent (Silver) and Gules (Red)

A Lion of Rampant (Standing in a Stricking Pose),
Ermin (Black) Crowned or (Gold)

Supporters	On either side A Lion Ermin (Black) Ducally Crowned or (Gold)
Gorged	With a Collar Gamel Gules (Red) and Supporting a Tilting Spear Proper
Motto	En Dieu Est Non Esperance – Gules (Red), on Argent (Silver) Ribbon.

Sign commemorating Dr. Thomas Gerard, Esq. at Colton's Point
with St. Clements Island in the background.

GERARD FAMILY

The history of the Cheseldine family in America may well begin with Thomas Gerard since the first Kenelm Cheseldine in this country married Gerard's daughter, Mary and their respective political careers in the Maryland Province closely paralleled each other. The first Gerard to arrive in Maryland was Richard. He came on the Ark and the Dove in 1634. Richard, as will be shown later in this account was a younger brother of Thomas Gerard. Richard returned to England in 1635 and became quite famous in the service of the King.

Thomas Gerard born at Winwick, December 10, 1603, arrived in Maryland in 1637 and was chosen a burgess from St. Mary's Hundred on February 16. 1638. He married in England, Susannah, the daughter of Abel and Judith Snow and had five children at the time of moving to Maryland. Namely, Susannah, Justinian, Frances, Temperance and Elizabeth, and he claimed 2,000 acres of land for transporting them into the Province.

Thomas Gerard was a doctor and practiced both in Maryland and Virginia. He also took an active part in the affairs of the Province. Space limitations do not permit a repetition of all his activities here. They may be reviewed in the Archives of Maryland, copies of which are on file at the National Archives and the Library of Congress in Washington, DC. It is interesting to note that Gerard was a member of both the Assembly, appointed in 1638 and the Council, appointed November 17, 1643. A copy of this later appointment is included with this account. The grant provided for the establishment of a Court Baron and a Court Leet and the records of St. Clement's Manor are the only ones of this unusual type of Baronial Court proceedings known to be in existence in Maryland. They may be reviewed in the Maryland Archives.

Gerard, in addition to being a prominent member of the Assembly and Council was one of Calvert's Captains in the difficulties with the Puritans in 1654-56. During this trouble he and William Eltonhead (who possibly was his son-in-law) were among those captured in the Battle of Herring Creek on the Severn River and although quarter had been promised, Eltonhead and three others were executed by the Puritans. He took part in several expeditions against the Indians and on June 18, 1644 was appointed a member of a Commission to deal with the Susquehanna Indians. It is evident from a review of the Provincial records that he was held in high esteem by the Calverts.

It was noted (Proceedings of the Assembly 1637-1644 Maryland Archives) that on March 23, 1641 "The petition of the Protestants was read complaining against Mr. Thomas Gerard for taking away the key of the chapel and carrying away the books out of the chapel and such proceedings desired against him for it as to justice appertaineth. Mr. Gerard being charged to make answer the house upon hearing the prosecutors and his defense found that Mr. Gerard was guilty of a misdemeanor and that he should bring the books and key taken away to the place where he had them and relinquish all title to them or the house and should pay a fine of 500 pounds of tobacco toward the maintenance of the first minister as should arrive." In this connection, it is interesting to note that the Provincial Council on December 16, 1696 ordered "the vestry of King and Queen Parish in St. Mary's County make inquiry of Captain Gerard Slye concerning 100 acres of land said to be given to the church by Mr. Thomas Gerard, Sr., and that said vestry take care to get the bounds thereof run out before the said Captain Slye depart the country and that they be served by the said Sheriff with this order." Gerard Slye denied that Thomas Gerard ever made this gift and demanded payment for the land.

Gerard was a Catholic but his wife and children and many of the people he had transported into to the Province were Protestants. Although there has been much speculation as to just what was back of this difficulty, no theory has been substantiated. It is probable that his pastor, Father Francis Fitzherbert, objected to Gerard's building the Anglican Chapel and persuaded him to close it.

It was noted also (Proceedings of the Provincial Council 1658-1662 Maryland Archives) in October 1658 the Attorney General accused the Rev. Francis Fitzherbert of mutiny and treason in trying to prevent musters and for having said if Thomas Gerard of the Council did not come and bring his wife and children to church he would come and force them to his church. "Gerard said upon oath, that having a conference with Mr. Fitzherbert as they were walking in the woods and in his own orchard, touching the bringing his children to the Catholic Church, he gave Mr. Fitzherbert reasons why it is was not safe for himself." Just how much weight these religious difficulties carried in Gerard's decision to break with Lord Baltimore in 1659

(Fendall's Rebellion) is problematical.

On October 5, 1658, Gerard was "accused by Richard Smith, Attorney General, of violating the secrecy of the Council and saying Governor Fendall would do anything requested by the people of Ann Arundel, saying the whole Council were a bunch of rouges and he would not sit with them." Lord Baltimore let this suit fall but advised Gerard he could ask for a trial, if he desired. In view of this it is difficult to understand how Gerard could have thrown in with Fendall when the show-down came in 1659. It appears certain also that he could not have had any love for the Puritans, who sided with Fendall, after his experience at Herring Creek in 1655 when William Eltonhead, Thomas Hatton and others were executed and he narrowly escaped the same fate. Sparks, in his book, "Maryland Revolution 1689", says "The real cause of the disturbance that now arose (Fendall's Rebellion of 1659) are scarcely explained by Maryland historians. Governor Fendall is charged with being the chief cause of the rebellion. It is true that Fendall tried to keep in favor with the party of resistance (The Ann Arundel Party) and that he was intimately connected with Gerard whose party was destined to triumph in 1689 but it was really the question of taxation that caused the so-called Fendall's Rebellion. It is sometimes said it was a Puritan movement and so it was in one sense but Gerard who seemed to be the real leader, was a Catholic who had been and was then a member of the Council. In 1647 an Act was passed by the Assembly granting the Proprietor (Lord Baltimore) a duty of 10 shillings on every hogshead of tobacco exported from the Province, this Act by the admission of the Proprietor was the cause of the complaints". There were several other like acts and it appears likely that these acts eventually galled the large landholders to open rebellion.

On January 12, 1659, "Mr. Gerard, our dear friend and Counselor" was ordered by Phillip Calvert, Secretary of the Province, to attend an Assembly to be held at Gerard's home at Longworth Point (now Colton's Point) on February 28, 1659. This Assembly was continued at Robert Slye's (Gerard's son-in-law) home at Bushwood until the middle of March and involved a struggle between the Lower and Upper House. The Lower house claimed themselves to be a lawful Assembly without dependence on any power in the Province and the highest court of Judicature. There was considerable maneuvering back and forth between the two Houses and finally

Fendall took the position that the Burgesses (by intent of the King in his patent) could make and enact laws by themselves, publish them in the name of the Proprietor and they would be in full force, provided they were agreeable to reason and in no case repugnant to the laws of England. The Secretary, Phillip Calvert, brother of the Proprietor, of the Upper House disagreed and held that the assent of the Proprietor or the Governor, lawfully authorized by the Proprietor was necessary. "Thomas Gerard being asked his opinion, sided with the Governor". Calvert withdrew in a huff and the rebellion of 1659 was on. The rebellion collapsed in May, 1660 when Charles II returned to the throne of England and the Proprietor was restored to favor at the Court. Lord Baltimore in a letter dated August 24, 1660 instructed his brother, Phillip Calvert, the Governor, to deal harshly with Gerard, Fendall, etc., taking their lives, if necessary, seizing their property, banishing them from the Province, etc. Gerard's lands (including St. Clement's Manor, over 11,000 acres) and other property were seized and he was banished in November 1660 but in the following February he petitioned the Governor and the Council to restore his estates and withdraw banishment and this was immediately granted but with the provision that he could not hold office. It is interesting to note that his grand-daughter Elizabeth married Benedict Calvert.

With the restoration of his estates Gerard continued to live in Maryland until 1666 when. after the death of his wife, Susannah, to whom he was very devoted, he moved to Machodac, Westmoreland County, Virginia, to escape as he stated, the religious difficulties plaguing the Province. It was here that together with Henry Corbin, John Lee and Isaac Allerton, that never-to-be-forgotten quartet of bon-vivants, was entered into a contract in 1670. Later duly recorded, to build them "a banqueting hall" at or near the head of Cherive's (now Jackson's) Creek where their estates cornered. It was agreed that each party to the contract should "yearly, according to his due course, make an honourable treatment fit to entertain the undertakers thereof, their men, masters and friends...." "Bishop Meade cited this as an example of riotous living".

It was here also that he married Rose Tucker, a widow with two children, Sarah who married   Blackistone and Rose who married William Fitzhugh. He died here in 1673, but in compliance with a request contained in his will his body was taken to Longworth Point (Colton's Point) his old home in Maryland, and buried there in the private burial grounds by the side of Susannah. This private cemetery still existed until a few years ago when one of the late owners of Longworth Point threw the tombstone over the bank into the Potomac River (adjacent to St. Clement's Island) and leveled the plot. Not satisfied with this act of desecration, it is reported that a guest at the hotel there was permitted to open one of the graves and remove a skull. In a terrific storm in the summer of 1933 the hotel was wrecked and much ground washed away so that in 1946 there was no evidence whatsoever of the Gerard home or burial ground.

Rose Tucker, after the death of Thomas Gerard, married John Newton and had 3 children,

(1) Gerard born 1677

(2) Thomas

(3) Elizabeth

On July 8, 1709 she stated that she was about 80 years of age. Her will was dated December 12, 1712.

Thomas Gerard owned some 3,500 acres of land in Westmoreland County, Virginia, known as Gerard's Reserve He acquired most of this land around 1650.

The Gerards were a very ancient and distinguished family of Lancashire, England and some fortunate discoveries in our research had removed any doubt that Thomas Gerard was of this family. In the Virginia Historical Magazine, Vol. 33, page 302 the family history of the Newton family is reviewed and it is stated that "John Newton married Rose Tucker Gerard, the widow of Thomas Gerard of Westmoreland and Maryland and formerly of New Hall, Lancashire, England." William Playfair in his "British Family Antiquity" Vol. 6 printed in London, 1811, (copy in the Congressional Library) traces the family genealogy in Lancashire and states that Sir Thomas Gerard, of Kingsley and Brynn born 1431 was an ancestor of Thomas Gerard of Maryland. There is an account of Richard Gerard coming to Maryland with Calvert in 1634 when he was 21 years of age, his return to England in 1635 and his subsequent services to the King. In 1641 Thomas Gerard claimed land for transporting John Gerard and in 1658 he claimed land for transporting Winifred and Bridget Gerard who undoubtedly were relatives.

According to William Playfair's account the Gerard family derives its origin from Otho, a rich and powerful Lord in the time of King Alfred (848-899), and descended from the Dukes of Tuscany, who came from Florence or Norway and passed into Normandy and thence to England where they flourished. A descendant Otho, was a Baron of England in the time of King Edward the Confessor (1004-1066), and was the father of Walter Fitzotho. (The eldest son was generally surnamed Fitz.)

Walter Fitzotho, at the general survey of the Kingdom in 1078 was Castellan (Commander) of Windsor. He married Gladys, the eldest daughter of Rywall Ap Conyn and had three sons, (1) Gerald, (2) Robert and (3) William. Gerald, the eldest son, surnamed Fitz was Constable of Pembroke Castle, which he fortified and defended with great courage against the Welsh. He had by Nesta, his wife, daughter of Rees, three sons, (1) William, (2) Maurice and (3) David. William Fitzgerald, the eldest son, was possessed of the Castle Carrio, in Carmathenshire, the inheritance of his mother. He died in 1173 and left issue (1) Otho, (2) Raymond Crassus, (3) Silvester, (4) Henry and (5) William. The last named William had his name corrupted from Gerald to Gerard and became the direct ancestor to the family Gerard. He was Justice in Eyre, in Chestershire, and was the father of:

William Gerard (1)

He was one of the jury on the death of Sir Hamon Massy in 1255 during the reign of Edward I (1239-1307). He married Emme, daughter of heir of Sir Richard Kingsley of Chestershire and through this marriage the Kingsley estate came into the Gerard family. Issue:
1. William (2)
2. John

William Gerard (2)

Did homage to Edward II (1284-1327) for his lands in Chestershire and died at Eaton Hall in 1338 during the reign of Edward III (1312-1377). He married Matilda, daughter of Henry De Glasehouse. Issue:
1. William (3)
2. Thomas

William Gerard (3)

Married Joan, daughter and heir of Peter De. Bryn and through this marriage the estate of Bryn or Brynhill in Lancashire came into the family. Issue:
1. Peter De Bryn (4)

Peter De Bryn Gerard (4)

He died in 1381 and left three sons. Issue:
1. Thomas (5)

2. Peter who married Isabel, daughter of Thomas Strangeways in the time of Henry IV (1367-1413) who overthrew Richard II (1367-1400).

3. John who married Helen, daughter of Richard DeInce.

Sir Thomas Gerard (5)

Thomas Gerard of Bryn was knighted for valiant service to Richard II (1367-1400) in 1384 in the Scottish Wars. He was a member of Parliament from Lancashire. Issue:

1. Thomas (6)

Sir Thomas Gerard (6)

Was married and left two sons. Issue:

1. Thomas (7)
2. John

Sir Thomas Gerard (7)

Sir Thomas Gerard of Bryn served England in the wars against France in the reign of Henry VI (1421-1471) and fought with great valor in the siege of Montereau in 1437. He died without issue and was succeeded by his kinsman Sir Thomas Gerard of Kingsley who was great grandson of Peter Gerard (before mentioned) who married Isabel Strangeways and had John who died in 1432 and was father of Peter who died in 1490 who was the father of Thomas.

Sir Thomas Gerard (8)

Sir Thomas Gerard of Kingsley who succeeded his kinsman of the same name of Byrn was recorded as being 14 years of age in the 18th year of the reign of Henry VII (1457-1509). He married Dowse, daughter of Sir Thomas Asheton of Lancashire. Issue:

1. Peter (9)

Peter Gerard (9)

Married Margaret, daughter of Sir William Stanley of Hooten who was heir to her grandfather Sir John Bromley and received from him the estate of Bromley in Straffordshire. He died in 1492 prior to his father's death. Issue:

1. Thomas (10)
2. Joan, married Richard Done
3. Isabel, married Richard Langton
4.   , married Com. Ratcliff
5.   , married John Southworth

Sir Thomas Gerard (10)

Succeeded his grandfather to the estates of Byrn, Bromley and

Kingsley and other land holdings. He employed the famed Lancashire Archers against the Scots in 1513 to aid Thomas, Earl of Surrey while Henry VIII was busy in his wars in France. He is credited with behaving with great valor at Flodded Field when the Earl of Surrey defeated and killed James IV of Scotland. He married Margaret, daughter of Sir Edmund Trafford of Trafford in Lancashire. Issue:

1. Thomas. (11)
2. William.
3. James.
4. Henry of Rainhill.
5. Pyers.
6. Margaret. Married Peter Legh.
7. Catherine. Married Thomas Hoghton.
8. Elizabeth, married Richard Asheton.

Sir Thomas Gerard (11)

(Succeeded to Family title. Brother of William shown below.) He is recorded as a Knight and High Sheriff of Lancashire in 1548 during the reign of Queen Elizabeth (1533-1603). He married Jane, daughter of Peter Legh. Issue:

1. Catharine. Married William Tarbock.
2. Thomas (12)

William Gerard (11)

Of Newhall, married Constance. Newhall was conveyed to him and his son Thomas in 1542 by his brother, Sir Thiomas Gerard shown above. Died in 1558. Issue:

1. Thomas (12)

Thomas Gerard (12)

Of Newhall in Ashton-in-Makerfield, Lancaster County, Gentleman. Died December 29, 1628. Buried at Winwick. Married Jaine, who was living in 1632. Issue:

1. John (13)
2. Joseph
3. Marye
4. Anne
5. Jaine

John Gerard (13)

Of Newhall in Ashton-in-Makerfield. Married Isabel at Winwick February 16, 1607-1608. Living at Warrington in 1641. Issue:

1. Thomas (14)
2. Marmaduke
3. William
4. Francis

Thomas Gerard (14)

This Thomas Gerard of the 14th generation in England is the subject of this account and his story is told in the beginning of these notes. It is hoped that someday some of his personal papers may be discovered so that we may know something of his private life as well as his public life in Maryland and Virginia. As before mentioned, he married Susannah Snowe and their issue was as follows:

1. Justinian,born about 1634 in England, married Sarah, widow of Wilkes Maunders of Westmoreland County, VA. He died without issue in 1688. He was left St. Clement's Manor (that portion not already settled on his sisters) and Bramly (originally spelled Bromley) by his father. In 1678 the Lord Proprietor proved in Court that the original grant was only intended to be about 6,000 acres and the resurvey showed 11,400 acres. Justinian was defended by Nehemiah Blackistone and the Lord Proprietor by his attorney general, Kenelm Cheseldyne Apparently Justinian was able to satisfy the Court and he was allowed to keep the manor intact. Justinian left his property to his widow Sarah, who later married Michael Curtis and they sold St. Clement's Manor on May 18, 1711 to Charles Carroll and moved to Prince George's County, Maryland.

2. Thomas, born about 1638 in St. Mary's City, married Susannah Curtis, a widow. He died without issue in 1686. Thomas was given Westwood Manor and lived there until his death. Apparently Susannah died before 1686, as Thomas left Westwood to Justianian. Upon his death it passed to his wife Sarah who also sold it to Charles Carroll on May 18, 1711.

3. Susannah, born about 1627 in England, married (1) Robert Ellyson, (2) Robert Slye and (3) John Coode. She was given Bushwood by her father at the time of her marriage to Slye. There were two sons, Gerard and Robert and two daughters, Elizabeth (1669-1722) who married (1) Luke Gardiner and (2) Edward Cole (1657-1717), and Frances, who married (1)   Wheeler and (2) Peter Mills. Robert Slye, Jr., married his first cousin, Percilla Goldsmith. Judith Gerard was apparently the daughter of John Gerard. Susannah died 1716.

4. Anne, born about 1642 married (1) Walter Broadhurst. They had;

> A. Walter, who returned to England, married and had a family and died there in 1707.
>
> B. Gerard, died before 1676.

Ann married (2) Henry Brett in September, 1665 or 1667. No issue. Ann married (3) John Washington, great grandfather of George Washington in 1669. It is interesting to note that John Washington came from Lancashire, England as did the Gerards. The probabilities are that the families knew each other in England. No issue.

5. Frances, born about 1640 in England married (1) Col. Thomas Specke. in 1659. They had;

> A. Thomas, died 1659. (Died young)

Frances married (2) Col. Valentine Peyton. They had;

> 1. Gerard, born about 1661, married   Hardwick, daughter of William Hardwick No issue. Left everything to his half sister, Elizabeth Hardwick.

Frances married (3) Captain John Appleton. No issue. Died 1676. Frances married (4) Col. John Washington. Married May 10, 1676. No issue.

Frances married (5) William Hardwicke (Hardidge). They had;

> 1. Elizabeth, born 1678. Married about 1700 to Col. Henry Ashton, born July 30, 1671, died November 3, 1731. She died February 25, 1722. They had;
>
>> (A) Frances, born 1699, married 1718 to George Tuberville. She died in 1718. Had a daughter Elizabeth.
>>
>> (B) Anne, born 1701. Married 1725 to Captain William Aylette. She died in 1731. They had (a) Elizabeth, married William Booth.
>>
>>> (b) Anne, married 1743 to Augustine Washington, brother of George Washington. They had;
>>>
>>>> (1) William Augustine
>>>> (2) Elizabeth, married Alex Spottswood.
>>>> (3) Jane, married Col. John Thornton.

(4) Ann, born April 2, 1752,
married December 19, 1768.
Burdett Ashton. She died
June 3, 1777.

(C) Elizabeth. Did not marry.

(D) Grace, married Richard Lee of Charles
County, Maryland.

6. Temperence, born about 1646 in England married (1) Daniel
Hutt, in 1669. They had;

A. Ann

B. Gerard, married Ann. He died in 1739, and in his
will named his wife and children.

(1) Gerard

(2) Daniel

(3) Frances

(4) Elizabeth

(5) Susanna

(6) Anna

(7) Thomas, married   , had a son,
Thomas, born January 30, 1766, married
September 11, 1792 to Mary Young
Sturman, born February 29, 1764. Both
died in 1805. Had son, William, born
December 11, 1801. Married January 27,
1828, Elizabeth Jane Harvey. He died
April 14, 1850. Had a son, Joseph Warren.
born May 18, 1829. Married March 8,
1854, Elizabeth Elbert Costin. He was
living in Westmoreland County, Virginia in
1907.

Temperance married (2) John Crabbe.

7. Elizabeth, born about 1636 in England married (1) Ralph
Rymer, (2) Joshua Guilbert and (3) Nehemiah Blackistone, May 6,
1669. She was given St. Clement's Island, Longworth Point (now
known as Colton's Point) and Dares Neck, about 400 acres of ground.
She died 1716 in St. Mary's, MD.

8. Janette, born about 1648 married (1) Richard Eltonhead
who was shot after being captured during the trouble with the Puritans
in 1654-56. Married (2) Thomas Smyth, (3) Philip Taylor and (4)
William Eltonhead.

9. John, born about 1644 in St. Mary's City, MD, married Elizabeth   . His father in his will provided December 15, 1673, left Basford Manor to John and his wife Rose Tucker Gerard with the reversion to John. However, by a decision of the Provincial Court, December 2, 1676, Thomas Gerard, Jr. of Westwood Manor obtained possession of Basford Manor and sold it April 18, 1677 to Governor Thomas Notley*. John died 1678, and his widow married James Johnston of WestmorelandCounty, Virginia, in this year, and had five children from this marriage. He left a daughter, Susannah, and a son John, who married Jane, and had a daughter, Elizabeth born February 24, 1730. Since the second John Gerard had no sons, the family name became extinct at his death.

10. Mary, born about 1652 in St. Mary's City, married in 1677, Kenelm Cheseldine. **Her father gave her as a dowry, before he died in 1673, four seats of land in Maryland, including Westwood Lodge (100 acres). He had given Westwood Manor (1,600 acres) to her brother, Thomas, Jr. The other three tracts were St. Katherine's Manor, including the Island, White's Neck and Mattapany.

*Maryland Historical Magazine Vol. 33
**Sandra Harrison letter

Thomas Gerard

and His Sons-In-Law

Thomas Gerard and his Sons-in-Law

Published In the Maryland Historical Magazine
by Edwin W. Beitzell

Maryland historians have given scant attention to one of the most important political figures and also one of the largest landholders in the Province during the period 1637-1673. He was Dr. Thomas Gerard, Gentleman, born about 1605, at New Hall, Lancashire. England, son of Sir Thomas Gerard. The Gerards were an ancient and distinguished Roman Catholic Family of Lancashire. John Gerard, brother of Sir Thomas, was a Jesuit Priest, and was tortured in the Tower during one of the religious upheavals in England. He later founded a College at Liege. A daughter of Sir Thomas, Frances, became a Nun at Graveline in Flanders. The family history has been traced back to the time of the General Survey of the Kingdom in 1078. (1) The first of the Gerards to arrive in the Maryland Province was Richard. He arrived with the first colonists on the Ark and the Dove in 1634. Richard returned to England in 1635 and became famous in the service of the King. Thomas Gerard, cousin of Richard, arrived in Maryland in 1637 and was chosen as a Burgess from St. Mary's Hundred on February 19, 1638. (2) He married in England, Susannah, the daughter of Abel and Judith Snow and had five children at the time of moving to Maryland, namely, Susannah, Justinian, Frances, Temperance and Elizabeth, and claimed 2,000 acres of land for transporting them into the Province. (3) Five more children were born to Thomas and Susannah after they were established in the Province.

On March 16, 1639, Cecillus, Lord Baltimore, elected St. Clement's Hundred and appointed Thomas Gerard as "Conservator of our Peace" within the Hundred. (4) Probably the first game conservation law in the Province was contained in this curious old document, which provided that severe penalties were to be assessed against "all persons whatsoever that shall unlawfully trespass upon any of our game of Deer, Turkies, Heron or other wild fowl or Shall destroy them their nests or eggs, wither upon our land or waters". On November 3, 1639, the St. Clement's Manor grant was made to Gerard, which made him one of the largest land holders in Maryland as has been noted by Mr. J. Hall Pleasants.(5)   With subsequent additional grants of land, the Manor included the whole neck of land extending from the head of St. Clement's Bay over to the Wicomico River, totaling some 11,400 acres of land. Also included in the grant were the Heron Islands of St. Clement's, St. Katherine's and St. Cecilla's, afterwards called St. Margaret's. (6) The grant provided for the establishment of a Court Baron and a Court Leet and the records of St. Clement's Manor are the only ones of this unusual type of Court proceedings known to be in existence in Maryland. (7)

In addition to the practice of medicine in both Maryland and Virginia, Gerard was active in provincial affairs from the time of his arrival. His selection as Burgess from St. Mary's in 1638 has been noted. On July 19, 1641 he was chosen Burgess :from St. Clement's Hundred. (8) Sometime between these dates he removed his residence to Longworth's Point, (now known as Colton's and also Kipel's Point), a high bluff on St. Clement's Manor overlooking St. Clement's Island and commanding a sweeping and beautiful view of the Potomac River, St. Clement's Bay and the Virginia shore. Because of his duties at St. Mary's City, he retained a Town House, Porke Hall, at the city. (9) It appears likely that the Manor House at Longworth Point was erected about 1644, for on November 1, 1643 Gerard made an agreement with Cornelius Canedy, a brickmaker, whereby Canedy agreed to make brick for Gerard for a period of three years. (10) This house was destroyed by Richard Ingle, during the Ingle Invasion. (11) The second house was destroyed by the British on June 13, 1781, during the Revolutionary War, and one of Gerard's descendents, Herbert Blackstone, was carried off as a prisoner of war.(12)

On the morning of March 23, 1641 an incident occurred which has caused the name of Thomas Gerard to be remembered in Maryland history at the expense of his many worthwhile contributions to the growth of the infant Province and his achievements in many fields. A complaint by the Protestants against Gerard was read before the Assembly "for taking away the Key of the Chappel and carrying away the Books out of the Chappel and such proceedings desired against him for it as to Justice appertaineth. Mr. Gerard being charged to make answer to the house upon hearing of the Prosecutors and his defence found that Mr. Gerard was guilty of a misdemeanor and that he should bring the Books and the Key taken away to the place where he had them and relinquish all title to them or the house and should pay for a fine 500 pounds tobacco towards the maintenance of the first minister as should arrive."(13)   It is generally believed that the chapel mentioned is one that Gerard erected on St. Clement's Manor, although the petition of the Protestants was presented by David Wickliff of St. George's Hundred which might indicate that the chapel in question was located in St. Mary's City or St. George's Hundred. In any event, Gerard, despite his prominence in the Province, was dealt with promptly and severely for his interference with Protestant worship. Although there has been much speculation as to the reasons for Gerard's closing the Protestant Chapel no theory has been substantiated. Thomas Gerard was a Roman Catholic but his wife and children were Protestants. It is a matter of record that Gerard erected a chapel on St. Clement's Manor for his family, friends and servants. John Walter Thomas has written that this chapel was located on St. Paul's Creek, a little below the present All Saint's Protestant Episcopal Church and was the third Protestant Church to be erected in Maryland. (14)   All Saints Church is located on Tomakokin creek, now commonly called Cobrum creek, approximately eight miles from Longworth Point, the original home of Thomas Gerard on St. Clement's Manor. The writer has been puzzled for some years as to why Gerard would have located the chapel, erected for his familly, friends and servants, eight miles from his manor house, in what was then the forest or backwoods, approximately 3/4 of a mile from a boat landing.   A review of the early Maryland maps at the Library of Congress answered this question. The Gerard chapel was not located near the present All Saints Church nor on St. Paul's creek, except due to a map maker's error. St. Patrick's Creek is located about one mile from Longworth Point, the Gerard home, and this name is mentioned in the sale of 220 acres of land in 1666 by Gerard to Edward Connery. (14a) The earliest Maryland map at the Library of Congress, showing the creeks in question is dated 1794 and shows the name St. Paul's creek for St. Patrick's creek. (14b)   This error was repeated on subsequent maps until 1940. (14c)   The error was repeated again on maps dated 1841 and 1852 but finally corrected in 1865 (14d) and appears correctly as St. Patrick's Creek on all subsequent maps.   It appears from this that the Gerard chapel was erected at the head of a branch of St. Patrick's Creek, in King and Queen Parish, about a mile from the Gerard home, which was convenient by land or water to the whole community living on this neck of land. On December 16, 1696 the Provincial Council ordered that "the vestry of King and Queen parish in St. Marie's County make inquiry of Capt. Gerard Slye (grandson of Thomas Gerard) concerning one hundred acres of land, said to be given to the Church by Mr. Thomas Gerard Senr (15) Slye attempted to deny this gift but was unsuccessful for in 1750 the vestry of King and Queen Parish was authorized to sell the glebe land given by Gerard and to purchase a glebe nearer the center of the parish (15a) The Maryland Assembly, on June 1, 1750, in view of a petition that "the Parish Church is so situated that the said petitioners cannot, without riding a great distance attend the service of God there" authorized the purchase of one acre of land near Tomakokin Run for a Chapel of Ease. (15b) It is evident from this that the Gerard chapel was not located on Tomakokin Creek, the present site of All Saints Church, but was located away from the center of the parish, namely down near the tip of St. Clement's Manor and undoubtedly on St. Patrick's Creek. Also it would appear that the Gerard chapel was standing in 1750 and continued to be the Parish Church for some years although it eventually disappeared and its location was forgotten. But history has a way of repeating itself for in 1895 an Episcopal Mission House was opened at Colton's (Longworth's) Point. (15c) Services were conducted by the Reverend Mr. Sohnnig. In 1900, the parochial Chapel of St. Agnes was erected near Palmer's on St. Patrick's Creek, undoubtedly near the location of the old Gerard Chapel. (15d) The Reverend Mr. LaRoche was the first Minister to officiate and Miss Nell Palmer was in charge of the Sunday School. A staunch supporter of the Chapel was Mrs. Jennie Husemann, whose youngest daughter, Elsie, was the first child to be baptised in the new Chapel. On the same day her three older children, Julia, (Mrs. George Knott), Charles and Ethel (Mrs. William Petti) were received in the Episcopal Church. One of Mrs. Knott's most cherished possessions is a silver medal awarded her as a child for excellence in her Sunday School work at the Chapel.

Considerable difficulty with the Indians on St. Clesent's Manor was experienced by the Colonists, particularly in the stealing of cattle and corn, which caused Lord Baltimore on October 29, 1642 to grant a Commission to Gerard to take whatever action, including "the killing of any of them if it shalbe necessary" required to put an end to the trouble.(16)

On November 17, 1643, Lord Baltimore appointed Thomas

Gerard as a member of the Provincial Council for "his diligent endeavors for the advancement and prosperity of the colony". (17) Other appointments and commissions followed, such as, to look after his Lordship's property, to advise concerning Indian problems and the like. Gerard continued as a member of the Council until the time of Fendall's Rebellion in 1659 and also served as a Judge of the Provincial Court during this period.

It is apparent that Gerard, as a member of Lord Baltimore's government, suffered damage at the hands of Richard Ingle during Ingle's Invasion in the years 1644-1646 because after the difficulties he obtained through court action part of Ingle's loot in settlement of his claim. Gerard was then sued by Thomas Cornwaleys who claimed that he had prior right to recover from Ingle.(18) This dispute dragged through the courts for several years.

Thomas Gerard, as is borne out by the Archives of Maryland not only was active in the practice of medicine, as a member of the Council and a Judge of the Provincial Court but he was also an able farmer, a manufacturer of liquors, particularly peach brandy, and a breeder of fine cattle. Apparently he was also an excellent sailor for his many trips between Longworth Point at St. Clement's Manor and St. Mary's City were made by boat, although the type of boat is not mentioned. He might also be described as one of the first realtors in Maryland for the Provincial Court records record the sale of many pieces of land and other property.(19) In fact due to his many activities he was involved in more court actions than any other man of his time. Perhaps this is the reason that he provided in his will that "if it shall hereafter happen at anytime hereafter yt any ambiguity, doubt, question or controversy doe gro or rise concerning ye true meaning and intent of this my will and testmt, I will therefore yt my Extors and Extri choice each of them a judicious prson and according to there verdict lett ye doubt and dispute be ended without comencing a sute at law".(19a)

During the Puritan Uprising (1654-1656) Gerard was appointed as one of Governor Stone's Captains and took part in the battle at Herring Creek on the Severn River where he was captured with the rest of Stone's force. Although quarter had been promised, four of the men were executed by the Puritans and Gerard narrowly escaped with his life. (19b) After the difficulties with the Puritans had been resolved, Gerard returned to his duties as a.member of the

Council under the Govenorship of Josias Fendall.

One of the men executed by the Puritans was William Eltonhead, a member of the Council and close associate of Gerard. There are indications that Eltonhead married Jane, the daughter of Thomas Gerard, but conclusive evidence is lacking at this time. Mrs. Jane Eltonhead, the wife of William, is a fascinating character and her life, if the whole story could be pieced together, would be a highlight of life, love and adventure that came to many of the Provincial ladies of the Seventeenth Century. Jane, (nee Gerard ?), as it appears from the record, married first Thomas Smith (Smyth) who was captured by Governor Leonard Calvert after the reduction of Kent Island and hanged as a pirate for his part in leading the attack on the fleet of Captain Thomas Cornwaleys.(20) She was left a widow with two daughters, Gertrude and Jane. (21) Soon afterwards she married Captain Philip Taylor, who was an associate of her former husband and was indicted with him, but who was lucky enough to avoid hanging. Apparently he died a natural death prior to 1649, and left two children, Sarah and Thomas. (22) Sometime after this, Jane, perhaps acting on the basis that if you can't lick the opposition, you had best join it, (although it was probably true love), married William Eltonhead of his Lordship's Council and became sister-in-law of Cuthbert Fenwick, who had valiantly fought her two previous husbands as Lieutenant of Captain Cornwaleys "in the good pinace called the St. Margarett in the harbour of great Wighcocomico in the Bay of Cheseapeack on the tenth day of May in the year of our Lord one thousand six hundred thirty and five".(23) As we know, Jane soon lost her third husband, on March 28, 1655, after the battle of the Severn. There seems to have been no issue from this marriage as Jane testified that William Eltonhead "left all his lands with all his other goods and chattles to her disposing, for the good of her and her children and desired her to allow unto Robert Fenwick and Richard Fenwick (nephews) some part of the lands according to her discretion".(24) It is interesting to note that Cuthbert Fenwick's will which is cited in Footnote 23 was witnessed by Elizabeth Gerard, a daughter of Thomas Gerard and that both the Gerard and Eltonhead families were from Lancashire. It is difficult to piece together the ancient records and particularly so in the case of Jane Eltonhead who is often confused with her sister-in-law Jane Eltonhead Fenwick. This difficulty is compounded by the fact that as many as five marriages were not uncommon in the early days. In this, the ladies of those days were not so different from their sisters today, except that the ladies in the early days buried their husbands instead of divorcing them, which perhaps is not a bad idea in a good many cases.

On October 5, 1658, Thomas Gerard was the central figure in another religious controversy for on that date the Attorney General of the Province preferred charges against Father Francis Fitzherbert "that he hath Rebelliously and mutinously sayd tht If Thomas Gerard (of the Councell) did not come and bring his wife and children to his Church, he would come and force then to his Church, Contrary to a knowne Act of Assembly in this Province".(25) In his testimony, "Thomas Gerard Esqr. sayth uppon oath, That having conference with Mr. ffitzherbert as they were walking in the woods, and in his owne Orchard, Touching the bringing his children to the Roman Catholque Church, Hee gave Mr. ffitzherbert reasons, why it was not safe for himselfe and this Depont, and the sd Mr. ffitzherbert told this Depont That hee would compell and force them and likewise he sayd, that hee would excommunicate him, ffor hee would make him know tht hee had to doe wt the bringing up of his Children, and his Estate" Gerard's testimony that it was not safe for him or Father Fitzherbert if the children were brought to the Catholic Church is inexplicable. Whether this religious difficulty carried any weight in Gerard's decision to break with Lord Baltimore In 1659 (Fendall's Rebellion) is problematical. The chances are that it did not because the Court adjourned before the case was completed and it was finally settled until 1662 when Father Fitzherbert was acquitted.(26)

On the same day that Gerard's religious difficulties with Father Fitzherbert were aired, Richard Smith, the Attorney General made some very serious charges against Gerard before the Council. (27) He was accused of violating the secrecy of the Council, of saying that Governor Fendall was a tool of the people of Ann Arundel and was not above helping himself to the Provincial revenues, that Capt Stone, Job Chandler and Dr. Luke Barber were secretly playing into the hands of Richard Bennett, Lord Baltimore's opponent, that the whole Council was a bunch of rogues and he would not sit with them and finally he was accused of drunkeness. Gerard asked for and was granted time to answer the charges against him but the Attorney General let the suit drop, which caused Gerard to write a letter of complaint to Lord Baltimore who ordered the Council to give him satisfaction.(28) It is of interest to note that in connection with the charges of drunkeness, Henry Coursey testified that "he was on board of Covill's ship with Mr. Gerard, that he came from on board with him to Mr. Packer's landing, that the said Gerard had drunke some-thing extraordinary but was not so much in drinke but he could gett out of a Carts way and further saith not".(29) Whether the other charges against Gerard were true or not is unknown as the Council did not persue the matter. Probably there was a good deal of truth in the charges since they had been overheard at the home of his son-in-law, Robert Slye, at Bushwood. In view of the long, trusted, and friendly relationship between Gerard and Lord Baltimore, extending over a period of more than 20 years, it is difficult to understand how Gerard could have thrown in with Fendall when the show-down came in 1659. Certainly he had no love for the Puritans of Anne Arundel, who sided with Fendall, after his experience at Herring Creek in 1655 when several of his close associates and friends were executed and he narrowly escaped the same fate. Keeping this fact in mind it is easy to understand the statements attributed to him in the charges before the Council. In the absence of any of his personal papers (which the writer is still endeavoring to locate) perhaps the best conjecture has been made by Mr. F. E. Sparks, in his book "Causes of the American Revolution of 1689", wherein he states, "The real cause of the disturbance that now arose, (Fendall's Rebellion) are scarcely explained by Maryland historians. Governor Fendall is charged with being the chief cause of the Rebellion. It is true that Fendall tried to keep in favor with the party of resistance (The Ann Arundel Party) and that he was intimately connected with Gerard whose party was destined to triumph in 1689 but it was really the question of taxation that caused the so-called Fendall's Rebellion. It is sometimes said it was a Puritan Movement and so it was in one sense, but Gerard who seemed to be the real leader, was a Catholic who had been and was then a member of the Council. In 1647 an Act was passed by the Assembly granting the Proprietor a duty of 10 shillings on every hogshead of tobacco exported to any other port.(30) Fendall, in order to promote the rebellion, advised the Assembly and the people that Lord Baltimore had ordered that if the Act was not passed, then he, Fendall was to put into execution the Act for Customs of 1646, (which had never been in force), for the payment of ten shillings per hogshead on all tobacco exported out of the Province. In reality also, Lord

Baltimore had written Fendall to ask the Assembly to repeal the Act for Customs of 1646 and provide instead a straight duty of two shillings per hogshead of tobacco, which fact as Lord Baltimore wrote, "he wickedly concealed from the people". It is significant that Gerard in his petition for a pardon, after the Rebellion, used the following words "Upon mature deliberacon (being) Sensible that through Ignorance something hath been done by him while this Province was without Government", which indicates that he had been taken in by Fendall.(32)   At the same time the Assembly also was deceived because the Speaker delivered a paper to Fendall which read "whereas the howse hath had certaine information that the Lord Proprietary hath sent to the secretary a Warrant and demand annexed to it to repeale the Act of Ten shillings per hogshead. The Howse do therefore desire and request the said warrant and demand be exhibited to the publick viewe of this Assembly forthwith".(33) There to no record that such a paper was produced and since Lord Baltimore had directed the letter to Fendall, he must have concealed it.

Another event occurred in 1659 which may have influenced Gerard in his decision to break with Lord Baltimore. He had, in the right of his wife, laid claim to 1,000 acres of land (Snow Hill) which had been granted in 1640 to Abel Snow, his brother-in-law, who was now deceased. The land was repossessed by Lord Baltimore under the Act for Deserted Plantations and had been granted by him in 1652 to Richard Willan and James Lindsey.   Apparently there had been litigation for sometime and finally Philip Calvert, Secretary of the Province, appealed the case to Lord Baltimore who ruled against Gerard and in his own favor.(54) It should be remembered also that only a few years had elapsed since the time of the Ingle Invasion and the Puritan Uprising and that the Government of the Province was far from secure. Under such conditions it was a great temptation to any strong man to take the Government into his own hands rather than again risk the loss of all of his possessions.

It seems fairly evident that Gerard was faced with such a decision and with at least some fancied justification for his action. After he had reached a decision, it is evident that Gerard maneuvered to have the Assembly and the Council meet at a location where he would have a better opportunity to dominate the meetings. The ideal location was at St. Clement's Manor, which was far removed from the usual meeting place, St. Mary's City, and where Gerard would be sure of the attendance of all his friends and adherents. The first and second meetings were held at the Gerard Home at Longworth Point on February 28, 1659.(35) All subsequent meetings including the final meeting were held in the home of Robert Slye (Gerard's son-in-law) at Bushwood on St. Clement's Manor.(36) During a period of two weeks a struggle went on between the Upper and Lower Houses of the Assembly. The Lower House claimed themselves to be a lawful Assembly without dependence on any power in the Province and the highest Court of Judicature. There was considerable manuevering back and forth between the two Houses and finally Fendall on March 13, 1659 came out in the open and took the position that the Burgesses (by the intent of the King in Lord Baltimore's patent) could make and enact laws by themselves, publish them in the name of the Proprietor and they would be in full force, provided they were agreeable to reason and-not repugnant to the laws of England. The Secretary, Philip Calvert, brother of the Proprietor, of the Upper House declared that it was not in the power of the Burgesses by themselves without assent of the Lord Proprietary or the Governor to enact any laws. Calvert then proceeded to poll the Upper House or Council. In addition to Fendall and Calvert only four members were present; Gerard and Col.Nathaniel Utie supported Fendall and Baker Brooke and John Price supported Calvert. The following day Fendall expressed himself as being willing to sit with the Lower House as Governor on their terms. Calvert and Baker Brooke "departed the howse (after leave asked) and given in these words or to this effect (vizt) you say if you please, wee shall not force you to goe or stay, uttered by the Governor". The Rebellion was on.

The Rebellion collapsed in May 1660 when Charles II returned to the throne of England and the Proprietor was restored to favor at the Court. Lord Baltimore, in a furious letter dated August 24, 1660, instructed his brother Philip Calvert, then Governor, to deal harshly with Gerard, Fendall, Hatch, Slye and others who took a leading part in the revolt. They could be sentenced to death, be banished from the Province and suffer the loss of all the property.(37) Gerard's Manor lands and other property were seized and he was banished from the Province. He temporarily retired to his lands on the Machodoc River in Westmoreland County, Virginia, a 3500 acre holding known as Gerard's Preserve.(38) In a few months, however, applied to the Maryland Council for a pardon which was promptly granted. He was restored to citizenship in the Province but forbidden to hold office or to have a voice in elections and his lands and other property were restored to him.(39) It is significant that while Fendall was required to pay a fine of 50 pounds Sterling, Gerard was required to pay 100 pound Sterling and 5,000 pounds of tobacco, and in addition required to post 10,000 pounds of tobacco as collateral for his good behavior.

After the restoral of his estates Gerard returned to live in Maryland, where he continued his practice as a Physician, looked after his lands and completed more sales of property. His large family consisted of three sons and seven daughters. Perhaps this is why St. Clement's Manor was often referred to as Bedlam Neck. He had many friends on both sides of the Potomac River and several of his daughters married Virginians. In addition to enjoying the favorite provincial drink of "burnt brandy" Gerard was not averse to cards and dice. One incident in the latter game resulted in a law suit which is recorded in the Maryland Archives.(40) In 1666, after the death of his wife, Sussannah, to who he was very devoted, Gerard moved to his lands of Machodoc, in Westmoreland County, Virginia.(41) A fine old two-story brick house, set between two outside chimneys still stands there. The original widely overhung eaves of the hipped roof have been changed in recent years. The home is now owned by Mrs. Margaret A. Roberts. John Gerard, the only grandson to credited with having erected this house about 1685.(42) It was here that Thomas Gerard together with Henry Corbin, John Lee and Isaac Allerton, "that never-to-be-forgotten quartette of Bon-Vivants," entered into a contract in 1670, later only recorded, to build a "Banquetting House" at or near the head of Cherives (now Jackson:s) Creek, where their estates cornered. It was agreed that each party to the contract should "yearly, according to his due course, make an honorable treatment-fit to entertain the undertakers thereof".(43) Bishop Meade cited this an example of "riotnus living".

After settling at Machodoc, Gerard married Rose Tucker, a widow with two children, Rose, who married   Blackistone and Sarah who married Wm. Fitzhugh.(44) Gerard died here in 1673, but in compliance with a request contained in his will, his body was taken to Longworth Point, his old home in Maryland, and buried there in the private burial grounds by the side of his first wife, Susannah.(45) This private cemetery still existed until a few years ago when one of the late owners of the land threw the tombstones over the bank into the Potomac River, adjacent to St. Clement's, Island, and leveled the plot. Not satisfied with this act of desecration it has been reported that a guest at the Hotel there at the time was permitted to open one of the graves and remove a skull, perhaps-that of Thomas Gerard. In a terrific storm in the summer of 1933 the Hotel was wrecked and much ground washed away so that now there is no evidence whatsoever of the original Gerard home or burial grounds.

Although Gerard made elaborate provisions in his will for any children that might be born of his second marriage there was no Issue. The children of his marriage to Susannah Snow were as follows:

  1. Justinian, married Sarah   widow of Wilkes
     Naunders (47)
  2. Thomas, married Susannah Curtis (48)
  3. Susannah, married (1) Robert Slye (49)
                       (2) John Coode (50)
  4. Anne, married (1) Walter Broadhurst (51)
                   (2) Henry Brett (51)
                   (3) John Washington (51)
  5. Frances, married (1) Col. Thos. Spoke (52)
                      (2) Col. Valentine Peyton (52)
                      (3) Capt. John Appleton C52)
                      (4) Col. John Washington (52)
                      (5) Wm. Hardwick (52)
  6. Temperance, married (1) Daniel Hutt (53)
                         (2) John Crabbe (53)
  7. Elizabeth, married (1) Nehemiah Blackistone (54)
                        (2) Ralph Rymer (54)
                        (3) Joshua Guibert (54)
  8. Jane or Janette, married
  9. John, married Elizabeth   (55)
  10. Mary, married Kenelm Cheseldine (56)

None of Gerard's three sons long survived him. John died first, prior to 1678, leaving a son John and daughter Rebecca, who married Charles Calvert in 1722. The second John had no sons and his only child, Elizabeth, married Benedict Calvert in 1748. (58) Since his uncles died without issue, this branch of the Gerard family in this country became extinct at his death. Consequently, the Gerards of

294

America most be descendants of William Gerard, probably of the same family In England, who obtained a grant of 125 acres of land in Westmoreland County on January 31, 1716. (57) The family name continues in England and the present holder of the title is Baron Frederick John Gerard, N.C. of Lancashire. -Thomas Gerard, Jr. was given Basford Manor and Westwood Manor by his father. He sold Basford Manor to Gov. Thomas Motley in 1677 and upon his death in 1696, since he died without Issue, Westwood Manor passed to his brother, Justinian. Justinian was left St. Clement's Manor (those portions not already settled on his sisters) by his father. He died without issue in 1688 and left everything to his widow, who later married Michael Curtis. They sold both Westwood and St. Clement's Manor to Charles Carroll on May 18, 1711. (59)

Two of Gerard's daughters married Col. John Washington, the great grandfather of George Washington, although he had no issue by either of them. The first was Anne Gerard who married him in 1669. After her death, Col. Washington married her sister, Frances on May 10, 1676. She survived Col. Washington and then married for the fifth time. A great grandaughter of this fifth marriage, Ann Aylett, married in 1743 Augustine Washington, a brother of George Washington. It is interesting to note that Col. John Washington came from Lancashire, England, as did the Gerards. The probabilities are that the families knew each other there. (60)

Temperance Gerard married-Daniel Hutt of Virginia. Hutt was originally a New England Sailing Master and was convicted in 1659 of illegally trading with the Indians in Maryland and his Bark, the Mayflower, was confiscated through action of the Provincial Court. Although not an inhabitant of the Province at this time he was present at the sessions at St. Clement's Manor and Bushwood which preceded Fendall's Rebellion. He subsequently was Master of vessels engaged in the Barbados trade and made his home in Virginia. (61) After the death of Hutt, Temperance married John Crabbe, a prosperous Virginia merchant. (62)

Walter Broadhurst who was the first husband of Anne Gerard first appears in the Maryland records in 1642 and was closely associated with Thomas Gerard from this time until he moved to Westmoreland County, Virginia in 1657. He appears to have been an adherent of Capt. Edward Hill, following the Ingle Invasion. Their son, Walter, returned to England where he married and had a family and there died in 1707. Henry Brett the second husband of Anne, whom she married in 1665 or 1667 was a Virginian. He died prior to 1669. There was no issue. As previously mentioned Anne's third husband was Col. John Washington of Virginia. (63)

The first and fifth husbands of Frances Gerard, Col Thos. Speaks and Wm. Hardwick (Hardidge) were closely associated with Walter Broadhurst and Thomas Gerard, father of Frances. Both Speaks and Hardwick are first mentioned in Maryland records in 1642 (64) when they were sent with an expedition of soldiers to Kent Island. Subsequently Hardwick, Broadhurst and Gerard testified against Richard Ingle and a warrant was issued to Hardwick to arrest Ingle for high treason. They testified to Ingle's traitorious utterances when his ship lay anchored at St. Clement's Island, Just off Longworth's Point. (65) Gerard was amply repaid by Ingle later when he burned Gerard's home. Undoubtedly Hardwick and Broadhurst were subjected to like treatment. It was noted that Broadhurst, like Gerard, became involved with Cornwaleys, in the effort to recover property-after the affairs in the Province had quieted down. After Col. Speake's death Frances married Col. Valentine Peyton, a Virginian, and moved there. (66) After Col. Peyton's death, she married Capt. John Appleton, another Virginian, who died in 1676, whereupon she married Col. John Washington. Upon the death of Col. Washington, she married Wm. Hardwick, who had moved to Nomini in Virginia in 1650. Hardwick was described by Nathaniel Pope, formerly of Maryland but then of Virginia as "a well-beloved friend".(67)

There are indications that Janette or Jane Gerard, another daughter of Thomas Gerard, married Wm. Eltonhead, who was shot after being captured during the Puritan Uprising, although there is such confusion on this score. Some writers have indicated that she married Richard Eltonhead and others that she was the first wife of Cuthbert Fenwick, famous in early Maryland history, who subsequently married Jane Eltonhoad, the sister of William Eltonhead. There were so many Janes and so many marriages that it will probably take another 300 years to completely unscramble them.

Robert Slye married Susannah Gerard who was the oldest of the Gerard girls.(68) She was given Bushwood Manor by her father at the time of her marriage, which subsequently descended to her son Gerard and grandson George, who willed it to his nephew, Col.

Edmund Plowden. (69) Robert Slye, although he was the son-in-law of Thomas Gerard, accepted a position on the Puritan Council and as a Commissioner of the Province in 1654-1655.(70) This action within the family given some idea of the turmoil in the Province during this period. As previously noted the Assembly met at Slye's home preceding Fendall's Rebellion and there is no doubt that he played an important role in this uprising also. Although Slye died considerably before the Rebellion of 1689, the family penchant for rebellion was to be carried on, this time strongly and successfully. According to Spark's theory it was a continuation or revival of the so-called Fendall Rebellion of 1659. After the death of Robert Slye, Susannah married John Coode who organized and led the successful rebellion of 1689. (71) His chief lieutenants were two other Gerard sons-in-law, Kenelm Cheseldine and Nehemiah Blackistone. Kenelm Cheseldine married Mary, the youngest daughter of Thomas Gerard. Her dowry included St. Katherine's Island, White's Neck, Broad Neck, Westwood Lodge (100 acres) and Mattapany. The latter tract of land should not be confused with Mattapany-Sewell on the Patuxent River. (72) Nehemiah Blackistone married Elizabeth Gerard, whose dowry included St. Clement's Island, Longworth Point (the original Gerard home on St. Clement's Manor) and Dare's Neck. She subsequently married Ralph Rymer and Joshua Guibert, both of Maryland.

The history of the Protestant Rebellion-of 1689 and the activities of Coode, Cheseldine and Blackistone are too well known to be repeated here. The details may be reviewed in the Maryland Archives of this period. The success of this rebellion put an end to religious freedom in Maryland for almost eighty years. It was not until the American Revolution that Maryland again became the "Free State". Strangely enough, within a comparatively few years after the Rebellion the Coode, Cheseldine and Sly families were brought into the Roman Catholic Church. This was the work, largely of a great missionary priest of early Maryland history Father William Hunter of the Society of Jesus. (74) George Slye built the first Sacred Heart Church at Bushwood, which Is mentioned in his will dated 1773. (75) He is buried there as are many of the Cheseldine family. Many of the Coode family also are buried in the Sacred Heart Cemetery and at old St. Inigoes in the lower part of the County. Most of the Coode descendants are now living in Nashville, Tenn. Many of the Cheseldine descendants are still living at White's Neck and in nearby

Washington. This is true also of the Blackistone descendants. In recent years the beautiful old Blackistone home at River Springs has been restored and one of the family now owns Upper Brambly, which adjoins Bushwood. The original name was Bromley, named by Thomas Gerard after one of the Gerard Family manors in England.

Thomas Gerard of Maryland and Virginia

Old World Roots

By David Spalding, C.F.X.

The following is part of the material submitted by Brother David, who has done extensive research on Dr. Thomas Gerard, to The Chronicles of St. Mary's.

The career of Dr. Thomas Gerard provides us with an excellent example of the adventurer who sought to better his position politically, socially and economically by taking advantage of Lord Baltimore's offer of a manor in the New World. Unfortunately, not many facts are available on Gerard's life in the Old World. From a few scattered sources, however, enough information can be pieced together so that certain conclusions can be drawn about three important points: Gerard's social and economic status in England, his motives for wishing to emigrate, and the immediate influences that persuaded him to cast his lot with the Maryland adventurers.

Only one serious attempt has been made to trace the family connection of Dr. Thomas Gerard in England, and that incorrectly. He is asserted to have been the son of Sir Thomas Gerard of Bryn and the brother of Richard, one of the original adventurers. 1. There is undoubtedly a relationship between Thomas Gerard the emigrant and the family of Sir Thomas Gerard, but not nearly so close as the author in question would have it. The importance of the influence of this family (the Gerards of Bryn) on the career of the Maryland adventurer stems not so much from kinship as from other considerations, of which it is necessary to have some knowledge.

About 1340, William Gerard of Kingsley Cheshire, acquired by marriage the manor of Ashton in Lancashire. 2. From this point on the family fortunes increased rapidly and the name acquired some importance. By a series of well-planned marriages many other manors and estates in several counties came into the family's possession. The summit of the family fortune was reached shortly before the reign of Elizabeth with the marriage of Sir Thomas Gerard to the heiress of Sir John Port, lord of the manor of Etwell and possessor of considerable estates. It was during the lifetime of the same Sir Thomas Gerard, however, that the Gerards of Bryn fell on evil days. 3. Unfortunately,

299

Sir Thomas Gerard, a somewhat adventurous individual, espoused the cause of Mary Stuart. For his complicity in the Ridolfi and Babington plots he was twice thrown into prison. The price of his freedom on the first occasion was the forced sale of one of his most prized manors, Bromley, to his Protestant cousin, Sir Gilbert Gerard. 4. In addition, Sir Thomas was compelled to sell or mortgage several other lordships in Leicestershire, Derbshire, Cheshire and three holdings in Lancashire. 5. At the time of his second imprisonment in 1586 he was faced with the loss of most of his remaining estates to his half brother, or more exactly his base brother, whose name was also Thomas. 6. To prevent such a loss and to obtain his freedom, Sir Thomas renounced his faith for a time and supplied evidence for the Crown against Philip Howard, Earl of Arundel. 7.

Sir Thomas had two sons, Thomas and John. John was the noted Jesuit. 8. Thomas, the elder son, succeeded to the family estates at the death of his father in 1601. In two years time the situation improved for the Gerards of Bryn when James I ascended the throne of England. On his journey to London James conferred the honor of knighthood on Thomas Gerard, expressing his gratitude to the family for their services to his mother. In 1611, he bestowed on Sir Thomas the title of baronet. 9. The reigns of James I and Charles I were times of comparative peace and security for the Gerards of Bryn, though they were compelled on occasions to pay large fines in accordance with the penal statutes enacted against recusants. The family estates, which now consisted of the manors Ashton and Windle in Lancashire, Etwall and Hardwicke in Derbyshire, and several smaller holdings, remained intact during this period.

The second baronet (whose name was also Thomas) enjoyed his title for only nine years. At his death in 1630, he left several sons and a daughter. Three of the sons call for special mention. The eldest, Sir William Gerard, succeeded to the title and to the family estates. The second son, Richard, was among the first Maryland adventurers and was, like his great-grandfather, an adventurous and romantic character. 10. Among the four remaining sons was a Thomas Gerard, but he could not have been (as the above mentioned author states) the Thomas Gerard of our study. The son of the second baronet died in England without issue. 11.

Who, then, was the Thomas Gerard who sailed to Maryland in 1638? One valuable clue in the Maryland records enables us to place him geographically in England and thereby gain some knowledge of his family connections and his background. In two instances he is referred to as Thomas Gerard of New Hall, Lancashire. 12. The County of Lancaster contains (or contained) many estates so named, but the New Hall with which we are concerned was located upon the manor of Ashton, principal estate of the Gerards of Bryn. That this is the New Hall in question can be proved from the baptismal records of Winwick parish (of which Ashton was a part). From these we learn that Thomas Gerard, "son of Mr. John Gerard of New Hall," was baptized December 10, 1608. 13. This is undoubtedly our Dr. Thomas Gerard. The fact that he named one of his earlier holdings in Maryland "Ashton" further validates the connection. 14.

What, then, was the relationship of Dr. Thomas Gerard to the Gerards of Bryn? Though his residence upon the manor would seem to indicate a close kinship, he was certainly not a direct descendant of Sir Thomas Gerard the Elizabethan. Though Sir Thomas had both son and grandson named John, neither could have been "Mr. John Gerard," the father of Dr. Thomas Gerard. 15. Of the several freeholders of Ashton Manor, however, listed for 1600,. the first named was a Thomas Gerard of Garswood. 16. This man was undoubtedly the grandfather of our Thomas Gerard, since Garswood and New Hall were the same. 17. Moreover, it is probable that Thomas Gerard of Garswood was the base brother (or son of the base brother) of Sir Thomas Gerard the Elizabethan above mentioned. 18.

To these facts we are able to add one or two others, and a general picture emerges of Dr. Thomas Gerard's social and economic status. The fact that he was a surgeon would presuppose a university education, provided that he were a licensed one. 19. He married into a Staffordshire family of some means. Economically Gerard was well off, since his estate was a large one (though he probably possessed little liquid capital). Also Gerard undoubtedly enjoyed the status of "gentleman". 20. In short, Dr. Thomas Gerard was a man of some education, a man of property, a member of the gentry. Though not a member of the greater gentry. he was (perhaps for this very reason) an ideal prospect for Lord Baltimore's Maryland venture. Besides being a gentleman of substance, Gerard was a Catholic and was connected with a family whose name Baltimore was pleased to have associated with his undertaking. 21.

What considerations, then, moved Thomas Gerard to cast his

lot with Maryland colonists? Since Gerard was a Catholic, a religious motive might be deduced. 22. Undoubtedly there were religious considerations in Gerard's case. The story of the sufferings of the Gerards of Bryn for their faith was undoubtedly still vivid in the minds of those who dwelt upon Ashton Manor. The penal laws against recusants, though relaxed, were still a source of menace, if not actual hardship, for Catholic landholders. Moreover, no Catholic could hope for political preferment in England. In spite of a somewhat persistent feeling of insecurity and frustration, however, the Catholic gentry of England during the middle period of the reign of Charles I were enjoying a brief period of prosperity and peace that they had not enjoyed since the time of Mary Tudor nor would again enjoy until the nineteenth century. 23. Though religious considerations might eventually have induced Gerard to break all ties with England, at the time of his first voyage to America in 1638, they were, if anything, secondary. The principal reason, then, for Gerard's wish to emigrate must be sought elsewhere.

In addition to the religious motive there was another very compelling reason that prompted the Englishman of the seventeenth century to emigrate to America, and that was to better his position. This he would achieve primarily by the acquisition of land, which to the English mentality of the time meant economic gain and social advancement. To those who had already attained a degree of wealth and station in England, it meant also political preferment, for undoubtedly men of rank and substance would be chosen to guide the political destinies of the new colonies. From what we shall see of Gerard, he was definitely a man of ambitions, a man who was most anxious to better his station in life. Though already a man of means, he was, nevertheless, a member of that restless group, the lesser gentry, who lived for the day that they could take their place beside the more prominent members of the gentry with whom they associated. Living as he did, a tenant upon a 6000 acre manor of a baronet, Gerard's aspirations were undoubtedly centered on just such a station as that of his kinsman, Sir William Gerard. But the acquisitions of a 6000 acre manor was unlikely. Manors at this time were not easy to come by even if Gerard had the capital to purchase one, which he undoubtedly did not. The offer of a manorial estate in Maryland at comparatively little expense would obviously be most attractive to men like Thomas Gerard. Perhaps the most cogent argument for this motive in Gerard's case was the great avidity with which he subsequently possessed himself of large tracts of land in Maryland, the tireless energy he there displayed in enlarging his manorial estates to impressive proportions. Before considering this phase of Gerard's career, however, there remains another very important consideration to be taken into account.

What were the immediate influences that caused Gerard to translate this wish for manorial status into action? Here it is not necessary to search far to discover two important agents that contributed to Gerard's decision, in this case two families with whom Gerard was intimately connected. One was the Gerards of Bryn; the other was the Snow family of Ferny Hill in Staffordshire.

When Richard Gerard, the second son of the baronet, sailed to Maryland in 1633, it was not the first time that the attention of the Gerards of Bryn had been drawn to that section of the world. The tradition of a New World haven for English Catholics had its beginning with Sir Thomas Gerard the Elizabethan, the great-grandfather of Richard. This Elizabethan knight had been largely responsible for turning the second expedition of Sir Humphrey Gilbert into a Catholic venture. 24. This fact undoubtedly accounts for the ready response of the Gerards of Bryn to Lord Baltimore's appeal in 1633. Richard, however, was evidently not too pleased with prospects in Maryland. He returned to England within a year's time after having sold his Maryland estates to the Jesuit fathers "at a deare raite". 25. Dr. Thomas Gerard could not have been insensible to this reawakening of interest in the New World, caused by the departure and return of Sir William's brother. Undoubtedly he received a first hand account of the new colony from his distant cousin. It was not Richard, however, who provided the principal stimulus to Gerard's decision.

Gerard was married to Susannah Snow, the sister of three Staffordshire gentlemen who were closely connected with Lord Baltimore in his Maryland venture. The most prominent was Abel Snow, who held an important post in the Cursitor's Office of Chancery Land in London. 26. The other two, Justinian and Marmaduke Snow, had sailed to Maryland sometime before 1638. Justianian had been appointed by Lord Baltimore Chief Factor in the proprietary fur trade. 27. Undoubtedly it was the brothers-in-law of Thomas Gerard who persuaded him to share with them the opportunities that America presented.

The story of Gerard's decision, however, does not end here. Gerard seems to have gone to Maryland with some misgivings, for he sailed without his family and with no capital for establishing himself there. 28. He did not sell his estate in England until ten or more years later. Perhaps an unfavorable account of Maryland by Richard Gerard had cautioned him as to the advisability of immediately casting his lot with the Maryland adventurers. His first voyage in 1638 seems to have been of a purely exploratory nature. Wholly unforeseen circumstances, however determined Gerard's subsequent career in the New World. Justinian Snow, who had made a trip to England sometime in or before 1639, died on his return voyage. Marmaduke, his brother, soon after fell ill, and Gerard was name administrator of the Snow estate in Maryland by a commission from Lord Baltimore. 29. Gerard seems to have profited no little from his office as administrator, for he was able thereby to secure for himself a manor in the New World. 30.

Once he found himself the possessor of a thousand acre estate in Maryland, Gerard evidently resolved to convert it into a profitable holding, for in the summer of 1640, he returned to England on the ship Blessing to secure additional servants and capital. The latter was provided by his brother-in-law, Abel Snow, in the form of a loan of f178 9s.9d. 31. In connection with this transaction there occurred October 5, 1640, a meeting in London at which were present Lord Baltimore, Thomas Cornwallis and John Langford (both prominent colonists), Abel Snow and Thomas Gerard. At this meeting a commercial agreement between Snow and Gerard was witnessed, and important affairs of the colony were undoubtedly discussed. 32. Soon after this meeting Gerard returned to Maryland where he prospered.

It does not appear, however, that Gerard was at this point prepared to give up his estate in England. Two likely suppositions here present themselves. The one is that Gerard wished to develop fully his holdings in Maryland and make a name for himself there before selling out in England and bringing his family to America. The other is that Gerard intended his Maryland holdings as an auxiliary source of income or as a means of acquiring sufficient wealth to purchase a manor in England. The latter surmise seems to be the more probable since Gerard attained in Maryland economic stability and political preferment long before the final decision to abandon England was made. It was perhaps not clear even in Gerard's mind just what the eventual decision would be. Events both in England and America, however, tipped the balance in favor of Maryland as the sole center of Gerard's future endeavors.

In spite of any prejudices that Gerard might have once entertained concerning Maryland as a fit place to establish himself, he was prospering in this new land. On the other hand, conditions in England were rendering and aspirations for betterment there more and more untenable. Soon after Gerard's return to America in 1640, England was engulfed in the onrush of the Puritan upheaval. As the struggle progressed, there undoubtedly occurred on the part of Gerard a gradual shift of interest from the Old to the New World in proportion to the decline of the Royalist cause. 33. The Puritan victory in England (which occurred shortly after Gerard's appointment to the important position of Councilor in Maryland) forestalled any hopes that Gerard might have entertained for himself in England.

But Gerard waited a few more years before acting, perhaps vainly hoping for the fall of the Puritan power in England. From the latter part of 1647 to 1650, however, he made at least two trips to England. 34. In 1650 he sold his estate New Hall to the Launder family and brought his own family to Maryland. 35. Two important considerations undoubtedly determined Gerard in this course of action. The complete failure of a second Royalist uprising in 1648 shattered any hope that he might have had for the removal of Puritan control. Even more important, the ravages of this second campaign bore most heavily on the southern section of Lancashire. The area about the manor of Ashton was the center of greatest desolation. Destruction, famine and pestilence caused the people of Wigan and the township of Ashton to address to Parliament a petition for succor. 36. In the face of such dire conditions as these, Dr. Thomas Gerard undoubtedly acted as quickly as he could in disposing of his Lancashire estate and moving his family to a corner of the world where he had already created a comfortable place for himself. About the beginning of 1650, he took passage for America with family and servants. There is no record that he ever saw England again.

And thus it was that, though Gerard might have preferred to advance his station as a lord of the manor in England, events drew him inexorably toward America. Instigated by his brothers-in-law, he came to Maryland and evidently liked what he found there. Though the decision to uproot himself may have come later, once Gerard achieved the status of lord of the manor in the New World, he made the most of his position By the time of his final break with the Old World, he was well on the way toward the goal of his aspirations - political, social and economic advancement. And the key to this goal was land, particularly the manor.

Notes

1. Edwin Beitzell, "Thomas Gerard and his Sons -in-law," MHM, XLVI (1951, 189. Referring to a little known but important figure in Maryland history, Beitzell says, "He was Dr. Thomas Gerard, Gentleman, born about 1605, at New Hall, Lancashire, England, Son of Sir Thomas Gerard.   There Gerards were an ancient and distinguished Roman Catholic Family of Lancashire.   John Gerard, brother of Sir Thomas, was a Jesuit priest and was tortured in the Tower during one of the religious upheavals in England. He later founded a college at Liege. Frances, a daughter of Sir Thomas, became a nun at Gravelines in Flanders. The family history has been traced back to the time of the General Survey of the Kingdom in 1078." Dr. Thomas is also given by Beitzell as the brother of the first Gerards to arrive in Maryland in 1634; "Richard and his sister, Anne, the widow Cox." Ibid. Several inaccuracies in the above information will be later pointed out.

2. The following information on the Gerards of Bryn was obtained principally from two works: The Victoria History of the Counties of England: A History of Lancashire, London, Constable and Company, 1911, IV, 142-147, and William Playfair, British Family Antiquity, London, Reynolds and Grace, 1811, VI, cxix ff. See also Phillip Caraman (ed.) The Autobiography of a Hunted Priest, New York, Pellegrini and Cudahy, 1952, pp1, 213. Bryn was the capital messuage and the manor house of Ashton Manor.

3. Like his father, Sir Thomas had served as Sheriff of Lancashire and was a member of Parliament from that county in 1562. Victoria County History of Lancashire, IV, 144.

4. Bromley in Staffordshire had also come into the family by marriage about the end of the fifteenth century. In Gilbert Gerard we find a good example of the rise of a Protestant family at the expense of a Catholic one in Reformation England. Sir Gilbert Gerard was one of the Gerard's of Ince (most of whom remained Catholic), a family that originally stemmed from the Gerards of Bryn. From his staunch support of Elizabeth, even before her accession to the throne, Gilbert

was knighted and further rewarded with the offices of Attorney-General and Master of the Rolls. DNB, VII, 1097-1099. He was the progenitor of two branches of titled Gerards, both Protestant. His son, Thomas, was raised to the peerage as Baron Gerard of Gerard's Bromley. Through a second son descended the Earls of Macclesfield, a title created after the Restoration. Both titles have become extinct, and Bromley eventually reverted to the Gerards of Bryn. See Sir John Burke, A Genealogical History of the Dormant, Abeyant, Forfeited, and Extinct Peerages of the British Empire, London, Harrison and Sons, 1883, and DNB, VII, 1091-1097, 1102-1103.

5. Playfair, British Family Antiquity, VI, cxxii.

6. The base brother had become a Protestant in order to obtain the Lancashire estates. Victoria County History of Lancashire, IV, 144, 144n.

7. Ibid., p. 144. By the time of his death Sir Thomas was reconciled to the Catholic Church. The family has remained staunchly Catholic to the present day.

8. Supra, p. Though continually hunted, John Gerard made many famous converts in England. Caraman (ed.), Autobiography of a Hunted Priest, passim. His name was associated with the Gunpowder Plot. DNB, VII, 1101-1102.

9. The younger Sir Thomas Gerard was one of the first to benefit from the creation of that honor. In Gerard's case, James remitted the f1000 usually exacted from the conferee in consideration of the family loyalty to Mary Stuart. The title of baronet was hereditary and was the highest that could be held by a member of the gentry.

10. Richard was born in 1613. After his return from Maryland in 1635, he entered into the service of the Spanish King in the Low Countries. With the outbreak of civil war in England he raised a troop to escort Queen Henrietta Maria, then at the Hague, back into England. He also attended the King at Hurst Castle and was the last person to carry a message from King Charles to the Queen. At the end of the Interregnum Richard was created Cup-bearer to the Queen Mother. He purchased from Thomas Gerard of Ince the manor of Ince and established another prominent branch of the Gerard family there. He died in 1686. DMB, VII, 1103; Royalist Composition Papers (ed. J. H. Stanning; Publication of the Record Society of Lancashire and Cheshire, Vol. XXIX). London, 1896, III, 25n.

11. Playfair, British Family Antiquity, IV, cxxii; Sir William Dugdale,

Visitation of the County Palatine of Lancaster, (Chetham Society Publication, Vol. LXXXV), London, 1872, p. 116. Another son was Gilbert, who became a Jesuit. The daughter was Frances, the nun mentioned (supra, p.   ). In his account Beitzell confuses the first and second baronet, ignoring the existence of the latter. Father John Gerard was not the uncle but the great uncle of William, Richard and Frances. Nor did these three have a sister named Anne (Cox), as stated by Beitzell.

12. The Snow papers, MA, XLI, 543, 546.

13. Victoria County History of Lancashire, IV, 147n. This bit of information is to be found in connection with a discussion of the Launder family, who came into possession of New Hall about the middle of the seventeenth century. They undoubtedly acquired it from Gerard. The Gerards of Ince also owned an estate called "New Hall", but at the time in question it was owned by a James Gerard. Ibid., p.103n. The manors of Ince and Ashton were both in the barony of Makerfield. The township of Ashton is about five miles south of the city of Wigan in southern Lancashire.

14. Snow papers, MA, XLI, 544.

15. One was   , the Jesuit already mentioned; the other died without issue. Dugdale, Visitation, p. 166.

16. Victoria County History of Lancashire, IV, 146.

17. In 1796, The Gerards of Bryn acquired New Hall from the Launders. They made it their principal residence and thereafter designated it Garswood.

18. Supra, p.   . The base brother of Sir Thomas undoubtedly lived upon the manor. For several years he acted as trustee of Ashton. Victoria County History of Lancashire, IV, p.146.

19. See Wallace Notestein, The English People on the Eve of Colonization, New York, Harper and Brothers, 1954, pp.101-102, 105. Ordinarily a Catholic could not obtain a university education or a license to practice medicine. There were, notwithstanding, a considerable number of Catholic Physicians in England at this time. David Mathew, The Age of Charles I, London, Eyre and Spottswoode, 1951, p. 139.

20. Members of the gentry in England were usually referred to by mention of their name followed by that of their principal estate. The Launder family seemed to have achieved armorial status by the acquisition of New Hall.

21. Richard Gerard's name appeared high on the list of original adventurers, following those of Baltimore's brothers and the commissioners, Cornwallis and Hawley. See prospectus published by Baltimore in 1635, Clayton C. Hall (ED.) Narratives of Early Maryland, New York, Charles Scribner's Sons, 1910, p.101.

22. Though Gerard was a Catholic, his wife and children were not. Sometime shortly before 1658, Father Francis Fitzherbert said of Gerard, "allthough hee professed himselfe a Roman Catholique, yett his life and conversaon was not agreeable to his profession." Provincial Court proceedings, MA, XLI, 145. The principal reason given for this assertion was that Gerard refused to bring his wife and children to church. It is very possible that Gerard was a convert. Besides the probable descent from the Protestant half-brother of the old Sir Thomas, there is also the fact that Gerard's baptismal record was to be found in a parish of the Established Church.

23. Mathew, The Age of Charles I, p. 195. The response of Catholic gentlemen to Lord Baltimore's appeal was not nearly so great as expected. This was undoubtedly due to the fact that the domestic picture was at the time looking much brighter to the once-beleaguered Catholic gentlemen. See Charles M. Andrews, The Colonial Period of American History, New Haven, Yale University Press, 1936, II, 291, and Edward P. Cheyney, English Background of American History, New York, Harper and Brothers, 1904, pp.213-215.

24. Wesley Frank Craven, The Southern Colonies in the Seventeenth Century, Baton Rouge, Louisiana State University Press, 1949, pp.36-37.

25. Thomas Hughes, S.J., History of the Society of Jesus in North America, London, Longmans, Green and Co., 1908, Text I, p. 346.

26. Abel Snow's principal contribution was probably in drawing up the numerous documents needed by Baltimore for his undertaking. In 1640, he was rewarded by Baltimore with a manor in Maryland, which he named Snow Hill. Gerard acted as Snow's attorney in presenting the demand for this manor in the colony itself. "Land Notes", MHM, VI (1911), 198. Abel Snow, however, never saw his Maryland estate.

27. Provincial Court proceedings, MA, IV, 5.

28. Even his passage money of six pounds had been provided by Justinian Snow. Provincial Court proceedings, MA, IV, 85.

29. Ibid., pp. 55-56.

30. Infra p.   . Justinian's personal estate in Maryland was valued at

29,776 pounds of tobacco or about f375. Inventory, MA, IV, 79-84. Marmaduke evidently returned to England shortly after the death of his brother. He undoubtedly left in Maryland much in the way of building material. tools, and servants (all mentioned in Justinian's inventory) which Gerard acquired.

31. Snow papers, MA, XLI, 542.

32. Snow papers, MA, XLI, 543. The terms and the importance of the commercial agreement will be discussed in the following chapter. This meeting was undoubtedly very important in contributing to Gerard's later advancement. It is the only recorded instance of personal contact between Gerard and Cecil Calvert.

33. Besides being a Catholic, Gerard was connected with a family known to be committed to the Royalist cause. Both the Catholic and Protestant Gerards in England were considered by the Puritans notorious Royalists. Sir William Gerard of Bryn was governor of Denbeigh Castle, the last of the Royal strongholds to fall to the Puritans.

34. In 1647 and 1648, John Hatch and Guiles Brent successively acted as Gerard's attorney in several court cases. There is one definite reference to Gerard's being out of the province. Assembly proceedings, February 23, 1648, MA. I, 225.

35. "Land Notes", MHM, VIII (1913), 262, and infra p. .

36. Ernest Broxap, The Great Civil War in Lancashire, 1642-1651, Manchester, University Press, 1910, p. 173. A second battle near Wigan in 1651 marked the lowest ebb of the fortunes of the Gerards of Bryn. In a last desperate gamble Sir William Gerard contributed f10,000 (obtained from the sale of his manors in Derbyshire) to the Scottish campaign of Charles II (whom he entertained on one occasion in his home). Being declared both delinquent and recusant, his remaining estates were sold by Parliament to John Wildman, the collector of manors (supra, p. 11n.). The estates in Lancashire were returned, however, after the Restoration, and with the opening of the coal fields in that area, the Gerards of Bryn enjoyed renewed prosperity. The title of baron was conferred on the fifteenth baronet in 1876.

Permission to reprint from Joyce Bennett, St. Mary's Historical Society. May, 1999.

Addendum

Register

OF

Maryland's Heraldic Families

PERIOD FROM

1634--March 25th to March 25th--1935

Tercentenary of the Founding of Maryland

By ALICE NORRIS PARRAN
Author and Editor

The Tercentenary Edition is Sponsored

BY THE

Southern Maryland Society Colonial Dames

Founder and President, Mrs. Francis J. Parran.

(Memb. of the Md. Tercentenary Commission of Md.)
(Memb. of the Md. Historical Society and the Genealogical Dept.)
(First State Registrar of Md. State D. A. R.)
(Present Historian of the Baltimore Chapter D. A. R.)
(Former Historian of the Baltimore Chapter, U. D. C. and also
Former Md. State Director of the Children of the U. D. C.)
(Life Memb. of The American International Academy, Heraldry Section)
(Md. State Registrar, of the Nat. Soc. Daus. War of 1812.)
(Memb. of The Women's Literary Club of Baltimore, Md.)

Printed by
H. G. ROEBUCK & SON,
119 W. Mulberry Street
Baltimore, Md.

315

— CHESELDYNE —

CHESELDYNE—(BLACKISTONE—KNOTT—NORRIS)

Registrants: Under the dignity of notable ancient Welsh lineage to the famous Marylander, KENELM CHESELDYNE*, powerful orator of his time, Ambassador to Eng. for Md. A Founder of the new Capitol of Md. in 1694, at Annapolis. The Commissary - General. A Founder of the first Free School in Md., 1696 (and likely in America), King William College at Annapolis, now St. John's. A keeper of the Great Seal of Md. Speaker of Assembly. Noted Attorney-General. His home was at "Mattapany," at St. Mary's, Md. He received through marriage to Thomas Gerrard's dau—, Mary, St. Katherine's Island, in the Potomac, one of the three islands granted to Sir Thomas Gerrard with St. Clement's Island and MANOR in 1633. Sir Thomas Gerrard, or Dr. Gerrard, as he was also called, gave as wedding dower to his several daughters upon their marriages, one island a MANORIAL, part of the vast acreage of ST. CLEMENT'S MANOR, of which he was full Lord. Kenelm Cheseldyne's first wife was Chloe ——; his second, Mary Gerrard; his son was also named Kenelm Cheseldyne.

CHESELDYNE

Hon. **Kenelm** Cheseldyne, Esq., Gent., of St. Mary's Co., Prov. of Md:, Barrister; Orator; Organizer, Member of the Lower House of the Assembly (1676-1704); "Of His Lordship's Honorable Council (1704-to time of his death 1708). He served as Burgess of St. Mary's Co.; "His Lordship's Attorney of Provincial Court; Attorney Gen.; Speaker of The House; Chairman and Orator of Grand Committees; into which the House Dissolved itself; Commis. of St. Marie's; Chairman and Speaker of General Conventions of Representative Bodies of The Provinces in 1690 with John Coode, Agent and Commissioner (Deputies) from the late Convention of Protestants of Prov. of Md. to Her Majesty, the Queen of England; 1694, Member of Committee to Constitute a Court of Equity or Chancery; also, for erecting "Free Schools in the Province;" Division of Counties, etc.; Commissary General of the Prov.; Recorder of St. Mary's City; Mr. Attorney General and Solicitor General; Master in Chancery; one of Her Majesties Chief Justices for St. Mary's; A Vestryman of William and Mary Parish; Judge for the Probate of Wills; In latter part of Life he was appointed (against his will) to Ride the Circuit and act as Judge of Assizes. (P. 377—St. Ann's Parish Records, Annapolis, Md. and Hist. Soc. 1708, was buried Kenelm Cheseldyne, Esq., one of Her Majesty's Hon. Council.)

Hon. Kenelm Cheseldyne, Esq., Gent., of St. Mary's Co., Prov. of Md: is the only person of the Surname recorded among the First Settlers of Maryland, in fact, the Colonies of America, so far as has been ascertained

That he was a young man of means is deducted from the fact that he paid his own passage to Maryland, possesed an unusually fine education and was learned in the Law.

By Warrant and Patent he acquired 2,401½ acres of land. The earlier tracts were on the Eastern Shore of Md. By his 2nd marriage to Mary Gerrard four large Plantations were added to this number of acres, all of which passed to their only son, Kenelm Cheseldyne. There was ST. KATHARINES MANOR, or LODGE, Charles Co., WHITE NECK and MATTAPANAI, adjoining each other in St. Mary's Co., which last was the residence of Kenelm

Cheseldyne, The Immigrant, and his wife, Mary Gerrard; as well as their son Kenelm Cheseldyne.

Sign erected by the Optimist Club of St. Mary's County, MD.

Tour of St. Clements Manor
for Theresa Saylor and Thomas Brent (Cheseldine)
By Alton F. (Fred) Cheseldine
June 2, 1997

1. **Chaptico** - Was designated as a port in 1683 by an act of the Maryland Assembly. This marked the northern most boundary of St. Clement's Manor, if Basford Manor is included. The Key family of Bushwood moved to Chaptico in the 1790's. Phillip Key died a very wealthy man. At his death his personal property was valued at $8,711.43 and included sixteen slaves. His real property consisted of two thousand nine hundred acres of land.

2. **Christ Church** - A National Register Historic Site, it was erected in 1736 and is the burial ground for many of the early Protestant settlers.

3. **Basford Manor** - Site of. Thomas, the second Gerard son was given Basford Manor. He sold the manor to Governor Notley in 1677.

4. **Notley Hall** - The home of Governor Thomas Notley, was built on 500 acres of land purchased from Thomas Gerard, Sr., in 1677. Only the east wing remains, as the center and west wing were destroyed by fire. The site has a magnificent view of the Wicomico river and the mouth of Chaptico Bay.

5. **Bushwood Manor** - Susannah, the eldest daughter of Gerard, was given Bushwood, a 1,000 acre tract of land, when she married Robert Slye in 1654. George Slye willed Bushwood to Edmund Plowden, which remained in the Plowden family until 1872. It was destroyed by fire January 4, 1934.

6. **Sacred Heart Church** - The burial ground of Catholic families in the area.

321

7. **Ocean Hall** - The home of John Blakiston, built about 1667. Until her death in 1972, it was the home of Mrs. Alice Blakistone.

8. **Whites Neck** - When Mary Gerard married Kenelm Cheseldine in 1677, her dowry included Whites Neck, St. Katherine's Island, Westwood Lodge, and Mattapany.

9. **Fosters Neck** - Was home to many of the Cheseldine's, and the site of a private burial ground.

10. **Mattapany** - Was the home of Kenelm and the old house survived until 1926 when it was destroyed by fire.

11. **White's Neck House** - This was the home of many generations of the Cheseldine Family. It was torn down about 1950.

12. **River Springs** - Home site of Nehemiah Blackistone.

13. **St. Catherine's Island** - Included in the dowry of Mary when she married Kenelm. Was the home to many of the Cheseldines, including Fred, who has many happy memories of living on the Island.

14. **Gerards Chapel** - Site of.

15. **Colton's (Longworth's) Point** - Site of Gerards Home.

16. **St. Clement's Island** - Site of the landing of the Maryland colonists.

17. **Hatches Thicket** - A large tract of land owned by the Cheseldines.

18. **Collingwood** - Home to early Cheseldines, Beitzells and Mattinglys.

19. **Burlington** - Home of the Dents.

322

20. **Barton Hall**

21. **Broad Neck** - A 300 acre tract given to Mary and Kenelm who gave it to their daughter Mary Hay, who in turn gave it to her daughter who married Thomas McWilliams.

22. **All Saints Church** - Burial ground for many of the Protestant members of the family.

23. **St. Winifred's Freehold** - On Tomakokin Creek off the head of St. Clement's Bay.

24. **Clement's** - The farthest point north on the east boundary of St. Clement's Manor. The road west follows an old Indian trail to Chaptico which marks the northern boundary of St. Clement's Manor.

25. **Westwood** - Now called Charles County.

Westwood Lodge by Sandra Harrison

November 22, 1998

Dear Mr. Brent Cheseldine,
     I am writing to share some very interesting 1600's history that includes Kenelm Cheseldine and his wife, Mary Gerard Cheseldine.
     My husband, Phillip Harrison and I bought a 35 acre parcel of land in Charles County, Maryland in 1995. We are located near Allens Fresh just off of Route 234 at the south end of Penns Hill Road. Indeed, very close to the water and the location of the original town of Allens Fresh, a 6 acre town of the 1600's with a mill and other dwellings. Our 35 acre parcel was originally part of a 100 acre section called "Westwood Lodge" that wasn't divided into 3 parcels until approximately 1973. The 100 acre parcel called "Westwood Lodge" was part of a 1,600 acre parcel called "Westwood Manor". This manor was given in a land grant to Dr. Thomas Gerard, Mary Gerard Cheseldine's father in the early 1600's.
     I have spent many hours researching our property and have found a patent on "Westwood Lodge" dated 1649. I have rent rolls dated 1661. I have a survey that describes the location of "Westwood Lodge". This was the proof I was looking for so I could be sure. The Lodge was given to Mary Gerard Cheseldine as a dowry before her father died in 1673. Her brother, Thomas Gerard, Jr., was given "Westwood Manor" containing 1,600 acres. It appears "Westwood Lodge", 100 acres, was within "Westwood Manor" but always separate. I just found the patent and survey after our last conversation.
     In addition to the land, my husband and I have found many artifacts. When we were digging our footings to build our house we saw a piece of pottery. My husband then dug down 5 feet and found a 10 x 10 x 1 inch brick floor. We found 2 house keys, beautiful pottery pieces, horse stirrups, horse bits, wine bottles, pipes, cooking crocks, pieces of stem ware, window glass, caming, 2 digging hoes, 2 measuring weights with the kings stamp, bag of nails, bricks, floor tile bricks. door locks, boar tusks and teeth, cow bones, oyster shells, teeth of animals, flint, gun parts, medicine vials, plaster pieces and

100's of other items. We find things laying around in the yard all the time. We don't know what a lot of it is or what it was used for. The floor tile was also found in the Lord Calvert House. We feel that the occupants were wealthy for the time period.

The site has been registered with the State of Maryland Historical Trust. Ed Chaney and Julia King from Jefferson Patterson Museum came out in April of 1996 and did the site work but things have changed since then as we have found a corner brick structure that looks like a foundation in a different spot which would make the Lodge much bigger than they thought. We also just found another site full of artifacts in the middle of our vegetable garden down 2 feet. My husband was digging a hole to bury some of our food scraps and found it. In just that small place there were 2 pottery bowls, nails, brick, fish bones, small bird bones, misc. bones, metal pieces and oyster shells. There is much more in the ground. I think it must be one of their trash piles but the nails and charred wood are confusing.

We just found this new site a few days ago. It's also possible that the Gerard's and Cheseldine's could have rented the Lodge as a store.

We tapped into the spring beside our house to do all our brick work as we had no well at first and now we know that it once ran above ground and was called "Westwood Lodge Run" according to the old survey. It's amazing how we seem to be doing the same things the settlers did some 350 years ago but in a much more comfortable, easy way.

I will send you what information I have that you may be interested in. Please send me what ever you find.

Very Sincerely,

Sandra Harrison
10955 Earnshaw Lane
LaPlata, MD 20646-9741

November 22, 1998

HARRISON'S WESTWOOD MANOR - SUMMARY REPORT
By Edward Chaney

On April 18, 1996, Julia A. King and Edward E. Chaney of the Southern Maryland Regional Center at Jefferson Patterson Park and Museum conducted a field check of a site which had been discovered by Philip and Sandra Harrison while they were constructing a house. The Harrisons stated that the site, located near the head of Allen's Fresh Run in Charles County, had originally been part of Westwood Manor. Westwood Manor had been patented by Dr. Thomas Gerard in 1651, and he built a house there. In 1664, the property was leased to Capt. William Boreman. In 1672, Gerard gave Westwood Manor to his son Thomas Gerard, Jr., except for a 100 acre parcel which had been leased to a merchant named John Pryor. Pryor may have eventually lost his lease, because in 1677 Dr. Gerard gave as a dowry to his daughter Mary a 100 acre parcel called Westwood Lodge. It is possible that Westwood Lodge was John Pryor's leasehold. In 1708, Westwood Lodge was passed on to Mary's daughter, Mary Cheseldyne Hay. By 1682, John Pryor was keeping his store at Thomas Gerard Jr.'s house. Westwood Manor was inherited by Thomas Gerard Jr.'s brother, Justinian, in 1686. When Justinian died two years later, Westwood was left to his widow Sarah. In 1711, Sarah sold Westwood Manor to Charles Carroll of Annapolis.

The Harrison's discovered the site when they uncovered a tile floored cellar while building their house. The site is located at the foot of a terrace overlooking the Allen's Fresh Run floodplain. A fresh water spring is at the south end of the site. (The Harrisons report that the water table is just below the depth of the cellar). The tile floor was approximately 5 feet below the current ground surface. The unglazed redware tiles were 10 inches on a side, and 1 inch thick. One tile was pulled up, revealing that they were laid on a thin bed of mortar, and mortared together. Below the mortar was a 1 inch thick band of dark loam, which contained some charcoal. This would appear to be the original cellar floor, with the tile being a later addition. The tile appeared to cover the entire floor at the north and west end of the cellar, but no tile was evident at the south end (the floor was not uncovered at the east end). The tiled area measured approximately 15 feet north to south. The cellar continued untiled for at least 6 feet to the south, with the south edge yet to be uncovered. The east-west dimension of the cellar was approximately 16-18 feet. According to the Harrisons, they removed a row of bricks which formed the western edge of the tiled area. This brick course was probably used to finish the paving at the west end of the cellar. The north end of the tile floor was overlain by a layer of silt wash containing numerous micro bands of soil and some artifacts, but no rubble. The wash layer was about 4 inches thick at the north end, but eventually tapered out towards the south. Above it was a 6 inch, mottled clay layer containing large amounts of brick rubble. It too tapered out toward the south. Above the clay was a dark loam layer containing rubble and artifacts, which was overlain by a thick brown loam layer containing few artifacts of any sort. This upper layer was probably produced in part by erosion from slope above the cellar to the east. The fill varied elsewhere in the cellar, but was generally layers of dark loam containing artifacts and rubble, with occasional bands of charcoal.

The Harrison's construction excavations revealed only the westernmost 3 feet of the cellar. However, they also excavated a small exploratory test hole which came down on the northeast corner of the cellar. This corner was defined by dark fill which abutted subsoil walls (the floor was not revealed), and lined up with the north end of the tiled area. By contrast, north of the tiles in the northwest corner of the cellar there was no subsoil wall, but rather dark loamy fill. The absence of a subsoil wall in the northwest corner of the cellar, and the presence there (above the tile) of erosional bands and clay fill layers which taper off to the south, suggests the possibility of a bulkhead entrance to the cellar north of the northwest corner. The erosional bands would have washed into the cellar from the bulkhead entrance (probably while the building was still in use, since they appear to contain no rubble), while the clay and rubble layer may represent fill which was used to later close off the entrance.

The Harrisons have not uncovered any evidence of a foundation, suggesting that the house was an earthfast structure. However, they have found the remains of at least one, and probably two, fireplaces. In their exploratory hole at the northeast corner of the cellar, they found a large quantity of brick, almost exclusively Dutch yellow. This brick type was most commonly used in fireboxes. A fragment of charred hearthstone was also found there. The bricks still visible in the exploratory hole were not articulated, suggesting that the fireplace fell into the cellar as the building decayed. The other possible fireplace was found at the south end of the cellar, in the untiled area. It was indicated by a large quantity of unarticulated red brick, the recovery of several charred hearth tile fragments (similar to the cellar floor tiles), and the presence of a charcoal band in the cellar fill.

King and Chaney were able to make a cursory examination of the artifacts recovered by the Harrisons. They included a rich variety of ceramics, table and bottle glass, tobacco pipes, and metal objects, along with animal bone and oyster shell. The assemblage was notable for its high percentage of tin-glazed earthenware and Rhenish blue and gray stoneware. Lead-glazed or unglazed coarse earthenware was less common, with, for example, only a few shards of North Devon gravel tempered ware. Staffordshire slipware and white salt-glazed stoneware were absent from the collection, but English brown stoneware and a small amount of Buckley or Buckley-like earthenware were present. The glass consisted mostly of round bottles, with some stemware and other table pieces, along with some medicine vials. The metal objects included iron and pewter knives, forks, and spoons; copper-alloy buckles; iron horse bits and a stirrup; an iron hoe; and architectural hardware such as nails, door hinges, and pintles. Other architectural artifacts included window glass and lead cames, and a piece of plaster with a whitewash finish coat. The most notable artifacts were two hockey puck-sized brass scale weights, stamped with various assay symbols. They were found together at the south end of the cellar. A small brass pan, possibly a balance pan, was found nearby.

The ceramic assemblage, along with the near absence of case bottles, Dutch tobacco pipes, or terra cotta pipes, suggests a beginning occupation date for the site in the 1670's. The presence of English brown stoneware, with the absence of white salt-glazed stoneware, suggests the site was abandoned by 1720. There is nothing to suggest the presence of a house on the site in the early 1650's, when Dr. Gerard patented the property. The artifacts have not been studied closely enough to indicate whether this was the building Capt. Boreman leased in 1664, but it appears most likely that Thomas

Gerard Jr. built the house when he acquired Westwood Manor in 1672. The house was apparently abandoned by 1720, and may have been vacated in 1711, when Westwood was sold to Charles Carroll, who maintained his residence in Annapolis. The rich artifact collection recovered from the site, including a high percentage of imported stoneware and tin-glazed tableware, along with the scale weights and possible balance pan, may be best explained by the presence of merchant John Pryor at Westwood Manor house in the 1670's and 1680's. (An alternative explanation, at least for the scale, the glass medicine vials, and the tin-glazed apothecary jars, is that they originally belong to Dr. Gerard). The wealth of the Gerard family (one of early Maryland's most prominent families) would only add to the richness of the artifact assemblage. It is tempting to suggest that the tile floor was added to the cellar to protect John Pryor's mercantile goods from the damp earth, but this is of course just speculation.

Construction of the Harrison's house should have little additional impact on the site, so they have agreed to cover the exposed sections of the cellar with plastic and then backfill it. Mrs. Harrison will come to JPPM when time permits for assistance in cataloging the artifact collection. We will encourage her to write a short report on her findings for publication in Maryland Archaeology.

Sources: Edwin W. Beitzell, "St. Clement's Manor", Chronicles of St. Mary's, April 1964
    David Spalding, "Thomas Gerard; The Study of a Lord of the Manor and the Advantages of Manor Holding in Early Maryland", Chronicles of St. Mary's, July, 1959.

From "The Colonial Ancestors of Francis Scott Fitzgerald"
by his daughter, Frances (Scottie) Fitzgerald

All his life - which may seem odd in one who is sometimes
called "the historian of Jazz Age" - my father was fascinated by
the the poetic aspects of early times. His first success, at age
sixteen, came with the production in Saint Paul of a Civil War
play, *The Coward*....He knew of course that he was related to
Francis Scott Key, but he dubbed him great-great uncle
whereas he was, in fact, only a distant cousin. The snob in him
dropped the names of some Dorsey and Ridgely forebears into
his preface to Don Swann's *Colonial and Historic Homes of
Maryland,* but they were hopelessly confused. I do wish he
had been familiar with Adam Thoroughgood, **Kenelm
Cheseldyne**, Marmaduke Tylden, and the other intrepid souls
who set sail from England in the seventeenth century to settle
along the rivers of tidewater Maryland and Virginia, for surely
he would have contributed their improbable-sounding names to
literature.

The Bench and Bar of Maryland

by C. W. Sams

Kenelm Cheseldyne

May 27, 1676, Kenelm Cheseldyne appeared before the upper house as one of the managers of the lower house in the impeachment of Major Thomas Truman for permitting the execution of several Indians whilst they were prisoners under his command. In 1688 Mr. Cheseldyne was Speaker of the house of delegates, a body that bravely maintained its right to have an oath of fidelity administered to it before it began its session, and not ignominiously, at the whim of the governor, as a reflection upon it, in the middle of the assembly's meeting. The members replied manfully to an insinuation of rebellion, and declared that the house was deprived of its "inherent and just right" by "not having the last writs of election and journals returned as desired by this house". The contention was so sharp between the governor and the lower house that he prorogued the assembly. The matter was afterward amicably arranged.

Mr. Cheseldyne was one of those who, on the 27th day of March, 1689, signed a "Declaration of Remonstrance" to quiet the fears of a "Popish plot" and "Indian conspiracy" to murder the Protestant settlers. The whole report was declared "notorious false." Public documents, signed by "leading citizens," were the order of the day; and again, on July 25th of the same year, Mr. Cheseldyne was of those who underwrit the Protestant Declaration. The reasons were publicly given for seizing the government of Maryland and depriving Lord Baltimore of his authority. Our brother Cheseldyne had the courage of his convictions, for he was of the party, who., with the notorious John Coode, demanded of the governor the surrender of the province into the hands of the Protestants, August 1, 1689.

In 1692 the lower house entered the august presence of the upper house and presented "Mr. Kenelm Cheseldyne for the speaker, who (after some discourse to disable himself and render him uncapable to perform so great a charge) is approved of and allowed by his

Excellency. He then in the name of the House prays freedom and Protection of Persons and attendants from Restraint, &c., free liberty of speech in their house with due reverence and moderation upon all. Occasions free access to his Excellency, & for any Imperfections in himself desires that it may not be imputed as the house but favorably construed and excused in him. Which being assured them, the oaths of allegiance and supremacy is tendered unto them and by them severally taken." (L. H. Proceedings, 1692, p. 252.)

During the same year Mr. Cheseldyne was appointed to the office of commissary general. From the position he was dismissed August 25, 1697, for carelessness and negligence in office. Drink was the cause of his downfall.

ALL SAINTS BRAUNSTON
A brief guide

Braunston Church was a chapel dependent upon Hambleton Church in the early 12th century. From this time, date the nave, the responds of the chancel arch and the font. In the 13th century the south aisle and the doorway were added, together with the south arcade and the chancel. The north aisle was built in the 14th century and the clerestory and the tower in the 15th. The tower seems to have been rebuilt from the foundations in 1728-9 when it was buttressed.

If you walk straight up the nave to the chancel, you will see the carpets worked by the Mother's Union in th 1950's. The chancel windows are by Kemp and are in memory of those who died in the First World War. On the south wall of the sanctuary is a piscina and, usually in this position an aumbry. The narrow Priest's door is now unused. The tile floor dates from the 19th century when the vestry was built on the north side.

Returning to the nave, on your right, is a stained glass window to the village carpenter and undertaker showing scenes in the life of St. Joseph, the carpenter. The window has a strangely stepped sill; at one time it had an arch of five stones but nobody can tell us why. On the left, in the east corner of the south aisle, are two brasses to the <u>Chesilden</u> family. Above is a fragment of wall painting dating from the 15th century. It was the reredos for an altar and probably depicted Christ in Majesty. The bracket for the statue remains. The circle on the left contains instruments of the Passion. On the south wall another fragment (14th – 15th cnetury) shows part of a wheel, originally eight feet in diameter, with an altar, candlesticks and chalice suggesting a connection with the seven sacraments. The writing is part of a late 16th century list of the ten commandments.

Walk on and you will see the font, one of the oldest parts of the church, it dates from the 12th century and is a good example of Norman work. It was discovered in the churchyard during the 19th century repairs and was reinstated in 1890. The Vicar's son George Barratt (later to be killed in 1916) was the first baby to be baptised in it after its recovery. In the west corner is a stone coffin but we do not know whose it was or why it is here. Part of the lid is set in the wall of the north aisle. Here also you may see the surround of the north door, probably blocked in the 1890's when the nave was restored and the box pews and west gallery were removed. The pews in the north aisle and also the war memorial recall the men from the village who were killed in the First World War. The memorials to Major Hanbury and Tiptafts were moved from the east end of the aisle when the organ was installed in 1965.

Going out of the door, turn right and look back at the fine dog tooth arch and the remains of the mass clock above the west door jamb. The benches in the proch seated those who were entitled to bread and ale at Christmas when a bell was rung at noon on St. Thomas' Day.

In the churchyard, turn right and look up at the tower. You will see the dates it was restored, the initials would be those of the churchwardens at that time. There is a peel of six bells, the two newest added in 1967. We do not know why the spire is so truncated, although in a mid 18th century water colour it sppears higher.

At the west end of the tower stands Sheela Nargigs, a Celtic fertility goddess. In Christian times, her hideous features were supposed to put the devil to flight. These figures are generally seen in Ireland and there is no good reason for her to be in Braunston. She was found face downwards as a doorstop during the restorations.

On the north wall, you can see clearly where the north door has been blocked up.

The small window to the east of the vestry is the only 13th century one remaining – the others have all been altered at different times.

In a mid 19th century drawing of the church, there is a large sundial on the southeast corner of the chancel.

The clock was installed on the tower at the turn of the century by Mr. Hanbury at the Manor for his farm men to see the time from the Brooke Road.

We hope you have enjoyed your visit to Braunston Church,
and may
GOD DO WITH YOU.

Note: This information is from a brochure obtained from All Saints Braunston.

Braunston Manor - A Trip from London
(A letter from Thomas Brent Cheseldine
   to Wilda & Joseph Cheseldine)

Matunuck, RI 02879
February 7, 1990

Dear Wilda and Joe,

The trip over took 6 hours and trip back 9 hours, Pan Am. I think the difference is in the model plane or the winds; it was very inexpensive for me at this time of year - $280.00 round trip and room w/bath was $40.00 a night in Paddington Square area. Royal Eagle hotel; it was okay but I think you could find a nicer one at same rate. Saw some shows; sun came out 4 or 5 times sort-of (that is normal for January); but I did pick a good day to go to Braunston; no rain and tho chilly some sun; generally the temperature was in the 40's the 2 weeks I was in England.

The train leaves <u>Kings Cross Road.</u> Buy a ticket for <u>OAKHAM</u>. Train is British Rail line. Change at <u>Peterboro</u> for Oakham. It takes about an hour to get to Peterboro and about 20 minutes to get from there to Oakham, as I recall. I think its about 80 miles or so north of London in the EAST MIDLANDS section. Train has lots of "dining cars" where you can get a sandwich, lunch or dinner. Also, in the coaches they come around with a food cart, coffee, etc. if desired. The waiting room in Peterboro has a snack bar.

It is best when looking at schedule to take a train that meets the train in Peterboro; then there is little or no wait.

At Oakham I got off the train and walked 5 blocks to the library; this is a nice way to see the old town; nice library and it has a tourist section; but I got there at 1 PM and it was closing on that day at that time tho regular time was 5:30 PM. Anyway they gave me a few folders. I then took a cab 2 miles to Braunston Manor, across from which is All Saints Church. Cab cost 1 pound + 80 pence. A pound then cost $1.75. (There are 100 pence to 1 pound).

The "manor" is a disappointment as it is not a huge stately home as one sees on TV. It looked more like a long stone warehouse, directly on the sidewalk, with no windows on 1st floor; has 2 courtyards; I went into one and was met by the son of the owner (in his 40's I would say); told him my mission and he appeared to be

341

amazed a Cheseldine was before him. He had never met one before. He went to get his father (probably in his 70's) and called a local woman, Joanna Stevens, who seems to be the local historian. They arranged to meet me in 1/2 hour in the church which is across the way and which I wanted to take pictures of. So we did.

I took some pictures of this manor. It was changed over the years, naturally. I did not go inside, tho was invited. It has a wing on it and the pictures that I have show the courtyard area of part of it. I am sorry to say I did not get as many pictures of the building as I should have. It had a sign outside: "Furniture Manufacturing".

The church is as stated, the bronze covered graves inside and the bodies buried underneath. There is more detail, etc. which is explained in the two papers I am enclosing herewith to you. A table had postcards and a history of the church; it is still used for services; still an operating church. The three people met me and we talked for about 45 minutes. They were all excited to see a Cheseldine. They thought they had all died out or disappeared, as they had never had a visitor with that name nor met any one with it, though they certainly knew the name, as it is a part of the church. Also, about 1 mile away is a Cheseldyne Spinney as is shown on the map. Spinney means woods. I imagine this is a park. I did not go there.

Each of the three told me what they knew about the place. The owner has been there since 1940's. It was difficult for me, alone, to grasp all that was said; little overwhelming for me to digest it all. Then I went with Joanna and walked a few blocks to a house which was called Cheseldyne farm house. On its outside wall there is the name Cheseldyne and the coat of arms. She explained about the dog being, I believe, a Dalmatian and that is why the spots showed on it; also it has a long cord; because the dog ran along the carriage and if the rope was short it would hurt itself-thus the long rope. House is very old. She remembers as a child it was still a working farm. It looks like it is now either apartments or a private house.

She offered to drive me to Oakham so I would not have to take a cab and did so. Around 4 PM I got a train back to London. She had offered to drive me to Northampton and other places to see things related to Cheseldine. but it was so overwhelming for me and I wanted to get back to the city, so I very nicely declined. But I did mention that you two may come over this summer and she was excited about that. I also said I would write her and send her some things.

342

Eventually I plan to send her the history of what happened to the family after it left England.

I gave her a copy of the enclosed History of the Cheseldine Family in England and they made copies of it and they did not know all that information. I could see it was all fascinating to them as it was to me.

I am going to write to her about getting all these things together and getting them to her and then she can put them or a copy of them, in the local library for others that some day may be interested in this.

If I had it to over again, I would go over and go directly to Leicester, spend a week there, and then get around to the various places. Leicester is a large city and is about 5 or 10 miles the other side of Braunston. Oakham has hotels and is a tourist area but much smaller. I did not get to Leicester. It has a famous theatre there. Nearly every town has a legitimate (live) theatre.

My suggestion is, if you do go over, you would naturally go US to London, the go to Oakham. Intend to spend at least one night there in the hotel. Have arranged to meet with Joanna, and, knowing her, she will help line up a tour of the places, etc., related to the trip.

As we know, at one point Kenelm's father (also named Kenelm) sold the manor and moved to Bloxham where he was a vicar of a church there. We also know - which I forget to mention to them, but now remember - that Mr. Beitzell met with a Mamie Cheseldine in Lincoln who took them all around to the places. So obviously there are some of the family still in England, about whom I will have to let Joanna know.

The whole area you would want to cover would be within a 35 mile radius of Oakham, I would think, tho on the maps it looks larger. I would have done more if I had been with someone but being alone it was a bit overwhelming and tiring and that is the reason I did not do more. Also, it is better to go when the weather is better, like spring or summer or fall. Winter is not the time to go sightseeing over there.

I will send you what pix I took when I have copies made. Enclosed is a postcard of the inside of the theatre and various copies of maps, etc. If you do decide to go and let me know then I will be glad to send you actual maps and folders, etc., that I picked up which will give more explicit information including train schedules, etc.

343

It was quite an experience but, as I said, it would be more enjoyable doing it with someone else, same about London. I just did not want to have to travel with a friend 24 hours a day, would rather go alone than that. If I had known people over there it would have been better. But I did make one good contact and this Joanna and I am putting her name at the end of this letter. When I write I will get the names of the two men – owners of the Braunston manor – which I neglected to get. They were very cordial.

Before, when I sent you material, much of it was not correct. Lo and behold, I found there were twon Braunstons and one not far from the other. One is the one I had pointed out to you before, it is about 3 miles south of Rugby – I thought this was the correct one. But it is not. The correct one is the one 2 miles from Oakham. The Rugby Braunston is near Stratfor-on-Avon. Yet it appears only to be about 30 miles from the Braunston I visited. Maybe they are connected in some way.

Joanna said there were originally three Braunston Manors where she was. A "manor" is not only a house, it is like an estate or a whole town or village of which there is the owner or proprietor who lives in the manor house – I gathered from the conversation. I really don't know much about all this.

It was a rewarding experience and I am glad I went and did it. It seemed my destiny to go there. Even tho I did not have much enthusiasm to make the trip, alone, I am glad I did.

Love,

PS   The round trip fare from London to Oakham on British Rail is:
Before 9:30AM Mon-Fri – 32 lbs
After 9:30AM Mon-Fri – 18 lbs
The pound cost 1.75 to 1.63 per fluctuation. Big difference traveling after 9:30 AM though.

Miss Joanna Spencer
22 High Street
Braunston-in-Rutland
Oakham, Leies, England
LE15, 8QU
Telephone: Oakham (0572) 72-2073

Addendum Notes

About a visit to Braunston

Except of letter from Jean Beitzell Quinnette to Thomas Brent Cheseldine, dated August 3, 1999:

But to get to the story of my trip to Braunston. When I worked at the Smithsonian, I had the good fortune to accompany a number of their travel programs to England as a staff rep. As I think you know from my Dad's account, he had located John and Maisie Cheseldine in Lincoln, and he and Mother met them in 1980 and were delighted to be driven by John to see the Cheseldine Farm and burials in the church. He (Daddy) also found a number of places linked to Gerards in other areas, but I've not had the opportunity to follow up there. At any rate, I worked a trip to Yorkshire in 1987 and then got permission to stay on when my charges went home. I took the train from York to, I believe, Doncaster where I changed for a train to Lincoln. I had called ahead to John and Maisie so they came to my hotel for dinner the evening I arrived. Next day we set out in their car, passing one of Alfred Lord Tennyson's homes on the way, along some very windy roads. Eventually we arrived at Braunston, and I was positively thrilled to see Cheseldine Farm, 1604, chiseled into the stone wall along the road. I believe they said at the time that the farm was being turned into a trade school or experimental agricultural center. We then visited the church, and I tried taking photographs of the brasses, but it was so dark, they did not turn out very well. Ever since that day, I've honestly felt that I had a firmer grasp on who I am and where I came from than ever before. And it's a splendid feeling that I'd love to share with my children and grandchildren. When I got home, I checked in the Cheseldine genealogy and found out they'd owned that farm since the 1300's and sold it in the 1600's.

ENGLAND – Map of Oakham & Braunston Area

346

William Cheselden (1688-1752) wore silk turban during his operations, an elegant precursor of surgeon's cap.

The driving power behind these reforms was William Cheselden. His connections with the London hospitals had been a close one since his boyhood. At 15 he was apprenticed to a Mr. James Ferne of St. Thomas Hospital. (Surgeons were not called Doctor and still are not in England.) At 23 he started his own lecture course in anatomy, switching bodies away from the executioner and dissecting them in his own home. Cheselden's dexterity as a surgeon was based on sound anatomical insight. This enabled him to bring an operation like "cutting for the stone" to such a pitch of perfection that he could perform it in a record time of 53 seconds. The death rate, too, was amazingly low. He lost only 3 patients out of the first 53 cases.

In spite of his acknowledged mastery, Cheselden always tensed with fear before an operation — an experience probably shared by many of his confrères.

Cheselden attended Newton in his last sickness. He was surgeon to Queen Caroline until he lost favor due to an experimental ear operation performed on a criminal. The prisoner had been promised his freedom provided he let Cheselden perforate his ear drum. The Queen who had agreed to this arrangement was forced to dismiss her surgeon when the patient died.

Percival Pott (1714-1788) of Pott's disease fame, a big surgeon but a small man, was an impeccable dresser.

Eighteenth century instrument table.

Dainty Percival Pott, an elegant gentleman and scholar, moved among London's aristocrats and intellectuals and showed that surgery had arrived. His sterling honesty, kindness of heart and great professional skill made him the head of the profession after Cheselden's death. The Royal Society recognized his scientific merits by electing him as a member. Many names familiar to the modern doctor keep his memory alive: Pott's disease (curvature of the spine caused by tubercular caries), Pott's puffy tumor and Pott's fracture.

Dr. Pott deepened his knowledge of fractures by his own sufferings. On a frosty January morning in 1756, his horse slipped as he was riding to Lock Hospital and the doctor was thrown to the ground. He suffered a compound fracture of the leg — not the fracture known by his own name, which is a fracture plus dislocation of the ankle joint.

To prevent aggravation of his injury Pott instructed his rescuers to carry him on "the door from a nearby house." The doctors who were quickly summoned to their colleague's bedside advised immediate amputation. While they were greasing their saw, Dr. Nourse, Pott's old master, arrived and pronounced that the limb could be saved. During his long recovery, Pott started his books on fracture, tumors and spinal curvature which are acknowledged as masterworks to this day.

This article published in "A Pictorial History of Medicine" by Otto L. Bettman. Xmxmxmxmxmxmxm Charles C. Thomas, Publisher, Springield, Illinois. 1956

William Cheselden - apprentice physician, London England, age 15.

Photograph of bust of William Cheselden at St. John's Hospital –
1688-1752 in London, England. He was the first to wear a silk turban
during his operations, an elegant precursor of the Surgeon's Cap. At
age 15 he was an apprentice to Mr. James Ferne. St. Thomas Hospital
surgeons were not called Doctors in England.

Letter from Frank Geoffrey Cheseldine, England to Thomas Brent Cheseldine, USA

April 15, 1996

237 Wrugby Road
Lincoln
Lincs
LN2 4PZ
01522-520865

Dear Mr. Brent,

I was pleased to hear from you we are family. I am Frank Geoffrey Cheseldine. I am 80 years old and have spent all my life in or about Lincoln. I have one brother. Peter. He has no family. I also have one sister, Joyce. She was married to Reginald Burns who is dead. I have several relatives who were brought up at a small village (West Abbey), there were nine brothers and sisters_____. Harry, Fred, Joseph, John, Charles and my father Frank. Also, Louie, Harriet amd Lizzie. When they grew up they all migrated to Lincoln where they found employment. I myself worked for Ruston & Hornsbey as a fitter. I have one son Colin and daughter, Anita. They have two daughters.

Find much more, but I should think the part about West Abbey would be of interest to you. It is about 5 meters from Horncastle. I will close now. Wishing you success in your search.

F. G. Cheseldine

THE RUTLAND RECORD SOCIETY

(conserving the heritage of the Ancient County of Rutland)

Patron: Col. T. C. S. Haywood, O.B.E., J.P., H.M. Lieut. for Leicestershire
(with special responsibility for Rutland)

President: G. H. Boyle, Esq.

Please reply to:

QUAINTREE HOUSE
BRAUNSTON-IN-RUTLAND
OAKHAM,
RUTLAND LE15 8QS

RUTLAND COUNTY MUSEUM,
CATMOS STREET,
OAKHAM,
RUTLAND, LE15 6HW
Tel. Oakham 3654

10 April 1990

Dear Mr.Brent Cheseldine,

We were so thrilled that you should have made contact with Braunston.

Everything that you left with Joanna Spencer has been passed to me
as Chairman of the Rutland Society and as historian of Braunston.

It must have been so exciting for you to have seen the Cheseldine
tombs in Ridlington and Braunston. What you have yet to see is the
family tree drawn about 1603. The original used to hang in Cheseldine
farm on the High Street. But only three years ago the then owner -
a Mr>Solomons sold it without anyone in the village knowing.
Fortunately I had had it photographed some years previously and
also coloured. If only I can find the negative you can have another
copy made.

We know a lot about the Cheseldine family and long to sit down with
the next member of your family who comes over.

Braunston was a parish divided into three small properties - hardly
worthy of the title of 'manors' of which one belonged to younger
sons of the main family. Another branch moved to Somerby (about
3 miles from Braunston). They produced a famous British scientist
who in about 1770 was made a Fellow of the Royal Society. I have
have a print of him.

I was interested to hear about the Lincoln Cheseldines. I will be
writing to those who appear in the telephone book.

May I suggest that you join the Rutland Record Society as an overseas
member (subcription £10 - ten pounds) and you will have access to
our publications in which from time to time there references to
your family. I enclose a current price list.

Yours sincerely,

Prince Yuri Galitzine
Chairman,Rutland Record Society

Letter from Rutland Record Society

354

Regarding Kent County, Maryland:

The Kenelm Cheseldine Family

Information on this family has been expanded by the notes kindly forwarded to me by Thomas Brent of Matunuck, RI. He and others have been compiling information on the Cheseldine Family for a future book.

1. KENELM CHESELDINE has been largely associated with St. Mary's County, however he was a large landowner of property on the eastern shore which some of his descendents continued to possess. Kenelm Cheseldine the immigrant, was the sone of Kenelm Cheseldyne and Grace Dryden of Braunston Manor in Rutland County, England. (She is the daughter of Stephen Dryden, son of John Dryden and Elizabeth Cope, who descended of royalty through Edward I, King of England (1)) In 1655, his father sold Braunston Manor which had been in the family foir 250 years. In that year he was appointed Vicar of Bloxham in Lincoln County where he died in 1667. Kenelm, after the death of his father. moved to the Eastern Shore of Maryland in 1669 bringing with him an excellent law library and his father's divinity books which he willed to his descendents. Kenelm had studied law and practiced for many years in England.

Kenelm Cheseldine received a patent of "Grantham" for 500 acres in 1674 in Kent County, MD. Kenelm Cheseldine (presumably the grandson) was still listed as the owner of "Grantham" in 1733 Kent County, MD in the debtor books.

By patent and warrant he acquired 2,401 1/2 acres.

(1) Ancestral Roots of Certain American Colonists 7th Edition p. 18

3. KENELM CHESELDINE III, son of Kenelm (2) was born about 1713 (age 4 in 1717).

Kenelinn Cheseldine of St. Mary's County, son and heir of Kenelinn Cheseldine vs. George Gordon and Kenelinn Greenfield Jowles, execs of George Forbes and Ann Greenfield exec. of Thomas Trueman Greenfield, Dryden Jowles now called Dryden Forbes exec. of Henry Peregrine Jowles. The bill of complaint says that Kenelinn

Cheseldine father, made his wife Mary, mother of the complaintant, his exec. and appointed his brothers in law Thomas Trueman Greenfield and Henry Peregrine Jowles guardians of the complaintant after his mother's marriage. At his father's death, the complaintant was about 4 years. After his father's death, George Forbes late of St. Mary's County, merchant, intermarried with Mary, eldest sister of Kenelinn Cheseldine, father. Thomas Trueman Greenfield's first wife was Susanna, another of the complaintant's father's sisters. Henry Peregrine Jowles intermarried with Dryden, another sister of the complaintant's father. Dryden Jowles later intermarried with John Forbes now decd. Dec. 14, 1740 (MSA Vol. 8 p. 339)

The answer of George Gordon states that Kenelinn Cheseldine, father of complaintant's father, died in 1708 and mentioned in his will a son, Kenelinn Cheseldine and 3 daughters Mary Hayes, Susanna Greenfield, and Dryden. Kenelinn Cheseldine, complaintant's father, died in 1717. George Gordon believes that Mary Phippard, mother of complaintant and Kenelinn Cheseldine, father of complaintant, were never married. May 23, 1743 (MSA Vol 8 p. 344)

Present were George Hamilton who intermarried with a daughter of George Gordon; Kenelinn Trueman Greenfield, oldest son and heir of Col. Thomas Trueman Greenfield; and James Forbes, only son of Mrs. Dryden Forbes; in above case. (MSA Vol. 8 p. 369)

James Bowles owned "Cheseldine" in 1733-1769 in Kent County (3)

DEED: George Plater of SM County Esq. conveys to Nicholas Smith of KE County the tract "Grantham" 500 acres defending against other claims including Elinor, Mary, and Jane, daughters and coheirs of James Bowles (Jowles?) Esq. dec and against Kenelm Cheseldine. Nov. 6, 1753 (KELR JS #27:361)

(3) Inhabitants of Kent County, MD 1637-1787 by Henry Peden.

PARRIS N. GLENDENING
GOVERNOR

ANNAPOLIS OFFICE
STATE HOUSE
100 STATE CIRCLE
ANNAPOLIS, MARYLAND 21401
(410) 974-3901

WASHINGTON OFFICE
SUITE 311
444 NORTH CAPITOL STREET, N.W.
WASHINGTON, D.C. 20001
(202) 638-2215

TDD (410) 333-3098

October 5, 1997

Dear Friends:

As Governor, I am delighted to extend my greetings and warmest welcome to The Cheseldine Family as you gather to celebrate your first family reunion in Maryland! This is certainly an historic occasion as you honor your ancestor, Kenelm Cheseldine, in recognition of his significant contributions not only to your family, but to the State of Maryland.

On behalf of the citizens of Maryland, I salute you on this very special occasion. We are honored to host your family this year and hope your stay here is enjoyable for all the Cheseldine generations in attendance.

Today, as you gather with loved ones from all over the country, you celebrate a most meaningful and valuable American institution, family. Your recognition of the importance of your lineage and heritage is an honor and a tribute to all those who came before you and to your family's future generations.

Please accept my heartfelt congratulations on this momentous event. You have established a wonderful tradition today, and you have my best wishes for many joyous reunions to come.

Sincerely,

Parris N. Glendening
Governor

358

United States Senate
Washington, D. C.

October 5, 1997

c/o Thomas Brent Cheseldine
11700 Perry Branch Road
Newburg, Maryland 20664

Dear Friends:

I am writing to welcome and to congratulate the members of the Cheseldine family as you gather in Newburg, Maryland for your first family reunion.

It has long been my belief that the family structure is the bedrock of our society, producing the strong values, morals, and community ties necessary to carry our nation forward into the future. Since the day your ancestors settled in Maryland, your family has done a remarkable job in preserving both its unity and integrity.

Again, it gives me great pleasure to join the members of the Cheseldine family in celebrating this event and in wishing you continued success in the years to come.

Sincerely,

Paul Sarbanes
United States Senator

SENATE OF MARYLAND

Resolution

Be it hereby known to all that

The Senate of Maryland

offers its sincerest congratulations to

the descendants of Kenelm Cheseldine

in recognition of

their first historic reunion to commemorate 328 years
of residency in Maryland, and to honor the significant
contributions made to the State of Maryland
by their ancestor, Kenelm Cheseldine.

The entire membership extends best wishes on

this memorable occasion and directs this resolution

be presented on this 5th day of October 19 97.

Thomas V. Mike Miller
President of the Senate

Sponsor

Senate Resolution 1063

360

ANNAPOLIS, MARYLAND 21401-1991

THOMAS V. MIKE MILLER, JR.
PRESIDENT

September 17, 1997

STATE HOUSE
WASH. AREA (301) 858-37
BALT. AREA (410) 841-37

Thomas Brent Cheseldine
11700 Perry Branch Road
Newburg, MD 20664

Dear Mr. Cheseldine:

Congratulations on the great ingathering of Cheseldines from all over the country returning to southern Maryland on October 5, 1997. I know this will make some history on its own, as the first family return to Maryland, while it will bring new knowledge to younger descendants.

Such reunions are among the most joyous of American institutions. And they are also just plain fun.

As a life-long student of Maryland history, the family name has been familiar to me though I had forgotten that the roots went so far back into the 17th Century. Of the many accomplishments, I take my hat off to anyone capable of handling the Speaker's office in those tumultuous times.

In my lifetime, I know the family has continued to be an important leader in the business and social life of southern Maryland.

I wish the gathering well.

Sincerely,

Thomas V. Mike Miller, Jr.

TVMM:jrw

SENATE OF MARYLAND

ANNAPOLIS, MARYLAND 21401-1991

THOMAS MAC MIDDLETON

STATE SENATOR
28TH LEGISLATIVE DISTRICT
CHARLES COUNTY
BUDGET AND TAXATION COMMITTEE

ANNAPOLIS ADDRESS:

ROOM 210 SENATE OFFICE BUILDII
ANNAPOLIS, MARYLAND 21401-19
PHONE: (410) 841-3616
(301) 858-3616 (DC)
1-800-492-7122 EXT. 3616

October 5, 1997

To the descendants of Kenelm Cheseldine:

It is with great pleasure that I am
sending you this Senate Resolution to
celebrate the Cheseldine Family Reunion.

Kenelm Cheseldine was truly remarkable
in his devotion to our State of Maryland.
His accomplishments are well documented and
deserve the appreciation of all our citizens.

Enjoy your celebration!

Very truly yours,

Mac Middleton

Thomas McLain Middleton
State Senator

ANNAPOLIS, MARYLAND 21401-1991

ROY DYSON
SENATOR

September 29, 1997

1-800-492-7122
WASH. AREA (301) 858-3673
DIST. OFFICE (301) 994-2826
P.O.BOX 229
GREAT MILLS, MARYLAND 20634-0229

Mr. Thomas Brent Cheseldine
11700 Perry Branch Road
Newburg, Maryland 20664

Dear Mr. Cheseldine:

I am honored to offer to you, and to the hundreds of descendents of Kenelm Cheseldine, my sincerest welcome as you gather together for the first historic reunion of the Cheseldines.

The Cheseldine name has long been recognized for the outstanding contributions made to our State and community. Begining with Kenelm Cheseldine, an honorable and brave gentleman, whose knowledge and leadership helped to mold the future of our great nation; to the many present day descendents who have dedicated themselves to serving their communities in numerous ways, we recognize their contributions to society.

As you honor Kenelm Cheseldine today, I extend the appreciation of our community, and my personal good wishes for a very successful day.

With kindest regards, I am

Sincerely,

Roy Dyson
District 29

363

MARYLAND
HOUSE OF DELEGATES

House Resolutions

Be it hereby known to all that

The House of Delegates of Maryland

offers its sincerest congratulations to

THE DESCENDANTS OF KENELM CHESELDINE

in recognition of

KENELM CHESELDINE SIGNIFICANT CONTRIBUTION TO THE STATE OF MARYLAND
AND TO HIS FAMILY CELEBRATING 328 YEARS OF MARYLAND HISTORY
ON THIS HISTORIC OCCASION OF THEIR REUNION.

The entire membership extends best wishes on

this memorable occasion and directs this resolution

be presented on this ___5th___ day of ___October___ 19 _97_ .

Speaker of the House

Chief Clerk

SPEAKER AND ALL MEMBERS

Sponsor

House Resolution ___1034___

364

ANTHONY J. O'DONNELL
LEGISLATIVE DISTRICT 29C
CALVERT AND ST. MARY'S COUNTIES

———

JUDICIARY COMMITTEE

———

FAMILY LAW SUBCOMMITTEE

HOUSE OF DELEGATES

ANNAPOLIS, MARYLAND 21401-1991

HOME ADDRESS
P.O. BOX 865
SOLOMONS, MARYLAND 20688

———

OFFICE: (410) 326-0081
FAX: (410) 326-0472

———

ANNAPOLIS ADDRESS:
LOWE OFFICE BUILDING
ROOM 217
ANNAPOLIS, MARYLAND 21401-1991
PHONE: (410) 841-3314 / (301) 858-3314
1-800-492-7122 EXT. 3314

October 5, 1997

To all who have gathered to celebrate the first historical reunion of the Cheseldine family.

It is with great pleasure that I welcome each Cheseldine family member as you gather to celebrate the rich historical significance of your family heritage. As the descendants of Kenelm and Mary Gerard Cheseldine, you share in a vast wealth of Maryland history.

Sir Thomas Gerard made tremendous contributions throughout the state of Maryland. He held a prominent position in the Maryland Assembly and Council. He was a mediator with the Indians and the Puritans. His medical expertise benefited both Maryland and Virginia. Sir Thomas Gerard's daughter Mary married Kenelm Cheseldine.

Kenelm Cheseldine was an impressive orator. His contributions to the state are far reaching and certainly impressive. He represented the great state of Maryland as Ambassador to England. He was the founder of the new Capitol of Maryland when it moved to Annapolis as well as the Honorable Speaker of the Assembly and the Attorney General. Additionally he was the founder of the first Free School in Maryland, King William College, which we now know as St. John's College.

I am hopeful that each member of the Cheseldine family will cherish their great historical significance. I welcome each of you to the first Cheseldine family reunion.

Sincerely,

Anthony J. O'Donnell
Delegate, District 29C

365

STENY HAMILTON HOYER
5TH DISTRICT, MARYLAND

October 5, 1997

The Cheseldine Family
C/O Mr. Thomas Brent Cheseldine
11700 Perry Branch Rd.
Newburg, MD 20664

Dear Friends,

It is with great pleasure that I congratulate you as you come together to celebrate your first historic reunion in Maryland. The Cheseldine family has quite a firm root in Maryland. Mr. Kenelm Cheseldine contributed so much to our state and I cannot think of a better way to honor his memory than for all his descendants to come together.

I wish you the best for a celebration filled with the warmth and joy you can bring only to each other. You should be proud of your efforts to maintain and nurture the relationships that make your family special.

Again, congratulating you and with kindest regards, I am

Sincerely yours,

STENY H. HOYER

NOT PRINTED AT GOVERNMENT EXPENSE

SHH:cb

366

(1)   William Playfair, British Family Antiquity, Vol. 6, London,
        1811. Reverend Horace Edwin Hayden, Virginia Genealogies,
        p. 490 reprinted Washington, DC. The Rare Book Shop 1931
        Edwin W. Beitzell, The Gerard and Cheseldine Families,
        Revised 1950.
(2)   Archives of Maryland, I, 29.
(3)   Maryland Historical Magazine, Vol. 8.
        Archives of Maryland, XLIX, Letter of Transmittal, xxvi
(4)   Archives of Maryland, III, 89
(5)   Ibid, LVII, Introduction, xiii
(6)   Ibid, LI, 506
(7)   Ibid, Liii, 627 and Introduction "Maryland Manorial Courts"
        by J. Hall Pleasants
(8)   Ibid, I, 105
(9)   Archives of Maryland, IV, 143, XLI, 265, 533, 544.
(10)   Ibid, X, 214; XLI, 52
(11)   Bernard Christian Steiner, Beginnings of Maryland, p. 54
(12)   Archives of Maryland, XLV, 295
(13)   Ibid, I, 119
(14)   Chronicles of Colonial Maryland, p. 198
(14a)   Archives of Maryland, LVII, 283
(14b)   Library of Congress, Maps Division, Early Maryland Maps,
        Map of Maryland, 1794 Issued by US Constitution
        Sesquicentennial Commission
(14c)   Library of Congress, Maps Division, Map of Maryland, 1840
        Issued by John H. Alexander
(14d)   Ibid, Map of Maryland 1865, Issued by S. J. Martenet
(15)   Archives of Maryland, XX, 584
(15a)   Historical Records Survey, Works Project Administration,
        Inventory of Diocese of Washington Archives of the Protestant
        Episcopal Church, Vol. 1, p. 232
(15b)   Archives of Maryland, XLVI, 476
(15c)   St. Mary's Beacon, Leonardtown, MD, October 4, 1895
(15d)   Historical Records Survey, Works Project Administration
        Inventory of Diocese of Washington Archives of the Protestant
        Episcopal Church. (Missing)

(16)   (Missing)
(17)   Archives of Maryland, III, 138
(18)   Ibid, X, 218
(19)   Ibid, XLI, 142, 188; XLIX, 573-582, 586-587; LVII,
        Introduction xiii, xiiii, 220-226, 330-333, etc.
(20)   Archives of Maryland, I, 16-19, IV, 23, 527, (not legible)
(21)   Archives of Maryland, IV, 507; LVII, 249
(22)   Ibid, IV, 23, 507, 527
(23)   Ibid, IV, 23, 527; X, 496; XLI, 178, 261, 263
(24)   Ibid, XLI, 178, XLIX, 206
(25)   Archives of Maryland, XLI, 144
(26)   Ibid, XLI, 566
(27)   Ibid, III, 354
(28)   Archives of Maryland, III, 384
(29)   Ibid, III, 357
(30)   Archives of Maryland, I, p.420
(31)   Archives of Maryland, I, p.421
(32)   Ibid, XLI, 429
(33)   Ibid, I, 383
(34)   Archives of Maryland, XLI, 265, 373
(35)   Ibid, I, 382
(36)   Ibid, I, 383-391
(37)   Archives of Maryland, III, 396
(38)   William and Mary Quarterly, Series 2, Vol. 12, p.13
        Nugent, Cavaliers and Pioneers, p198, 324, 424, 532
(39)   Archives of Maryland, III, 406-407
(40)   Ibid, XLI, 585
(41)   Ibid, (not ligible)
(42)   Virginia, A Guide to the Old Dominion, p. 557
(43)   Westmoreland County Records
        Virginia Magazine of History and Biography, Vol. 8, p.171
(44)   Ibid, Vol.1, p. 269
        William and Mary Quarterly, Series 1, Vol. 4, p. 35, 41
(45)   Ibid, p. 80
(46)   Edwin W. Beitzell, The Gerard and Cheseldine Families,
        Revised 1950
(47)   William and Mary Quarterly, Series 1, Vol. 4, p. 36

(48) Ibid
(49) Archives of Maryland, XLIX, 575
(50) Archives of Maryland, XX, Preface xiv
      Ibid,XXIII, p. 443
(51) William and Mary Quarterly, Series 1, Vol. 4, p. 35, 76
      Ibid, Vol. 17, p 226
      Tyler's Quarterly History and Genealogical Magazine, Vol. 4,
      p. 35, 76
      Ibid, Vol. 9, p. 70
(52) William and Mary Quarterly, Series 1, Vol. 4, p. 36
      Ibid, Series 2, Vol. 3, p. 99
      Ibid, Vol. 17, p. 111
      Virginia Magazine of History and Biography, Vol. 15, p. 430
      Rev. Horace Edwin Hayden, Virginia Genealogies, p. 486-488
(53) William and Mary Quarterly, Series 1, Vol. 4, p. 36
      Ibid, Vol. 15, p. 49
      Virginia Magazine of History and Biography, Vol. 20, p. 249
(54) Archives of Maryland, XXIII, Preface, xviii
      Ibid, LI, Letter of Transmittal xivi
      James Walter Thomas. Chronicles of Colonial Maryland, p. 13
(55) William and Mary Quarterly. Series i, Vol. 4, p. 36
      Ibid, Vol. 5, p. 68
      Ibid, Series 2, Vol. 10, p. 68
(56) Thomas Gerard in his will, probated Oct. 19, 1673, left his
      daughter Mary, White's Neck, Mattapany, St. Katherine's
      Island, Westwood Lodge (100 acres) and Broad Neck. In the
      will of her husband Kenelm Cheseldyne, dated Dec. 6, 1708,
      (on file at the Hall of Records at Annapolis) he left the same
      tracts of lands to their son Kenelm II and daughter Mary.
(57) William and Mary Quarterly, Series 1, Vol. 5, p. 142
      Ibid, Series 2, Vol. 12, p. 13
(58) Ibid, Series 1, Vol. 4, p. 35-36, 80, 87
      Ibid, Vol. 5, p. 68-69
      Ibid, Vol. 23, p. 77
      Virginia Magazine of History and Biography, Vol. 33, p. 300
      (not legible)
      Probate records, Hall of Records, Annapolis, MD (not legible)
(59) Maryland Historical Magazine, Vol. 33

(60)   William and Mary Quarterly, Series 1, Vol. 4, p. 35
       Ibid, Vol. 17, p. 226
       Ibid, Series 2, Vol. 3, p. 99
       Tyler's Quarterly History and Genealogical Magazine, Vol. 4,
          p.322, vol. 9, p. 70
(61)   Archives of Maryland, XLI, p. 287, 302, 344, 410
(62)   William and Mary Quarterly, Series 1, Vol. 4, p. 56
(63)   William and Mary Quarterly, Series 1, Vol. 4, p. 35
       Archives of Maryland, II, p. 234, 324
(64)   Archives of Maryland, III, p. 119-122
(65)   Ibid, II, p. 234, 237; IV, p. 231-233
(66)   William and Mary Quarterly, Series 1, Vol. 4, p. 36
(67)   Archives of Maryland, X, p.39, 122
(68)   Archives of Maryland, XLIX, 575
(69)   Helen W. Ridgely, Historic Graves of Maryland, p. 30
       Archives of Maryland, LIII, Maryland Manorial Courts, lxv
(70)   Ibid, III, p.315; x, 412
(71)   (missing)
(72)   (missing)
(73)   (missing)
(74)   Archives of Maryland, XXIII, p. 448, 463
(75)   St. Mary's County Court House, Leonardtown, MD

E.W. Beitzell
Dec. 1, 1950

BIOGRAPHICAL INDEX

ANDERSON
Denise E 576
Donna L 574
Julie G 577
Mary A H C 507
Richard D 575
ARNOLD
Mary C C 129
BAGGETT
Beverly J 482
Burton A 592E
Danielle N 592C
Joyce L 560Z1
Larry E 483
Luke C 592B
Mark D 560Z
Martha M 302D
Matthew C 592D
Richard A 560Z2
BAILEY
Alice E 350
Ann E 550A
Ann M 265
Bernard A 350K
Bernard A Jr 550X
Beverly S 550T
Catherine E 264
Catherine E C 136
Catherine M 350H
Donna L 550U
Eleanor B 350F
Fay M 550Q
Jacqueline 550W
James A 262
James T 349W

BAILEY (cont.)
Janice M 350A
John T 350E
Kenneth A 350D
Lulu K 349Y
Mark A 550S
Mary S T G 349A
Mazie R C 198
Maud R 268
Philip R 349X
Robert P 266
Robert P Jr 350C
Samuel M 267
Samuel M Jr 350I
Samuel M III 550R
Susie E 263
Susie E 350B
Thelma L 350G
Virginia C 170
Walter B 269
William E 350J
William E Jr 660V
BARBOUR
Julia C 183
BARLOW
Chester 247A
Elizabeth C 132A
BASILE
Alice R O 376
Brenda T C 539
Courtenay A 591A
David P 591D
John J 558Z3
Joseph A 591C
Joshua J 501F

BEITZELL (cont.)
William B 359
William B 368S
William B Jr 558T
BICEUSKIS
Ashleigh E 591T
Catherine M K 560N
Megan A 591U
BIGGS
Constance 412
Dorothy I 414
Robert G 415
William W Jr 413
BLACKISTONE
Mary C 14
BLAKISTONE
Joanna C 57
BOSTIC
Elizabeth A 606
Evelyn M S 550
Scott M 590E
Sean M 590E
BOWLING
Lydia C 38
BOWMAN
Brian M 568
Lisa A S 503
Michael E 567
BRAGG
Allen J 565
Mary T C 502
William P Jr 564
BRANSON
Charlotte R G 518
Daniel P 578A

BRANSON (cont.)
David L 578B
Dorian L 578C
Raquel M 578F
Sharon A 578D
Stephen P 578E
BRECKENRIDGE
Pearl F C 344
BRUSE
Ann L G 349B
Sue A 550B
BUCKLEY
Kristen E G 560Z16
BUSH
Dorothy I B 414
Linda A 558Z27
BUSWELL
Edward A 583A2
Elizabeth E 583C
Jacqueline N 593
Joyce M S 544
Karen H 583B
Maureen L 583D
William E 593A
CARNEY
Bessie D 220
CARTER
Cari L S 560F
Charles A 591I
Jeannette F 310
Mark A 591J
Nettie C 186
CARTWRIGHT
Elaine K Y 478

CATTERTON
Kevin A 592J
CAVEY
Bridget M C 542
Sean P 582
CHAUNCEY
Tilly C 184
CHESELDEN
Edward 10
Edward 18
Elizabeth 11
Eusebius 12
George 14
James 17
John 2
John 3
John 5
John 7
John 16
Richard 9
Robert 1
Thomas 8
Thomas 19
William 4
William 6
William 13
CHESELDINE
Addie 89
Adeline 53A
Alamedia 126
Alfred W 86
Allison M 590
Alton F 333
Alton G 244

CHESELDINE (cont.)
Andrew F 139
Andrew F 272
Andrew J 74
Andrew J 250
Ann L 82
Ann M 75
Ann R 157
Ann S 114
Ann V 100
Anna 92
Anna E 236
Annie 283T
Annie E 121
Ataway 107
Audrey 318
Augustus D 87
Barbara E 306
Ben 557
Bernard E 335
Bertrand F 501
Bessie 230
Beth 556
Betty L 287
Biscoe K 54
Biscoe 120
Brenda T 539
Bridget M 542
Caleslenleys N 13
Carl C 196
Carl C Jr 301
Carla 463
Carrie 213
Cary 494

Catherine 98
Catherine E 136
Charles 22
Charles 27
Charles 35
Charles 69
Charles 119
Charles B 192
Charles C 48
Charles E 106
Charles F 561
Charles G
Chloe 30
Clara 93
Clara 112
Colleen E 589
Cora 88
Cyrenius 17
Cyrenius 39
Cyrenius 70
Cyrenius 132
Daniel M 603
David 54
David S 165
Dennis P 548
Dewberry A 554
Diane H 493
Dick 313B
Donald 231
Donald R 467
Doris 270
Dorothy E 302
Dorothy L 331
Edna H 338

Edna H 338
Edward K 233
Eileen E 332
Eleana 177
Eleanor 59
Eleanor M 320
Elijah 66
Eliza 31
Elizabeth 16
Elizabeth 33
Elizabeth 128
Elizabeth B 117
Elizabeth E 340
Ellen 102
Ellen E 108
Elmer B 215
Elmer H 297
Elmer H Jr 466
Erin M 587
Etta B 243
Eva 171
Everett 245
Everett A 296
Everett A Jr 465
Everett A III 560A
Florence 197
Frederick 285
Garrett F 142
Garrett Jr 365
George B 284
George F 156
George F 314
George F 349V
George W 79

Josephine 94
Judith L 455
Julie 183
Kathleen 312
Kathleen A 581
Katie A 543
Kenelm (V) 19
Kenelm 25
Kenelm (VI) 40
Kenelm 68
Kenelm G 37
Kenelm G 56
Kenneth G 234
Kim 495
Leddy 104
Lelia 140
Leonard 366
Lillian 294
Lillian 459
Lily G 164
Linda 317
Linda D 536
Lorraine 364
Louisa 190
Lucinda 152
Ludwell 182
Lydia 38
Mabel L 282
Madeline D 588
Marchal 178A
Margaret 295
Margaret L 289
Maria 273
Maria S 116

Marie 199
Marion 345
Marjorie 286
Martha 313
Mary 14
Mary 103
Mary 469
Mary A 32
Mary A 135
Mary A 163
Mary A 300
Mary A 507
Mary B 137
Mary B 279
Mary C 129
Mary E 80
Mary E 162
Mary E 271
Mary E 458
Mary G 343
Mary I 141
Mary J 81
Mary J 151
Mary J 159
Mary L 73
Mary M 90
Mary M 188
Mary M 193
Mary M 337
Mary N 21
Mary S 58
Mary S 134
Mary T 45
Mary T 502

CHESELDINE (cont.)

Mary W 161
Maude R 251
Mazie R 198
Megan V 602
Melissa A 601
Michael R 538
Nelson A 178
Patricia G 537
Patty 195
Pearl F 344
Phillip H 179
Posey 55
Raymond M Jr 305
Raymond M 233
Rebecca 109
Rebecca 115
Rebecca 153
Reginald K 168
Richard 36
Richard 67
Richard B 242
Richard H 127
Richard T 123
Robert 63
Robert 138
Robert B 166
Robert B Jr 290
Robert G Sr 280
Robert L 361
Robert L 443
Robert L Jr 553
Robert 460
Ronald 461

CHESELDINE (cont.)

Rose M 508
Roseanna 96
Rosemary 468
Rubin 10
Samuel D 118
Sarah E 76
Sarah F 194
Sarah M 110
Saundra B 563
Seneca N 24
Seneca 111
Stanley 292
Stanley 462
Sterling 232
Steve 555
Sue 303
Susan 85
Susan F 122
Susan L 540
Susie 181
Susie 363
Susie E B 263
Theresa N 342
Thomas A 175
Thomas B 341
Thomas E 95
Thomas P 101
Tilly 184
Ursula 15
Virginia 170
W Marshall 189
W Wallace 293
Wendy M 560B

CHESELDINE (cont.)
William 12
William 23
William 34
William 176
William 180
William A 84
William C 51
William C 97
William D 246
William E 62
William F 133
William F 248
William H 43
Wilmer 169
CHESELDYNE
Alice 22
Ann 21
Anthony 24
Cyrenius 8
Dryden 5
Edward 20
Edward 27
Everard 25
Elizabeth 28
Kenelm (I) 31 & 1
Kenelm (II) 4
Kenelm 15
Kenelm 23
Kenelm (III) 6
Kenelm (IV) 9
Lyon 26
Mary 2
Mary 7
Rubin 10

CHESELDYNE (cont.)
Seneca 11
Susannah 3
Thomas 30
Wynborow 29
CIPRIANO
Noella J 560H
CLEMENTS
Carl C 471
Mary A C 300
Mary T C 45
Samuel B 470
COMPTON
Annie B R 255
Milton E Jr 349I
CONWAY
Mary E B 368C
CROMWELL
Alice C 22
CRYER
Margaret P 475
Olive L Y 302A
CULLENS
Agnes D 222
Richard 301U8
Wallace 301U7
William 301U9
CULLISON
Mary L C 73
Elizabeth 132A
Lucy 132B
CURTIS
Robin R R 560Z4
DAVIS
Heather L 578

DAVIS (cont.)
Rose M C 508
DENT
Evelyn S 178B
DE WAARD
Lily G C E 164
DINGEE
Agnes 222
Bessie 220
Carrie 224
Edith 221
Henrietta 113
Ida 223
James L 225
Lida 226
Minnie M 228
Nell 227
DODD
Alice 349
Maud R C 251
DONNELLY
Christopher N 604
Eric N 590A
Heather L 605
Joan T S 549
Mark O 590B
Michelle T 590C
DOVE
Gerald T R 560Z5
Jason K R 560Z6
DOWNS
Charles D 557N
Elizabeth J H 368 H
Grace A 558Z21

DOWNS (cont.)
James M 557L
Margaret R L 403
Melanie A 558Z22
Sharon E 557M
DREW
Dolores J 558Z14
Ruene M 558Z13
Ruene M N 400
DUDLEY
Mary N N W 283G
DUNNIGAN
Martha N 283R
DYSON
Eva C 171
ELLIS
Ada 200
Addie E 178C
Ann M C 75
Bernard 173C
Charles A 178B1
Daisy 201
Delmas 296F
Edward 173E
Eliza C 31
Ernest 178G
Eva 178F
Fenny 204
Gilbert 296E
Harry 203
Jane M 178B2
John N 178B3
Josephine C 94
Mary A 178B5

ELLIS (cont.)
Mary E 173A
Mary E C 80
Mary M C 90
Minnie 202
Randolph 178H
Rebecca C 109
Richard 173B
Susan 175B6
Susan 178
Thomas 173D
Thomas 178E
William N 142A
EIBEL
Lily G C 164
EMBREY
Audrey C M 318
Joyce L B 560Z1
Matthew C 592D
EMMERT
James D Jr 591X
Lori P G 560T
FARR
Carol A 550M
Joseph 550N
Thelma L B 350G
FISK
Carol 525
Caroline L W 325
James 527
Robert 526
FISSELL
Barbara E L 406
Steven L 558Z26

FLORENCE
Mary M C 337
FORBES
Dryden C J 5
Mary C H 2
FRASER
Anna E C 236
Jeannette 310
Maxine C 309
Peggy L 311
FRASS
Jane M C 125
FROESCH
Annette L R 258
FULTON
Elizabeth C 16
FUNGE
Patricia L S M 560E
GARDINER
Alemedia C 126
GARDNER
Donna L A 574
GARVER
Dorothy E C 302
Dorothy 472
Earl C 474
Raymond 473
GERMAN
Kenneth L 428
Judith A 429
Mary A N 283K
Raymond C Jr 427
Robert N 430

GIBSON

Alan D 520
Andrew J Jr 550C
Ann L 349B
Ann R 207
Andrew J 349C
Bernice 301K
Catherine V 349D
Cecil F 211
Cecil F Jr 301Q
Charles F 350L
Charlotte R 518
Doris C 270
Dorothy N 349P
Eleanor 301L
Elizabeth 301H
Essie M O 282P
Frances D 389
George B 349E
George R 301I
George W 210
Gordon P 301F
Helen C 391
Helen R 349F
Ida P R 257
James A 352
James E 301G
James H 388
James R 301E
James S 209
John E 301C
John W 301J
Joseph 301M
Joseph E 208
Joseph H 351

GIBSON (cont.)

Katherine E B M 253
Leah E 301N
Margaret A 301D
Margaret A 354
Mary A 301B
Mary A 349Q
Mary C 349G
Mary E 390
Mary J 517
Mary L 301O
Mary L 349O
Mary S 349A
Sarah A 301P
Sara E 212
Sarah M C 110
Sidney A 519
Sherry M 550D
Shirly M 353
Sophie R R 321
Thelma B 355
Thomas L 387
William J 205
William T 301A

GLENN

Linda D C S 536
Sommer A S 580

GOODE

Dorothy K 302G
Joyce 486B
Penny 486A
Skip 486C

GRANT

Bonnie J Y 480
Elizabeth C 33

GRANT (cont.)
Lori P 560T
Mary A C 32
Robert D 560S
GRAVES
Eleanor M C 320
Francis W 515
Glen D 516
Joseph D 514
GREEN
Ann C
GREENFIELD
Susannah C 3
GIUBBINI
Barbara S J 496
Kristen E 560Z16
Mark R 560Z15
GUINARD
Barbara E 558N
Frances A 558M
Mary A B 368P
William J 558O
HALL
Eva C D 171
Gladys M C 167
HANBACK
Evelyn 524
Mary B R 323
Virginia L 523
HANCK
Marguerite B 296D
HANCOCK
Lillian C 294
HARTMAN
Katie A C 543

HARTMAN (cont.)
Robert J V 583
HASKINS
Ursula C 15
HAY
Mary C 2
HAYDEN
Charles 367
Henrietta C 20
Mabel L C 282
Mary C T 550G
Richard 368
HERMAN
Ann 438
Bernadette L 439
Mary 437
Olive N 283P
HEWITT
Barton A 558Z6
Donald A 558Z12
Helen C G 391
Joanne P 558Z11
Laurie A 558Z8
Mark C 558Z9
Mary B 558Z10
Michael P 558Z7
Rose E 558Z4
William B Jr 558Z5
HINSON
Brittney E 600
Bruce E Jr 583G
Cheryl H 583E
Debra L 583F
Jean F S 545
Keith A 583H

HIRST
Brenda L 448
Darlene M 450
Dawn L 451
Linda A 449
Marjorie C N 286
HOGUE
Bessie 219
Bruce 217
Clara C 112
Mamie 218
William 216
HOPKINS
Bonnie 529
Caroline L W F 325
Glenn 530
Peggy 528
HUNTINGTON
Elizabeth 489
J Wallace 490
Jeanne 491
John S 487
Priscilla 492
Sue C 303
Sue C 488
HUSEMANN
Charlene A 557E
Charles A 557D
Charles R 368F
Donald A 557C
Elizabeth J 368H
Francis J 557 H
Harry B 368G
Harry B Jr 557K

HUSEMANN (cont.)
Jeffrey L 557I
Karen A 557J
Mary A B 282B
Michael R 557G
Richard B 557F
Walter D 557B
William J Jr 557A
IRVIN
Margaret C 295
JAVINS
Minnie M D 228
JOHNSON
Ida C 185
JONES
Barbara E C 306
Barbara S 496
Catherine E 497
Owen W 498
JOWLES
Dryden C 5
JOYNER
Debra L H 583F
Gary M Jr 599
JUSINO
Bertito 557Y
David 557X
John 557Z
Joseph 557W
Mark 558
Mary J B 368L
KERSHAW
Bonnie J T G 480
Victor S 560U

KHOURY
Hayley N 592G1
Heather R R 560Z7
Travis J 592G
KIMBLE
Carol A Y 477
Carrie K 560M
Catherine M 560N
Jacob R 591V
Kevin R 560O
Matthew K 591W
KNOTT
Andrew 509
Ann S C 114
Biscoe 302I
Dorothy 302G
Fern D 486I
George B 228A
Jane E 302J
Joseph D 302F
Lida D 226
Linda C 317
Maria 228B
Samuel 510
LACY
Linda 457
Susan 456
Margaret L C 289
LASLIE
Kathryn M Q 558X
Lauryn E 590H
LAWRENCE
Barbara A 558Z20
Barbara E 406
Charles 402

LAWRENCE (cont.)
Charles E 558Z17
Frances R 404
Francis D 401
George E 558Z19
Grace G T 282V
James F 558Z15
Margaret R 403
Mary E 405
Rose F 558Z16
William D 558z18
LE BARRON
Masie B 296A
LEE
Marie M 301U3
LESAN
Maxine C F 309
LONG
John B 486J
Marie C O 199
MADDOX
Elizabeth E B 583C
MAHONEY
Etta B C W 243
MATTINGLY
Alfred 361K
Alton F 534
Annie E C 121
Beatrice 362
Dorothy L C 331
James 361J
James D 398
Mary B C 279
Mary E O 282S

MATTINGLY (cont.)
Michael W 399
Nellie 239
Robert 361L
Scott 579
MAYER
Robert C 557V
Rose M B 368K
Susan K 557U
MAZURE
Mary C 469
MC CUMBER
Helen M 301U1
MC DONALD
Eileen E C W 337
Thomas A Jr 535
MC WILLIAMS
Andrew J 361G
Charles H 361E
George 361A
Ida C 361 C
James J 361D
Mary A 361B
Mary A B 274
Rose M 361F
William P 361H
MELLON
Betty L C 287
David M 454
James S 453
James S Jr 559
Richard P 452
MEUSHAW
Bessie S 301U
Catherine 301U5

MEUSHAW (cont.)
Edith M D 221
Harold 301U6
Helen 301U1
John 301U2
Marie 301U3
Melba 301U4
Richard 471B
Wallace 471A
William 471C
MILES
Amanda L 591G
Joycelyn E 591H
Patricia L S 560E
MILLER
Audrey C 318
James 513
MORGAN
Anna 178B10
Ann E 178B7
Eugene III 550I
James C 178B8
Jane C 91
Judith A 550J
Katherine B 253
Louise 252
Mary S C 134
Mary L G 349O
Nettie 186
Thomas D 178B9
MORRIS
Dora 296I
Earl 296G
Ernest 296H

MURRY
Patricia G C 537
NAIL
Jeffrey A 447
Marjorie C 286
Michael D 446
William D 444
Winnie F 445
NELSON
Mary E C 162
NEWMAN
Nell D S 227
NORRIS
Alma 283C
Bernard E 283F
Betty 283S
Charles E 283J
Charles E Jr 426
Darlene 432
Edna G 283L
Eldridge 282U
Frances L 146
Irving 283O
James B 149
James R 283E
James R Jr 416
James S 283M
Jane A 77
Jane A 283Q
Jane N 147
Janet 423
Jay R 435
Joan 422
John E 150

NORRIS (cont.)
John F 282T
John L 148
John L 283I
John L III 424
John R 283N
John W 283H
Joseph A 145
Joseph L 418
Joyce 433
Lucy R 144
Martha 283R
Mary A 283K
Mary E 143
Mary N 283G
Olive 283P
Rosemary 419
Ruene M 400
Sarah E C 76
Sharon I 425
Shirley M 417
Stephanie L 436
William A 283D
OLIVER
Daisy E 201
Marie C 199
Mary W C 161
OSWALD
Betty 308
Izora 235
Kenneth 307
OWENS
Alice R 376
Aloysuis M 395
Annie R 371

OWENS (cont.)
Benjamin 378
Bernita 380
Charles L 282Q
Daisy D 282M
Essie M 282P
Grover R 282N
James B 282O
James I 372
Jane A 282K
John 377
John J 282L
Joseph M 282R
Joseph W 385
Joseph W 395
Lois R 373
Lucy R N 144
Mary E 282S
Mary I 369
Mary L 384
Mary L 397
May R 392
Melba M 396
Robert W 383
Shirley 381
Sophie B 393
Teresa 386
Vivian 382
Walter 379
William A 370
William L 282J
PALMER
Angela 486L
Larry B 486K
Lielia 302L

PALMER (cont.)
Maria K 228B
Mary W 486M
Windsor 302K
PARVIS
Carrie L K 560M
Jennifer R 591R
Joshua R 591S
PAYNE
Mary G C 343
PHILLIPS
Barbara S J G 496
POGUE
Billingsley G Jr 486N
Lielia P 303L
POLING
Andrew C 346
Dorothy 348
Grace B 249
Osborn 347
PROSKE
Joseph M 591K
Lisamarie 591K1
PUMPHREY
Susie C 181
QUINN
Frances R L W 404
QUINNETTE
Charles D 558Z
Emma N 590L
Jean I B 368U
John J 558W
Joseph R 558Y
Kathryn M 558X
Kathryn N 590I

QUINNETTE (cont.)
Richard R 590J
RASMUSSEN
Edna G N 283L
Halvar P Jr 431
REDMOND
Margaret P C 475
Terry D 560C
RENNER
Beverly J B 482
James D 560Y
Kelly A 560X
RICARDI
Jane A N 283Q
Patricia 440
Ralph 441
RICE
Etta B C 243
Florence 521
George G 324
Mary B 323
Richard 322
Sophie R 321
RICHARD
Brian D 560Z3
Debra J 486
Fred D 484
Gerald T 485
Gerald T 560Z5
Heather R 560Z7
Jason K 560Z6
Katherine J 302E
Kayla M 592F
Robin R 560Z4

ROBBINS
Christi S 566
Mary T C B 502
RUFNER
Deborah K 500
Peggy L 311
Richard K 499
RUSSELL
Ann L C 82
Annette L 258
Annie B 255
Barbara A 349U
Betty J 349S
Christian 349K
Edward N 173F
Edward W 256
Edward W G Jr 349M
Eleanor 349T
Garrett 261
Ida P 257
Joseph L 259
Lillian M 254
Martha 349L
Mary A C 135
Mary H 349R
Milton J 349
Priscilla 173G
Ruene M N D 400
Shirley 349N
Theresa 260
SABAT
Cheryl H H 583E
Christina H 598A

SAITIA
Sidney A G 519
SAVAGE
Daniel 504
Geraldine L C 315
Jason D 570
Lois A 503
Mary J 505
Megan A 569
SAYLOR
Evelyn M 550
Joan T 549
Theresa N C 342
SESSO
Edna H C 338
Jean F 545
Joyce M 544
Patricia 545A
SHYMANSKY
Denise E A 576
SIMPSON
Brandon K 560Z13
Christina J 560Z9
Cody G 592I
David W 486G
Deborah L 560Z10
Dennis C Sr 560Z8
Dennis C Jr 592H
Donald A 486E
James R 486F
Jason D 560Z11
John F 302H
John F Jr 486D
Kathleen M 560Z14
Michael K 486H

SIMPSON (cont.)
Michael K 486H
Michael K 560Z12
Nell D 227
Ryan M 592K
SMINKEY
Jamie M 597
Jenna M 598
John A 596
Maureen L B 583
SMITH
Ada E 200
Addie C 89
Bessie D C 220
Christina E 557R
Daniel K 557O
Donna L 590P
Evelyn 178B
Linda L 557P
Mary B R 323
Melenia A 557Q
Minnie L 202
Rachel R 522
SPENCE
Andrew D 560G
Cari L 560F
Margaret P C R 475
Patricia L 560E
Tommye Dawn 560D
STANLY
Linda D C 536
ST. CLAIR
Joseph E 349H
Josephine 240
Lillian M R 254

ST. CLAIR (cont.)
Susan F C 122
STILWELL
Kelly A R 560X
Jessica L 592A
Taylor J 592
STOWELL
Karen H B 583B
Matthew C 593
Nicholas W 594
STREET
Susan L C 540
SULLIVAN
Ethel M 228C
Maria S C 116
SWANN
Annabelle 283B
Frances A 550P
Laura V 283A
Jane N N 147
Nancy L 550O
SWEENY
Dorothy L C M 331
TAYLOR
Edward 247B
Emma 132E
James 132C
Mary L C C 73
Mary T C B R 502
Sarah 132D
TENNENT
Lois A S B 503
THOMAS
Elizabeth R W 329
Mary A H C 507

THOMAS (cont.)
Mary J 533
THOMPSON
Donald 409
Edgar F 282X
Elizabeth C 128
Frances E 408
Frances L N 146
Grace G 282V
Joseph H 411
Leonard A 282Z
Mary E L 405
Mary F 410
Ruth L 282W
William A 407
William L 282Y
William L 558Z25
TIPPETT
Bernard A 550F
Brenda K 550H
Catherine V G 349D
David 550L
Eleanor B B 350F
James T 550E
Mary C 550G
Richard 550K
Susan C 85
TURNER
Betty 301Y
Elizabeth B C 28
Henrietta 301X
Ida V D 223
James L 301V
Katie A C H 543
Raymond 301Z

TURNER (cont.)
Virginia 301W
William J 583A1
VAN HORN
Daniel 560
Judith L C 455
WARDER
Eugenia R 558Z24
Frances R L 404
Joseph R 558Z23
WEST
Benjamin F 326
Caroline L 325
Elizabeth R 329
Etta B C 243
Grace S 327
Nalley F 330
Nancy 532
Thomas 531
William R 328
WIBLE
Allan 420
Eileen E C 332
Gary 558Z29
Mary N N 283G
Robert 421
Sandra 558Z28
WILD
Beverly J B R 482
WILLIE
Christina K 560P
George S 560R
Kathleen K 560Q
Sandra K Y 479

WOODBURN
Jane A O 282K
Edwin 374
Mary A 375
WORTZ
Olive L Y C 302A
WYANT
George C 301T
James D 301S
Robert L 301R
Sarah E G 212
YATES
Bonnie J 480
Brantley D 591N
Carol A 477
Carrie L 224
Devin E 591E
Elaine K 478
Emily E 591Q
John W 560K
John W 591P
Katherine J 302E
Logan T 591M
Martha M 302D
Michael C 591O
Michael L 560J
Olive L 302A
Pamela A 560L
Ralph A 302C
Ralph E 481
Sandra K 479
Thomas I 302B
Thomas I Jr 476
Thomas I III 560I

YATES (cont.)
  Timothy A 560V
  Tyler C 560W
YOUNG
  Elizabeth 117
ZELESKI
  Carol A 557T
  Charles L 557S
  Elizabeth H B 368J

www.ingramcontent.com/pod-product-compliance
Lightning Source LLC
Chambersburg PA
CBHW070539270326
41926CB00013B/2143